SURVEY OF
INTERNATIONAL AFFAIRS
1963

The Royal Institute of International Affairs is an unofficial body which promotes the scientific study of international questions and does not express opinions of its own. The opinions expressed in this publication are the responsibility of the author.

SURVEY OF
INTERNATIONAL AFFAIRS
1963

BY

D. C. WATT

Issued under the auspices of the
Royal Institute of International Affairs

OXFORD UNIVERSITY PRESS
OXFORD   LONDON   NEW YORK
1977

Oxford University Press, Walton Street, Oxford OX2 6DP

OXFORD LONDON GLASGOW NEW YORK
TORONTO MELBOURNE WELLINGTON CAPE TOWN
IBADAN NAIROBI DAR ES SALAAM LUSAKA ADDIS ABABA
KUALA LUMPUR SINGAPORE JAKARTA HONG KONG TOKYO
DELHI BOMBAY CALCUTTA MADRAS KARACHI

ISBN 0 19 214733 1

© *Royal Institute of International Affairs 1977*

Printed in Great Britain
at the University Press, Oxford
by Vivian Ridler
Printer to the University

PREFACE

THE present volume is the last in the annual series of *Surveys of International Affairs* to be published by Chatham House. This series—which was begun under the direction of Professor Arnold Toynbee in 1924—has always sought to go beyond the task of providing a work of immediate record by a multiplicity of expert hands, in the manner of the *Annual Register* and other valuable works of reference modelled on it. Its aim has been to supply, fairly close to the events which it records, an objective historical narrative written from a non-national viewpoint, which subsequent generations of professional historians would be expected to develop and enlarge.

Among other things, this has involved the imposition on each volume of a single historical viewpoint, and although contributions to the text have come from several authors, the material ultimately presented to the reader has all been filtered, so to speak, through a single pair of eyes—those of the editor and main writer to whom the attribution of responsibility is made on the title-page. Thus the reader knows where he is. However, from the writer's point of view, the task of effective synthesis and interpretation of the whole world's affairs, as national and international centres of power have proliferated and identifiably significant events have multiplied, has become less and less feasible. It gradually became clear that it would in future not be possible to master all this variegated material year by year, within a timescale which would make it useful to the reader, and the Council of the Institute then decided that with the production of the 1963 volume the series should be discontinued. The annual volumes of *Documents on International Affairs*, which have been linked with the *Survey*, are also being discontinued. The Council's decision, it should be said, was not a reflection of any deterioration in the quality of the volumes produced, but was prompted by the profound change in the character of international relations which required that a different analytical treatment be applied to it.

Chatham House will of course continue to make its contribution to the writing of contemporary history. We do not propose to establish any successor to the *Survey* as a special and distinct department of the Institute's activities. Rather, our intention is to conduct from time to time, as part of our general research programme, large-scale studies of particular aspects of international relations, covering longer time periods than the *Surveys* though with a somewhat narrower focus. We believe that this is a more appropriate way in which the Institute can henceforth serve the serious student of international affairs.

Thanks are due to those who have worked on the present volume, including not only the editor and his co-authors, but also Miss Cornelia Navari, who assisted with research, Mrs. Judith Gurney, who prepared the text for the printer, and Mr. F. N. Crofts, who compiled the index. More generally, the Institute is grateful to the outstanding scholars who have contributed over a period of more than forty years to the production of the *Survey*, which was a pioneering project in its early years and has continued to bring distinction to Chatham House. The venture has benefited from the support awarded to it in recent years by the Social Science Research Council. In addition to the special recognition due to Arnold Toynbee, whose recent death is mourned by the Institute, and of Mrs. Toynbee, his faithful collaborator in the venture over many years during which he edited the series, the Institute records its appreciation for the work done by Mr. Peter Calvocoressi, Professor Coral Bell, Professor Geoffrey Barraclough, and Professor Donald Watt, who between them have carried the main burden of writing and editing all the subsequent volumes which have appeared.

ANDREW SHONFIELD

SOURCE ABBREVIATIONS

Cmnd.	Command Papers (London, HMSO)
DSB	*Department of State Bulletin* (Washington DC, USA, GPO)
Documents	*Documents on International Affairs* (Oxford University Press for the Royal Institute of International Affairs)
Documents on Disarmament	*Documents on Disarmament* (Washington DC, USA, United States Arms Control and Disarmament Agency)
FAZ	*Frankfurter Allgemeine Zeitung*
GAOR	United Nations, *General Assembly, Official Records*
HNA	Hsinhua News Agency
HC Deb.	Hansard's Parliamentary Debates, House of Commons
HL Deb.	Hansard's Parliamentary Debates, House of Lords
NYHT	*New York Herald Tribune* (Overseas edition)
NY Times	*New York Times* (Overseas edition)
NZZ	*Neue Zürcher Zeitung*
OFNS	Observer Foreign News Service
Public Papers	*Public Papers of the Presidents of the United States* (Washington DC, USA, GPO)
SCOR	United Nations, *Security Council, Official Records*
SWB	*Summary of World Broadcasts*, British Broadcasting Corporation monitoring service
Survey	*Survey of International Affairs* (Oxford University Press for the Royal Institute of International Affairs)
USIS	United States Information Service

CONTENTS

CONTENTS

PART I

THE GREAT POWERS:
EAST AND WEST
IN CONFLICT AND
DÉTENTE

CHAPTER I

EAST-WEST RELATIONS:
THE COLD *DÉTENTE*

IF 1962 was the year of confrontation, the year in which the danger of nuclear war between America and the Soviet Union came nearest to realization, then 1963 was to bring a very distinct easement to the tension that had produced that danger. That that easement was partial rather than complete lay less in the inevitable state of competition between the two super-powers than in the dilemma in which each of them found itself *vis-à-vis* the other powers they claimed to lead. The Soviet Union had to cope with the problem of a 'bloc' torn apart by the ideological challenge of the leadership of Communist China. The United States faced a trio of second-rank powers, Britain, France, and West Germany, whose coming together in a single European entity was a major plank in US policy, but whose anxieties, whether collective or individual, were to prove a constant inhibition on American freedom of action and a constant misdirection to American thinking. Both super-powers were in addition hampered by fears of a largely ideological origin and by ideological or quasi-ideological doctrines which were to prove a barrier to an accurate perception of their opponent's position.

That 1963 saw only a partial *détente* was certain to make it a year of disappointed and frustrated hopes. But it was also to prove a year of endings. In Britain, the government of Harold Macmillan, the culmination of twelve years of Conservative rule, reaffirmed through three successive general elections, was disintegrating in scandal and back-stage manœuvres over the succession to the premiership. Macmillan himself was driven from the stage by a stroke in October, and was to be succeeded by Sir Alec Douglas-Home, chosen by a procedure so mysterious as to drive several of the ablest in the Tory leadership to refuse to serve under him. In West Germany, the ageing Chancellor, Dr Adenauer, found himself increasingly at odds with his putative successor, Dr Erhard. His attempts to impose an alternative successor on his party were thwarted by a major revolt in its ranks; and his last words before his resignation in October were still bitterly contemptuous of the policies with which Dr Erhard was coming to be identified. Only President de Gaulle was to remain in power, serene and unruffled, for most of the remainder of the decade, a decade which was to see the triumph of social democracy in Britain and West Germany.

The real tragedy was to come in the United States. President John F.

Kennedy was a man of many imperfections and his method of government left room for divided policies and overweening and self-defeating arrogance among his advisers. But he was a man of charisma, capable of embodying hopes, aspirations, confidence, in a style of oratory which, however easily it lent itself to parody, gave him a capacity for movement and initiative lacking to all but a handful of his predecessors. His tragic death in Dallas, at the hands of a mentally disturbed nobody, put paid to the hopes of a generation that any very substantial change in the style and content of international politics could be hoped for, and dealt a profound shock to the self-confidence of his nation.

(a) *Towards a* détente: *the initial check, January–March 1963*

The initial moves towards what was to prove the highest point of the American-Soviet *détente*, the establishment of an immediate priority teleprinter link between the White House and the Kremlin, the so-called 'hot line', and the signature of the treaty barring further tests of nuclear weapons on land and sea, in the atmosphere and in the stratosphere, were taken in December 1962. On 19 December Khrushchev addressed a letter to President Kennedy proposing 'an end once and for all' to all testing of nuclear weapons. He argued that agreement had already been reached that national means of detection were sufficient to control all nuclear tests save those conducted underground. On these latter, he reiterated the Soviet view that 'national means' were equally adequate for the detection of illicit underground nuclear tests, and that, consequently, the obstacle to the signature of an agreement was the American insistence on international control and inspection on the territories of the nuclear powers. He pointed out that the Soviet Union had, notwithstanding its own views, accepted a British proposal that automatic seismic stations should be placed on Soviet territory and agreed that three such stations should be located in Central Asia (near the city of Kokatchev), in the Altai republic (near the city of Bodaibo), and in the Soviet Far East (near the city of Yakutsk). Nuclear tests in the two other zones of seismic activity in the Soviet Union, in the Caucasus and the Carpathian mountains, could be ruled out because of the density of population. He went on to say that the Soviet Union would even be prepared to accept up to three on-site inspections a year in cases where underground disturbances could not definitely be identified as of seismic origin. This figure, he alleged, had been mentioned as acceptable to the United States by Arthur Dean, the US representative in matters of arms control and disarmament, in a conversation with the Deputy Foreign Minister of the Soviet Union, Vasily Kuznetsov, on 30 October 1962. On this basis he called for the signature of a test-ban treaty.[1]

---

[1] For previous developments in negotiations for a treaty banning the testing of nuclear weapons, see *Survey, 1962*, pp. 18–30, 34–7, 42–3, 74–8.

This letter, with perfect timing, reached President Kennedy while he was engaged in discussions with the British prime minister, Harold Macmillan, at Nassau in the Bahamas.[1] Both men were delighted. Macmillan had already received a rather similar missive from Krushchev at the end of November 1962 which offered, in addition, talks with Lord Home, the British foreign secretary, on the issue of Berlin. The letter to Macmillan made no mention of any concessions on on-site inspections.[2] Macmillan himself regarded the possibility of achieving a treaty banning further nuclear tests, with what he saw as its essential concomitant, a treaty banning the dissemination of nuclear weapons, as the crown of his political career, which was clearly drawing to its end. President Kennedy was obsessed by the idea of so massive a proliferation of nuclear powers that nuclear conflict would be almost inevitable. 'I am haunted', he remarked in March 1963, 'by the feeling that by 1970, unless we are successful, there may be ten nuclear powers instead of four, and by 1975, fifteen or twenty.'[3]

On the Berlin issue, both Premier and President were prepared to wait on the order of events. If Krushchev chose to step up the pressure again they were reasonably confident of their ability to withstand it. On the nuclear issue, however, they were the prisoners of American political circumstance. And here there were three developments or currents of opinion which were to make for considerable difficulties. The first was that there was apparently considerable disagreement amongst their scientific and technical advisers on the number of annual seismic events which could not be identified as such with sufficient certainty to obviate the need for on-site inspection. The argument itself involved no little confusion between the number of seismic events which might require on-site inspections to give the United States authorities a 100 per cent guarantee against Soviet treachery, and the number of on-site inspections necessary to deter the Soviets from embarking on underground testing of nuclear weapons, a confusion which made the argument, as the wiser scientists advised their heads of government, political in nature. Independent scientists of great prominence in the United States, including Dr Hans Bethe of Cornell, Professor Bruno Rossi of the Massachusetts Institute of Technology, and Professor Donald Glaser of California, were to lend their weight in April 1963 to the belief that three on-site inspections were enough. The British view was similar.

There was, however, enough scientific disagreement to stir considerable feelings of unease in the Senate. A hard core of Republicans had always found the idea of signing agreements with the Soviet government (who,

[1] *Survey, 1962*, pp. 160–8.
[2] Harold Macmillan, *At the end of the day* (London, 1973), p. 484.
[3] Arthur J. Schlesinger Jr., *A thousand days: John F. Kennedy in the White House* (Boston, 1968), p. 867.

it was, in their view, axiomatic, would break any agreement when it seemed in their interest to do so) both repugnant and silly; more found the abruptness of the transition from the Cuban missile crisis to possible *détente* more than a little difficult to accept. And from mid-January their feelings were beginning to surface with increasing strength. They were not lacking scientists of hard-line anti-Communist views, such as the former Hungarian physicist, Edward Teller, who had played so prominent a part in persuading the US Government to embark on the development of the hydrogen bomb, to provide them with scientific backing. On 25 January 1963, for example, Representative Craig Hosmer, a Republican member of the Congressional Joint Committee on Atomic Energy, gave it as his view that the United States was 'losing its nuclear shirt'. Since any treaty banning the staging of further nuclear tests would have to run the gauntlet of this Committee before ratification by the Senate, the Kennedy administration and any foreign governments involved in the negotiation of such a treaty had good reason to be wary of such views.

President Kennedy's reply[1] to Khrushchev's letter was therefore on the cautious side. He chose to take issue with several of Khrushchev's points, including the allegation that Dean had said that the United States would be content with not more than three on-site inspections, the British origin of the automatic seismic stations proposal, the exclusion of such stations from the seismically active areas of Kamchatka and Tashkent and the limitation of on-site inspections to seismically active areas. But he went on to propose American-Soviet talks at the expert level. Khrushchev's reply of 7 January,[2] while reiterating the Soviet position, accepted the invitation. And talks duly took place, firstly between American and Soviet representatives, and then with British participation. These talks, in which Mr William Foster represented the United States, Messrs Kuznetsov, Fedorenko, and Tsarapkin the Soviet Union, and Sir David Ormsby-Gore, the British Ambassador in Washington, led the British team, lasted from 14 to 31 January. To maintain the initiative, President Kennedy suspended underground testing in the United States on 26 January, despite mounting criticism in Congress, echoed by Governor Nelson Rockefeller on 29 January speaking to a conference of Republican members of the House of Representatives. But on 31 January the Soviet representative proposed that the talks be referred to the Eighteen Nation Disarmament Committee, due to reconvene in Geneva on 12 February. President Kennedy promptly rescinded his suspension of underground nuclear tests and the American series began again on 8 February in the deep caverns prepared in Nevada.

The Soviet leadership had clearly decided on a change of strategy.

[1] 29 Dec. 1962. *DSB*, 11 Feb. 1963, pp. 200–1.
[2] *DSB*, 11 Feb. 1963, pp. 201–2.

The indications are that this was based on two gross errors in their interpretation of Western policy in addition to their failure to make any headway with their initiative on nuclear tests. The first of these errors lay in their interpretation of President de Gaulle's press conference of 14 January,[1] and the subsequent conclusion of the German-French treaty. The second lay in their interpretation of American proposals for the setting up of a multilateral naval force in NATO of ships to be manned by crews drawn from a mixture of the various nationalities members of NATO and armed with medium range nuclear *Polaris* missiles. Both of these errors centred on their fixation on Western Germany as a potentially revanchist power determined to secure nuclear arms and allies with which to unify Germany by force or the threat of force and reverse the verdict of 1945. Those fears bore so little relation to the real state of West German opinion that it was tempting to regard them simply as Soviet propaganda designed to maintain Soviet control over East European satellites. This temptation was rendered particularly strong when the Soviet propaganda machine indulged itself in idiocies such as the accusation by Mr Tsarapkin that the French nuclear test of 20 March was 'American-inspired'.[2] This picture was reinforced when the Soviet leadership alternated its bitter attacks on the West German government with blatant efforts to lure West German politicians and industrialists with promises of major trade and investment opportunities in the Soviet home market.

The Soviet attacks on the Franco-German treaty were bitter and persistent.[3] On 23 January Tass commented that it offered 'even more freedom to the West German militarists', talked of 'collusion to step up the arms race' and called it 'a new step made by the French government towards a new Munich'. On 24 June V. Zhukov writing in *Pravda* spoke of the 'shadow of Bismarck in the Elysée'. An official note of protest was presented on 5 February to the French and West German ambassadors in Moscow. The coincidence of the opening of Franco-Spanish talks on military co-operation in Madrid the previous day (an empty gesture by General Franco towards President de Gaulle's dreams of weaning Spain away from reliance on US military aid) fed Soviet nightmares of what the DDR propagandists called a new 'Axis treaty'. The French reaction was to cancel the showing of two interviews Khrushchev and Marshal Malinovsky had granted the official French television service ORTF. Soviet attacks on Gaullist views of a Europe united from the Atlantic to the Urals as 'pure adventurism'[4] followed. The French and West German

---

[1] *Documents, 1962*, No. 128.

[2] Tass denounced the French tests as 'links in the common chain of the peace-jeopardizing military preparations of this aggressive bloc' [i.e. NATO]. UN Documents, ENDC/80, 5 Apr. 1963.

[3] See for example, *Current digest of the Soviet press*, No. 4, p. 21 and No. 7, p. 15.

[4] *Izvestiya*, 17 Feb. 1963.

replies of 1 April and 29 March did nothing to assuage Soviet wrath. On 5 April Moscow radio, broadcasting in German, alleged that the Franco-German treaty contained secret clauses providing for co-operation between the governments of Bonn and Paris in the sphere of the manufacture of nuclear weapons.[1] Kuznetsov made similar attacks at the Eighteen Nation Disarmament Committee conference at Geneva.[2] A new Soviet note of 17 May[3] repeated these accusations, 'the French-West German Treaty reeks of gunpowder and field-hospitals—the government of the Federal Republic . . . is subordinating everything to a single aim; to even the score for the lost war'. Those views were dutifully echoed by the Czech and Polish governments. They found very little conviction, however, outside the Soviet bloc. And yet the evidence of those whose professional or other business took them into less formal contact with Soviet representatives at this time suggests that the Soviets had to a considerable extent become convinced by their own propaganda. The Franco-West German Treaty of Alliance and the welcome given by German opinion to American proposals for a multilateral nuclear force seemed to them to represent not the desperate strivings of a Chancellor haunted by the failure of his German policy and the nightmare of abandonment, the sacrificial victim on the altar of *détente*, but an accession of strength and leadership reminiscent of Stalinist fears of a capitalist crusade.

The American proposals for a multilateral force were admittedly singularly well adapted to awaken Soviet fears. The original scheme, as related in earlier volumes of this series,[4] had been produced as a European reaction to fears of an American nuclear monopoly which could well lead to a revival of isolationist ideas of the withdrawal of American power into an unassailable 'Fortress America'. It had been abandoned fairly early on in his term of office by President Kennedy as irreconcilable with the ideas of centralized control under evolution by the secretary of defence, Robert McNamara, and expounded in his speeches to the NATO Council in May 1962 and at Ann Arbor the following month. It was, however, to attract new and more determined sponsors that year in a group of State Department advisers headed by the redoubtable George Ball.[5] To these men the MLF, as it came to be known, fulfilled a variety of purposes. It was to provide the European members of NATO with a single force of strategic importance and significance. Its control would provide the Europe of the Six, enlarged by British membership, with a common

[1] *SWB*, SU/1222/A1/2, Apr. 1963.

[2] Speech of 12 Feb. 1963. *Cmnd. 2184*, miscellaneous No. 16 (1963). *Further documents relating to the conference of the 18-Nation Committee on Disarmament (session Feb. 12, 1963 to June 21, 1963)*, pp. 72–9.

[3] *Soviet News*, 20 May 1963.   [4] *Survey, 1961*, pp. 45, 48, 65, 81; *Survey, 1962*, p. 137.

[5] See his remarks in *The discipline of power* (London, 1960), pp. 205–7 and *passim*.

instrument with which to achieve and to celebrate their new-found unity. It would absorb the separate and, to American eyes, puny British and French national nuclear forces. It would provide West Germany with the equality of status and rights in the matter of national armaments which the historical experience of the 1920s and 1930s had convinced them was the compelling goal of German nationalism, its denial the seed-bed of Nazism.

George Ball and Dean Rusk had both put a great deal of energy into the proselytization of their European allies before the events of December and January.[1] It was Ball who believed that, at the Nassau meeting between President Kennedy and Macmillan, the British had been forced to commit themselves to a multilateral force as a *quid pro quo* for the American agreement to supply them with *Polaris* missiles.[2]

The French refusal of the offer of *Polaris* missiles, President de Gaulle's veto on British accession to the EEC and the signature of the Franco-German treaty added a new urgency to the advocacy of the MLF. Unconsciously echoing Russian suspicions, the State Department's 'MLFophiles' saw in this the spectre of Franco-German nuclear co-operation and the erection of a European power both narrowly, chauvinistically nationalist and beyond American influence. At the same time, McNamara reached and began publicly airing the conviction[3] that the right of a NATO ally to influence NATO strategy varied directly with its willingness to make a special contribution to the cost of deterrence. A European contribution to a new multilateral European nuclear force would involve just such a new contribution, whereas a formal regrouping of existing nuclear forces such as the British had accepted at Nassau did not.

The dispatch of an American mission to put the new proposals for a multilateral nuclear force for NATO to its other members was announced by President Kennedy on 24 January. The issue was discussed with the new German defence minister, Kai-Uwe von Hassel, when he visited Washington in February. The American mission, headed by Livingston Merchant, and including Gerard Smith of the State Department and Rear-Admiral John Lee, who had taken part in an earlier mission in September 1962, actually embarked on its work in March. The scheme was publicly aired by Mr Ball in a speech to the Princeton National Alumni Association in Washington on 26 April 1963.[4]

The new American proposals were for a seaborne force of surface ships armed with *Polaris* medium range missiles and manned by crews of

[1] See *Survey, 1962*, pp. 153–4.
[2] On the misunderstandings arising out of the Nassau meeting see ibid., pp. 166–8.
[3] See Mr McNamara's statement before the House Committee on the Armed Services, *Documents on disarmament, 1963*, pp. 17–22.
[4] *Documents, 1963*, pp. 28–31.

mixed nationality. The force would be assigned to NATO, incapable of withdrawal from NATO and controlled by a collective decision of all fifteen NATO members. How this control would work (the Americans rejected von Hassel's proposal for a majority vote) was never quite explained. The many European audiences to the American missionaries of the MLF were left with the uneasy conviction that this problem had never been thoroughly faced by the authors of the proposals.

It is worth pausing here for a moment to consider the appalling blindness of the originators and proselytizers of the MLF scheme to the realities of the situation. They were attempting to force upon their allies a form of military organization which they would reject for themselves. Their estimate of the political situation among their allies was wildly wide of the mark, being constructed on a set of *a priori* assumptions that had only limited correspondence with reality. Of their major associates in NATO, they knew that neither Britain nor France would touch the scheme with a bargepole unless forced to. The MLF by their own admission served no military need. Yet they were determined to secure its adoption. Their determination could only have succeeded if their allies had been prepared to accept demotion to the role of satellites, that is by an exercise in naked imperial power. President Kennedy was never prepared to exercise such power.

It is hardly surprising in the face of all this that the Soviets got the MLF proposals as wrong as they did the Franco-German treaty. They saw in it a competition between Paris and Washington for the favours of the West German 'militarists', a competition in which nuclear weapons played the role of flowers and boxes of chocolates in more conventional courtships.[1] They protested long and bitterly[2] at the arming of the West German militarists. And their misconceptions coloured the whole of their conduct at the Eighteen Nation Disarmament Committee at Geneva.

The Eighteen Nation Disarmament Committee resumed its deliberations on 12 February. The Soviet representative, Kuznetsov, swept aside the initial, rather optimistic statement by Mr Foster,[3] his American opposite number, with its suggestion of discussion on measures to reduce the risk of war. Instead he swept into a denunciation of the Nassau agreement, the MLF proposals, the Franco-German treaty and the American resumption of nuclear testing underground and insisted[4] on submitting a draft declaration on the renunciation of the use of foreign territory for the stationing of nuclear missile sites.[5] This rather crude attempt to make a virtue out of the withdrawal of Soviet missiles from

[1] See *SWB*, EE/1147, 12 Jan. 1963; SU/1161, 29 Jan. 1963; *Izvestiya*, 26 Feb. 1963.
[2] Soviet Note of 8 Apr. 1963, UN Documents, ENOC/84, 17 Apr. 1963. Khrushchev's interview with *Il Giorno, Soviet News*, 25 Apr. 1963.
[3] *Documents on disarmament, 1963*, pp. 32–58. *Cmnd.* 2184, pp. 66–71.
[4] Speech of 12 Feb. 1963, op. cit.   [5] *Documents, 1963*, pp. 156–7.

Cuba the previous November was followed by a second proposal[1] (an equally old nag in the Soviet stable) for a non-aggression pact[2] to be signed between the members of the Warsaw Pact and of NATO.

Neither proposal struck the neutral members of the conference with any enthusiasm or as anything but manœuvres designed to keep the conference alive. The American delegate spent some time explaining the American viewpoint privately to Kuznetsov; in the course of these private conversations he in fact reduced the American demand for on-site inspections to seven annually. But attempts to renew tripartite discussions on the test-ban treaty were rejected by Tsarapkin, the Soviet deputy. Any chance of a further reduction in the US position seemed impossible in the face of increasing Republican criticism in Congress of the Administration's alleged willingness to sacrifice American interests in the search for an agreement.

By the beginning of March the obvious stalemate at Geneva was beginning to try everyone's temper. The Canadian delegate delivered an ill-tempered attack on both super-powers. On 4 March *The Times* attacked the British delegation for incompetence, a denunciation promptly pounced on by Tsarapkin and read into the record. In Washington the Government was obliged to defend itself against charges of a 'sell-out', Dr Long of the Arms Control and Disarmament Agency and Mr Foster being obliged to make long statements of the American position to the Congressional Joint Committee on Atomic Energy,[3] while Mr Rusk appeared before the Senate Foreign Relations Committee.[4] In Geneva the eight neutrals met regularly to try to evolve some joint approach. Gromyko cultivated the Norwegians, and Godber was observed in close conversation with the Swedish representative in London. The eight neutrals were, however, unable to agree on any compromise proposal. Desultory discussions continued on the more long-term proposals for a progressive reduction in nuclear armaments. All the signs of a stalemate were to hand. The atmosphere was exacerbated by the French nuclear test (in the Sahara) on 18 March. A partial break in the deadlock seemed to have been secured when on 5 April Kuznetsov announced Soviet willingness to consider the American proposal for a direct teleprinter link between the White House and the Kremlin. But this was so little regarded that on 10 April the Egyptian, Nigerian, and Indian delegates proposed that the conference should adjourn indefinitely and reassemble only when the American and Soviet co-chairmen had decided that the presence of the non-aligned countries could be of some value. On 20 April, in an interview with *Il Giorno*, Khrushchev spoke candidly of his disappointment.

[1] Speech of 20 Feb. 1963, *Cmnd.* 2184, pp. 80–8.   [2] *Documents, 1963*, pp. 157–8.
[3] On 10 and 11 Mar. *Documents on disarmament, 1963*, pp. 77–98, 99–106.
[4] On 11 Mar. Ibid., pp. 101–2.

The hopes aroused by the end of the Cuba missile crisis, in his view, had proved unjustified. America persisted in the illusion that she was negotiating from strength and could bully and press the Soviets into further concessions. Everywhere was American and British obstruction. If there was no change, he said, the Soviet offer of three on-site inspections would be withdrawn.[1]

In addition to the Geneva Conference Khrushchev complained bitterly of Western behaviour in Berlin. Since the collapse of Soviet pressure on Berlin in the aftermath of the Cuban missile crisis, the Soviet authorities, needled by an East German government confronted with the failure of its hopes of rule over West Germany or at least over West Berlin, had showed themselves extremely sensitive over Berlin. The East Germans suffered further blows to their hopes when their representative at the meeting of the UN Economic Commission for Africa, Wolfgang Kiesewetter, was expelled from Leopoldsville by the Congolese authorities, and hopes of the establishment of a Ghanaian trade mission in East Berlin fell through. The East German foreign minister toured Africa, being received by Nkrumah, Modibo Keita and Sékou Touré. But no formal recognition of the DDR followed. On 28 February the Social Democratic administration of Willy Brandt was re-elected to rule Berlin.

At the beginning of March a fresh storm in a teacup blew up over the introduction of a new law into the Berlin Senate governing the conduct of judges and making the Federal German disciplinary court the last court of appeal for judges against whom disciplinary action was being taken. A flurry of notes followed but to no avail. The West Berlin House of Deputies listened on 17 March to a declaration of policy by the governing Social Democrat-Free Democrat Coalition which, with its unvarnished rejection of links with the DDR or a United Nations presence and its call for a strengthening of links between Berlin and Bonn, can have afforded very little comfort in East Berlin or Moscow.[2] At American initiative, exploratory talks were held between Rusk and Dobrynin, the Soviet ambassador in Washington, on 20 March, but to no avail. By the end of March, Berlin had been added to the Soviet catalogue of 'militaristic' activities directed against the Soviet Union.

(b) *Towards a* détente: *the British initiative, April–July 1963*

Behind the scenes, however, a new initiative was under preparation. Macmillan was, like President Kennedy, obsessed with the dangers of a proliferation of nuclear weapons. He was also convinced that the only way to break the Russian front was by a direct approach to Khrushchev. From 16 March onwards he had been urging on President Kennedy the

---

[1] *Soviet News*, 22 Apr. 1963.   [2] *Documents, 1963*, pp. 187–90.

need for a new initiative, possibly in the form of the dispatch of special emissaries to Moscow.[1] Discussion followed between the two on the draft of a common letter to Khrushchev. The final text was sent on 15 April, but not delivered until 24 April. It proposed a reopening of tripartite talks on a test-ban treaty either in Geneva or in Moscow.[2] Khrushchev replied on 8 May, and after a further message from the two Western statesmen on 29 May, he finally agreed on 8 June to open negotiation and to receive the emissaries. It cannot be said that the British initiative was welcomed at the lower levels of Washington officialdom.[3] For the scientists and theorists of the Arms Control and Disarmament Agency, the State Department, the Pentagon, and Congress, the process of negotiation had as always tended to confer upon the American position the rigidity of theological dogma. But President Kennedy never quite trusted his experts' lack of pragmatism. His own fears (he was quoted as saying that a new round of tests would be 'a great disaster . . . the genie will be out of the bottle and we will never get them back again')[4] drove him on. And in Lord Harlech, the British Ambassador, Macmillan had permanent access to the President himself, an asset which the President's advisers were quite unable to counter.

Before the emissaries of Britain and the United States arrived in Moscow, however, there were very considerable difficulties to be surmounted. On the Berlin issue the East Germans were extremely active. On 9 May an American convoy was delayed for four hours on the way to Berlin by an officious insistence by the Soviet military authorities that its personnel dismount from their vehicles to be checked. On 27 May DDR police blocked off the tiny enclave of Steinstücken, an American-occupied enclave within East Berlin, withdrawing after protest. On 7 June they imposed long delays on civilian traffic coming from West Germany at Babelsberg outside Berlin, allegedly as a reprisal for the arresting of an East German journalist. And on 22 June they established a forbidden zone along the eastern side of the Wall.

On 10 June, in a speech at the American University, Washington,[5] President Kennedy announced the decision to send Averell Harriman to Moscow to open negotiations on the early conclusion of a comprehensive test ban. The sticking point was still the number of on-site inspections. The American position had, however, been obviously undermined.

[1] For his message of 16 Mar. 1963 to President Kennedy, see Harold Macmillan, *At the end of the day*, pp. 456–64.

[2] *NY Times*, 23 Apr. 1963; Schlesinger, *A thousand days*, p. 898. For the text see Macmillan, *At the end of the day*, pp. 466–8.

[3] See the reported bad-tempered reaction of American officers, who were quoted as saying of the British proposal, that it was 'ill-timed and will possibly fail', reported in *NY Times, Times*, 24 Apr. 1974.

[4] In a presidential press conference held on 8 May 1968, *Public papers, 1963*, p. 343.

[5] *Documents, 1963*, pp. 14–19.

Several prominent American scientists had already issued a statement saying that three inspections on site would be quite adequate. On 18 May
Lord Home, the British foreign secretary, had spoken of alternative
offers, a comprehensive test ban with limited on-site inspection or a ban
on nuclear tests in the atmosphere without inspection. In Lord Home's
view the most important element was the coupling with either of these
of a treaty prohibiting the transfer of nuclear weapons from one power
to another, a non-proliferation treaty. But the US Senate had submitted
to it on 27 May a resolution calling for a simple unilateral commitment to
the banning of atmospheric tests.

In the meantime Khrushchev was starting two of his own hares or
rather starting one and continuing to exercise another. The older of the
two was the non-aggression pact to which he was to give a new lease of
life in the fortnight before the Moscow talks began. The new was a series
of proposals for nuclear-free zones. The first of these to surface was the
proposal to declare all of Scandinavia a nuclear-free zone, a proposal
designed by the Soviets both to appeal to Swedish traditional attitudes to
neutrality and to lure Denmark out of NATO. The original proposal
was contained in a press communique of 25 April[1] issued after talks
between Suslov, usually regarded as the keeper of the Soviet Communist
party's ideological conscience, and a delegation from the Danish Communist Party. This provoked the Danish foreign minister, Mr Haekkerup,
in an interview printed in *Izvestiya* the following month, to deny that
Denmark was proposing to join the MLF. At the end of May, presumably
on Soviet prompting, President Kekkonen of Finland, in an interview in
The Times, pointed out that Scandinavia in fact formed a nuclear-free
zone and suggested this fact be confirmed in writing. The Norwegians and
Swedes were a good deal less than enthusiastic about playing the Soviet
propaganda game. Mr Lange, the Norwegian foreign minister, said on
7 June that the proposal should be left to find its own solution in the
proposed test-ban treaty and in the negotiations for a general disarmament convention. Mr Erlander, the Swedish Premier, said that Sweden
did not wish to limit her freedom of action in matters of defence without
some kind of indemnification, while in Denmark the majority of the
Danish parliament remained overwhelmingly opposed to the proposal.
Mr Haekkerup said Danish policy remained unchanged.

The reactions of the Scandinavian powers were no doubt confirmed
when, a little belatedly, the East German Government chose to put it at
the forefront of their propaganda, Herr Bolz, the East German foreign
minister, referring to the proposal repeatedly.[2] The West Germans
rejected the idea completely as clearly directed against membership of the

[1] Tass communique of 25 Apr. 1963, *SWB*, SU/1235/A1/3, 29 Apr. 1963.
[2] *Neues Deutschland*, 1 June, 25 June, 8 July, 1963.

MLF and to the exclusion of ships of the MLF from the Baltic.[1] With this the proposal lapsed temporarily to be revived by Mr Kekkonen in September.[2] It was given a decorous *congé* by the Swedish foreign minister, Torsten Nilsson, in the Swedish parliament on 6 December, as requiring as 'a necessary condition . . . some relaxation in tension in Europe' before it could be taken up in earnest.

In May the Soviets chose also to resurrect the old Polish scheme for a denuclearized zone in Central Europe and a degree of military disengagement. The initial step was taken in a *Pravda* interview of 16 May with the Polish deputy foreign minister, Marian Nosznowski. Mr Cyrankiewicz called for a nuclear-free zone in Central Europe during his visit to Berlin in July and Gomulka raised the issue in September and again during Herr Ulbricht's visit to Poland in October. The Czechs, Hungarians, and Yugoslavs all expressed themselves in favour. The only Western echo came from the British Labour party which had been enamoured of disengagement ever since Gaitskell, their lost leader, had embraced it in the late 1950s. The annual Pugwash Conference held at Dubrovnik in Yugoslavia in September also passed a resolution supporting the idea. But its chances of adoption by any Western government in the age of ICBMs were never very real.

The genuine stimulus to these various Soviet moves had been provided independently of Soviet action by the Latin American states members of the Eighteen Nation Disarmament Committee. On 30 April the representatives of Mexico, Brazil, Chile, Ecuador, and Bolivia had proposed a declaration making the whole of South America a nuclear-free zone.[3] The proposal did credit to the sentiments of the signatories; but it was a little difficult not to equate it with the denial of an intention to commit adultery by a group of fifty-year-old spinsters. There was no threat to their nuclear virginity from any state equipped to do anything about it. And the effort of creating their own nuclear capacity would, in all but a handful of cases, have been beyond their capacity.[4]

The main Soviet effort in the drive to create nuclear-free zones in areas where the Soviet felt sensitive was in the Mediterranean. A Soviet note of 20 May,[5] sent to all the Mediterranean littoral states, as well as to the United States and Great Britain, specifically referring to the MLF scheme, proposed that the Mediterranean should be declared a nuclear-free zone, with no sea-borne nuclear weapons or missiles deployed anywhere along its waters. Given the range of the *Polaris* missile, such a

[1] Interview by von Hassel with *Berlingske Tidende*, 3 June 1963.
[2] Interview with Danish journal *Politiken*, 16 Sept. 1963.
[3] *Documents, 1963*, pp. 161–2.
[4] The Latin American proposal was copied by the member states of the Organization of African Unity meeting at Addis Ababa on 25 May 1963.
[5] *Documents, 1963*, pp. 162–4.

proposal, if adopted, meant greatly increasing the area of southern and central Russia that lay beyond the range of NATO's IRBMs.

The proposal attracted support predictably from Syria, Egypt, and Yugoslavia. Just as predictable were its rejections by Greece, Israel, Turkey, and Cyprus. Khrushchev made a special effort where Italy was concerned, warning Italian opinion in an interview with *Paese Sera* on 7 June that the presence of *Polaris* submarines in the Mediterranean would make all countries on its shores 'hostages'. Russia was the more annoyed in that, although the (now obsolete) *Jupiter* missiles, whose removal from Greece and Turkey had been proposed the previous November as part of a *quid pro quo* for the removal of Soviet missiles from Cuba, were now being removed, their replacement by *Polaris* submarines, 'weapons of aggression' in Soviet parlance, made the Soviet situation worse.[1]

The Soviet proposals did nothing to interfere with the development of the American MLF proposals, nor to enhance the distaste with which Britain and France regarded them. They merely constrained the British and French into rejecting them at a time when both powers shared with the Soviet Union a desire to slow down the US offensive.[2]

The real American worry came from Germany. The prospect of an American-Soviet agreement over the heads of the European powers was one that haunted Adenauer at least since the onset of the second Berlin crisis two years earlier. Whether in retrospect the burden of anxiety felt by German politicians was as great in reality as it was adjudged in Washington is impossible now to say. The visit that President Kennedy paid to Germany, Italy, Britain, and Ireland in June 1963 was only in part intended to soothe their anxieties. It was just as deliberately intended to 'sell' President Kennedy himself to the non-Communist left in Europe as the embodiment of democracy and the forces of progress. The interest of the President in Italy, where the Socialist Party of Signor Nenni seemed about to abandon its long-standing objections to a coalition with the Christian Democrats and where even the Communist Party appeared to be striking out on its own, was equally important. The *apertura a sinistra* (opening to the left) so much discussed in Italian political circles, seemed the embodiment of President Kennedy's own belief, enshrined in his inaugural, that under his presidency the United States should be counted as a progressive country rather than one stuck in defending the *status quo*. It is significant, therefore, that he chose to make his biggest impact in Berlin, not only to guarantee the citizens of that beleaguered

---

[1] Moscow radio broadcasting in Italian, 8 June 1963; *SWB*, S4/1271/AI/2, 11 June 1963.

[2] The British rejection was made in a statement to the House of Commons by Mr Godber on 28 May 1963, 678, *HC Deb.*, cols. 1115–18, and confirmed in a note of 26 June 1963; *Cmnd.* 2184, pp. 30–1. The US rejection came on 31 May in a speech by Mr Stelle, then American delegate to the Eighteen Nation Disarmament Committee, Geneva, *Cmnd.* 2184, pp. 171–5. It was confirmed in a note of 24 June 1963, *Documents, 1963*, pp. 166–8.

city that America would stand by them but because Berlin was governed by a Social Democratic leader, one much more to Kennedy's taste than the ageing Adenauer or the portly peripatetic, Dr Erhard.

The president's tour of Europe was therefore essentially a showing of the flag, a flag designed to win goodwill for the United States and support for the American position. It has to be said that as such it was enormously successful. A series of speeches in Bonn, in the Assembly Hall of the Paulskirche in Frankfurt where the constitutional assembly of 1848 had deliberated, and in the Rudolph Wilde Platz in Berlin[1] established the President unshakeably in the hearts and emotions of his European audience. Diplomatically his visit was less of a success, though by no means a failure. Both the German and Italian governments were induced to sign communiques[2] indicating a more positive attitude towards the proposed MLF. With Macmillan, the President was less successful. His brief visit to Macmillan's private house on 29 June committed him to a definite effort to secure at least a partial test ban treaty in Moscow. And Macmillan was easily able to evade any pressure on the MLF scheme.[3]

The real measure of Kennedy's success can be seen in the Soviet reaction. Khrushchev had welcomed Kennedy's speech of 10 June to the American University in Washington in a statement printed in the form of an interview in both *Pravda* and *Izvestiya* on 14 June. He had, however, made no bones about his final rejection of any on-site inspections. Kennedy's speech, he said, had made a 'favourable impression', a formula to be repeated to Julian Amery, the British minister for aviation, currently visiting Moscow, the next day.

Kennedy's tour of Europe, however, brought him running. Under enormous pressure from the Chinese[4] he organized a visit to East Berlin four days after President Kennedy's visit. For a day or two, *Pravda* floated a hint that a Kennedy-Khrushchev meeting in Berlin was on the cards.[5] This was then abandoned for reports that the visit was to celebrate Herr Ulbricht's 70th birthday and that Khrushchev was to be accompanied by other Communist leaders. In fact Gomulka of Poland, Novotny of Czechoslovakia, Zhivkov of Bulgaria, and Kadar of Hungary attended him in Berlin on 28 June. The Romanian leader, Gheorghiu-Dej, was conspicuous by his absence. Schoolchildren and factory workers were paraded to greet them but their sullen regimented appearance contrasted very badly with the more than a million who had turned out to greet President Kennedy. The summit conference of Communist leaders opened on 30 June on an excursion boat on a lake in East Berlin.

---

[1] *Documents, 1963*, pp. 34–40, 200–1.   [2] *Documents, 1963*, pp. 33–4.
[3] For Macmillan's account of the meeting see *At the end of the day*, pp. 471–5. For the joint communique issued after the meeting, see *Documents, 1963*, pp. 41–2.
[4] See Chapter II below.   [5] *Pravda*, 25 June 1963.

Khrushchev tried publicly to pin the Order of Lenin on Ulbricht, but after several minutes' struggle to get the pin into the lapel of Ulbricht's coat could only get it on crooked. The summit broke up after a single day.

In his speech in Berlin Khrushchev came out heavily for a partial test-ban treaty to be united with a non-aggression pact between the two blocs.[1] With this, morale in Washington sank to a new low. Senator Jackson had already commented on 23 June that the prospects for an agreement were 'virtually hopeless'. Kennedy, under British urging, decided that half a treaty was preferable to no treaty at all. But the prospect of being caught in Moscow by a British negotiator hell-bent on a treaty (they knew little of Lord Hailsham, the British negotiator, save that the eccentricity of his behaviour could on occasion match the strength of his intellect), they found alarming. Macmillan's scheme called for a Test-Ban Treaty to be followed by a Non-Proliferation Treaty and an agreement on a series of summits. For the non-aggression treaty he had no time at all. On 11 July he saw Mr Soldatov, the Soviet ambassador in London, and made it plain that to link the proposed non-aggression pact with the Test-Ban Treaty was to make the Test-Ban Treaty impossible.

This Khrushchev, to judge from the record kept by Mr Spaak, the Belgian foreign minister, of his remarks at Kiev on July 8,[2] had already concluded, since he made no attempt to convince Mr Spaak that the one could not be obtained without the other. The impending choice between China and an intensification of East-West tension or a *détente* with the United States with very little positive gain to Russia was one that could well have shaken his position in the Politburo very badly. But the Chinese choice meant an enormous increase in the internal strains of Soviet society and within the Soviet bloc in East Europe, and again the pay-off to the Soviet Union would be little or nothing of advantage. The choice was duly made[3] and the Moscow talks duly opened.

(c) *The Moscow agreements*

The Moscow negotiations fell essentially into two parts, the opening phase in which each of the three parties stated its maximum position and went through the motions of urging acceptance, and the closing phase in which the Soviet and Anglo-American drafts of a partial test-ban treaty were cobbled together to produce the document initialled on 25 July. Of the three negotiators, Harriman had the most difficult task since overt opposition to anything less than a complete Soviet acceptance of the American position was strong and vocal both within the American

---

[1] Speech of 2 July, *Documents, 1963*, pp. 144–56.
[2] Paul-Henri Spaak, *The continuing battle* (London, 1971), pp. 428–32.
[3] The critical date was 14 July, the date of the publication of the open letter of the Central Committee of the Communist Party of the Soviet Union to its Chinese equivalent. The British and American delegations arrived in Moscow that same day.

administration and in the country. He had the added burden of knowing that there was considerable opposition to the treaty among America's associates, particularly in France and Western Germany. Khrushchev laboured under a similar burden in relation to China and to the ideological opposition which China represented. He too seemed, from his utterances, to be arguing with a point of view which would settle for nothing less than total acceptance of the Soviet viewpoint. He also appeared to feel a need to soothe German (in his case, East German) susceptibilities. There are indications, too, that Soviet military circles were in need of appeasement as, for example, in the withdrawal of even the concession of three on-site inspections annually.

The negotiations began after Harriman, on arrival at Moscow airport, had publicly set a two-week period for the conclusion of the treaty.[1] At the opening session Khrushchev, who himself headed the Soviet delegation, submitted a simple three-article draft banning nuclear tests in the atmosphere, in space and under the water (the 'three environments', so-called). It bore a strong resemblance to drafts submitted in October 1958 at the opening of the original Geneva Conference and to the draft treaty of 28 November 1961. It had no withdrawal clause. It did, however, include provision for the accession of other powers. In submitting this draft Khrushchev made it clear that he ruled out all on-site inspections and a comprehensive test-ban treaty with this, if the Western powers would not accept such a treaty without on-site inspections. Lord Hailsham made a valiant effort to get the issue of on-site inspections referred to discussion between the scientific experts, but in vain. In reply Harriman made it clear that while a partial test-ban treaty could be signed in a few days a non-aggression pact would require extensive discussion with other NATO members and the chance of a test-ban treaty might be lost. In any case he did not see how such a treaty could be signed without assurance that interference with access to West Berlin would be classed as aggression. In turn, at British urging, he presented the idea of a non-proliferation treaty, something which took the Russian premier a little by surprise. Harriman did not pursue this: which was hardly surprising in view of the strength of the MLF supporters in the State Department and President Kennedy's forthcoming attempt to propitiate the French.

The behaviour of the three participating governments during the negotiations left little doubt that, despite the apparent cliff-hanging aspect of the negotiations, there was more concern in the three capitals with the expected objections and possible obstructiveness of their associates

---

[1] On the negotiations see W. Averell Harriman, *America and Russia in a changing world* (London, 1971), pp. 91–9; Macmillan, *At the end of the day*, pp. 476–85; H. K. Jacobson and Eric Stein, *Diplomats, scientists and politicians* (Ann Arbor, 1966), pp. 454–6; Schlesinger, *A thousand days*, pp. 905–9; Sorensen, *Kennedy* (London, 1965), pp. 735–6.

than there was anxiety about the outcome of the negotiations. Khrushchev chose to interrupt the negotiations to receive Kadar, the Hungarian premier, and Herr Bolz and Herr Hoffmann, respectively the foreign and defence ministers of the DDR, who arrived in Moscow on 17 July. On 20 July he employed a speech of welcome to lambast opponents of nego- tiation with the West and to publish the full agenda of his *détente* proposals, which included in addition to the test-ban treaty, provision of inspection against surprise attacks, mutual and balanced force reductions within the two Germanies, a non-aggression pact between the two blocs, a settlement of the problem of West Berlin and a peace treaty with the two German states.[1]

The initial American reaction to the speech in Washington was more than a little suspicious. Khrushchev, it was felt, was manœuvring towards a breakdown in the talks by introducing so many wider issues. The an- nouncement of the arrival in Moscow of the DDR's minister of defence provoked as answer the announcement in Washington that talks on the MLF were to be resumed.

On 18 July Gromyko again took up the issue of a non-aggression pact. The idea took some hold of Harriman and of the rest of the American delegation but foundered again on the anxieties felt in Washington as to French and German reactions. In the end the matter was dealt with in the final communique[2] in a clause of British drafting. The most difficulty arose over the drafting of the withdrawal clause (Article 4) and the pro- vision (Article 3, clause 1) opening the treaty to all states who wished to accede. The discussion was hard and bitter and gave rise to much anxiety in London. But it was essentially concerned with the conclusion of a treaty and the reconciliation of two conflicting theories of treaties not with whether or not a treaty should come into existence at all.

The draft of the treaty was initialled in Moscow on 25 July amidst much expression of hopes on both sides that it would prove but the first step in the negotiation of a far-reaching *détente* between the Soviet Union and the states of the Western alliance. The final signature did not take place until 5 August in Moscow; by which time it was already clear that the hopes voiced so piously in the first communique were doomed, for the time being at least, to remain pious aspirations.

On the Soviet side the principal difficulty lay, as always, in the Soviet commitment to the DDR and to the guarantee of security which the stationing of Soviet troops in Central Europe on DDR territory provided for the Soviet Union. Bound up with this was the question of the status of Berlin, one insisted on by the DDR, which could only be settled if the Soviets felt strong enough in their relations with the Federal Republic to be able to override the DDR's position.

[1] *Documents, 1963*, pp. 168–70.   [2] Ibid., p. 170.

On the American side the problems were of two kinds, those internal to the Kennedy administration and to its relations with Congress, and those bound up with relations with West Germany and anxieties over President de Gaulle's attempt to outbid Washington for the leadership of Western Europe. President Kennedy had begun worrying about this latter point almost as soon as Harriman had arrived in Moscow. On 16 July he had intimated to Macmillan[1] his intention of sharing with France all those vital nuclear secrets which had hitherto been withheld from both Britain and France. Macmillan had responded with enthusiasm[2] for the general idea, but with detailed proposals as to how advantage should be extracted from the offer which President Kennedy seems originally to have thought of as unconditional. Kennedy welcomed this and duly made an offer along these lines to President de Gaulle in a letter of 25 July.

It is doubtful whether even an unconditional offer would have been reconcilable with de Gaulle's sense of national pride. As it was, M. Couve de Murville had indicated the French refusal to be associated with the treaty in a statement to the Foreign Affairs Committee of the Assemblée Nationale on 25 July. The test-ban treaty, he said, could not be said to be a measure of disarmament since it sought simply to perpetuate and crystallize the difference between the nuclear 'have' and 'have not' states. 'En l'absence d'un accord sur un désarmement efficace et contrôlé, le gouvernement n'entendent pas sacrificier l'armement atomique de la France, donnée fondamentale de sa défense', he added.[3] This view was thoroughly confirmed by President de Gaulle in the press conference he gave on 29 July.[4] A question directed to the sense of Kennedy's highly confidential offer he dismissed as being 'une serie d'hypothèses dont aucune jusqu'a présent n'a reçu le moindre commencement d'exécution...' As for the more general sense of President Kennedy's European policy, he dismissed this in the course of a long historical disquisition on Franco-American relations in which he contrasted the friendship for and alliance with America on which French policy was based and the American policy of attempted integration of France into an American command and control system which was not, in his view, consonant with either the reality or the dignity of France.

The Moscow agreement provoked a much more divided reaction in Western Germany. To Adenauer and the hardliners around him the treaty was at best a partial success and one which had been obtained by excessive Western concessions. Talk of a non-aggression treaty worried them still further. But their major worry was over the terms of Article 3. If the DDR acceded to the treaty (as she clearly would) would the

---

[1] Macmillan, *At the end of the day*, p. 476.   [2] Ibid., pp. 477–9.
[3] *Le Monde*, 25 July 1963.   [4] *Documents, 1963*, pp. 46–54.

coincidence of accession by the Federal Republic constitute recognition of the DDR. Anxieties such as this provoked Hase, the German press spokesman, to reiterate on 2 August the Federal German claim to be the sole legal representative German state (*Alleinvertretungsrecht*). Assurances given them by Britain and statements made by Kennedy that co-signature did not imply recognition were far from automatically accepted by the West Germans. Reassuring visits by McNamara on 4 August and by Rusk on 10 August were less than entirely successful. The signature of the treaty by the East Germans on 8 August alarmed the West Germans still more, and was followed by a series of outspoken attacks on the treaty by Franz-Josef Strauss, the leader of the Bavarian CSU, which made matters no better. The final decision was taken by a reluctant West German cabinet on 16 August after fresh Anglo-German talks had taken place in London.

The Kennedy administration also anticipated great difficulty in getting the treaty through the Senate. Harriman defended the treaty at the National Press Club on 1 August as the 'signal event' in the discovery of areas in which America and Russia, despite the irreconcilability of their basic aims, shared a common interest. Dean Rusk was quick to knock the idea of a non-aggression treaty on the head despite Kennedy's indication at his press conference of 2 August that he was attracted to the proposal. In fact the Senate proved much more amenable to the treaty than had been expected. The main opposition lay as before in the State Department and the Pentagon.

(d) *The* détente *slips away, August–October 1963*

The Test-Ban Treaty[1] consisted of four separate articles. The first bound the signatories not to carry out tests of nuclear weapons or any other kind of nuclear explosion in the atmosphere, in outer space, or under water. The second provided for a procedure by which the treaty could be amended. The third provided for accession by any state so desiring. The fourth made the treaty of unlimited duration and protected the signatories' right to withdraw in the case where 'extraordinary events related to the subject matter of this treaty have jeopardized the supreme interests' of the signatory. In itself, as President Kennedy pointed out in his message to the Senate of 8 August,[2] it inhibited rather than prohibited the nuclear arms race; it curbed the pollution of the atmosphere; it did not alter the status of unrecognized regimes; it did not halt American (or Soviet) nuclear progress; nor was it a substitute for the maintenance of Western or American military strength.[3] What it did do was open a way to further

---

[1] *Documents, 1963*, pp. 170–3.   [2] *Public Papers*, 1963, pp. 622–4.

[3] This view was echoed in the statements made to the Senate Foreign Relations Committee on 13 Aug. 1963 by McNamara and on 18 Aug. by General Taylor, Chairman of the US Joint Chiefs of Staff, *Documents on disarmament, 1963*, pp. 312–26, *American foreign policy: Current Documents, 1963*, USA, Department of State, Washington, D.C., pp. 1016–20.

agreements and serve as an important wedge in efforts 'to get the genie back into the bottle' (i.e. to control the spread of nuclear weapons). Khrushchev made rather similar points in the formal interview he gave on 27 July to *Pravda* and *Izvestiya*.[1] Yet by the end of October, only three months later, the Berlin issue was alive again with American convoys being interrupted on their way to and from Western Germany. Hopes of *détente* appeared to have died in their infancy.

In retrospect it is clear that the signature of the treaty could not have come about without the conjunction of Kennedy's own willingness to override his advisers, Khrushchev's need for some major success in the West to set against the breakdown of his attempts to contain China's activism, and the decided push provided at a crucial stage by Macmillan. Against them were ranged all the forces of the institutions which had come to solidify their attitudes during the height of the Cold War, the State Department and the Pentagon, the Soviet military advisers, the ambitions of the East German government, the fears and disappointments of Dr Adenauer and his followers in the Christian Democrat Union in West Germany, President de Gaulle's refusal to accept any external inhibitions on France's drive for great power status.

Khrushchev's programme included, as has been said, a non-aggression treaty, the freezing of military budgets, measures against surprise attack, an exchange of military observers, and a reduction in the number of foreign troops stationed in Germany. The Soviet spokesman, Tsarapkin, in fact introduced proposals covering most of this ground when the Eighteen Nation Disarmament Committee reassembled in Geneva on 12 August.[2] He added to this mix, however, two other measures, the proposal to make the Mediterranean a nuclear-free zone and the abolition of bases and missile sites on foreign soil;[3] the appearance of this last in Tsarapkin's statement of 20 August marked a transition back to the previous Soviet policy of making the conference a platform for propaganda purposes.

Khrushchev sought to measure the degree of American and Western readiness to move a step further on the road to *détente*. He had certainly grounds for believing that the British and American delegations at Moscow had taken the matter seriously and had promised to open discussions as soon as possible with the allies. It was here that the greatest difficulty lay. Dean Rusk himself was far from convinced of the desirability of such an agreement. On 5 August he told Khrushchev that it was far down the list of priorities. It is therefore hardly surprising that he made little or no effort to urge the idea upon his West German allies or upon the NATO standing council which had rejected the idea earlier. All

---

[1] UN Documents, ENDC/103, 30 July 1963.
[2] Statement of 14 Aug. 1963, *Documents on disarmament, 1963*, pp. 334–43.
[3] Ibid., pp. 377–89, statement of 16 Aug. 1963; pp. 394–404, statement of 20 Aug. 1963.

had before them the example of de Gaulle who, at his press conference of 29 July,[1] had dismissed the idea of a non-aggression pact between the members of NATO and of the Warsaw Pact as entirely unnecessary.

Khrushchev had not lost his deep abiding suspicion for Adenauer's Germany. The Federal German cabinet on the other hand, while greatly divided on whether to accede to the Test-Ban Treaty or not, were almost uniformly sensitive to what they imagined to be the Anglo-American failure to consult them or brief them during the negotiations of the treaty. Gerhard Schroeder, the new Federal German foreign minister, who was in favour of signing the treaty, found himself under strong pressure from the old centre and right of the CDU, especially from Krone, von Brentano, Strauss, Barzel, and von Guttenberg. The British reassurance given on 4 August[2] and repeated on 14 August[3] when Schroeder visited London, that there had been no change in British policy and that no recognition of East Germany was involved or planned, did nothing to assuage the feelings of this group. Rusk's version of the talks he had had in Russia, according to which the Soviets refused to include in their proposals for a non-aggression pact any guarantees of the security of West Berlin, confirmed the right in their opposition.[4] On 12 August therefore the Federal cabinet decided to delay a decision until they had listened to Rusk's statement to the Senate Foreign Relations Committee and Schroeder had visited London. On 16 August the Federal cabinet, in a meeting attended by Franz-Josef Strauss, as leader of the parliamentary party, decided without enthusiasm to sign the pact. They insisted, however, on accompanying the act of signature with a statement saying that they did so 'being entitled to speak on behalf of all Germany'. On 21 August the Soviets refused to accept the statement, which, in a statement of their own, made on 4 September, they described as a 'bluntly [sic] revenge-seeking, statement' showing that Federal 'duplicity' would continue.[5] The British and American governments felt obliged to reject the Soviet notice of the accession of the DDR to the treaty, provoking an equally ritualistic statement from Moscow which certainly did nothing to improve matters.

At the end of August the Soviets attempted to push the Western allies greatly over Berlin. In a meeting in West Berlin between Sir Frank Roberts, the British ambassador in Bonn, and his Soviet opposite number, Mr Abrassimov, the Soviet authorities pressed for the establishment of a Soviet trade mission in Western Berlin. The move represented an attempt to establish some kind of Soviet political presence in West Berlin while at the same time developing direct relations with the West Berlin city

[1] Op. cit.
[2] Foreign Office statement, 4 Aug. 1963.
[3] Foreign Office statement, 14 Aug. 1963.
[4] See von Brentano's interview in *Süddeutsche Zeitung*, 10 Aug. 1963.
[5] *Soviet News*, 6 Sept. 1963.

government. The Soviets had no doubt been impressed by the very critical statements made of West German policy by Herr Albertz, deputy to Herr Brandt, the head of the West Berlin government, in a broadcast on Hesse radio on 13 August, in which he accused Bonn of wanting to turn Germany into a Rhenish state at the expense of Berlin and attacked their all-or-nothing policy on reunification. Khrushchev appeared to be toying with the idea of treating West Berlin as a third German state, an idea which was equally unwelcome in Pankow as it was in Bonn. A proposal to this effect was made to the vice-president of the Bundestag, Dr Dehler, by Gromyko, during the former's visit to Moscow on 2 September.

Another promising development was knocked on the head on 21 August when a majority of the NATO Council, led by France and the Netherlands, rejected the idea of guarding against surprise attack by stationing Soviet and Western observers at critical centres of communication on each other's territory. Initial discussion on this had begun at Geneva between Stelle, the American representative, and Tsarapkin. Here again there had been no previous consultation with the West Germans, or indeed, any other of the members of NATO. The NATO vote was therefore at least in part an expression of alarm at the extent to which discussion between the two super-powers was developing over the heads of the European powers. The effect, however, when taken with the Western protest over the DDR was to put an abrupt stop to any further progress on *détente*. In frustration *Pravda* was driven to denounce the Federal German government as 'political Neanderthalers'.

At the end of August, the Eighteen Nation Disarmament Committee adjourned its discussions to allow report and debate in the annual meeting of the UN General Assembly. On 19 September the Assembly heard Gromyko call for further moves to reduce the danger of war and accuse the Western states of using the Geneva meeting simply as a sounding board for propaganda. His speech had a wearisomely familiar ring about it, the same virtuously whining recitation of Soviet virtues and generosity rebuffed by the warmongering West. Gromyko was, in fact, up to the old Soviet game of attempting to embarrass the Western states into turning up at the conference table in a mood to make concessions. He did not refer to the bellicose claims of Soviet nuclear supremacy made by Marshal Malinovsky a fortnight earlier in an interview with *Komsomolskaya Pravda*. Nor did he refer to the fact that the very day before he had met Stevenson, his American opposite, or to the talks between Rusk and Dobrynin at which the Americans agreed to explore again the question of measures against surprise attack.[1]

---

[1] Rusk had in fact spoken of possible further American-Soviet agreements being reached through new discussions in a speech to the American Legion Convention at Miami Beach on

Mr Rusk was already in enough embarrassment. At a long conference between Dr Adenauer, Dr Erhard, Herr von Brentano, and Herr Schroeder at Adenauer's Italian villa at Caddenabia on 14 September, Schroeder had secured the reluctant agreement of his colleagues to supporting further American-Soviet talks. But Adenauer had chosen to pre-empt the conference's decisions by publishing his own views on West German television the previous day; he did not see the slightest sign of the Soviet Union being prepared to make any significant concession and accused Kennedy and Macmillan of wanting to claim a reduction in East-West tension for reasons of purely domestic politics. And Schroeder could only obtain his colleagues' agreement on condition that anything likely to perpetuate the division of Germany or weaken the position of West Berlin was to be opposed. On the other side, Rusk found equally embarrassing the continuous prodding of Lord Home, the British foreign secretary, speaking for a united cabinet and always able to use the British ambassador's privileged access to the President as a means of going behind Rusk's back. Lord Home was particularly pressing on the subject of a non-proliferation treaty, something he tried vainly to convince both Rusk and Gromyko was not irreconcilable with the setting up of a multilateral force.

The talks between Gromyko, Lord Home, and Rusk lasted into the first week in October. They did have two results: an agreement was reached between Russia and the United States not to station nuclear weapons in orbit around the world, one of the most unpleasant possibilities opened by the Soviet-American space race; and Gromyko did assure his Western interlocuters that, even if the multilateral force was set up, talks on the relaxation of tension would continue. He was not, however, prepared to discuss a non-proliferation treaty unless the MLF was abandoned. Rusk and Lord Home in return assured him that control over nuclear weapons and a consequent veto on their use would be retained in London and in Washington. No nuclear secrets would be imparted to West Germany and the balance of nuclear power would not be disturbed. British hopes of a further agreement on the exchange of observers were dashed when Gromyko refused to discuss the issue save in the context of a larger agreement on force reductions in Germany.

Gromyko gave the Soviet view of these talks on 24 October in an interview with *Izvestiya*. They were useful, he said. The West was divided and there were more progressive elements to set against the influential forces striving to continue the arms race from which the powerful capitalist monopolies could extract such vast profits.

The British government were a good deal less happy. On his visit to

10 Sept. *DSB*, 30 Sept. 1963, pp. 490–6. For Gromyko's speech of 19 Sept. see *Cmnd.* 2353, miscellaneous No. 12 (1964). *Further documents relating to the conference of the 18-Nation Committee on Disarmament (July 30–August 29, 1963)*, pp. 78–96.

America from 23 September onwards, Schroeder had made it clear that West Germany had no objection to the continuation of talks on what he described as peripheral problems, such as disarmament, control posts against surprise attack and so on, but on core problems, such as Berlin and German unification, West Germany remained opposed to any sacrifice of her interests. He remained adamant on the point despite being given the full treatment designed to overawe visitors with American strength, including a parade in New York, a guided tour of the Strategic Air Command headquarters in Nebraska and a personal interview with President Kennedy. More ominously from the British viewpoint, he declared Germany's support for the MLF and willingness to go ahead with the project even without British participation. The experience of the summer had convinced the German government that they could not afford either to oppose the project or to remain outside it. Fear, not concern for equal rights, drove Germany to embrace the MLF. Faced with this the British government capitulated. On 1 October Macmillan's office issued a statement of Britain's willingness to discuss a mixed nuclear force, though the question of British participation was still, by implication at least, given a negative answer.[1]

The firming of the West German position made the Soviet decision to use Berlin as the point of pressure on the West even more maladroit than normal for the Soviet authorities. Unless they seriously believed that the Western allies could be forced out of Berlin (something they singularly failed to achieve in 1948–9), they should have realized that pressure on Berlin was the one sure way to re-establish Western solidarity and play into the hands of the hawks in Washington and Bonn. Nevertheless, this is what the Soviet did. It may of course be that the Soviets were angered by the uncompromising tone of the West Berlin city government's statement of policy made to the House of Deputies on 3 September,[2] and the defeat of that attempt to concentrate all the various Soviet offices in West Berlin, Tass, *Intourist*, *Sovfilmexport*, etc. in one building which would in effect create a Soviet diplomatic presence in the free city. But whatever their reasons their tactics were singularly inept.

Trouble began on 26 September with harassment by the East German authorities of civilian traffic on the *Autobahn* to Berlin. On 28 September an American convoy was halted at Helmstedt. There was then a brief lull. On 12 October Soviet tanks and armoured cars were used to block an American military convoy for fifty-two hours. This was ended after Kennedy had personally spoken to Gromyko. On 17 October a British military convoy was delayed for nine hours on the *Autobahn*. The following day Gromyko, on his way back from New York, stopped over in East Berlin to see Ulbricht. The prospects of an East-West settlement, he said

---

[1] *Documents, 1963*, pp. 42–3.   [2] *FAZ* 4 Sept. 1963.

in a press conference at Prestwick, passing through Britain, could not
be worse. This statement he later denied and press reports of it were
castigated as contradictory and tendentious. Harassment in Berlin, however, continued with fresh incidents at Marienborn on 5 November. On
7 November Khrushchev said publicly that if the Western powers attempted to force their way through to Berlin it would be over the bodies
of Soviet soldiers.

The incidents then petered out in an angry exchange of notes and a
procession of Western eminences to Berlin, including Mr Butler, the new
British foreign secretary (10 December) and Dr Erhard. At the end of the
year tensions relaxed as the Erhard government moved into a new policy
of bilateral talks with the DDR authorities. A press agreement and an
agreement on Christmas traffic between East and West Berlin was reached.
This cannot really be considered much of a triumph for what was in fact
the burial by the Soviet authorities of the remnants of the summer's
détente.

The Soviet Union scored one other gain from the period of détente.
This was the American agreement to allow up to 10 million tons of surplus
grain to be sold to Russia. Kennedy piloted the agreement firmly through
Congress, despite denunciation from the American right and more distant
if still more vehement denunciations from Adenauer in the final week
before his retirement. It was no doubt of major advantage to the over-
strained Soviet economy. But it seems in retrospect rather little to set
beside the postponement of any further moves towards a détente for the
next six years.

(e) *The end of the regimes: Adenauer, Macmillan, Kennedy*

The year which saw the first major step in the easing of the confrontation between the Soviet empire and the American-led Atlantic bloc saw
also the passing of three of its major figures. Dr Adenauer, chancellor of
West Germany since the foundation of the Federal Republic in 1949,
went in bitterness and defeat. His promise to resign was forced out of
him; his party's choice of successor, Dr Erhard, for so long his deputy, a
man he disliked and despised. There had been a major row between the
two men in March, as a result of Dr Erhard's attempt to mitigate the
effects on Anglo-German relations of the French veto on British entry into
the European Community. Dr Adenauer did his utmost to secure the
succession for Herr Krone. But even the most prominent supporters of
Dr Adenauer's policy, Franz-Josef Strauss, Herr von Brentano, and Herr
Dufhues, were forced to tell him that Dr Erhard was the party choice.
The chairman of the party organizations in the various *Laender* supported
him by ten to one. And the parliamentary party, voting by secret ballot,
gave him 158 votes out of a total of 225. In August Adenauer was forced

to announce a date for his retirement, 15 October. To the last he remained outspokenly critical of the atmosphere of *détente*, saying of the Western sales of grain to the Soviet Union 'only the stupidest calves choose their own butchers'. 'What', he added, 'does this word détente mean? Nothing.' The Federal German Republic owed his firmness a great deal. And he set his stamp, what the Germans have called 'Chancellor democracy', as firmly on the Federal Republic as Washington did on the United States. But his retirement was too long delayed; and his successor's ability to exploit for Germany the less rigid international alignments of the 1960s showed how much his rigidity in old age had disadvantaged his country.

Dr Adenauer's actual retirement was followed within three days by that of Harold Macmillan, struck down at the very moment of his decision to lead his party into a new election. Although his control over the domestic political scene had slipped rather in 1963, a year of political scandal of a Rabelaisian nature and scale, the rapport which he had established with President Kennedy enabled his country to continue to exercise a degree of international influence altogether disproportionate to the decline in its physical strength and to its continuing economic and financial weakness. In 1960 his skill and firmness had saved the day after the collapse of the 1960 Summit, he had acted as a wise restraint on President Kennedy throughout the dangers of the Berlin crisis of 1961–2, and now the signature of the Test-Ban Treaty could hardly have come about without his sense of timing and his unique ability to lay himself alongside the American President. Had he stayed in office and had Kennedy served out his full term in office, it is tempting to believe that the more rigidly defensive elements in the American administration could well have been curbed and 1964 have seen not decline into the South-East Asian imbroglio but a further step towards the relaxation of tensions in Europe.

The death of President Kennedy at Dallas on 22 November 1963 removed from the scene the one remaining figure of power and vision. The extravagance of his court historians and others inevitably provoked a reaction after his death in which serious historical judgement of his abilities and achievements was largely impossible. His control over the gigantic and diffuse machinery of American government was far from complete. And his quasi-monarchical ability to tolerate widely different and conflicting views among his admirers, treating them as advocates of alternative policies rather than executants, with himself as the judge, made it difficult often to distinguish his true line of policy amidst the babel, often carefully orchestrated on Wagnerian lines, produced by his advisers. His style of government, however, was inseparable from the monarchical model of the US presidency. And if it was tempered with caution always, it was usually decisive. He suffered, it was true, from his countrymen's tendency to confuse oratory with action. Nor were all his advisers of equal merit, and he was prepared to tolerate in office men of whose drive and abilities he had no very high opinion, preferring to find alternative channels of action rather than alternative candidates for their position. His nerve was excellent and his ability to resist pressure, to stand back from the conduct of daily business and wait until the time was ripe for action, was unusual in occupants of the American presidency. His strength in most things (and his weakness in others) was his detachment. His Grand Design suffered essentially from his feeling that in the end its success or failure would affect him and America very little. And he was the victim on several occasions, as over the Bay of Pigs and the cancellation of Skybolt, of that other curious import from the patterns of thought of European autocracy, the total separation of the military and political spheres of governmental activity.

He had, however, in addition to his merits as a governor and arbiter between conflicting advice, an enormous capacity for embodying the hopes and aspirations of the political masses whose active participation in politics is largely minimal. The enormous success of his European tour in producing this effect outside his own country can be measured by the titanic scale of the reaction to the news of his assassination. It took on, wherever the news came, the quality of a personal tragedy for whoever heard it. It is given to very few figures in history to command this kind of reaction, one much deeper than reason or argument can uncover. His untimely death was mourned the world over in a way few others have been in this century.

His achievements, however, remain. He outfaced the Soviet nuclear power in the Cuban missile crisis without in any way creating the kind of victory which inspires the defeated with the lust for revenge. He stood unmoved through the worst Soviet pressure over Berlin. He turned his country along the road to a lessening of tension. It is difficult not to think of his death as a disaster for his own country, for Europe, and for the world.

(f) *Europe after the French veto*

For much of 1963, matters within the European Community, in the sphere of Franco-German relations, were largely frozen—frozen with shock at the enormity of the unexpected last-minute French veto of Britain's application to join the Community. As Dr Schroeder, the German foreign secretary, said in his address to the Council of Ministers of the European Community on 2 April 1963:[1]

The hopes of the Community, the hopes expressed in the rest of free Europe... have been dashed to the ground . . . the shadow of uncertainty about the future

[1] *Documents, 1963*, pp. 74–80.

hangs over the Community . . . the sequence of events in question up to 29th January ended up by causing a serious deterioration in mutual feelings, and I do not think I am exaggerating when I speak of a crisis of confidence . . .

The immediate reaction of the rest of the Community to the French veto and to the signature of the Franco-German treaty was one of anger. Its members felt deceived, cheated, out-manœuvred in a game not of their choosing. Their anger was voiced by Spaak, the Belgian foreign minister, in an interview with West German radio[1] in which he attacked the notion of a Franco-German bloc within the EEC as contrary to the spirit of the Community. The Luxembourg foreign minister, Eugene Schaus, speaking on 12 March, said that such bilateral pacts were remnants of a now bygone era. Dr Hallstein, the president of the High Commission of the Economic Community, added his warnings in a speech made on 27 March to the European Parliament.[2] Many others added their voice, among them George Ball, under-secretary in the State Department, in a letter of 15 February 1963 to Senator Paul Douglas, who opined that the effectiveness of the 'European partner' in NATO would be 'greatly enhanced' if Britain had succeeded in joining the Community. By implication, therefore, America had suffered a mild reverse which it was not prepared to allow to affect American policy.

The only country in a position to do anything about the treaty actually was Germany, where it soon became clear that Adenauer had overplayed his hand. Reconciliation with France was one thing. Reliance on French military strength to replace that of the United States was not a prospect to gladden the hearts of even the most devoted of President de Gaulle's German supporters. In the debate on the ratification of the treaty in the Bundestag, its members, angered and disturbed by the president's neglect to consult France's new ally, were in a position to do something about it. It became, therefore, extremely important to square everyone beforehand. State Secretary Dr Carstens went to Washington early in February. It was there suggested to him that a preamble might be attached to the treaty or that a declaration maintaining German faith in NATO should be passed by the Bundestag.

Adenauer took up this suggestion early in April. At Caddenabia, his Italian country villa, on 4 April, meeting his CDU and FDP ministerial colleagues, he agreed that the Treaty should have a preamble. This crucial decision was announced on 25 April, as the chancellor faced a disturbed and anxious Bundestag. The Bundestag duly approved the treaty on 16 May. The new preamble[3] specifically mentioned the alliance with the United States and the drawing of Britain and other European states into the Community. Adenauer himself was a good deal less than

---

[1] Belgian Foreign Ministry Press Release, 8 Mar. 1963.
[2] EEC press release, 27 Mar. 1963.   [3] *Documents, 1963*, pp. 54–5.

happy about this. But he was no longer a free agent. His resignation had been announced; and his struggle to choose a successor whom he could trust was useless in view of the support enjoyed both in the country and the Bundestag by Erhard. He was to have his moment of glory when President de Gaulle came to Germany at the beginning of July.[1] The meeting was an occasion for great pomp and ceremony; but the final communique found little positive to mention outside the moves towards a common agricultural policy and various cultural and youth contacts. Indeed, it was difficult to see what advantage Federal Germany could derive from the treaty with France unless America withdrew entirely from Europe: a contingency the possibility of which was steadily denied in Washington.

The main moves made by the European Commission were announced in June and July. On 25 June the Council of Ministers of EEC announced that moves were to be initiated towards a harmonization of grain prices within the Community. And on 11 July, over French protests, the Council hit upon the idea of regular quarterly meetings with Britain within the framework of the old Brussels treaty of 1948, that which established Western European military co-operation.[2] The British government accepted the idea immediately as some small salvage of their wrecked hopes. The first meeting of the WEU Council took place at The Hague on 25–6 October.

The year was therefore one in which little movement took place in European affairs. President de Gaulle's power was revealed as essentially negative. And his warnings against too great a reliance on the United States, for fear the lure of agreement between the super-powers would seduce her into abandoning her allies, fell on the whole on deaf ears. Germany had no choice but to rely on the United States. No other power could provide the force adequate to restrain the Marshal Malinovskys of the Soviet world. For the five it became a question of waiting out de Gaulle in the hope that a post-Gaullist France would return to the European ideas of Pleven and Monnet.

[1] There is a long account in his unfinished memoirs, pp. 221–30. For the final communique see *Documents, 1963*, pp. 55–7.

[2] Ibid., pp. 83–4.

CHAPTER II

THE SINO-SOVIET COLLISION

THE year 1963 saw the stripping away of all the veils from the conflict which had been developing between China and the Soviet Union over the previous decade. Before that year the antagonism between the Soviet leadership and that of the People's Republic of China had been couched in terms which were easily penetrable by the knowledgeable non-Communist student, but which, nevertheless, observed a curiously formal, almost Victorian, respect for fraternally Communist sensitivities, and an equally Victorian desire to avoid that most dread of Victorian social disasters, an 'open scandal'. As a result it was still possible as late as 1962 to maintain that 'it was easy to exaggerate the practical significance of the Sino-Soviet dispute',[1] and to quote with approval the verdict of *The Times* on the 1960 Moscow conference of eighty-one Communist Parties that the outcome was 'something more forceful, more confident and more exhaustive . . . than the mere resolution of Sino-Soviet differences which precipitated the gathering', something 'backed by a new and expanding force'.[2]

All this was to change in 1963 as the two parties principally involved, the Chinese making the first move, abandoned secrecy and began to publish lengthy and thoroughly documented accounts of the clashes between their two leaderships.[3] In 1961 and 1962, the Chinese had directed their assault on the Soviet leadership ostensibly against Yugoslavia and, more latterly, against the Italian Communist leader, Togliatti,[4] for their various offences against the doctrines and interests of the Communist world. The principal Soviet target had been the minute state and equally absurd Communist party of Albania (absurd, that is, not in the impact of its tyranny on its unfortunate subjects, but in its claims to be taken seriously as an embodiment of Marxist revolutionary traditions and doctrines).

In this contest the principal Soviet figure had undoubtedly been that of Nikita Khrushchev. By turns embattled and bellicose, benign and expansive, he had veered and turned in his struggle to maintain his own position and initiative at the head of both the Soviet state and the international Communist movement against the assaults and manœuvres of

---

[1] *Survey, 1959–60*, p. 568.   [2] Ibid., citing *The Times*, 7 Dec. 1960.
[3] See Alexander Dallin, ed., *Diversity in international Communism* (New York, 1963), and John Gittings, *Survey of the Sino-Soviet dispute 1963–1967* (London, 1968).
[4] See, for example, *People's Daily*, 31 Dec. 1962.

his principal rivals among the others of the late Joseph Stalin's *diadochi*, Malenkov and Molotov especially. Not for him the placid unimaginative inactivity of his more stolid comrades on the party presidium—nor for that matter the Calvinist devotion to first principles of the party 'ideologist', Mikhail Suslov. It was hardly surprising therefore that he should take the lead in the development of the conflict with China—nor that, for a time, the Chinese should believe it possible to divide him from the rest of the Soviet leadership. The events of 1963 were to show them that this hope was based on illusion. The rivalry between the two major powers of the Communist world went a lot deeper than personalities.

To the non-believer, much of the disputation between the respective Communist parties of China and the Soviet Union, and virtually all of the press polemics exchanged between *Pravda* and *Izvestiya* on the one hand and the *People's Daily* (*Jen-min jih-pao*) and *Red Flag* on the other, must seem as arid and incomprehensible as the conflicts which rent latter-day Byzantium between the supporters of the respective doctrines of *homoousion* and *homoiousion*, about which Edward Gibbon made so merry, or the terrible internecine war between little-enders and big-enders discovered by Captain Gulliver in his first voyage. But the doctrinal disputes over the interpretation of the Communist sacred canon, Marx, Engels, Lenin, and Stalin (or not, as the case might be) hid a very real conflict, or rather grouping of conflicts, over issues the outcome of which could well influence the lives of generations to come.

These conflicts operated both at the subjective and objective levels. Subjectively, the conflict lay between two different interpretations of the effect the contemporary development of military technology in general and nuclear weapons technology in particular were having on the objectives and long-term aims of the revolutionary Communist movement. A parallel conflict lay at the level of the organization of that movement and the degree of individual variation from the doctrinal norm permissible without a qualitative (and therefore deviationist) change in the norms being affected. Questions of leadership, methods by which the conflict might be resolved, methods by which the goals of revolutionary socialism might be achieved in different parts of the world, and so on, formed essential parts of this conflict. Behind lay something much deeper—the hopes and frustrations of individual Communist parties and their perceptions of the tactics best suited in their own particular political situation to advance those hopes more closely to their goal.

At the objective level, that on which the large body of Western analysts and commentators on the Sino-Soviet split were to focus their attention, two different sets of conflicts could be identified. The first, on which self-styled 'realist'-minded analysts concentrated, was the struggle to command the loyalties of Communist parties and supporters in the rest of the world, the struggle which was all the 'realists' could perceive behind the exchange of denunciations, comminations, anathemas. The second, even more direct than the first, lay between Russia and China as individual great powers. One aspect of this latter area of conflict was the Soviet attempt to limit, obstruct, and constrain the Chinese acquisition of nuclear weapons and their means of delivery. Another led to direct armed collisions along their common frontiers, the ultimate form of conflict whether between competing and mutually antagonistic ideologies or territorially limited power systems.

To neglect the subjective levels at which the Sino-Soviet conflict was to manifest itself is, it has been argued, to distort historical reality and to mislead the reader. To dwell upon it at too great length, however, would greatly bemuse and fatigue him. In brief, therefore, the doctrinal essence of the Sino-Soviet differences stemmed from the reaction of the Soviet leadership to the frustrations of the nuclear stalemate and their fears of nuclear war, fears fed no doubt by their own personal experience of the otherwise inconceivable holocausts created by a nuclear explosion in the multi-megaton range.[1] They seem to have concluded, no doubt reinforced by their experience during the Cuban missile crisis, that the existence of nuclear weapons and the apparent willingness of elements among the American ruling élites to envisage their use made the physical destruction through nuclear war of all that the international revolutionary socialist movement, of which they believed themselves to be the head, had so far achieved, a possibility that had to be reckoned with. The policy of the socialist world had to adapt to this reality, especially in Europe. It had to adapt by doing all it could to lower the temperature and avoid incidents out of which hotheads might manufacture a war. And it had, too, to encourage the moderates, the nuclear faint-hearts, among its bourgeois, capitalist, imperialist adversaries, in a similar ap-proach to the problems of conflict. The notion of peaceful co-existence in the minds and mouths of the Soviet leadership was more than a pious adaptation of the long-standing ideals of the international peace movement to the aims of Soviet policy. It represented a definite and permanent limitation of the kind of conflict and rivalry they still expected to continue between the socialist and the imperialist worlds, to levels below those of armed conflict between Soviet forces and those of the United States and her allies.

The Soviet leadership were, however, able to extract a certain degree of positive reassurance from this. If, they argued, the dangers of nuclear annihilation operated to restrain them from an overt use of force in the

---

[1] It is not clear who among the Soviet leaders personally witnessed the 57 megaton explosion of 30 Oct. 1961 at Novaya Zemlya, *Survey 1961*, p. 273. The first Chinese nuclear test, of only 20 kilotons, took place on 16 Oct. 1964.

interests of revolution, it equally restrained the Americans from intervention with the territorial domains of Soviet Russia's friends and allies.
After all, as Khrushchev never failed to point out, the outcome of the
Cuban missile crisis had been an American pledge not to invade Cuba and
overthrow the Cuban revolution by force.

This acceptance of a stalemate in Europe had, however, further implications for Communist parties lying outside the protection of the
Soviet nuclear power. In the first place, argue as they might, the Soviet
authorities were in fact conceding that revolution within the more
powerful states of the Western world was impossible until or unless that
power was destroyed by the internal contradictions which the prophets
of Marxism-Leninism decreed to be characteristic of capitalism. The
bourgeoisie controlled the machinery of state repression, machinery of
which the generation at the head of the West European Communist parties
had only too often had personal experience during the period when Europe
was divided between Fascist and Stalinist rule. To seek to overthrow this
by violent revolution was to condemn several generations of revolutionary
socialists to frustration at best, imprisonment and repression at worst.
The West European communists were therefore seduced more and more
by ideas of acting through and capturing existing bourgeois parliamentary
institutions. At the very least they could compel the bourgoisie to carry
out measures beneficial to the working class and transcending mere
reforms. In the long run, by adroit manipulation and political manoeuvre,
they could capture a majority in parliament and obtain a peaceful transition to socialism by the parliamentary road. For West European Communist parties, with the very sizeable amount of electoral support they
could count on in, for example, Italy and France, the idea of subverting
capitalism from within was the only alternative to a sterile half-century
of frustration in which the working class would turn to other leaders.[1]
Moreover, although to question the doctrine of the inevitability of capitalism disintegrating as a result of its own internal contradictions was still
personally hazardous inside the Soviet Union, 'socialist' economists, even
in the Soviet satellites, could see no evidence to confirm the doctrine in the
two decades since 1945, and plenty to refute it.

To these heresies the Chinese turned a stern and unyielding face. To
the Soviet emphasis on the dangers of nuclear destruction they opposed a
reassertion of the traditional Marxist doctrine of the inevitable victory of
socialism. To question this 'inevitabilitarianism' was the act of a pusilla-
mous backslider. To go further and advocate a transition to socialism by
the parliamentary road was to reassert the heresy of the German re-
visionists, Kautsky and Bernstein, and to indulge in 'parliamentary

[1] Cf. for example, the speech of the French Communist leader, Waldeck-Rochet, at the
Annual Congress of the French Communist party, 6 Oct. 1963.

cretinism'. The reactionary classes would never abandon power voluntarily. As soon as they were seriously challenged they would resort to violence against those sections of the working class who challenged them. This was the meaning of Mao Tse-tung's famous aphorism—'all power grows out of the barrel of a gun'.

As for peaceful co-existence, as the Russians interpreted the phrase, the Chinese would have none of it. 'Normal' relations with non-Communist states on terms of equality and mutual respect were possible. But such a situation could not be achieved without maintaining the 'struggle against imperialism'. Nor did it mean the elimination of antagonisms between socialism and capitalism. This would be to 'substitute class collaboration for class struggle on a world scale'.

From the Chinese viewpoint neither the Soviet frustration in Europe nor the Soviet fear of American nuclear attack seemed particularly relevant or impressive. And they denied utterly the danger of nuclear obliteration. No matter what the death roll, socialism would survive. Indeed it would build a newer civilization on the ruins of the old.[1] What impressed the Chinese was that 'the international proletarian socialist revolution and the national democratic revolutionary movement in Asia, Africa and Latin America have become the two major historic trends of our time'. As for Khrushchev's observation that paper tigers have nuclear teeth, in the Chinese view, 'no matter what kind of teeth imperialism may have, whether guns, tanks, rocket teeth, nuclear teeth, or any other kind of teeth that modern science and technology may provide, its rotten, decadent and paper-tiger nature cannot change. In the final analysis, neither nuclear teeth nor any other kind of teeth can save imperialism from its fate of inevitable extinction.'[2] And again, 'the logic of survival in the nuclear age is in fact the logic of slaves'.[3] The people who attacked the paper-tiger theory have 'obviously lost every quality a revolutionary should have and are become instead as short-sighted and timid as mice'.[4] The doctrinal argument was inextricably interwoven with the question of the control and leadership of the international Communist movement, and of the various international front organizations, particularly those bearing an 'Afro-Asian label'. The rivalry between the Soviet and Chinese leadership here worked itself out at different levels. At the highest the Chinese strove to appeal to the Soviet military leadership, and to isolate Khrushchev from his colleagues. They were to pursue similar tactics in the other Communist parties wherever this was practicable. At

[1] 'More about the differences between Comrade Togliatti and us', *Red Flag*, reprinted in *People's Daily*, 1–4 Mar. 1963.
[2] These quotations are all from *People's Daily*, 'Differences between Comrade Togliatti and us', 31 Dec. 1962.
[3] 'Leninism and Modern Revisionism', *Red Flag*, reprinted in *People's Daily*, 5 Jan. 1963.
[4] *People's Daily*, 31 Dec. 1962.

the Afro-Asian level their aim was to label the Soviets as not rightfully qualified to be counted as Afro-Asians: while at the front level generally they did their best to resist Soviet capture of these organizations.

The reasons for the international Communist movement and the fronts beyond but attached to it forming the main arena for the Sino-Soviet struggle were both subjective and objective. The doctrinal formulation of the dispute obviously limited its sphere of activity to those to whom the doctrinal concepts were comprehensible. Christians do not argue the doctrine of transubstantiation with Moslems or Buddhists. But there was more to it than this glimpse of the obvious suggests.

For the Chinese, isolated from the United Nations, the only international platforms available to them were those provided by the Communist, Communist-front and Afro-Asian movements. These were the major part of their international world, the world of 'the people'. All outside them was inhabited and controlled by their enemies, the imperialists.[1] Naturally there could be no relaxation in the struggle between the two sectors. Even more important, however, was the maintenance of unity of purpose within the world of socialism and of the emergent peoples. Division meant a reversal of the tides of history in favour of the imperialists.

At the same time, however, the Chinese recognized, as the Soviets had since 1919, that the international Communist movement, through its constituent parties, reached deep into the territories under capitalist-imperialist control. This was to be expected in view of the role of leadership in the struggle of the peoples against imperialist-bourgeois power history had conferred on the Communist parties. Control of the movement, therefore, provided that centre of authority which exercised it with a valuable weapon by which capitalist-imperialist bourgeois governments could be inhibited and attacked on their own territories, in their own processes of decision-making and at the levels from which they claimed to derive and exercise authority. To win the support of the international Communist movement, of the various 'front' organizations or of the Afro-Asian solidarity movement was to add to one's military power and prestige a very potent weapon in international politics. To be deprived of

---

[1] The parallel with the *siyar*, the classical Islamic law of international relations, which divided the world into the *dar al-Islam* (the abode of Islam) and the *dar al-Harb* (the abode of war) between which the only acceptable relations were those of the divinely just permanent conflict (*jihād*), interrupted only by short intervals of recess (the Shafis limited this to ten years at most) is very striking. The *dar al-Harb* was strictly incapable of possessing a legal status in Islamic law. Some jurists of the *Shafi* school recognized, it is true, a third division, the *dar al-sulh* (world of truce) or *dar al'ahd* (world of covenant) with whose members treaties of peace were possible for limited periods, modelled on the *Hudaybiya* treaty between the prophet Mohammed and the government of Mecca, postponing war and prohibiting 'unbecoming acts' between the signatories for a period of ten years. Cf. Majid Khadduri, 'International Law' in Majid Khadduri and Herbert J. Liebesny, eds. *Law in the Middle East*, vol. i, *Origin and development of Islamic law* (Washington, D.C., 1955), pp. 349–72.

it, to be isolated within or excluded from these movements constituted a form of compelled disarmament. Thus the struggle for control of these three separate movements combined within itself both the doctrinal and the *macht politische* elements in the Sino-Soviet conflict. It is hardly surprising therefore that as the conflict between the Soviet and the Chinese leadership emerged into the open, it should manifest itself immediately within these separate international movements.

With the partial exception of the long-standing front organizations, the World Peace Council, the World Federation of Trade Unions, the International Union of Students, and the Women's International Democratic Federation being the most important, these movements were far from happy about being drawn into a struggle for control. Khrushchev's attack on Stalinism at the 20th Party Congress had begun a process of devolution of initiative and power that was more than a little welcome to them. The attack had destroyed the doctrines of quasi-papal succession and infallibility, which they had hitherto laboured under, and all opinions now had an equal chance of advancement. Small chance, therefore, of the Italians or the others willingly returning to the days when the international Communist movement was governed by a series of *ex cathedra* fiats issued by a single self-elected embodiment of the voice of 'inevitabilitarianism'. The European parties were more opposed to the Chinese leadership's fundamentalism than to the pragmatism of Khrushchev. But they were to resist obstinately the idea of a new Council of Nicea which by expelling the Chinese would re-establish the power of Moscow.

Afro-Asian governments were equally unwilling to be drawn into the wake of one or other of the powers, if they could avoid it. But the Afro-Asian movement included among its ranks a number of personalities whose status and stature both in their own eyes and within the minute élite groups then existing in their separate countries depended on the 'representative' roles they could secure for themselves in the various subordinate organizations which the movement could be induced to foster. The room for manipulation, even invention, of 'representative' personalities within some of these gatherings would require the pen of an Evelyn Waugh to do it full credit. The Soviets 'exposed' such characters and goings-on when it happened to suit their book.[1] But the representative nature of some of the 'third world' figures at similar Soviet-organized gatherings was not always immediately apparent to the independent observer. For a time there was quite a profitable gravy-train for such 'representatives'.

[1] Cf. *Izvestiya*, 17 Aug. 1963, for a letter from a Zanzibari, alleging that the two self-styled Zanzibari 'representatives' at the World Conference against Atomic and Hydrogen Bombs, held that month at Hiroshima, were long-standing *émigrés* resident in Peking and paid employees of the Chinese government, with no political standing in Zanzibar whatsoever.

The contrast can be seen when the Soviet and Chinese attempts to enlist governmental support for their side of the controversy are compared with these more unofficial front gatherings. Both sides were to make a major effort, for example, at the Afro-Asian People's Solidarity Conference which met at Moshi in northern Tanganyika between 4 and 11 February 1963. The organizing body, the Afro-Asian Peoples' Solidarity Organization, AAPSO, had its headquarters in Cairo and drew its rather limited financial support equally from China, the Soviet Union, and the UAR. The Soviet Afro-Asian Solidarity Committee, headed by a Soviet Moslem from central Asia, Mirzo Tursun-Zade, issued some markedly anti-Chinese statements before the conference. The Chinese concentrated their efforts on lobbying the countries sending delegations to Moshi. When the conference met, the Chinese successfully vetoed Soviet proposals to seat observers from Eastern Europe, Malaya, and Singapore, and the pro-Soviet Turkish exile, Nazim Hikmet. At the conference itself Tursun-Zade stressed the importance of peaceful co-existence and the consequent switch in great power expenditure that might be expected from armaments to aid to the underdeveloped world. Liu Ning-i, the principal Chinese delegate, head of the Chinese Trades Union Federation, in the course of a ferocious assault on 'imperialism', attacked a number of well-known Soviet proposals, including the diversion of money from armaments to aid to the third world, the 'attempt to decide major problems of the world and to manipulate the destiny of the world by one or two powers', and 'big powers bullying, oppressing and giving orders to the small powers', and advocated the settlement of Afro-Asian affairs by the Afro-Asians themselves.[1] His audience remained unimpressed. Delegates from the so-called Pan-African Freedom movement for East, Central, and Southern Africa pleaded that the conference should not be involved in remote and irrelevant arguments. The *Ceylon Daily News* of 9 February 1963 commented acidly that the Afro-Asian countries being only recently emancipated from one form of foreign domination, were now being turned 'into pawns on a fratricidal chessboard'. The final resolutions consisted of a patchwork of conflicting ideas culled equally from the Chinese and Soviet sides.

China was able to make a certain headway thereafter, mainly with Indonesian support, in the establishment of professional internationals on an Afro-Asian basis. An Afro-Asian Journalists Association, AAJA, was founded at Bandung in Indonesia in April, as a challenge to the Soviet front organization, the International Organization of Journalists. The Chinese worked hard to set up an Afro-Asian Trades Union movement to challenge the WFTU, and when the AAJA met for its first Conference in Bandung in September, the Soviet Union was excluded

[1] *Documents, 1962*, pp. 631–5.

from full membership. They also organized a branch of the World Federation of Scientific Workers, whose intention was to prepare a world symposium of scientists from Asia, Africa, and Latin America to be held the following year.

The Soviet authorities regarded these moves with alarm, with anger, and with suspicion. The lead in the subsequent polemics was taken by the Soviet journalist, Mirsky. Writing in *Izvestiya*, for example, on 15 July 1963, on 'Socialism, Imperialism and Afro-Asian solidarity' he denounced as 'intolerable' Chinese efforts to replace the solidarity of East and West against 'the common enemy, imperialism' by 'some sort of geographical, national, or racial principle', suggesting to the peoples of Africa and Asia that 'white people remain white people' irrespective of their doctrinal or social colouration. This was, he wrote, only 'one step from an appeal for a split in the World Communist movement and for the setting up of a new international Communist centre'. In subsequent radio propaganda directed to Africa the attack was continued on the idea that the world was divided into white peoples, who had brought with them coercion and suppression, and coloured peoples, who personified all the virtues, as inverted racialism and a degeneration of the 'healthy anti-imperialist nationalism of the oppressive peoples'.

The Soviet authorities were therefore justifiably cock-a-hoop at their success in preventing the Chinese from capturing the main executive committee of AAPSO, meeting in Cyprus from 8 to 10 September 1963. The Soviet delegation, eight strong, again led by Mirzo Tursun-Zade, successfully secured the seating of observers from Eastern Europe and from the various front organizations. They felt themselves unable to oppose the Chinese proposal for an Afro-Asian workers' conference, but succeeded in establishing that this would take place under the sponsorship of the WFTU. The Indonesians, China's only reliable ally, protested and announced their intention of holding a preliminary conference in Djakarta. But in the face of vigorous Soviet denunciations and a direct threat from the Soviet trade unions leader, V. Grishin, of the withdrawal of Soviet support if Soviet trade unionists were not invited on terms of full membership, what support Indonesia enjoyed from other Afro-Asian groups largely disappeared.

If there were any in Moscow or Peking to lift their eyes from the immediate fog of battle and contemplate the over-all success or failure of their efforts not in defeating the machinations or exposing the false doctrines of their adversaries, but in securing the understanding and support of the governments and peoples of Africa and Asia, they must have thrown a veil of gloom over the much celebrated triumphs in the battle of doctrine. Neither the Soviet Union nor China could claim any real degree of success. The Soviet authorities were forced to acknowledge the loss of much of the position still enjoyed by Communism within the Arab world. In November 1962 the Algerian Communist party had been proscribed by the Ben Bella government on the grounds of its existence and operation as a separate party. Statements of Soviet 'bewilderment' and attacks on the proscription as 'undemocratic'[1] were simply ignored in Algiers. In January 1963 the Tunisian government followed the Algerian example and declared the Tunisian Communist party illegal, denouncing it in the pages of the government newspaper *Al-Amal* on 10 January for attempting to 'poison the atmosphere . . . spread dissension and discord' and alleging that it had 'fought against independence'. The Soviet press replied that the Tunisians were following the example of 'openly Fascist bloody dictatorships',[2] allegations that were hardly calculated to win the support of the Tunisian government.

Further disasters were to follow in the Arab world. The overthrow of the Qasim government in Iraq on 8 February 1963 was to be followed by severe repression of the Iraqi Communists by its successor, drawing protests from the Soviet press and a denunciation from the Soviet Central Committee of the 'rampage of anti-Communist terror', and a statement in protest by the Iraqi Communist leadership—or that part of it which escaped arrest—was broadcast in Arabic by one of the many Soviet controlled clandestine radios, in this case one located in East Germany, which usually transmitted in Persian, Kurdish, and Azerbaiani, but initiated broadcasts in Arabic with this statement. The overthrow of the Syrian government in March was also followed by repression of the surviving Syrian Communists.

Nor were the two protagonists much more successful in Africa or Asia. The Organization of African Unity, meeting in Addis Ababa in May, rejected a Soviet call to align itself with the Soviet bloc. In Africa, Communist parties were weak and non-existent. But of these which did exist only the extremist wing of the *Union des Populations du Caméroun* could be called pro-Chinese. The Chinese greatly increased Peking radio broadcasts to Africa, including daily broadcasts in Hausa, Swahili, and Portuguese. The military were made an especial target. But the only governments to listen sympathetically were those of Guinea and Somalia, both isolated among hostile neighbours. The Somali premier, Dr Sharmanke, visited Peking in August 1963.

Within Asia, Liu Shao-chi and Chen Yi, the foreign minister of China, were to visit Indonesia, Burma, Cambodia, and North Vietnam in April and May in a tour hailed by the Chinese press as of great importance in view of the experience of imperialist aggression shared by both visitors and visited. Only the North Vietnamese would play the Chinese game by

---

[1] Communique issued in Moscow after the meeting of the delegates of the Soviet and Algerian Communist Parties, 5 Feb. 1963.   [2] *Pravda*, 22 Jan. 1963.

denouncing Yugoslav revisionism. The Burmese refused to endorse the Chinese call for a new Bandung Conference. The Indonesians were most concerned to enlist Chinese support for their campaign against the setting up of Malaysia. And the Chinese visit was followed by widespread rioting in Indonesia, directed against the native Chinese minorities in the Indonesian archipelago. There was, in any case, no Chinese surplus of funds or resources to meet Indonesia's desperate need for aid.

Among the Communist parties of Asia, the Chinese scored the greatest success with those that lay along China's borders or where there were large colonies of overseas Chinese. The North Korean government and party marked their final accession to the Chinese side with a visit to Peking led by Choi Yong-kon, the President of North Korea, in June. Liu Shao-chi, who received him, praised North Korea for building its own independent economy and relying on its own strength, praise echoed in the North Korean press and reprinted in that of China.[1] The joint communique issued at the end of the visit pledged full support for China. Similar efforts were put into wooing Japanese opinion, and the Japanese Communist party remained pro-Chinese. The Indonesian party, the PKI, did its best to demonstrate its independence, its leader Aidit, rejecting 'the baton of any other Communist party'. But its condemnation of revisionism echoed that of Peking. The Cambodian and Laotian parties were practically Chinese puppets, dependent on Peking for supplies, radio facilities, etc. The Malayan party was entirely Chinese anyway. In Burma the more violent White Flag Communists inclined toward Peking. The small New Zealand party also looked to Peking. The North Vietnamese remained neutral. But this was the full extent of Chinese success though they cultivated splinter groups in Australia, India, and Cyprus. The Soviet Union retained the support of the official parties in Mongolia, India, Ceylon, Nepal, and the Philippines, as it did that of the United Workers Party in Burma.

A particular target for Chinese propaganda was Cuba. There can be no doubt that Castro greatly resented the Soviet role in the Cuban missile crisis of 1962 and that, given complete freedom of action, he would have echoed the Chinese denunciations of Khrushchev's willingness to sacrifice Cuban ambitions for a *détente* with the United States. A Cuban delegation did in fact visit China in February 1963 to negotiate loan and aid agreements. The visit coincided with a slight lull in Sino-Soviet polemics. But Cuba's need of aid in the face of the United States blockade was so great that China was quite unable to meet it. Castro was therefore forced back on the Soviet Union. In April he went to Moscow for a visit which was to last six weeks. On 23 May a joint Cuban-Soviet communique committed the Cuban government firmly to co-existence. All echoes of

[1] *Nodong Sinmun*, 12 June 1963, reprinted in *People's Daily*, 19 June 1963.

Chinese charges of 'capitulationism' in Moscow disappeared from the
Cuban press. 'World War', declared the communique, 'is not fatally
inevitable'. In return for this sale of his revolutionary birthright, the
Soviets agreed to support Castro's two Havana Declarations and his
Five Points. They also agreed to raise the price paid for Cuban sugar, her
one staple crop, from four to six cents a pound.

In fact the Soviets needed Castro's support as much as he did theirs.
He represented the one regime whose commitment to revolution won
universal acceptance. His endorsement of the Soviet position was the
best possible refutation of Chinese charges that the Soviet Union had
become a power of the *status quo*. Castro was, however, much too much
his own man to go over to the Chinese side. And so far as revolution in
Latin America itself was concerned, he preferred the revolutionary
parties to look to Havana rather than to either Moscow or Peking. On
his return to Havana he gave a radio and television interview which, in
belittling the Sino-Soviet dispute,[1] was most probably intended to maintain his own open commitment to guerrilla revolution in Latin America.
It was noticed that in Brazil he backed the extremist Peasant Leagues of
Senhor Juhão rather than the official Moscow-oriented Communist party.
In Venezuela he convinced the Soviet Union into overt support for the
guerrilla movement against the moderate left government of President
Betancourt. In September Cuba's failure to sign the Test-Ban Treaty,
and Castro's renewed allegations that an American attack on the island
was imminent showed a less than total willingness to follow the Soviet
line. And the authoritative articles of his Minister of Industries, 'Che'
Guevara, argued a thesis of the near inevitability of violent revolution as
opposed to peaceful change, which was far closer to the Chinese than to
the Soviet line, though his illustrations were confined purely to the case of
Latin America.

In the rest of Latin America the Soviets retained control of the loyalties
of all the largely urban-based Communist parties, though not without
difficulty. There were distinct murmurings in the ranks in the Mexican
and Peruvian Communist parties. In Ecuador the more militant Communists tried, and failed, to gain control of the party, apparently with
Chinese financial support. In Brazil, a dissident Communist party with a
membership of several thousand was established by the end of 1963. And
the Paraguayan party, in a statement published in September 1963,
argued that violent revolution was not incompatible with allegiance to
Moscow, no other course being possible in the conditions of Latin America.

Elsewhere the Chinese polemics were not without effect in unsettling a
section of the faithful in each party. In 1960 at the Moscow Conference
the Chinese had held out effectively for the maintenance of minority

---

[1] The interview was reprinted, with all references to China omitted, in *Izvestiya*, 8 June 1963.

views within the parties, 'factionalism' as it was known to the party theologians. But what they now practised, the covert lobbying of the rank and file, or dissident groups among the leaderships of the various parties ('factionalism' in the party jargon), was very different. They were to find fertile ground among the Italian, Belgian, Australian, and American parties. In general they appealed to the old dogmatists for whom Soviet theories of co-existence were a denial of the basic tenets of their faith and to the young whose impatience for change and unwilling-ness to compromise were the most potent forces binding them to the party in the first place. The Belgian Communist party was to expel a pro-Chinese faction in April 1963—and throughout all the other non-governing parties there was to be a constant ferment which the Chinese did their best to encourage and the Soviets to resist.

These were, however, the main areas in which the doctrinal battle was to rage. The *furor sinaica* displayed by Peking fed on grievances other than, and at least as solid as, the theological disputes over peaceful or violent revolution. They held that the Soviet leadership had deserted and be-trayed them for the imperialists on two issues, those of the Sino-Indian conflict of 1962 and the Test-Ban Treaty. On a third issue, that of their common borders, they held that the Soviet authorities were themselves behaving in a thoroughly and reprehensibly imperialist manner. Behind the ideological disputes and the struggles to control the front movements and the international amalgam of Communist parties lay the injured *amour-propre*, the sense of prestige denigrated and status denied which from time immemorial has been a most potent begetter of conflict.

It was this last factor more than anything else that seems to have precipitated the Chinese into open conflict with Russia, out of the conflict by proxy that had hitherto obtained. In its article of 31 December 1962 referred to earlier, 'Differences between Comrade Togliatti and us', the *People's Daily*, though mainly concerned to answer Khrushchev's speech of 12 December to the Supreme Soviet, still used Togliatti as a stalking horse, and referred to Khrushchev himself under the general rubric of 'some people' or occasionally as 'some self-styled Marxist-Leninists'. In his speech at the East German party congress at Berlin on 18 January 1963, Wu Hsiu-chuan still employed the same circumlocutions. But the treatment he then received from this audience was a little too much for Peking's self-control. On 27 January, the *People's Daily* named Khrush-chev directly as the man who had started the practice of using party congresses to attack another 'fraternal' party. For the time being, how-ever, both sides were restrained, possibly, by concern within the other Communist parties to avoid a full-scale break. In December 1962 the pro-Chinese New Zealand party and the anti-Chinese Indians had both called for a new international conference to reach a compromise. The call was to be repeated by the Communist Party of Great Britain in January and by the pro-Chinese parties of North Vietnam, Japan, and Indonesia the following month. At the East German congress Khrushchev expressed considerable pessimism as to the outcome of such a conference. But by the beginning of February opinion had begun to change. On 10 February *Pravda* proposed bilateral talks to prepare for a world summit conference of Communist parties. Five days later Khrushchev publicly embraced the Chinese ambassador at a reception held for the King of Laos. Gromyko, the Soviet foreign minister, held a luncheon party for the ambassador that same day. On 21 February the Soviet Party CC proposed an immediate high level meeting between Soviet and Chinese representatives. Two days later Mao Tse-tung received the Soviet ambassador, Mr Chervonenko, for the first time since his arrival in Peking in 1959, and on 9 March the Chinese Party CC replied, accepting the proposed meeting and agreeing to suspend polemics 'temporarily'.[1]

The undertaking to cease polemics was on the whole honestly observed by the Chinese for a couple of months or so. It was high time. On 24 February Thorez and Togliatti had reacted very strongly against their Chinese detractors, provoking a 14,000 word editorial in the *People's Daily* on 27 February, and an even more massive article in *Red Flag*, reprinted in four successive instalments in the *People's Daily*, 1–4 March 1963, under the title 'More about the differences between Comrade Togliatti and us'. On 8 March the *People's Daily*, stung by Soviet charges that Chinese toleration of Macao and Hong Kong belied its anti-colonialist zeal, attacked the US Communist party, which had echoed these charges, following the next day with an even less restrained attack on the Indian Communist leadership for its 'betrayal' of Marxism-Leninism and its ever deepening immersion in the 'swamp of class capitulationism and national chauvinism'.

From March until May, the two major participants remained fairly quiet. *Pravda* defended Togliatti in its issue of 26 March without provoking any Chinese reactions. The *New China News Agency* responded by giving wide circulation to speeches by Le Duan, First Secretary of the Political Bureau of the Democratic Republic of [North] Vietnam (on the 80th anniversary of the death of Karl Marx[2]) and by the PKI's second vice chairman, Njoto.[3] On 14 April the Indian Party CC passed a resolution critical of the Chinese. Negotiations meanwhile continued between the two protagonists, final agreement being reached early in May that bilateral talks should be held in Moscow early in July 1963.

By then the Chinese control had already begun to slip. On 10 May the *People's Daily* had attacked the new Yugoslav constitution as 'revisionist'.

[1] *People's Daily*, 13 Mar. 1963; *Pravda*, 14 Mar. 1963; *Peking Review*, 22 Mar. 1963.
[2] *Documents, 1963*, pp. 212–17.　　　　　　　　　　　　[3] *SWB*, 1963, FE/1247/C/1–2.

Two days later, in a speech made during his visit to Hanoi, Liu Shao-chi,[1] the Chinese party chairman, denounced co-existence, charged that the Soviets were violating their socialist responsibilities and expounded yet again the Chinese concept of the strategy to be adopted towards the West. On 23 May Khrushchev used a farewell party for Castro to retaliate,[2] and two days later a joint statement issued in the names of the Chinese and New Zealand parties condemned the Soviet line.[3]

At the beginning of June therefore it is reasonable to assume that each of the two leaderships was secretly looking for an excuse to break up the talks. But now a second element was about to be added—that of the Soviet-American partial Test-Ban Treaty.[4] On 10 June Tass announced that talks on the treaty were to be held in Moscow in July. That same day Kennedy's speech on the strategy of peace underlined the degree of the Soviet-American rapprochement.[5] Liu Shao-chi denounced it as 'a great conspiracy'.[6] *Pravda* and *Izvestiya* printed the text of an interview with Khrushchev welcoming the speech.[7] On 20 June the Soviet-American agreement on the setting up of the 'hot line' between Moscow and Washington was signed.[8] The evidence that the Soviet Union was prepared to put agreement with Washington in the place of its loyalty as a socialist state to the world revolution and to the interests of its Chinese 'fraternal state' was conclusive.

The Chinese had, in fact, already shown their hand. On 17 June, the *People's Daily* published[9] the text of the letter addressed three days earlier by the Chinese Party CC to its Soviet opposite number. In 22,000 words of highly polemical tone, it outlined no less than twenty-five separate points of principle they expected to be discussed at the forthcoming talks. The Soviet CC, meeting from 18 to 21 June, in a vain attempt to clamp down the polemics,[10] decided not to publish the text anywhere in the Soviet Union, a decision dutifully followed throughout the Soviet satellites, save in Bucharest, where excerpts were printed.

Baulked of their hopes of stirring up sympathy for their arguments, official Chinese representatives in Eastern Europe took it on themselves to distribute the text of the twenty-five points. The first protest against this extraordinary breach of socialist etiquette came from the East Germans. It was followed on 27 June by a Soviet demand for the recall of three Chinese diplomats and two other Chinese residents in Moscow, caught in similar activities in Moscow. A similar demand for the recall

---

[1] Ibid., FE/1248/A3/2–7.   [2] *Documents, 1963*, pp. 218–28.   [3] Ibid., pp. 228–31.
[4] See Chapter I above.   [5] *Documents, 1963*, pp. 14–19.
[6] Ibid., pp. 249–50.   [7] On June 14. Ibid., pp. 243–9.
[8] Ibid., pp. 164–6.   [9] For extracts see ibid., pp. 231–43.
[10] The Soviet press had published a carefully edited version of Marshal Tito's speech of 18 May to the Yugoslav party central committee, omitting Tito's attacks on China, *Pravda*, 26 May 1963.

of Chinese news correspondents in Prague was made by the Czechs on 7 July. In the meantime the World Congress of Women, one of the lesser known Soviet front organizations, was holding its annual jamboree in Moscow. Delegations from China and Albania attended. On 25 June the Chinese delegate made what was described in the *People's Daily* as a militant speech. It passed quite unheard. In scenes of disorder which would not have seemed out of place in an eighteenth-century political election in Britain, the Chinese delegate was shouted down. The conference ended in uproar, the delegations of China, North Korea, Albania, and Indonesia voting against the Congress's resolutions, those of Japan, Laos, South and North Vietnam abstaining. Thus did the principles and desirability of 'peaceful co-existence' triumph over the rhetoric of those who preferred a continuing 'struggle for peace' through revolutionary violence. The final seal was set on the episode by the breaking of the display windows at the Chinese embassy by Soviet citizens, apparently unable to restrain their indignation at the infamous conduct of the Chinese in seeking to publicize their disagreements with the Soviet leadership, and, for once, freed from the restraints on expressing their feelings that Soviet society normally imposed on them.

It may have been the hope of those whose inspiration lay behind those 'spontaneous' outbreaks that the Chinese delegation would abandon its intention of travelling to Moscow. But the traditions of the Chinese party, forged in the 'Long March' of 1934 and the inhospitable mountains of China's north-east where that march ended, let alone the weight of three thousand years or more of self-induced contempt for all those 'barbarians' whose abode lay outwith the bounds of Chinese civilization, made such a course unthinkable. After welcoming the expelled Chinese diplomats with full honours, a reception by Premier Chou En-lai and a full-scale rally, the Chinese delegation left Peking to the ceremonious farewell of over two hundred party dignitaries. On 5 July the talks duly began.

The Chinese delegation was led by the Party General Secretary, Teng Hsiao-ping, and his fellow CC member and Secretary of the Peking branch of the Party, Peng Chen. The Soviets had at their head the formidable figure of Mikhail Suslov, generally regarded as the guardian of Party doctrine and keeper of the Party's conscience (if such a word can legitimately be used in this context). Suslov was supported by two other members of the Soviet central committee, Yuri Andropov and Boris Ponemarev, and by Leonid Ilyichev, head of the 'ideological' department of the party secretariat.

The detailed course of the talks, held under maximum security conditions in a villa on the outskirts of Moscow, remain buried in the archives of the participants. In their letter of 14 June, the Chinese had recapitulated the whole sweep of their ideological dispute with the Soviets. The need to 'carry the revolution to the end' (Point I); the need to establish a new world without imperialism or exploitation by bringing the proletarian revolution through union with the oppressed peoples, 'step by step to complete victory' (Point II); the violation of the principles proclaimed by the congresses of 1957 and 1960 which had led to a 'one-sided' reduction of the general line of the movement to 'peaceful co-existence, peaceful competition and peaceful transition' (Point III); the existence of various 'fundamental contradictions' (Point IV); the absolute necessity of repudiating various of Khrushchev's views in support of 'peaceful transition' (Point V); the absolute necessity of loyalty within the 'Socialist camp'; the outright abandonment of attempts to 'entrust the fate of the people and mankind in [sic: to] collaboration with U.S. imperialism'; the renunciation of 'legalism' and 'parliamentary cretinism', or any kind of parliamentary forms of struggle save where of short-term advantage (Point X); the abandonment of attempts to base party thinking and 'policies for revolution' on 'the assumption that the imperialists and reactionaries will accept peaceful transformation' (Point XI); the inevitable replacement of 'leading groups' within any party who 'adopt' a non-revolutionary line and 'convert it into a reformist party' (Point XII); the abandonment of 'general and complete disarmament' as a 'deliberate deceit of the people and aid to the imperialists . . . World peace can only be won by the struggles of the people in all countries and not by begging the imperialists for it' (Point XIV); the abandonment of the argument that nuclear technology has made 'the basic principles of Marxism-Leninism and especially the theories of proletarian revolution and the dictatorship of the proletariat . . . outmoded' (Point XV); the basing of Socialist foreign policy on the development of 'proletarian internationalism' within the Soviet bloc, the confinement of 'peaceful coexistence . . . with countries having different social systems' only to countries free from the stigma of imperialism and oppression, aggression and war, and the full support of 'the revolutionary struggle of all the oppressed peoples and nations' (Point XVI); recognition that class struggle continues after the proletariat takes power and that to deny this 'violates Marxism-Leninism' (Point XVII); rejection of Khrushchev's theory that the state and party of the 'dictatorship of the proletariat' can be replaced by a state and party 'of the whole people' as a disarmament of the proletariat and 'tantamount to helping to restore capitalism' (Points XVIII and XIX); abandonment of the Soviet campaign against Stalin and the 'personality cult' as an attempt to 'counterpose the leaders to the masses, undermine the party's unified leadership . . . dissipate its fighting strength and disintegrate its ranks' (Point XX); the adoption of the principles of 'complete equality' in relations between socialist countries both in economic matters and in political relations and the

abandonment of all claims to be 'superior' or to impose a 'common programme' on fraternal parties (Points XX and XXI); the settlement of
Soviet-Albanian relations and the rejection of the 'Yugoslav revisionist
clique of traitors to Marxism-Leninism' (Points XXII and XXIII);
and, finally, full publication of the Chinese case in the Soviet press—
public polemics on a basis of fraternal equality (Point XXV).

With such principles there could be no compromise between the Soviet
and the Chinese leadership unless, as the Chinese phraseology in many
places suggested they hoped to effect, a split developed within the Soviet
leadership. If this was the Chinese hope, they had overplayed their
hand and had united rather than divided their opponents. The talks
were broken off on 20 July. But by that date their failure had been
openly acknowledged on both sides. On 14 July, the day after a rather
plaintive article in the *People's Daily* had proclaimed 'we want unity, not a
split', *Pravda* published the Chinese letter of 14 June together with a
lengthy 'open letter' in reply.[1] In this 'open letter', the Soviet leadership
accused the Chinese leaders, *inter alia*, of being prepared to sacrifice
hundreds of millions of lives in nuclear war, of advocating a return to
Stalinism, of organizing disruptive activities inside other parties and of
preaching nationalism and racialism rather than Communism. The open
letter breathed righteous anger rather than understanding: for its Soviet
drafters had convinced themselves of the dogmatic truth as well as the
pragmatic justifiability of their position. Dogma, they held, evolves
through the collective deliberations of the leadership. Doctrine, the
Chinese would reply, is enshrined in the fundamental writings of Marx
and Lenin. And in their maintenance of the view that there could be no
compromise with evil there is much of the sixteenth-century clash between
Calvinist protestantism and reforming Catholicism.

It was at this point in the polemic that the Soviet leadership compounded its infamy by the signature of the Test-Ban Treaty. On 6 June
the Chinese had issued one last private protest against the Soviet intention.[2] On 31 July the Chinese issued a violently worded statement
attacking the Test-Ban Treaty, initialled in Moscow six days earlier as an
attempt by the signatories to preserve their 'nuclear monopoly', as a
Soviet licence for 'U.S. imperialism to get military superiority', as a
'dirty fraud . . . diametrically counter to the wishes of the peace-loving
peoples', as a betrayal 'of the peoples of the Socialist camp' and a revela-
tion of 'the ugly face of U.S. imperialism—as well as the servile features of
those who are warmly embracing American imperialism'.[3] Two days
later, on 2 August, Chou En-lai sent identical letters to the heads of all

[1] *Pravda*, 14 July 1963.
[2] Statement by the Chinese spokesman, 15 Aug. 1963, *Peking Review*, 16 Aug. 1963.
[3] *Documents, 1963*, pp. 287–90.

the Afro-Asian states calling for a world conference of heads of government to discuss 'the thorough, completely total and resolute prohibition of nuclear weapons'.[1] This bold appeal was answered positively by the governments of North Korea, North Vietnam, and Albania, and by that of Pakistan, and by no one else. The break was now absolute and the polemics began again in real earnest.

To catalogue the exchange of theological abuse is something from which most historians of the Church shy away. The exegesis of doctrinal interchanges is of itself of little historical value and even to approach the endlessly verbose documents with which each side was now to bombard the other can cause all but the most earnest of *aficionados* of Communist polemics a considerable sinking of the heart. The Chinese took upon themselves to reply to the accusations contained in the Soviet open letter in a series of seven lengthy articles published between 6 September 1963 and 10 February 1964 in the *People's Daily* and in *Red Flag* and reproduced in a series of pamphlets in dozens of different languages by the Foreign Language Press in Peking. They also republished the Soviet open letter as 'superlative material for education by negative example'.

The main burden of the Soviet response to this abuse fell into three parts. The theoretical part of the dispute was taken care of by a number of articles in *Kommunist*,[2] while the widest circulation was given to statements by all those Communist Party leaderships and governments on which the Soviets could rely. The Chinese polemics against the Test-Ban Treaty were answered by a series of attacks on alleged Chinese nuclear bellicosity, made the more bitter by a long series of accusations from Chinese sources of deliberate delays and attempts to block the Chinese acquisition of a nuclear capability.[3] The third part of the Soviet response took the form of encouraging calls from other Communist Parties for a world Communist conference and an end to polemics.

This last campaign opened on 27 September when *Pravda* reprinted a call by John Gollan of the British Communist party for the summoning of a world conference (while omitting his plea for a resumption of bilateral talks). But it was soon made clear that the task of organizing such a conference would be long and difficult. In its opposition to Chinese fundamentalism and 'inevitabilitarianism', the Soviets could clearly count on the support of all but a handful of members of the international Communist movement, especially after the Chinese denunciation of the world peace and disarmament movement. Few if any felt strong enough, either nationally or internationally, to dispense with the additional support this could enlist for their general position. But a world conference

---

[1] *Peking Review*, 9 Aug. 1963.   [2] Notably on 31 July, 1 Oct. and 14 Oct. 1963.
[3] For example, the Chinese statement of 15 Aug. 1963; *People's Daily*, 15 Aug. 1963; *Peking Review*, 16 Aug. 1963.

at which China would be confronted with the necessity of conformity or expulsion would not confine that dilemma to the Chinese. Few were anxious to return to the period of ideological control which had followed the expulsion of Yugoslavia from the Cominform. No one dared come out and say this outright. But the expression of reservations as to the 'appropriateness' of such a conference in the near future, as expressed, for example, by the Italian party leadership, was another matter. By the end of the year *Pravda* had boxed the compass, summarizing the Italian position without comment (28 October), suppressing that part of the resolution passed by the Colombian Communist Party which called for a world party meeting (2 November), and even (6 December) proposing fresh bilateral talks, presumably in the safe conviction that much water would have to flow along the Yangtse before Peking would agree.

In these last months of 1963 the Chinese had, however, introduced a newer, more ominous note. It will be remembered that back in March 1963 the Soviet press had poked fun at the Chinese toleration of such colonialist outposts on its borders as Macao and Hong Kong. At that time the *People's Daily* had been stung into the retort that all so-called 'unequal treaties', forced upon China, would be reviewed and handled according to their merits. Among those treaties, it listed the Treaties of Aigun (1858), Peking (1860), and Ili (1881), treaties by virtue of which the Russians had set up the entire Soviet maritime province centred on Vladivostock and held part of Sinkiang. There had, in fact, been considerable local tension at various points along the Sino-Soviet frontier since 1960 when as part of the 'Great Leap Forward', the Chinese had vigorously pushed the policy of sinifying Sinkiang with its considerable minorities of Kazakh, Kirghiz, Uighur and other semi-nomadic communities. Increasing local resistance led to Chinese military pursuit of dissidents up to and across the Sino-Soviet frontier and to a degree of local alarm and sympathy among the peoples of the Soviet republics of Kazakhstan and Kirghizstan. Each side compiled its own list of such incidents, breeding resentment against the arrogance of its opposite numbers and suspicion that the incidents formed part of a deliberate policy. The Chinese naturally came to suspect the Soviets of encouraging and harbouring the dissidents. The Soviets, who in earlier days had had their own troubles with the native population of their Transcaspian provinces and had dealt with them by much the same means as the Chinese were now employing, displayed their characteristic indignation at the infamies of those who imitated them. There was also trouble along the Amur and Ussuri rivers over fishing rights and the ownership of the islands within the rivers. And the whole combined to play on the professional anxieties and arrogance of the frontier police on both sides.

On 13 September this arrogance—and no one who attempted to cross the European frontiers in the immediate aftermath of the German defeat will find the events which took place in anyway unfamiliar—boiled over. The Peking-Moscow train was stopped at the Soviet frontier by Soviet guards. The train was refused permission to cross, its Chinese passengers were detained, and its non-Chinese passengers provided with a Soviet train to speed them on their journey. The sheer pointlessness of the whole episode (trains were allowed to pass thereafter) demonstrates the familiar combination of bureaucratic incompetence and officialdom's bloody-mindedness. It was the cause of immediate protest from China. It may well have been a reply to accusations of Soviet subversive activity in Sinkiang which appeared in the Chinese press on 6 September 1963[1] as part of a reply to the Soviet open letter of 14 July. It was replied to by *Pravda* (19 September), by an official Soviet note printed in *Izvestiya* (21 September), with accusations of 'more than 5,000' Chinese frontier violations in 1962 and the deliberate fomentations of frontier incident in order to fan nationalist passions among the Chinese people. This was followed by allegations of Chinese repression in Sinkiang, including 'personal stories' by alleged refugees from that repression and persecution. It was said that 60,000 refugees had crossed into Soviet territory in 1962 alone. *Pravda*, in its issue of 19 September, linked this with Chinese charges of Indian expansionism, commenting that Chinese claims against the unequal treaties and Chinese frontier practices made it 'difficult to believe in the sincerity of Chinese leaders who give assurances that they are striving towards a peaceful settlement'. The Soviet Union, it added, with all the unctuousness of the publicly reformed sinner, at least understood that 'good neighbourliness was only possible where there is respect for the frontiers established between states'.

With this, the pattern of the next few years appeared to have been fixed. The opening of direct polemics between the two sides, the sealing of the Soviet rapprochement with the United States in the Test-Ban Treaty, which the Chinese could not fail to see as anything but an attempt morally to blackmail them into accepting permanently the status of a non-nuclear power, the Soviet support of India by military aid, and the open acknowledgement of frontier conflicts, all seemed enough in themselves to herald a long-standing rivalry such as that which had so long governed relations between the House of Bourbon and the House of Habsburg, or between France and Germany. *Irridenta*, it is true, were only partially present—though the position of Outer Mongolia seemed analogous in many ways to that of Belgium. But the real dispute lay in the theological-ideological conflict. It was to this that the Chinese appealed. Its concepts and terminology governed their intellectual processes and conditioned their choice of alternative courses of policy. Theocratically

[1] *People's Daily, Red Flag*, 6 Sept. 1963.

oriented states have never found it difficult to make peace, even to seek
the alliance of the unbeliever. But with the heretic or the schismatic,
peace can only be secured at the expense of the faith, and the achievement
of such peace is a measure of the overthrow of religion and the triumph of
rationalism.

CHAPTER III

THE FINANCIAL POLICIES OF
THE WESTERN POWERS

IN the recent history of the international economy, 1963 stands out as a
year of unusual stability and expansion. In contrast with the years immediately preceding not only was there a general rise in output among the
industrial countries and a larger expansion of world trade, but the value
of exports of the primary producing countries rose in line with world
trade, i.e. by about 9 per cent.[1] Apart from a short period of speculation
against sterling in February and March following President de Gaulle's
veto on British entry to the EEC, the year was also one of relative calm in
foreign exchange markets. The pattern of transactions resulted in a
substantial increase in international liquidity, total official reserves of all
countries rising by $3.4 billion, more than in any other postwar year.[2]
The year also witnessed considerable international activity in preparation for two major assaults on the world's trading arrangements, the
'Kennedy Round' of tariff negotiations within GATT, and the United
Nations Conference on Trade and Development (UNCTAD), both
scheduled for 1964. While these early negotiations were more revealing
of the obstacles to further trade liberalization than a possible solution, renewed confidence in the international monetary system at least meant
that, however sharp the differences over methods, the debate would be
conducted on the assumption of a generalized commitment to continued
international economic co-operation. Had the system of international
payments been under threat of imminent breakdown, this commitment
would have been inevitably undermined. In the sphere of financial
diplomacy itself, moreover, renewed confidence in the capacity of the
monetary system to adapt to change also provided the necessary background for the first official studies of long-term international liquidity
problems launched by the IMF and the Group of Ten at the IMF annual
meeting in October.[3]

But while in retrospect the record was one of expanding international
economic and financial co-operation, the year opened none the less in

[1] IMF, *Annual Report 1964*, p. 3.
[2] 'Three main features contributed to this improvement: (a) a $1.6 billion overall balance of
payments surplus by primary producing countries which generally keep a high proportion of
their international reserves in foreign exchange; (b) the rise in the gold production and Soviet
gold sales are on the open market, and (c) less hoarding than in 1962.' Ibid., pp. 6–7.
[3] See below, pp. 76–80.

a mood of profound uncertainty. In 1962 three themes had dominated the economic relations of the Western powers. First, there was the question of a continued expansion of world trade and investment in the face of the levelling off of growth rates in the EEC and the persistence of the US balance of payments deficit. Taken together, one consequence of these developments was the process, described in the previous volume in this series,[1] whereby the emergence of Western Europe as a commercial and financial rival to the United States began to impose severe strains on the structure and functioning of the Atlantic Alliance. Second, the related issue of the role of the developing countries within the international economic system continued to attract increasing attention, particularly after the decision taken on a Soviet initiative by the 17th General Assembly in 1962, to convene UNCTAD in 1964.[2] Finally, underlying both these issues, was the wider question of international liquidity; if world trade did begin to expand, as the optimists predicted, and if the USA succeeded in eliminating the US balance of payments deficit, as both her own government and her creditors insisted she must, would there be sufficient liquidity to cover the rising flow of international transactions?

With a significant difference of emphasis, these issues again provided the focus for international economic debate in 1963. In the previous two years the debate had been conducted against the background of the American Grand Design and of Britain's negotiations to join the EEC. The Grand Design had been conceived as a strategy for resolving the United States' economic difficulties, particularly the need for a rapid reduction of the balance of payments deficit,[3] on the basis of increased co-operation within the Atlantic Alliance. The Administration's chosen instrument for this purpose was the Trade Expansion Act under which the Executive was given authority to negotiate down to zero all tariffs on manufactured goods in which the USA and its trading partners accounted for over 80 per cent of world trade. In pressing for further trade liberalization, it was also stipulated that special attention should be paid in tariff negotiations to commodities of particular interest to developing countries. In this way the Kennedy administration hoped to resolve one of the central contradictions of American foreign policy—how to support the further integration of Western Europe without damage to US economic and commercial interests, while at the same time instituting a better deal for the 'Third World', an objective to which the administration was also committed.

The initiative to stage a further round of tariff negotiations within

---

[1] *Survey, 1962*, Chapter IV.

[2] For a discussion of the background and origin of the 1964 UNCTAD, see D. Cordovez 'The Making of UNCTAD', *Journal of World Trade Law*, vol. 1, No. 3, 1967, pp. 243–328, and B. Gosovic, 'UNCTAD: North-South Encounter', *International Conciliation*, No. 568, May 1968.

[3] *Survey, 1962*, pp. 184–7.

GATT, in which for the first time the 'contracting parties' would aim at a deep across-the-board cut in their respective national tariffs rather than at bargaining, as in the past, item by item, rested (at least in American eyes) on the assumption that the British government would be successful in its bid to join the EEC. Only on this assumption would the number of commodities in which the United States and an enlarged Western Europe would dominate world trade, be sufficiently high for the 'Kennedy Round' to result in the creation of a free trade area in industrial products, the condition under which the CET[1] would cease to pose a threat to American exports.

The prospect of an enlarged European Community was also linked, indirectly, with pressure for a World Trade Conference. Although, in Britain, it was often argued that accession to the EEC was necessary to ensure that the Community would adopt a liberal 'outward-looking' commercial policy, opinion in the Third World, with the exception of the francophone African states, was generally hostile. It is true that the results of the Dillon round of tariff negotiations, which ended in mid-1962, had generally been considered disappointing, but it had at least demonstrated the ability of the EEC to negotiate as a group on commercial policy and the general interest of the Community in trade liberalization. None the less the British application had originally aroused almost universal opposition from Britain's traditional Commonwealth trading partners, and, with the exception of Sierra Leone, the African Commonwealth states had interpreted the British offer to negotiate terms of association on their behalf as a slur on their sovereignty.[2] Much of the pressure which finally resulted in the decision to convene a World Trade Conference derived from these suspicions.[3]

For both the USA and Britain, however, acceptance was essentially a political gesture, and it was clear from the start that they did not expect much from the Conference. For substantive progress in trade liberalization, both in their own interests and for the developing world, they looked to the 'Kennedy Round'. If the US interest was primarily to find a way of reducing her payments deficit by creating a favourable climate for American exports and by sharing the costs of the alliance without disrupting it still further, Britain's traditional interest in liberal trade policies was made more urgent by the obvious need to minimize the cost of entry

[1] The common external tariff of the EEC.

[2] For a discussion on Commonwealth attitudes towards the British applications, see Pierre Uri, ed., *From Commonwealth to Common Market* (London, 1968).

[3] For example, the Cairo Economic Conference of Non-Aligned States, held in July 1962, came out strongly in support of a UN Trade and Development Conference. At the same time it expressed apprehension that 'regional economic groupings of industrialised countries will adversely affect the interests of their economies if conceived and operated in a restrictive and discriminatory manner'. *NYHT*, 23 Jan. 1963.

into the EEC and the damage to her overseas trading partners, particularly within the Commonwealth. Despite the broad similarity of the US and British positions—both after all managed reserve currencies in deficit—and of their objectives—an outward-looking low-tariff Community—British and American policies had diverged sharply in 1962, particularly in the monetary field.[1] But, so long as British negotiations with the EEC were in progress, the Grand Design provided a framework within which economic diplomacy could be conducted and the promise that, in the last analysis, it would be based, as in the past, on co-operative effort between the industrial states of Western Europe and North America.

President de Gaulle's veto on 3 January 1963 not only undermined this framework but called in question the assumption of future co-operation. For the USA, the continued co-operation of the European powers in monetary affairs was all the more important since the government was faced at the beginning of the year not only with an unusually high rate of capital exports,[2] and hence a continued strain on the balance of payments, but with evidence also of a reduced level of economic activity and consequently a persistently high level of unemployment.[3] In these circumstances there was clearly a danger that pressure would develop within the USA for a protectionist, if not isolationist, solution. If the French were to widen their opposition to Britain into a general attack on what they regarded as Anglo-Saxon domination of the international Monetary System, this pressure would be increasingly difficult to resist, with serious consequences both for the American economy and indeed for the economy of the Western world in general. At the same time, deceleration in the rate of economic expansion in Europe, which had provided one of the main foundations of the general growth in world trade during the 1950s, re-awakened fears that the EEC might develop along protectionist lines.

Per Jacobsson, Managing Director of the IMF, caught the prevailing mood of uncertainty in a speech delivered in New York in mid-February. With the end of postwar expansion in Europe, he suggested, 'a new situation has arisen which shows certain similarities with what happened in the early 1930s'. While it was not necessary 'to repeat the sad experience of those years . . . I do think that we will have to take definite measures that they are not repeated'.[4] As the course of events unfolded it became clear

---

[1] Cf. *Survey, 1962*, pp. 190–1 and 206–8.

[2] During the first six months of 1963, the outflow of US private long-term and short-term capital reached a peak equivalent to an annual rate of more than $5 billion. IMF, *Annual Report 1964*, p. 84.

[3] For most of 1962 the rate of unemployment remained unchanged, at about 5·5 per cent above the postwar average. Early in 1963, the rate rose further to about 5·9 per cent. Ibid., 1963, pp. 97–8.

[4] Mr Jacobsson's speech was delivered before the New York University Graduate School of Business Administration. Paradoxically, its main purpose was to express confidence in the underlying strength of the US economy and support for the Administration's recent programme of

that the governments of the major industrial states, including France, were indeed determined to avoid such a repetition; even so, the IMF felt constrained to include, in its annual report for 1963, an exhortatory plea to the European states that 'their regional arrangements remain outward-looking and thus contribute to the flow of trade, supporting both the recent progress toward equilibrium in world payments and the upward trend of exchange earnings of the less developed countries'.[1]

The progress which the IMF report noted did not result from any marked improvement in the United States balance of payments, but from a decrease in the balance of payments surpluses of the major European states. It was partly this deterioration in their relative positions which had served to soften European criticism of US monetary policy in 1962. It had also allegedly provided the background for co-operation amongst the group of ten states which had established, within the IMF, the General Agreement to Borrow in 1961,[2] and a growing network of 'swap' arrangements between their central banks which were devised to offset speculative pressure against any of their currencies. Although fully participating in these arrangements, the British government had isolated itself in 1962 from Washington and Western Europe by insisting that some more fundamental reform of the international payments system was required.[3] Now paradoxically, it was the speculative pressure on sterling after the French veto which proved the flexibility and strength of these essentially *ad hoc* arrangements (in which France was fully represented) and so helped to create the climate in which both the USA and the European powers could agree on the first tentative steps towards the introduction of more fundamental and ambitious reforms.

That this would be the outcome was not predetermined. Despite the political uncertainty to which the French veto gave rise, the immediate repercussions on the position of sterling were shortlived and easily contained. In anticipation of speculative pressure, the central bankers were reported to have devoted their monthly meeting in February to the preparation of contingency plans.[4] In the event the immediate outflow of funds from London was negligible and indeed the January gold reserve figures

tax cuts; these, he believed, would stimulate the economy without damaging the competitiveness of American exports in world markets. Yet, since the result of these expansionary policies would almost certainly be to prolong the period of budget deficits which, in another context, he described as the 'emanation of permanently unbalanced minds' the clear implication was that the twin problems of economic growth and the balance of payments could only be handled on the basis of continuing international co-operation amongst industrial states. *The Times*, 19 Feb. 1963; *Financial Times*, 20 Feb. 1963.

[1] IMF, *Annual Report 1963*, p. 5.
[2] For the background to the General Agreement to Borrow [GAB] see J. Keith Horsefield, *The International Monetary Fund, 1945–55: 20 years of international monetary cooperation*, vol. i, *Chronicle*, (Washington, 1969), pp. 510–12.
[3] *Survey, 1962*, pp. 206–8.   [4] *Observer*, 3 Feb. 1963.

showed an increase over the previous month. Even when, in the following weeks, pressure began to mount—on 11 March the pound fell below parity with the dollar on the Foreign Exchange Market for the first time since August 1961[1]—the movement out of sterling was kept within fairly narrow bounds. Although the authorities maintained their customary secrecy, it subsequently emerged that speculation against sterling had indeed been checked by central bank co-operation. In his budget statement on 3 April the British chancellor of the exchequer, Mr Maudling, announced that '$250m. have been advanced to us during the months of February and March, and these borrowings have, of course, been reflected in the published figures of the change in our dollar and convertible currency reserve for the two months'.[2] The chancellor himself gave no details of these loans, but the press reported that the Bank of France had, with Cabinet approval, advanced its full quota of $50m.[3] In any event, the announcement of this kind of support, with its implicit suggestion that day-to-day political tensions would not be allowed to undermine the general commitment to financial stability, was sufficient for the time being to restore confidence. Not only did the chancellor avoid calling up his second line of defence, the $1 billion immediately available from the IMF under standby arrangements, but the short-term loans had all been repaid by the end of June.

With a general election scheduled for 1964 it was, perhaps, not surprising that some experts forecast further sterling crises as a result of a government programme of expansion, heralded by a reduction of bank rate and purchase tax in January,[4] and confirmed by Maudling's 'Growth without Inflation' budget in April. Nevertheless, it was further evidence of the effectiveness of the European co-operation machinery, if also of the autonomous nature of currency speculation, that sterling recovered so fast despite an anticipated budget deficit of £687m. for the financial year ending in March 1964. Moreover, the support provided for sterling by European banks—the British evidently refrained from using their right to draw £50m. under the US 'swap agreement'[5]—was devised in such a way as also to ease pressure on the dollar.

[1] The loss of sterling on the same day was estimated by experienced observers as being 'over $40m and probably closer to $60m'. *Financial Times*, 12 Mar. 1963.

[2] *Documents, 1963*, pp. 84–5.

[3] It was also suggested that the terms allegedly attached to the loans, a 3–3½ per cent interest with a currency guarantee against devaluation, reflected the underlying strength of the major European countries currencies *vis-à-vis* both sterling and the dollar. *Sunday Times*, 7 Apr. 1963; *NY Times*, 18 Apr. 1963.

[4] Bank rate was reduced from 4½ per cent to 4 per cent on 3 Jan. 1963 and the highest rate of purchase tax from 45 per cent to 25 per cent.

[5] This agreement, one of a series between the Federal Reserve Bank and the central banks, was negotiated for a 12-month period from 31 May 1962, *Federal Reserve Bulletin*, Sept. 1963, p. 1216.

No doubt the improvement to the dollar's fortunes was primarily because, as we have seen, the major European powers, with the exception of France, eliminated their balance of payment surpluses during 1962. Still, despite the underlying strength of the US economy and the stability of the dollar in European foreign exchange markets, the persistence of the US deficit reduced the attraction of the dollar as a haven for hot money. Indeed, it was claimed at the time that one reason why support for sterling proved so effective was precisely because there was little incentive to switch from one vulnerable currency to another.[1] Meanwhile, however, dollars loaned by European central banks to Britain could not at the same time be converted into gold by purchases from the United States. The defence of sterling thus afforded a further measure of relief.

In the United States the problem of combining external stability with expansionary policies which aimed at stimulating the domestic economy, was compounded by the rate at which dollars continued to leave the country. It was the need to avoid the choice between domestic retrenchment and a weaker, even ultimately a devalued, dollar that had led the US government in August 1962 to negotiate a series of 'swap' agreements to a total of $700m. with seven foreign central banks and the Bank for International Settlements.

As the underlying problem, contrasted with the immediate stability of the dollar in foreign exchange markets, showed no signs of disappearing, this strategy was continued in 1963. Acting as agent of the US Treasury, the Federal Reserve Bank began to renew and extend the 'swap' arrangements negotiated the previous year. In December 1962 a $50m. 'swap' with the Bank of Italy was increased to $150m. By early March the network had been increased to a total of $1,100m.[2] In addition, the US Treasury continued the dual policy developed the previous year of issuing non-marketable securities, the so-called Roosa Bonds, to mop up surplus dollars while persuading its partners where possible to prepay outstanding debts to the USA.[3]

While there was little evidence to suggest that the European powers

---

[1] *Financial Times*, 12 Mar. 1963.   [2] *Federal Reserve Bulletin*, Mar. 1963, p. 311.

[3] The Bank for International Settlements gave the following account of the operational forms which US policies in defence of the dollar had taken. 'First, the US intervenes in the exchange markets, spot and forward, in order to forestall or damp down movements that lead to accumulations of dollars in the hands of foreign monetary authorities, for whom the dollars are convertible into gold at the US Treasury on request. Secondly, when such movements occur and it seems likely that they may be reasonably quickly reversed, the US authorities take steps to ensure the additional dollars in question are not converted into gold by relieving the holders of the exchange risk. Thirdly, in certain cases—either where unbalanced situations continued for longer than was at first expected, or, more generally, where a country has dollar reserves in excess of what it is likely to require in the short run—the US Government has issued non-marketable securities, expressed sometimes in dollars and sometimes in foreign currencies, with a life of between one year and five years'. Bank for International Settlements, *33rd Annual Report* (Basle 1963), p. 123.

were any more persuaded of the concept of 'burden sharing' than they had been earlier, it was 'now clear that their interests in maintaining the current gold price of the dollar would ensure continued co-operation with American strategy. After all, despite European resentment, particularly strong in the case of France, at having to finance the US deficit, it was the European states which held a relatively high proportion of their official reserve in dollars. In this respect, if no other, the mutual interests of the major powers always remained strong enough to offset the psychological damage of the West European political crisis.

Before long, European attitudes to the United States 'swap network' appeared to change from acquiescence to enthusiasm.[1] The stimulus for this was provided, on the one hand, by European fears of inflation, and on the other, by evidence of a movement of opinion within the US administration on the question of international liquidity. In general, most West European governments and central banks remained deeply sceptical of all plans for a major reform of the international monetary system, of which Maudling's 'clearing account' proposal[2] advanced in 1962, was the most recent. Inflationary pressures which had appeared in 1962 in most West European states were intensified in 1963, particularly in Italy and France where the rapid increase in effective demand provided, amongst other things, a stimulus to the West German economy and led consequently to the re-emergence of a German balance of payment surplus.[3] In this context the fact that wages 'continued to rise at a rate considerably higher than the gain in productivity'[4] was itself sufficient to confirm most European governments and central banks in their traditional belief in financial orthodoxy. But their scepticism also reflected a concern lest the question of structural reform, to which the British chancellor had addressed himself, should be used as a substitute for the elimination of the US, and to a lesser extent the British, balance of payments deficits which they regarded as the main problem confronting the international financial community.

European anxieties about inflation were no doubt in part projected on the United States; many European observers clearly found it difficult to accept at their face value American (and British) motives in raising the international liquidity issue. The references were seldom explicit but their general direction was clear. Thus in March Karl Blessing, President of the German Bundesbank, told a Basle audience that 'an indiscriminate increase of liquidity in the entire western monetary system would merely revive the process of creeping inflation in Europe in view of the level at which demand persists here'.[5] The existing network of financial defences

---

[1] *Financial Times*, 25 Feb. 1963.   [2] *Survey, 1962*, pp. 206–8.
[3] IMF, *Annual Report, 1963*, pp. 98–102; Ibid., *1964*, p. 46.   [4] Ibid., *1963*, p. 102.
[5] *Financial Times*, 12 Mar. 1963; *NY Times*, 13 Mar. 1963.

was, he concluded, adequate to cover any likely contingency in the international economy. But there was also a deeper resentment which found its most articulate and consistent expression in the Gaullist view that the entire structure of the Bretton Woods system discriminated against Western Europe and acted as a cover for the exercise of American power. In this sense, the French regarded the US balance of payment deficit as a means whereby Europe not only helped to finance the takeover of its own industry, but also American economic and military policy around the globe. There were, the French finance minister, Giscard d'Estaing, told the press on 21 March, two principles governing French financial policy. First, 'La France est favorable aux mesures qui ont pour objet de régler les problèmes et non pas d'en masquer la véritable nature'. Secondly, 'La France considère que dans l'ère de très grande liberté des transactions dans laquelle nous nous engagcons, un minimum d'organisation et de discipline commune est necessaire'.[1]

Yet France also was finally committed to a policy of financial co-operation with the USA. For her, like the other Western powers, the development of defensive co-ordination between central banks was a better alternative than a reform of the world monetary system which, by adding to the availability of international liquidity, would leave existing distribution, which the French regarded as inequitable, unaffected. Thus despite speculation that President de Gaulle would demand that the American government should control investment by US nationals in Europe as a *quid pro quo* for future co-operation, a new swap agreement of $100m. was negotiated in March without difficulty and apparently without conditions.[2]

The American position was not so clear cut. In 1962 Washington had been as cool as had the Europeans to the Maudling Plan. So long as the hope persisted of salvaging the Grand Design, the Kennedy administration had been unsympathetic to ideas for monetary reform which might put at risk European acceptance of 'burden sharing', while, by the same token, weakening the US bargaining position with her allies. But opinion within the American economic and financial establishment on the liquidity issue had never been unanimous. One consequence of President de Gaulle's veto was to open up the debate. As the year advanced three broad positions were discernible.[3] First, the official US Treasury view, advanced by Douglas Dillon, Secretary to the Treasury, at the IMF annual meeting the previous September, remained that the general problem of international liquidity (if it existed at all) should be tackled only when the United

[1] *Le Monde*, 22 Mar. 1963.
[2] The negotiations took place during the Paris meeting of the Political and Economic Committee of the OECD at the beginning of March, *NY Times*, 1 Mar. 1963; *Le Monde*, 24 Mar. 1963.
[3] For a contemporary account of the US domestic debate on this issue, see *Guardian*, 15 Aug. 1963.

States' balance of payments deficit had been brought finally under control. In 1962 US exports had increased by only 3 per cent while imports were up by 11 per cent. The administration thus faced a dilemma: how to stimulate the economy without damaging United States competitiveness in world markets.[1] The strategy devised for this purpose rested on the one hand on the administration's tax reform proposals which it was hoped would stimulate the economy without simultaneously leading to wage and price pressures,[2] and on the other on cutting the rate of capital outflow, preferably as the result of the development of a European market and voluntary European action to restrain borrowing on the New York market along the lines suggested by Dillon in his Rome speech of May 1962.[3] Second, against this orthodox position, were ranged not only the Bureau of the Budget and the Council of Economic Advisers, but elements within the US Treasury itself. Indeed, it is unlikely that the real lines of division anywhere coincided precisely with the departmental boundaries; both the intractability of the US deficit and the fact that, however desirable, changes in European markets were clearly not going to occur overnight inevitably meant that alternative strategies had to be considered.[4] For example, a report originally requested by President Kennedy in 1962, and commissioned from the Brookings Institution by all three bodies, concluded in mid-summer that it would be feasible to eliminate the US deficit between 1968 and 1970 on condition that certain reforms were instituted to allow economic growth at home to be combined with a continued expansion of world trade.[5] To this end the report advocated, as the ideal solution, the creation of a Payments Union with powers to create substantial international credit,[6] failing which it suggested the establishment of a sterling-dollar bloc[7] in juxtaposition to a European currency bloc. In this latter, and more likely, event it was suggested that while exchange ratios might fluctuate in transactions between the two blocs, they would be fixed within them.

The final compromise strategy was attributed to the Federal Reserve Bank, which having been largely responsible for the negotiation of the successful 'swap' network, was arguably in the best position to assess the tolerance of the European states whose co-operation would be necessary. By mid-August the Federal Reserve Bank was reported to favour an

[1] *Financial Times*, 25, 27 Feb. 1963.

[2] At the meeting of the Economic Policy Committee of the OECD at the end of February, the US delegation, led by Robert Roosa, the Under-Secretary to the Treasury, reportedly based their defence of American policy on the tax reform proposals.

[3] *Survey, 1962*, pp. 191, 193; for text of Dillon's speech, see *Documents, 1962*, No. 136.

[4] Despite Dillon's appeal, heavy foreign borrowing by European states, Canada, and Japan continued on the New York market. It totalled $1048m. in 1962 and in April 1963 it was estimated that the rate for the first quarter of the year was even higher. *NY Times*, 29 Apr. 1963.

[5] Walter F. Salant and others, *The US Balance of Payments in 1963* (Washington D.C., 1963). The report was submitted in Jan. 1963, although the final chapter of policy recommendations was added subsequently.   [6] Ibid., pp. 256–8.   [7] Ibid., pp. 258–62.

institutionalization of existing *ad hoc* arrangements which, together with a more regular use of the IMF credit system, would provide 'a blend of economic discipline and international credit'.[1] In other words, while the existing system should be continued and improved to cover short-term problems, attention should be turned towards making the IMF into a more effective agency for the creation of liquidity in the long-term.

The new United States position emerged only gradually as at different times and in different contexts the Kennedy administration took steps which appeared to be based on one or other of the three strategies outlined above. Since any international reform would take time to negotiate, let alone establish, these various positions did not, as the Brookings report acknowledged, really contradict one another. Where in 1962 the British government had been isolated in demanding a major reform, the American and British positions were now appreciably closer. While the 'swap' agreements had proved their value in containing speculation against sterling in the spring, the very magnitude of the dollar problem raised doubts in the USA whether a system of essentially short-term expedients could withstand a major assault on the Western payments system. Moreover, to the extent that the USA succeeded in reducing its deficit, and hence reduced the injection of more and more dollars into the system, these doubts were bound to grow. It was not surprising, therefore, that when, on 30 May, Maudling announced to the House of Commons[2] that an increase in the existing standby facility to $500m. had been negotiated with the Federal Reserve Bank, there was speculation that the deal was the result of a bargain. The British, it was suggested, had agreed to co-operate fully in the construction of a defensive network in return for an American undertaking to give a sympathetic hearing to British views on international monetary reform.[3] In any event, it was, as *The Times* rather cryptically noted,[4] a 'welcome strengthening of Anglo-American monetary cooperation which has not always been conspicuous'.

But if both reserve currency states shared a number of common interests *vis-à-vis* the EEC, for example in negotiating as deep a cut as possible in industrial tariff levels, neither state was in a strong bargaining position. This was, of course, a further reason for sterling-dollar co-operation, but it also meant the European states and their 'conservative allies' within the US administration could effectively dictate the pace at which the debate on international liquidity was allowed to develop.

Although the British government evidently now accepted this limitation, the leader of the opposition, Harold Wilson, did not. In a speech to the American Chamber of Commerce in London on 15 May[5] he warned

[1] *Guardian*, 15 Aug. 1963.   [2] 678 *HC Deb.*, cols. 1543–6.
[3] *Times*, 31 May 1963; *OFNS*, 4 June 1963.   [4] *Times*, 31 May 1963.
[5] *Guardian*, 16 May; *NY Times*, 16 May 1963.

against the dangers of concentrating excessively on defence rather than on economic strength. The result, he suggested, would be that 'we, in the West, are likely to find ourselves embedded in a nuclear citadel of impermeable strength, the foundations of which are being undermined by the onset of economic dry-rot'. In a three-point programme, Wilson appealed to the politicians of the Western world to overcome the natural conservatism of their central bankers. First, he proposed the convening of a world economic summit conference; secondly, that the IMF should be given full powers to issue certificates 'in terms of gold and equivalent to gold' to countries in payments difficulties which had unemployed resources; and thirdly, that the IMF should also be empowered to assign £200–300 million of these certificates a year to a new international investment fund which would link the needs of developing countries to the underemployed resources of the industrial nations.

Although to the 'pessimists' in the United States Wilson's speech no doubt came as welcome evidence of outside support,[1] it was mistimed and addressed to the wrong audience. For the time being the 'optimists' were making the running. Even Maxwell Stamp, to whose plan Wilson's proposals bore a close resemblance, expressed his reservations in a letter to *The Times*.[2] On the continent, the tide was still running strongly against ideas of radical reform. At the end of May, the Governor of the Banca d'Italia, Dr Guido Carli, explained that Italy's views on the liquidity issue were similar to those of France. There was no urgent need, he said, to strengthen the existing system of defences until these arrangements had been fully tested, but there was a need for EEC and other industrial countries to elaborate a common policy on the composition and administration of reserves to increase their effectiveness; if at this stage further reserves were still required, this could be achieved by an increase in IMF quotas.[3] Similar arguments were advanced at the beginning of August by four central bankers (from the United States, Switzerland, West Germany, and Italy) in an article in the *Financial Review* of the US Federal Reserve Bank. They rejected 'various theoretical plans which have been asking many of the right questions but so far suggesting unworkable solutions', expressed confidence in the new system of 'swap' arrangements, and called for its continuation.[4]

[1] Even the US 'pessimists' were not in favour of anything so radical as Wilson's proposals. One of them, Peter Kenen, published a report taking a highly pessimistic view of the availability of international liquidity but only calling for a big extension of the stand-by credit system (*Reserve asset preferences of Central Banks and stability of the gold exchange standard*, Princeton Studies in International Finance, No. 10, Princeton, 1963).

[2] *Times*, 20 May 1963. For Dr Balogh's letter supporting Wilson's initiative, see ibid., 27 May 1963.

[3] *Times*, 1 June 1963.

[4] *Financial Times*, 8 Aug., *NY Times*, 8 Aug. 1963. This article was seen as a direct riposte to the Brookings report mentioned earlier.

One of the main, if generally unstated, issues which lay behind these utterances concerned the future role of the IMF in any overhaul of the monetary system. Apart from the virtue, in the participants' eyes at least, of the *ad hoc* nature of the 'swap' network, these agreements were simple reciprocal arrangements for mutual support between sovereign governments. There was nothing automatic or supra-national about them. Any proposal which went beyond central bank co-operation was confronted immediately not only by President de Gaulle's objection in principle to supra-nationalism, but by a more immediate European suspicion that the new mechanism might release the US government from its commitment to eliminate the deficit. Moreover in doing so it was likely to perpetuate American control over the Bretton Woods system, within which, it was often felt, she had a dominant if not controlling voice. Paradoxically, US hegemony within the system was symbolized by the fact that, alone amongst the industrial powers which had suffered from balance of payments problems since 1947, the USA had never made any use of the IMF's facilities. The Fund was viewed by many Europeans, admittedly, as a mechanism for providing relief, but also for imposing a measure of discipline and control, which the United States helped to administer but itself escaped.

Despite a general desire to prevent any transfer of independent authority to the IMF so long as this situation persisted, it was the need to prepare for the Fund's annual meeting in September—when international liquidity would inevitably feature prominently on the agenda—which provided the stimulus to the preparatory debate in Europe as well as in the USA. Furthermore, the appointment of a Frenchman, Pierre-Paul Schweitzer, to succeed Per Jacobsson[1] as Managing Director of the Fund led to speculation about the possibility of an initiative in this field by the IMF itself. If the new Director had a developed position on the liquidity question, in his public pronouncements he was careful to offend neither camp. Before leaving Paris, he told the Press

Je crois a la possibilité d'améliorer le système monétaire actuel et d'accroître les ressources disponibles, mais je suis sceptique en ce qui concerne la possibilité d'inventer des systèmes monétaires entièrement nouveaux, et surtout autocratiques, qui apporterait miraculeusement la solution de tous les problèmes.[2]

Within the international financial community there was agreement on one thing, namely, that the American deficit constituted the most intractable of the problems to which Schweitzer had alluded. But on whether the deficit foreclosed the possibility of international action or necessitated it, there was no agreement at all. If, as we have seen, the

[1] Per Jacobsson died on 5 May 1963 during a visit to London.
[2] *Le Monde*, 23–24 June 1963.

Europeans took the view that there was nothing to worry about and that the USA should put her own house in order, the American reformers argued that while national action was necessary, this would rebound on the USA, and the West generally, if domestic and international policies were not reconciled. The Brookings report had concluded that, 'The present problem is not primarily a balance of payments problem. More fundamentally, the problem is the basic inadequacy of the international monetary mechanism in relation to the requirements of the Free World.'[1] This inadequacy reflected, in its view, on the one hand the fact that international liquidity was not sufficient to cover disequilibria resulting from structural change in advanced economies without damaging domestic economic growth, and on the other, the fact that the increase in world reserves in the form of liquid dollar claims could no longer be depended upon. Although these findings pointed unequivocally towards international action, the report also concluded that the major international financial problem facing the USA 'consists of the constraints imposed on the United States in its efforts to attain the more basic objectives of policy'.[2] It was 'the changed position of the dollar—the loss of foreigners' desire to continue accumulating dollars—which imposes these constraints',[3] and while it was suggested that this situation was irreversible, a function as much of the strength of European economies as of the US deficit, there was no doubt that the deficit had accentuated the change. In any case, if there was to be any hope of enlisting European co-operation in monetary reform along the lines proposed by the report, as a practical matter it was clear that the Administration would have to demonstrate its determination to reduce the rate of capital outflow.

This analysis of the US dilemma was confirmed by the prevailing attitudes of the European powers. Despite their commitment to short-term support for the dollar, it was evident that America's European creditors were not satisfied with the long-term prospects. In a slightly petulant tone, the BIS Annual Report published on 10 June 1963 concluded:

The United States authorities have tried, in a variety of ways, and with a moderate degree of success, to reconcile the opposing policy requirements of the external deficit and unused domestic resources. It is evident, however, that the situation calls for more vigorous measures. For some time it has seemed unlikely that the deficit will be resolved merely by a widening of the trade

[1] Salant, pp. 242–3.
[2] These were given as: (i) achieving domestic economic stability and sustained growth at full employment; (ii) maintaining the military strength of the Free World; (iii) promoting and supporting economic development of under-developed areas, and avoiding injury to the continued growth of other countries; (iv) assuring the greatest possible freedom of economic production and international transactions in the Free World. Ibid., pp. 241–4.
[3] Ibid., p. 241.

surplus; in fact the export trend will be quite favourable if it keeps pace with the rise in imports as the economy stands. Hence, contributions to equilibrium are needed from a reduction in net capital exports and in government dollar expenditures abroad.[1]

Nor, given the readiness of the authorities to deal with concrete problems as they arose, did Europe's central bankers see much point to the argument about shortages of liquidity.

The only real solution is to eliminate the external deficit. If, out of consideration for broader objectives, the government believe it necessary that this be done only gradually, then it is essential also to protect the international position of the currency by funding some part of the short-term liabilities. In effect, the issue of special securities has to some extent served this function. It is a useful technique, but it cannot be said too often that there is a vast difference between 'buying time' and 'marking time'.[2]

Similar concern was expressed at the July meeting of the Economic Policy Committee of the OECD. While the report submitted to the Committee was apparently optimistic about the revival of business activity in OECD member states, it also concluded that there was no likelihood of the US export surplus being significantly improved; further action by both the US and European governments was accordingly recommended.[3]

It was with this potentially critical audience in mind that President Kennedy framed the special message to Congress on the US balance of payments, which he delivered on 18 July.[4] With the credibility of his economic and financial policies at risk, his task was complicated by the fact that he had at once to underwrite the basic strategy which he had announced two years earlier for securing balance in the nation's international payments and economic expansion at home, while suggesting that new measures designed to achieve these goals would be more successful than those which had already been tried. Moreover, if the USA was to continue to discharge responsibilities deriving from her central position in the economy of the Western powers, the President had also to head off those critics at home who would always be ready to press a protectionist solution to American economic problems, and those abroad who argued for a return to the gold standard and a 'once and for all' upward revision of the gold price. The central position of the USA in the world monetary system was partly the result of a historical accident, the legitimacy of which the European states increasingly found it difficult to accept. It was equally the result of US economic power, of which, in a paradoxical

[1] Bank for International Settlements, *Thirty-Third Annual Report, 1 Apr. 1962–31 Mar. 1963* (Basle, 1963), p. 29.
[2] Ibid., p. 32. The same point was made in the annual report of the West German Bundesbank, which noted that 'devices for support of the dollar must not become a means of painless deficit-financing'. *NY Times*, 17 June 1963.
[3] *NY Times*, 10 July 1963.   [4] *Documents, 1963*, pp. 85–97.

sense, the US deficit was the reflection. With about half their reserves in dollars, the West Germans, for example, were clearly concerned that the Americans should not devalue. Whatever other States might do in similar circumstances, for the USA this course was not available. Thus President Kennedy first reiterated that:

in solving its international payments problem, this Nation will continue to adhere to its historic advocacy of freer trade and capital movements, and it will continue to honour its obligations to carry a fair share of the defence and develop-ment of the free world. At the same time, we shall continue policies designed to reduce unemployment and stimulate growth here at home—for the well-being of all free peoples is inextricably entwined with the progress achieved by our own people. I want to make it equally clear that this Nation will maintain the dollar as good as gold, freely interchangeably with gold at $35 an ounce, the foundation stone of the free world's trade and payments system . . .[1]

Apart from the announcement of an export promotion programme and of a series of measures to reduce official and private overseas expenditure through more rigorous screening by the Bureau of the Budget,[2] the Presi-dent announced three major policy changes in the monetary field. First, probably least important as it represented the area in which pressure had been most successfully contained, the Federal re-discount rate was in-creased from 3 per cent to 3½ per cent as a further disincentive to short-term outflow. Secondly, 'to stem the flood of foreign security sales in our markets and still be fully consistent with both economic growth and free capital movements', the President urged Congress to enact an interest equalization tax. Since the US regarded direct capital control as 'con-trary to our basic precept of freer markets' and since most European states were either unwilling or unable to dissuade their nationals from raising money in the USA, it was hoped that the tax—15 per cent on equity securities—would act as a disincentive to foreigners wishing to raise capital on the New York market. Thirdly, he announced that, for the first time, the USA had applied for support from the IMF. The negotia-tion of $500m. stand-by credit was essentially designed to meet a technical problem. This arose because countries which accumulated more dollars than they needed, used them to repay debts to the IMF, whose holding of dollars was consequently approaching the permitted ceiling.[3] The stand-by arrangement would therefore enable the USA to purchase foreign currencies with which to buy back dollars from countries wishing to repay the Fund; loans to the Fund could then, in turn, be repaid in foreign currencies other than dollars, hence conserving the US gold

---

[1] *Documents, 1963*, pp. 85–97.

[2] For details of the Bureau's Gold Budget Scheme, see *NY Times*, 2 Apr. 1963.

[3] 75 per cent of the original subscription, about $3 billion. For the text of the IMF announce-ment, see *DSB*, vol. xlix, No. 1259, p. 258.

supply. But if the problem was a technical one, the decision to apply for IMF support had none the less, as the European press pointed out, a deeper psychological significance: in a sense it was an official concession that the 'hegemony of the dollar was over', and it was welcomed as a sign that the USA, like other states, could apply for Fund support without this signifying a major crisis for the international monetary system as a whole.[1]

Finally, the President turned to the wider question of international monetary reform. While he expressed the administration's confidence in the network of reciprocal credit arrangements and their intention of strengthening them further, he concluded:

the U.S. interest in the continuing evolution of the system inaugurated at the time of Bretton Woods is not a result of our current payments deficit—rather it reflects our concern that adequate provision be made for the growth of international liquidity to finance expanding world trade over the years ahead. Indeed, one of the reasons that new sources of liquidity may well be needed is that, as we close our payments gap, we cut down our provision of dollars to the rest of the world.

As yet this Government is not prepared to recommend any specific prescription for long-term improvement of the international monetary system. But we are studying the matter closely; we shall be discussing possible improvements with our friends abroad; and our minds will be open to their initiatives. We share their view that the problem of improving the payments mechanism is one that demands careful joint deliberation. At the same time, we do not pretend that talk of long-range reform of the system is any substitute for the actions that we ourselves must take now.

Predictably it was on this last aspect of the President's message rather than on his intimation of change in the American position on international liquidity that European reactions were primarily focused. Judging by immediate reactions, it was clear that the major European states were satisfied that the USA had at last taken some decisive action. Although Belgium immediately increased her own short-term interest rates,[2] it was made clear that this was a special case—Belgium had also been suffering from a sustained outflow of capital—and no other European state followed suit. The Italians who were similarly in financial difficulties, although reportedly critical of the US proposals, did nothing.[3] Otherwise reactions were generally favourable. Dr Erhard, West German minister of economic affairs, issued a statement praising the decision to increase the Federal discount rate and the resort to IMF support.[4] The British chancellor took a similar line in a speech to the National Productivity Advisory Council on Industry on 19 July in which he suggested hopefully that by

[1] The Times, 19 July 1963; Le Monde, 20 July 1963.
[2] Le Monde, NY Times, 19 July 1963.   [3] NY Times, 22 July 1963.
[4] FAZ, 22 July 1963; Le Monde, 21–22 July 1963; Financial Times, 22 July 1963.

refusing to deflate the domestic economy, the US administration had chosen a strategy which would also help Britain's own effort at economic expansion.[1] In a statement which also expressed the hope that US efforts to stimulate the domestic economy would indeed prove effective, M Marjolin, Vice-President of the EEC Commission, stated that 'il est l'interêt de tous que le courageux programme de redressement de la situation extérieure des Etats-Unis annoncé par le Président soit couronné de succès'.[2] For Washington, however, it was the attitude of the French government which was most encouraging. On 19 July, Giscard d'Estaing, minister of finance and economic affairs, issued a statement in which he unequivocally approved US policy and appealed to the rest of the world to support it also:

... Pour le court terme, il lui paraît souhaitable que l'effet de cette décision ne soit pas annulé dans le reste du monde par des relèvements de taux injustifiés. Notre pays pour sa part n'a pas l'intention d'y procéder. Quant au long terme les autorités françaises, en décourageant depuis plusieurs années les entreprises françaises d'emprunter sur le marché de New York ont exercé leur action dans le même sens.[3]

It was symptomatic of the primacy of politics in international economic relations that reactions to President Kennedy's programme appeared to matter, at least in the short run, even more than results. While the success of his assault on the US deficit was necessarily unknown—the interest equalization tax was still pending before Congress at the end of the year—he needed to provide the Europeans with some immediate evidence of US determination. Although they generally preferred short-term monetary co-operation to structural reform, European support for the dollar was not finally guaranteed; some of the 'swap' agreements moreover were soon up for renewal. More important still, for the Americans, European co-operation was necessary if the 'Kennedy Round' of tariff negotiations, which hopefully would itself ease US balance of payment difficulties, was to have any hope of success, let alone if the Europeans were so to be wooed from their current negative attitude on the question of liquidity. But it was equally symptomatic of the Kennedy administration's political style that they appeared to have addressed themselves exclusively to Europe, where they had apparently prepared the ground in advance, while ignoring repercussions in other contexts which were likely to call in question the feasibility and hence the efficacy of the new measures.

As Dillon emphasized in his testimony on the President's proposals

[1] *Financial Times*, 20 July 1963.
[2] It was subsequently also revealed by Dillon in a testimony before a US Congressional Committee that it had been unanimously agreed by an OECD working party that no member state would take action to offset any increase in US short-term interest rates. *USIS Press Release*, 24 July 1963.   [3] *Le Monde*, 20 July 1963.

before the House Banking and Currency Committee on 23 July 1963, the interest equalization tax was a reaction to the slow progress made by European states in the development of their own capital markets.[1] But although Western Europe accounted for 18.4 per cent of US foreign investment in 1962, a total of $1,048m., Canada accounted for 42.3 per cent while Japan was also a major user of the New York market. In both these countries, neither of which was apparently consulted beforehand, the announcement of the new tax had the immediate effect of undermining business confidence; the Toronto and Tokyo stock markets recorded record falls,[2] and in an effort to control the situation, both governments announced their intention of seeking an exemption from the US authorities. After emergency consultations in Washington between the Canadian ambassador, Charles Ritchie, and Dillon—the Bank of Canada had been forced to intervene in the market to the extent of $250m. —the two governments issued a joint statement on 21 July[3] in which it was agreed that

... the draft legislation ... would include a provision authorizing a procedure under which the President could modify the application of the tax by the establishment from time to time of exemptions ... The President would thus have the flexibility to permit taxfree purchases of new issues needed to maintain the unimpeded flow of trade and payments between the two countries, and to take care of exceptional situations that might arise in the case of other countries.

In making this concession it was pointed out that Canada ran a current account deficit with the US which was traditionally financed by US capital exports; other considerations apart, therefore, US exports would suffer if Canada was denied access as in the past[4] to the New York market. Even so, it was clear that the Americans were sensitive to European interpretations of the concession as a retreat: not only was the Canadian government unable to secure the extension of the exemption to cover tax on outstanding securities,[5] but the US Treasury revealed on 23 July that as a *quid pro quo* for the exemption, the Canadians were pledged to take steps, including if necessary the reduction of Canadian interest rates, to stop any excessive flow of dollars to Canada.[6]

Viewed from Washington the Japanese situation looked entirely different. Although Japan absorbed $200m. US capital each year, unlike Canada she ran a substantial trade surplus and maintained a domestic

---

[1] *USIS Press Release*, 24 July 1963.
[2] *NY Times*, 19 July 1963; *Japan Times*, 20 July 1963.   [3] *Documents, 1963*, p. 97.
[4] According to Mr Gordon, the Canadian finance minister, this exemption represented 'a major change of course that would avoid increase in Canada's whole interest rate structure'. *The Times*, 22 July 1963.
[5] Mr Gordon pressed for this further extension when the full impact of the US proposals— Canada's official reserves fell by nearly $100m. in July—was revealed at the end of the month. *NY Times*, 7 Aug. 1963; *The Times*, 8 Aug. 1963.   [6] *NY Times*, 24 July 1963.

interest rate structure which, in the US view, was high enough to cover the extra cost of raising money in New York. Nevertheless, the reaction of the Tokyo stock exchange was so sharp—the average on the Dow Jones index fell 8.1 per cent in two days—that the government felt compelled to press for special treatment.[1] Understandably, their resentment centred on the fact that while there had been prior consultation with Western Europe, Japan had been ignored, an oversight which the US administration suggested as unlikely to recur if, as intended, Japan became a full member of OECD. However, although the prime minister, Mr Ikeda, urged that Japan should be given special treatment, it was clear that the object of his foreign minister, Masayoshi Ohira's emergency mission to Washington was primarily intended to restore confidence in the government rather than in the expectation that the Americans would give way. In this Ohira was reasonably successful. A joint communique on 4 August[2] stated that if serious economic difficulties resulted from the operation of the tax,

the US would consult with Japan on the appropriate measures that might then be taken to meet the problem, including consideration of some form of exemption from the proposed interest equalization tax for new issues of securities.

The Americans also agreed to set up a joint economic consultative task force to maintain liaison on this problem. But while nothing of substance was conceded, the finance minister, Mr Tanaka, announced that the agreement represented a 'considerable achievement for Japan'[3] and the Tokyo stock exchange obediently rallied.

Meanwhile, both in the USA and Europe, controversy over the desirability and efficacy of the US proposals tempered the initially favourable response. The decision to raise the short-term discount rate openly split the Federal Reserve Board.[4] Fear was expressed on both sides of the Atlantic that the interest equalization tax was evidence 'of the U.S. administration's reluctance to admit that it is qualifying, in however small a way and however temporarily, the principle of unqualified convertibility'[5] and represented a regression 'towards direct controls over capital and was probably unworkable anyway'.[6]

In retrospect, it seems clear that the new US policy did have some direct impact on capital exports in the second half of 1963: the outflow of private

---

[1] From the start the Japanese authorities seem to have viewed the US proposals with more equanimity than the Japanese financial and business communities. While the finance minister, Mr Tanaka, hinted that it might be necessary to re-examine financial and trade policies to attract foreign capital, he none the less emphasized that Japan still intended to implement Article 8 of the IMF Agreement under which Japan would abandon exchange control for balance of payments reasons. *Japan Times*, 20 July 1963.

[2] *Japan Times*, 4 Aug. 1963.　　　　　　　　　　　　　　　[3] Ibid. 5 Aug. 1963.

[4] For statements by board members see the *Federal Reserve Bulletin*, Aug. 1963.

[5] *Financial Times*, 23 July 1963.

[6] *NY Times*, 24 July 1963, 18 Aug. 1963.

long- and short-term capital fell from a peak equivalent of more than
$5 billion a year in the first half of the year to a rate of about $3 billion
in the second.[1] At the time the policy served two more immediate positive
functions. First, it acted as a cushion to the news, revealed at the end of
August, of the sharp increase in the rate of capital exports for the first
half of the year.[2] Secondly, it strengthened the position of those in Europe
who favoured the preparation of contingency plans to cope with a possible
future liquidity crisis. If few took seriously M. Monnet's appeal that
Britain should join the EEC immediately, 'setting aside the problems that
have blocked her entry for later negotiation', in order to provide Europe
with the basis for the rapid development of its own capital market,[3] it
was difficult to deny altogether the argument that with the levelling off of
an investment-led boom in Europe, and the prospect of a US surplus,
possibly even as early as 1965, Western Europe might be faced with severe
deflation. If this was a possibility, then it was also difficult to oppose, in
principle, the search for alternatives.[4] It could be argued, of course, that
the success of the US strategy was itself in doubt, that the administration
was spending $1 million a day in South Vietnam alone, which it was
unlikely to reduce quickly, that a cut-back in US capital exports was
likely to be accompanied by a cut-back in exports of goods and services,
and so on. None the less, the alternative possibility, and the attendant
risk, of a liquidity crisis could no longer be discounted.[5]

If within Europe it was now more difficult for the 'conservatives' to
argue against the American contention that the two issues—the US
deficit and international liquidity—could be kept entirely separate, for
the Americans the problem was how to direct the international debate
towards the formulation of contingency planning without reawakening
suspicions that the US was not serious about the commitment to reduce
her own deficit. The first official intimation of American support for a
compromise position midway between the Maudling plan of the previous
year and the conflicting European demands for either a continuation of
the *status quo* or a return to the gold standard, came in a statement on 18
September by the undersecretary to the US Treasury, Robert Roosa,
in which he advocated a study of international liquidity by the Group
of Ten.[6] Roosa, who was generally numbered among the US conservatives
on monetary affairs, developed his ideas further in an article in *Foreign
Affairs*.[7] Having surveyed the arguments deployed both by advocates of a
return to a reconstituted gold standard and those favouring flexible exchange rates, he made it clear that the USA supported a third approach

[1] IMF, *Annual Report 1964*, p. 84.   [2] Ibid.   [3] *Sunday Times*; *NY Times*, 22 July 1963.
[4] See, for example, the report from Brussels by Edward O'Toole in *NY Times*, 22 July 1963.
[5] See also *NY Times*, 18 Aug. 1953.   [6] *NY Times*, 19 Sept. 1963.
[7] Robert V. Roosa, 'Reforming the International Monetary System', *Foreign Affairs*, Oct. 1963,
pp. 107–22.

which 'would include in reserves a more flexible and larger volume of foreign exchange or internationalized credit than is used today, super-imposing this upon the slow accretion of gold that reaches the world monetary reserves'.[1] Roosa also stressed that any future inquiry would have to build on the foundations already developed by the governments and central banks within the Group of Ten. His conclusion was quite evidently an attempt to reconcile opposing positions:

Such an examination should lead to an evaluation of a wide range of pro-posals and suggestions, from a truly international point of view. The issue in such an international review is whether the present mixture of gold, dollars, sterling, and IMF facilities can in the future provide the ample supply of re-serves and credits that a healthy growing world economy should have, or whether major changes are going to be needed. The issue is also whether—if any particular change should be considered necessary—that change will be able to support added growth that is real, without contributing to monetary excesses and economic instability. The resolution of such a set of issues does not rest on the mere willingness of governments to vote yes or no on whether more international liquidity would be desirable. The primary task must be one of scrupulous preparation, within and among governments, looking toward a definitive appraisal by the governments themselves. Only in this way can these issues by resolved into a clear, reliable and workable consensus.

It was on such a basis that a compromise emerged between conserva-tives and reformers in both Europe and the USA. After a series of pre-liminary meetings in Paris between the members of the Group of Ten and OECD (the two overlapped) and the EEC financial ministers, it was agreed that a meeting should be held in Washington on 28 September, prior to the IMF annual meeting, to finalize arrangements for the study.[2] While the fact that control over the exercise was to be kept firmly in the hands of the Group of Ten reflected continuing suspicion of automatic credit creation on the lines envisaged in the Maudling plan, European acceptance of the desirability of the study also represented an important concession to the liberal position.

After these preliminary disclosures, the proceedings of the IMF's annual meeting in Washington between 30 September and 3 October were almost inevitably an anticlimax. For the time being the debate had been con-cluded; only the formal arrangements remained to be made. While con-ceding that 'other bodies, groups of countries and individual members' had a legitimate and independent concern, Schweitzer concluded his opening address with the announcement that the Fund was 'to develop and intensify its studies regarding international liquidity, the functioning of the inter-national monetary system and the effective role of the Fund in this field'.[3]

---

[1] *Foreign Affairs*, Oct. 1963, p. 109.   [2] *The Times*, 23 Sept. 1963; *Guardian*, 27 Sept. 1963.
[3] *Documents, 1963*, pp. 98–107.

But if, as it appeared, there were to be two simultaneous studies of the same subject, they were not to be regarded as rivals. In contrast with the previous year, the major speeches were, as *The Times* observed, 'a classic exercise in negative diplomacy'[1] with no states striking extreme positions and both conservatives and reformers careful to stress the common ground. While there appeared to be a general sentiment among the major powers, in favour of Herr Westrick's[2] view that any improvements in the existing system should be concentrated not only on the question of how best to *finance* balance of payments deficits but also on the even more important question of how to provide sufficient incentives for *curing* them, not even the French delegate, Giscard d'Estaing, stood out on grounds of principle against the proposed study. Nor did he suggest that France was necessarily committed to a gold standard solution.[3] Indeed, having noted that 'the attainment within an appropriate time of the balance in the external payments of the United States is indeed the precondition for our reaching decisions which do fall within our competence', he suggested 'a thorough examination of problems raised by the functioning of the international monetary system, particularly on the assumption that the development of world trade might require increased liquidity'.

On the other side of the international debate, Mr Dillon allowed himself a passing reference to the opportunities for surplus nations 'in instances where inflationary pressures are evident, to serve the interests both of their own domestic stability and of external balance by reducing or eliminating barriers to imports including those from the United States' and looked forward to the improvement of European capital markets which he had urged the previous year. But he was also careful to reiterate the official American view that the questions of the deficit and of international liquidity could and should be separated, and that nothing relieved the USA 'of the compelling and immediate task, of reducing the former'. Even Maudling was careful to emphasize that the UK was not wedded to his own Mutual Currency Account proposal. He was relatively more impatient than most speakers. 'What matters more than methods is the results and it is important to ensure that we do not spend so long looking for the ideal solution that we fail to make progress on improvements that can be achieved in the meantime.' In a sense even this appeal for urgency was beside the point. As the *Financial Times* observed, the British position at the Washington meeting was one of weakness. Whatever came out of the Group of Ten's deliberations would inevitably represent 'a balance of the continental and the American view'.[4]

[1] *The Times*, 2 Oct. 1963.
[2] Alternate Governor for the Federal Republic of Germany. *Documents, 1963*, pp. 124–6.
[3] On this subject only T. E. Donges, Governor for South Africa, sounded a discordant note.
[4] *Financial Times*, 7 Oct. 1963.

The announcement on 2 October by Dillon, on behalf of the Group of Ten,[1] reflected both the caution and the balance of the open debate. Thus while the Ten noted 'that the present national reserves of member countries, supplemented as they are by the reserves of the IMF, as well as by a network of bilateral facilities, seemed fully adequate in present circumstances to cope with possible threats to the stability of the international payments system', and that 'the underlying structure of the present monetary system—based on fixed exchange rates and the established price of gold—has proven its value as the foundation for present and future arrangements', they conceded the desirability of an inquiry into the functioning of the system and 'probable future needs for reserves and for supplementary credit facilities which may arise within the framework of national economic policies . . .'.

Outwardly little was changed by the commissioning of yet another study on international liquidity. But modest as the achievement was, it represented a significant advance on previous years. As one economic journalist noted, 'the vehicle for change, though not necessarily the will',[2] had at last been created. At first sight, it is true, the 'battle line' within countries as much as between them remained much as before. By the time the Committee met in Paris in December, for example, several of the European member states had reiterated that their primary interest in co-operation was to check inflation rather than to create new resources.[3] Within the United States also it was apparent that the debate between radicals and reformers had not been resolved. Thus Walter Heller, Chairman of the Council of Economic Advisers, and a leading reformer, told a Paris audience in November that 'the time has come for us jointly to give serious thought to the means for sharing the responsibility for providing international money',[4] a suggestion which echoed the British position but which seemed to go much further than the agreement reached in Washington. Roosa, on the other hand, as befitted the architect of the defences designed to maintain dollar supremacy, remained sceptical of proposals for major reform. In an address at the end of the year to the American Economic Association in Boston, he suggested that the unfortunate result of the official decision to study the liquidity problem had been 'to raise unrealistic hopes for the early solution of difficult problems through a simple monetary formula'.[5]

In the event, as Roosa had predicted, the reform of the monetary system was to prove a slow laborious process, which continued to occupy the governments of the major powers. It is clear that the 1963 agreement was a point of departure for later deliberation which took place in a significantly different context than in the past. As a result of the general

[1] *Documents, 1963*, pp. 128–9.   [2] George Cyriax in the *Financial Times*, 7 Oct. 1963.
[3] *Le Monde*, 18 Dec. 1963.   [4] *NY Times*, 9 Nov. 1963.   [5] *Guardian*, 31 Dec. 1963.

preoccupation with the US deficit on both sides of the Atlantic, an agreement had in effect emerged that it was safer to contain differences about the future development of the international monetary system within an officially recognized framework than to make prior agreement a precondition for its establishment.

In a sense, also, the fact that the motives of the major powers in supporting the IMF and Group of Ten studies so clearly diverged, probably strengthened the general commitment to future co-operation. It seemed all parties stood to gain from the establishment of a forum in which their official position could be advanced and defended. The IMF would clearly benefit from the establishment of a framework in which the Fund had a role, and the reassertion of its central position in the debate. If one result of the strategy of central bank co-operation favoured by the US administration and the European monetary authorities alike had been to bypass the IMF, the possibility that the USA would in future have recourse to the Fund, and be subject to its disciplines like any other state, reawakened European interest in the organization and to some extent redressed the balance.

For the US conservatives, a long-term study was the *quid pro quo* given to reformers at home and the European creditor states, in return for continued support for short-term defence of the dollar. The interests of these two parties, however, were significantly different. For the reformers, in the USA as elsewhere, the establishment of a framework was the only way whereby a problem, often regarded as the preserve of professional academic economists (and for this reason perhaps sometimes discounted by Central Bankers and national monetary authorities), could be brought within the realm of practical diplomacy. For the European conservatives, on the other hand, the review of the monetary system held out the prospect of a technical reform of the IMF, for example by an increase in IMF quotas, in which their own position could be strengthened. If this was to happen, and if the US continued to make use of the Fund, it might prove feasible to exercise a more direct influence than in the past both on the domestic policies of deficit countries, notably the USA, and on the amount of dollars that they themselves might at any time be asked to hold.[1] For one consequence of the high proportion of dollars which some of the European states held in their official reserves was, in the last analysis, to

[1] In his address to the Annual Meeting of the IMF Giscard d'Estaing, French finance minister, had made three criticisms of the position of the dollar in the international system. First, since dollar holdings in national reserves were built up on a bilateral basis, the country accumulating dollars had no voice—as in similar circumstances the IMF would have had—on the internal policies of the deficit country. Second, creditor countries had no effective control of the volume of dollars that they might be asked to hold. Third, as a consequence, some countries were holding a far higher proportion of their reserves in dollars than others, a situation which was held to be inequitable. For text see *Documents, 1963*, pp. 115–19.

force them into support for any scheme for the defence of the dollar which the US administration might devise. It is true that there was in any case considerable common ground between the US conservatives and European monetary authorities, both of whom preferred central bank co-operation to structural reform. None the less, as things stood, if psychological pressure failed, and if the US deficit continued, there were few sanctions which the Europeans could apply. Equally, if the US deficit was reversed, there would be few ultimate safeguards against the USA making damaging inroads into their own reserve positions.[1] In the event, therefore, the conservative case for the review was almost as strong as the reformist. While neither the structure of the world monetary system nor the under- lying problems confronting it had in any way been changed by the end of 1963, the diplomatic preconditions for future change had at least been set in train.

[1] Cf. *Survey, 1962*, pp. 204–5.

PART II

SOUTH AND
SOUTH-EAST ASIA AND
THE GREAT POWERS

CHAPTER IV

THE WESTERN POWERS AND THE INDIAN SUBCONTINENT: THE AFTERMATH OF THE SINO-INDIAN WAR

(a) *India and the West: attitudes and policies*

AFTER the shock of the Chinese military invasion in the autumn of 1962 and the humiliation of defeat which the Indian troops had sustained[1] it was inevitable that, for the Indian government, 1963 should be a year of stocktaking and reassessment both of India's position in the world at large and, in particular, of her relations with the major powers. It is true that, in the immediate aftermath of the fighting, the Indian government had looked stronger than for some time past, the people rallying behind Nehru's leadership at what must surely have been the weakest moment in his long political career. Yet, as the sense of crisis faded and factionalism reasserted its hold over Indian politics, it became increasingly clear that while Pandit Nehru's personal leadership had survived the crisis, Indian foreign policy, which had been so largely his own creation, together with the premises on which it was founded, had been virtually destroyed. Indeed, not only had the Chinese invasion forced non-aligned India to accept military support from the West, but it had also finally invalidated *Panch Sheel*[2] on which the structure of India's domestic policies, as well as the policy of non-alignment itself, had previously rested.

In a previous volume of this series[3] it was suggested that while non-alignment was usually presented to the world by Indian spokesmen, above all by Nehru himself, in broad moral terms as an independent stand for peace against the military blocs, more practical considerations of self-interest also featured in Indian calculations about foreign policy. The most important of these calculations concerned India's economic policies. From 1947 onwards the foremost aim of the Nehru administration had been to achieve rapid economic development to provide the impoverished mass of the Indian population with a standard of living above the bare subsistence to which they were accustomed. To achieve this end the government had embarked on a programme of industrialization carried

---

[1] For a discussion of the Sino-Indian War, see *Survey, 1962*, Chapter X.

[2] *Panch Sheel*, the five principles governing the Sino-Indian agreement on Tibet in 1954 were: non-aggression, non-interference, respect for territorial integrity, equality, and peaceful co-existence. See *Documents, 1954*, pp. 313–14.

[3] *Survey, 1961*, Chapter IX.

forward under the formula of the Five Year Development plan. It was a policy which, increasingly as time went on, dictated the curtailment of all non-productive public expenditure, so that even had it not appealed to him on other grounds, economic priorities would have necessitated keeping the defence budget within the strictest possible bounds. Alignment, in fact, in Nehru's view, was not only inconsistent with India's dignity as an independent nation, it was also beyond India's means.[1]

Moreover, on the military side, non-alignment had never appeared to the Indian leadership to involve unnecessary risks. The proximity of the two Communist land powers, they believed, was itself an argument against alignment with the West, and while ideological considerations on both sides similarly ruled out the possibility of a military alliance between India and either the Soviet Union or China, non-alignment, and its diplomatic counterpart, the *Panch Sheel*, had allowed India to achieve an acceptable *modus vivendi* with the Communist powers. It is true that with the gradual deterioration of India's relations with China towards the end of the 1950s, the government had been drawn perceptibly closer to the West, and Nehru himself had clearly envisaged a situation in which he would have to call on the West for support.[2] Nevertheless, before the Chinese invasion it was still widely held in India that non-alignment had rendered the possibilities of attack by a major power 'negligible, if not nil'.[3] It was a comforting belief, and given India's ambitious plans and slender resources, a necessary one also. The invasion, however, finally destroyed Indian illusions about the strategy of the *Panch Sheel* and since it necessitated a large-scale Indian rearmament programme, it also called in question the future course of India's development programme.

On the surface the Indian leadership emerged from its initial period of introspection after the crisis with its policies intact. In an article published in *Foreign Affairs* in April 1963, Nehru gave his own view that 'the challenge from China, as it has revealed itself, is not only to our foreign policy but to our domestic policy as well. Both are rooted in our needs and interests, and spring from the same cultural outlook and the same scale of moral values.' Whether the Indian objective of combining political democracy with economic justice could survive the shock of the Chinese invasion, depended only in part, as Nehru admitted, on India's own reactions to the crisis. Yet, understandably perhaps, Nehru himself had no new prescription to offer. The government's reappraisal, he concluded 'has convinced us that the basic policies we pursued in earlier years should not be changed but should only be adjusted to meet the new dangers that face us'.[4]

[1] Lane J. Kavir, *India's quest for security: defence policies 1947–1965* (Berkeley 1967), p. 39.
[2] *Survey, 1961*, p. 435.
[3] H. M. Patel, *The defence of India* (R. R. Kale Memorial Lecture 1963, Bombay, 1963), p. 3.
[4] Jawaharlal Nehru, 'Changing India', *Foreign Affairs*, vol. 41, No. 3, Apr. 1963, pp. 453–65.

Nevertheless, to outside observers, it seemed that these adjustments would, necessarily, be substantial. There was first the impact of the Chinese invasion on the issue of arms supplies. Prior to 1962, the Indian government had consistently refused to compromise its non-alignment policy by seeking arms aid. During the fighting in November 1962, however, this principle had been quietly abandoned when Nehru had sought and received military aid from several countries, but primarily from the United States and Britain. After the ceasefire there could obviously be no return to non-alignment as it had been previously interpreted: the old certainties were gone, and the government had no alternative but to revise its defence and diplomatic posture to safeguard against a second round of fighting. While the Indians were naturally reluctant to admit this blow to their independence, and attempted indeed to work out a new definition of non-alignment by balancing, wherever possible, Western military assistance with supplies from the Soviet bloc,[1] they were in no doubt that in order to push through a rapid rearmament programme, India would have to rely, as she had relied during the fighting itself, on supplies from the West.

In the longer run it was the indirect economic consequences of the invasion which threatened to prove more damaging. The diversion of resources to rearmament and defence would place an enormous additional strain on the economy at a time when India was already faced with severe economic problems. After two years, the Third Five Year Plan (1961–6) was already lagging badly. The Planning Commission's *Mid-Term Appraisal*, published at the end of the year, revealed that in the first two years of the plan, the growth of Indian national income had been only about 2.5 per cent a year as against the 5 per cent originally envisaged, a disappointing performance which reflected a failure to achieve most of the targets set in both the agricultural and industrial sectors of the economy.[2] Moreover, although the balance of payments improved as time went on, the year opened with one of the most acute foreign exchange crises in India's history, the reserves falling to around £73m. at the beginning of January, a situation which was itself related, at least in part, to the border fighting the previous year.[3]

The Indian government therefore had very little room for manœuvre. Whether or not they would be able to carry through the Third Plan, which was already heavily dependent for its implementation on foreign aid,[4] at the same time that they were adopting a new and vastly more expensive defence policy, would depend as much, if not more, on decisions taken in Washington and London, as on the position adopted by the Indian government in Delhi.

[1] Below, pp. 92–3, 103–4.
[2] *The Third Plan: mid-term appraisal* (Indian Planning Commission, Delhi, Nov. 1963), pp. 7–9.
[3] *Times*, 3 Jan. 1963.   [4] Below, pp. 110–12.

The western response to India's request for help at the time of the fighting had been swift, spontaneous, and united. At first sight, it appeared that the Chinese invasion marked a significant turning-point in India's relationship with the United States and Britain, a relationship which despite strong historical and economic ties, had been marred by recurring differences between the two sides over a variety of issues including the western alliance with Pakistan, the western stand on the Kashmir question, and the Indian occupation of Goa, which many in the West regarded as proof of Indian hypocrisy.[1] The Chinese invasion relegated these perennial sources of friction to the background, and created, for a time, a new sense of common purpose between India and the Western powers. Nehru noted:

Indo-American relations have seldom been so cordial as they are now. The deep sympathy and practical support received from the United States in meeting the Chinese aggression has created a wealth of good feeling and, apart from that, there is much in common between us on essentials. President Kennedy's vision of a world of free and independent nations freely cooperating to bring about a world wide system of interdependence, is entirely in accord with our own ideas.[2]

Mr M. C. Chagla, the Indian High Commissioner in London, made the point even more explicitly. 'From a global point of view', he said, 'the defence of India is the defence of South East Asia, democracy and the freedom of Asia. It is India which is the bastion of democracy. If India fails, democracy fails.'[3]

For the Kennedy regime, in particular, the idea of India as a beleaguered democracy, willing to learn from past errors, and resolutely determined to resist any further encroachments of Chinese power, held a special attraction. For the 'New Frontiersmen', with their determination to project a fresh and more pragmatic image of American policy in the Third World, Indian suspicions of American policy in Asia, and what they regarded as the doctrinaire self-righteousness of many Indian leaders, not least Nehru himself, had been a continuous source of frustration, the more so as Kennedy himself had long been convinced that India held the key to American policy in Asia. It was India, he believed, that would provide the vital test case of whether an overpopulated and desperately poor country could transform itself into a modern industrial state by non-communist means. 'We want India to win that race with China', he told the Congress in 1959; 'if China succeeds and India fails the economic-development balance of power will shift against us'.[4] While he remained

---

[1] *Survey, 1961*, pp. 432–5.   [2] *Foreign Affairs* (Apr. 1963).
[3] *Times*, 3 Jan. 1963. 'As a result of Chinese wanton aggression', Mr Chagla said on another occasion, 'all our differences with the United Kingdom during the last few years were forgotten.' *Hindu*, 3 Jan. 1963.   [4] Quoted in Schlesinger, *A thousand days*, p. 417

sceptical of the quality of the Indian leadership, Kennedy endeavoured to reach a new understanding with India based, on the one hand, on increased American financial commitment to India's economic development, and, on the other, on making clear American acceptance of India's neutrality. Yet opposition to India in the United States ran deep, particularly in Congress, where antipathy to both neutrality and socialism was prevalent. The Chinese invasion had the advantage of simplifying the issues involved in American support for India and thereby presented Kennedy, for the first time, an opportunity to secure the necessary domestic support for his pro-Indian policies.

Yet despite this auspicious start to the year, and despite—perhaps because of—India's increased dependence on the western powers, the hoped for new relationship failed to materialize. The issue which dominated India's relations with the West in 1963, and which provided the main source of tension, arose out of the question of Indian rearmament. Assistance with the reconstruction of Indian defences, to which Kennedy and Macmillan had committed themselves at their Nassau meeting in December 1962, raised two immediate problems for the British and American governments; first, the financing of large-scale purchases of military equipment for the Indian armed forces, whose deficiencies in this respect had been revealed during the fighting, and, secondly, the organization and co-ordination of emergency air defence measures in case the Chinese renewed their attack, and, as the Indians had feared the previous November, Indian cities were threatened with aerial bombardment. While the technical negotiations on both these problems were progressing at the beginning of the year, however, it became evident that they raised political and strategic issues on which the two sides were almost as much at variance as they had been before the invasion in October 1962.

Apart from the relief with which the cessation of hostilities had been greeted on all sides, the unilateral Chinese ceasefire of 19 November 1962 had provoked markedly different reactions in New Delhi and the Western capitals. Without at all diminishing their commitment to assist India in the event of a second attack (a commitment which on both sides was assumed rather than explicit), the ceasefire had provided both the United States and Britain with an opportunity to reassess their military assistance to India in the light of their own domestic preoccupations and of their other interests in Asia. This process itself assumed a degree of detachment from the crisis which the Indian government, for obvious reasons, could not possibly share.

As the immediate crisis faded, it became increasingly clear that the British and American governments were acting under three separate, although overlapping, restraints. First, in neither Washington nor London did there appear to be any great fear, as there was in Delhi, of a renewed Chinese attack in the spring. At the time of the invasion the United States State Department apparently concluded that amongst Chinese motives, territorial expansion was probably the least significant, and that the attack had been primarily inspired by Chinese nationalism, the purpose being to demonstrate by a forceful but limited response to India's forward strategy in the Himalayas,[1] where the true leadership of Asia and the Third World lay.[2] In the American view, the principal need had been to give the Chinese a clear indication that the West would not allow a full-scale invasion to go unchallenged, and this had been achieved by the Harriman mission to Delhi, in response to Nehru's urgent appeal for help, the previous November.[3] As one member of Harriman's party subsequently wrote, 'part of our mission was merely to demonstrate United States support for India and so to send the Chinese communists a signal of deterrence'.[4] Furthermore, as Harriman had also indicated, in the event of a second Chinese attack, the western powers would have no alternative but to intervene on the Indian side. In the American view, it was more important to construct an effective long-run deterrent to China for the subcontinent as a whole, than to be panicked into hasty commitments for the supply of military equipment, to meet an improbable short-run threat.[5]

Secondly, both the United States and Britain were anxious that any long-term programme of military assistance to India should not prejudice the Indo-Pakistan talks over the Kashmir dispute to which Nehru and President Ayub Khan had agreed under western pressure in November 1962.[6] In western eyes, the Kashmir dispute had always seemed an unnecessary disaster which diverted the attention of both disputants from their internal problems and from the 'real' external threat from the north. While the British were no doubt concerned with ending a family quarrel within the Commonwealth (one for which they felt partly responsible), the Americans were equally anxious to find a means of reconciling their policy of support for India with the legacy from the Dulles era of their military alliance with Pakistan. So long as the Kashmir dispute continued, Kennedy's Indian policies would never escape Congressional

---

[1] *Survey, 1962*, pp. 405–6.

[2] In the American view, as recorded by Roger Hilsman, the State Department intelligence chief, the Chinese aimed their attack not only against India but also against the Soviet Union in an attempt to make Moscow choose between Delhi and Peking. 'And the risk was relatively low. Britain and the United States might well intervene if China attempted to conquer and occupy India, but a carefully limited and quickly administered attack could be precisely managed and controlled, and the risks of outside intervention and escalation minimized. If Britain and the United States moved to intervene, the troops could be pulled back and the price for peace lowered. And if Britain and the United States hesitated, the attack could be pressed and the demands raised.' Roger Hilsman, *To move a nation* (New York, 1967), p. 324.

[3] *Survey, 1962*, pp. 429–30.   [4] Hilsman, p. 329.

[5] Ibid., p. 331.   [6] *Survey, 1962*, p. 430.

criticism that, by assisting both sides, the United States was engaging in an arms race against itself.[1] 'To nourish even in limited measure and, however indirectly, the two sides of the same dispute', Ambassador J. K. Galbraith told an Indian audience, 'does not appeal to the fiscal instincts of any elected body.'[2] And so long as the dispute continued, there could be no fully credible western defence against China in southern Asia. The Americans had no desire to force India into SEATO or any other military pact; indeed they had recognized from the start that India's formal non-alignment was likely to be a precondition of Russian neutrality.[3] On the other hand, the West could not merely abandon Pakistan whose leaders were convinced that any Indian rearmament would be inevitably directed against themselves rather than the Chinese. So long as the Indo-Pakistan talks continued, the desire to avoid alienating Pakistan provided Britain and the United States with an additional reason for delaying final decisions on military aid.

Finally, as the western powers considered the cost of supporting India militarily as well as economically differences of interest and capacity between Britain and the United States became apparent. The Kennedy administration, for reasons which were only indirectly related to the Indian situation, was anxious to extend the concept of burden sharing to military aid.[4] At the Nassau meeting in December 1962, this point had been met, after a week of hard bargaining, by balancing United States against Commonwealth aid. No official figure was given in the communique, but Mr Diefenbaker, the Canadian prime minister, revealed at a press conference that a figure of £45m. had been agreed.[5] This sum,

[1] Nor were his policies understood in India. In Aug. 1961 the American Ambassador, J. K. Galbraith, wrote to Arthur Schlesinger: 'Parliament assembled a week or two ago and during the recess two things happened: we had committed $500m in aid to India and the twelve F104 planes to Pakistan. The ratio of questions, words, comment and emotion has been no less than ten to one in favour of the planes. Such is the current yield of the Dulles policy.' See Schlesinger, p. 418.   [2] *Hindu*, 21 Feb. 1963.
[3] Hilsman, p. 331. See also the statement by Averell Harriman, Under-Secretary of State for Political Affairs, to the American Society of Newspaper Editors, 18 Apr. 1963. 'There are some people who think that we should not give aid to India unless they break with Moscow. I think that is a very stupid thing. I think it is pleasant to see Mr Krushchev on the horns of a dilemma between his friend India and his eternal brother China. Why should we relieve him of that embarrassment? I think that it is very much in our interest that the Soviet Union continue to give economic assistance to India. The Indians have indicated that they have no intention of being overrun by any outsider. They are determined to maintain their freedom and their way of life. If the Russians want to build a steel mill or give some other assistance, that will offset the obligation, the responsibility which will otherwise rest upon us and our European associates. . . . For that reason I suggest that we should in no sense attempt to interfere with India's foreign policy as it relates to Russia at the present time.' *American Foreign Policy: Current Documents, 1963,* pp. 764–5.   [4] Ibid., pp. 482–4.
[5] *Sunday Times*, 23 Dec. 1962. There were signs that both the US and British governments were embarrassed at this disclosure because they wished to withhold any final decision until the outcome of the Indo-Pakistan talks became clear; *Hindu*, 22 Dec. 1963. For the text of the Nassau communique, see *Documents, 1962*, pp. 482–3.

however, only covered immediate identified requirements. In any longer-term programme of military assistance, the need to match the aid given by the United States, which maintained large stocks of military equipment, would raise serious problems for Britain, which did not.

While the western powers were thus engaged in bringing discreet pressure to bear on Delhi over Kashmir and in trying to concert their own positions with regard to the future defence of India, the Indian government was attempting to conceal the near paralysis which had overtaken Indian policy. From Delhi, the Kashmir issue seemed an unimportant side-show, and the immediate danger the possibility of a spring offensive by the Chinese. Without assurances of military and economic aid, there was little the Indians could do by themselves. Nevertheless, in the highly charged atmosphere which persisted after the ceasefire, the government could not avoid taking basic policy decisions, or at least appearing to take them. To have announced, for instance, any major reduction in the Indian development effort to make way for rearmament, would have been to concede to the Chinese a political victory far beyond the military gains they had made. The government, in fact, adopted the opposite tactic, publicizing their determination to meet the economic as well as the military challenge with which the Chinese invasion had confronted them. Thus, on 3 January, when the Planning Commission met to review the prospects for the coming year, Nehru said that the government would not accept any large-scale revision of the Plan and was prepared to accept any sacrifice that might be necessary as a result of this decision.[1] 'From now on', Gulzarilal Nanda, the Minister of Planning, declared in a broadcast on 6 February, 'defence and development must be regarded as integral and related parts of the national economic plan.'[2]

The Indians were in no doubt about the need to rearm quickly. The Chinese refusal, as it was interpreted in New Delhi, to accept the Colombo proposals, lent weight to the view that they were not seriously interested in a negotiated settlement and might even be preparing to reopen the conflict.[3] But, if the prospect of 'a second round' added a sense of urgency to the government's deliberations, both the obscurity surrounding Chinese motives and uncertainty about the assistance that India might expect from the western powers, prevented the emergence of any coherent defence

---

[1] *Hindu*, 5 Jan. 1963.   [2] Ibid., 8 Feb. 1963.

[3] For a discussion of the Colombo proposals which were put forward by six non-aligned states, Ceylon, Burma, UAR, Indonesia, Cambodia, and Ghana in Dec. 1962, see *Survey, 1962*, pp. 435–7. While India accepted the proposals in their entirety, the Chinese had accepted them only as a basis for direct negotiations with India. Despite a voluminous correspondence between the two governments throughout 1963 this issue was never resolved and the direct peace talks envisaged in the Colombo proposals never took place. For the texts of these Sino-Indian exchanges, see *Notes, memoranda and letters exchanged between the Governments of India and China*, White Papers No. IX, Jan.–July 1963, and No. X, July 1963–Jan. 1964 (Ministry of External Affairs, Delhi).

policy. In the absence of such a policy, the government was faced with an undiscriminating demand for massive rearmament, which, in the political atmosphere, it was difficult for them to resist. By the end of January, the Indian press was speculating freely about the future divisional strength of the army, the intention of the navy to acquire a submarine arm, and the requirements of the airforce for supersonic jet aircraft.

The framing of a new Indian defence policy was complicated not only by the need for technical negotiations with the western powers, but by the fear that increased military dependency on the West might endanger India's relationship with the Soviet Union.[1] Within India, the Chinese ceasefire was widely regarded as a vindication of India's non-alignment policy. It was, Nehru was reported to have told the Congress parliamentary party in December 1962, 'as good during war as it was in peacetime. In fact it was better in times of war.'[2] The fact that the Soviet Union had not openly condemned Chinese aggression mattered less—Russia and China were after all still military allies—than that she had not openly sided with Peking or reduced her commitments to India. After the ceasefire, Nehru appeared more anxious than ever to balance between East and West, or rather to safeguard his relations with Moscow before committing himself further to the western powers. To many western observers, the Indian tendency, both during and after the war, to equate rather shadowy reports of support from Moscow with the material assistance already provided by the western powers, seemed exaggerated and hypocritical.[3] Yet in view of the uncertainty about Soviet policy towards the West after the Cuba missile crisis, Nehru's attitude was understandable. If, as then seemed probable, one consequence of the war would be a greatly increased western military presence, it was clearly in India's interests, as viewed from Delhi, to minimize the adverse effect of this development on relations with Moscow.[4]

[1] Indian fears were no doubt aggravated by the ambiguity of the Russian response to India's request for western military aid during the fighting. Thus, while Nehru apparently told Harriman in Nov. 1962 that 'the Soviets had said they understood both the request and the need for it' (Hilsman, p. 331), Khrushchev was reported to have told the Supreme Soviet on 12 Dec. 1962 that by accepting US military assistance India would be putting its neck into the 'imperialist noose'; *The Times*, 13 Dec. 1962. Earlier Tass had asserted that US motives in assisting India were to 'draw her into aggressive blocs' and to slow down her economic development plans; *Dawn*, 3 Dec. 1962.

[2] Cited in M. S. Rajan, 'Chinese aggression and the future of India's non-alignment policy', *International Studies*, July–Oct. 1963, p. 129.

[3] See for instance, Wayne C. Wilcox, *India, Pakistan and the rise of China* (New York, 1964), p. 73. 'In the heat of the battle India had called for help from the West, which with reference to her image as leader of the non-aligned states added insult to injury. Though large American planes droned over the cities of Northern India day and night, the Ministry of External Affairs asked newsmen not to photograph them, while the Ministry of Information issued statements noting that India remained non-aligned since she was seeking help from the USSR as well.'

[4] This was all the more important because, as Selig Harrison noted, 'India's leaders have built their whole foreign policy structure on the concept of a geopolitical community of interest

This need arose not merely out of a sentimental attachment to non-alignment, or a desire to derive maximum advantage from the Sino-Soviet rift, although clearly one aspect of this dispute, continued Soviet support for the uncommitted nations, was a factor which India could not afford to ignore. There were other reasons, both political and economic, for safeguarding India's relationship with the Soviet Union. After the United States and the World Bank (IBRD), the Soviet Union was India's third largest source of foreign aid. Moreover, despite the much larger American aid programme, and its wider spread throughout the economy, the Russians, whose aid was heavily concentrated in the public sector, had been generally more successful in identifying the Soviet Union with India's aspirations for industrial independence. The Soviet-constructed steelworks at Bhilai and the heavy engineering works at Ranchi stood as practical symbols of Indo-Soviet co-operation. Indo-Soviet trade had grown very rapidly and the five year trade agreement, signed in 1958, was due for renewal in 1963, providing indirectly another reason for caution in India's handling of her military relationship with the West. Moreover, the Russians enjoyed a clear diplomatic advantage by their unequivocal support of India in the dispute with Pakistan over Kashmir. This was of particular value to India at a time when the western powers were trying to persuade her, or so it was believed, to make concessions to Pakistan as a means of ending the quarrel.

It was against this background that the Indians sought, at the beginning of 1963, both to reassure the Russians on the issue of India's continued non-alignment, and to obtain from them some practical demonstration of support. Their efforts were concentrated on persuading the Russians to implement an agreement which had been negotiated the previous July by which the Soviet Union would supply India with twelve MiG-21 jet fighters and assist the Indians to set up a factory for their manufacture under licence.[1] Soviet delays over the delivery of the MiGs caused some impatience in Delhi and the secretary-general of the ministry of external affairs went to Moscow at the end of January to sound out Soviet intentions and also to see what other military equipment the Soviet Union might be prepared to offer.[2] At this point the Russians had not abandoned the attempt to resolve the ideological dispute with China, and there is some evidence that they were embarrassed over persistent Indian pressure for the supply of the MiGs. The Chinese air force was not equipped with these planes and since the official Soviet

between India and the Soviet Union with respect to China'. ('Troubled India and her Neighbours', *Foreign Affairs*, Jan. 1965, p. 325).

[1] See *Survey, 1962*, pp. 412–13. Also Ian C. Graham, 'The Indo-Soviet MiG deal and its International Repercussions', *Asian Survey*, No. 5, May 1964, pp. 823–32.
[2] *NY Times*, 26 Jan. 1963.

position on the Sino-Indian dispute was to encourage a negotiated settlement, it is, perhaps, not surprising that they drew back from a move which would inevitably aggravate their relationship with Peking.

However, Soviet anxiety over the MiG deal appeared to stem more from considerations of timing and publicity than from a desire to renege the agreement. In fact, while the Soviet Union appeared reluctant to involve itself heavily in the Indian rearmament programme, Indian pressure, or perhaps Soviet reluctance to leave the field entirely to the West, had produced an assurance as early as December 1962 that the Russians would honour the agreement. Early that month the Indian defence minister, Y. B. Chavan, had told the Lok Sabha that the first batch of MiGs would be delivered 'this month or a little later'.[1] But it was not until 11 February, after further prompting from Delhi, that the first four planes were delivered in Bombay with their armament (air-to-air missiles) following at the end of the month.[2]

There for the moment the Indian government let the matter rest. Having won their diplomatic point, they seemed prepared to let the agreement take its own course.[3] By this time the negotiations on the new trade agreement were already well in hand[4] and the Russians had also confirmed that their financial aid would be unaffected by the dispute with China.[5] The focus of discussion had, in any case, shifted from the acquisition of the MiGs to the manufacturing agreement. Since it would be at least two years before the Indian factories could start production, it was clear that whatever its other advantages, the MiG deal could not make any immediate contribution to India's air defence. The agreement had confirmed the Soviet Union's benevolent neutrality in the dispute with China, and by providing a counterpoise to military aid for the West, it had presumably restored Indian confidence in non-alignment. But its negotiation had also underlined the fact that it was still only the western powers that were likely to underwrite Indian security on any significant scale.

[1] *Soviet News*, 25 Feb. 1963.   [2] *Hindu*, 12 Feb. 1963.
[3] See for instance the dispatch from Prem Bhatia in the *Guardian* (9 Mar. 1963) in which he suggested that the government was no longer pressing the MiG issue. The four planes that had already arrived had not been assembled, their pilots had been sent on leave and there was no sign that work was about to begin on the factories.
[4] The second Indo-Soviet five year trade agreement was finally signed in Moscow on 10 June. It envisaged an annual exchange of goods worth about £160m. For the Indians this represented an advance over the earlier agreement in that the Russians agreed in principle to import more Indian goods, e.g. tea, pharmaceutical products, and insecticides, in an effort to balance the trade on both sides. Hitherto Indian imports from the USSR had always exceeded her exports. *Hindu*, 13 June 1963; *Times*, 11 June 1963.
[5] *Hindu*, 29 Mar. 1963. T. N. Kaul, India's ambassador in Moscow, was reported to have confirmed, in a speech delivered in Madras, both Russia's agreement to finance Fourth Plan projects when the time came and that Russian assistance to India would be unaffected by the Sino-Indian quarrel.

(b) *Indian rearmament: negotiations with the West, January–April 1963*

The triangular negotiations on arms aid between India, the United States, and Britain,[1] however, proved both slow-moving and difficult. They revealed from the outset, moreover, the distance between the three participants' perceptions of the threat itself, which have been outlined in the foregoing section.

Tension between India and the western powers became apparent soon after the arrival of a joint US-Commonwealth mission of air defence experts at the end of January.[2] Their precise terms of reference were never released, although it was widely assumed that they were concerned with arrangements for western air support in the event of a second Chinese offensive. After the fall of the Indian positions of Se La and Bomdila in the NEFA in November 1962, Nehru had apparently addressed an urgent appeal to President Kennedy for American air cover to guard Indian cities. Later in December he had confirmed, in a response to an American inquiry, that he still favoured the scheme, and the US-Commonwealth mission was set up to advise on its technical feasibility.[3]

It was clear at the outset that the mission had been set up at Nehru's own invitation. But the 'air umbrella' scheme, as it was dubbed by the press, ran into trouble as soon as it was exposed to Indian public opinion. In the face of left-wing criticism that the government was abandoning its non-alignment policy, Nehru began to waver. On 2 February he was reported to have assured a delegation of Congress party M.P.s that press accounts of the 'air umbrella' proposal were incorrect.[4] Unconvinced by such assurances, the Indian communist party passed a resolution a few days later condemning the proposed air defence arrangements, on which there had been no official announcement, as 'objectionable and dangerous'.[5] Why Nehru reacted so nervously to these criticisms remains unclear, although he was no doubt anxious to smother a potentially divisive issue before Parliament reassembled for the 'budget' session in the third week of February. In any event, on 16 February it was reported in the Indian and western press that Nehru had told a closed meeting of the Congress parliamentary party that there was no question of western air protection for Indian cities, that reports about the 'air umbrella' proposal were inventions, and that the sole purpose of the air defence mission was 'to examine Indian resources for self defence in the air and to recommend measures for strengthening them'.[6]

If his intention was to dispose of criticism, Nehru seriously miscalculated the strength of western reactions. Since it was widely known that the western mission had, in fact, been discussing air support facilities, the

---

[1] Canada and Australia also participated in a minor capacity in these negotiations.
[2] *Times*, 30 Jan. 1963.   [3] *Hindu*, 25 Jan. 1963.   [4] Ibid., 2 Feb. 1963.
[5] Ibid., 12 Feb. 1963.   [6] *Times* and *Hindu*, 18 Feb. 1963.

clear inference of his reported statement was that the western powers were pressing the 'air umbrella' scheme on a reluctant India. On 18 February the American ambassador, J. K. Galbraith, accordingly requested the Indian government to correct this impression.[1] He then followed his formal representations with a public speech to the Indian Institute of World Affairs on 20 February. After reminding his audience that the air defence mission was in India at the request of the Indian government, Mr Galbraith went on to state the official United States position on the 'air umbrella' proposal:

I have been firmly instructed to make clear to you that even the act of exploring the problem does not constitute a commitment. . . . On these difficult and highly technical matters I venture only one word. The choices, especially as concerns what can be done very quickly, are expensive and very few. Any course will be difficult. The best advice may not come from those whose ultimate preference is to do nothing.[2]

Any doubt that the air defence team was in fact exploring the feasibility of the 'air umbrella' scheme, or some variant of it, was now dispelled. Yet, when Nehru finally made a statement in the Lok Sabha on 21 February, it was so ambiguous as to satisfy neither those who wished to safeguard India's non-alignment at all costs, or those who favoured a more straightforward military relationship with the West. He first insisted that 'the air defence of the country is too vital a matter to be left to improvisation and delays inherent in any project like the "air umbrella" suggested in the press reports',[3] but then went on to announce that the government had already taken the decision to extend existing air strips and to improve the air force's ground control and communications systems in a way which would allow India to call on the western powers in an emergency.[4] But despite Nehru's vacillation, which was never more pronounced than when he was dealing with military questions, which he so profoundly disliked, it seemed fairly clear that he was also deliberately concealing his hand lest by expressing openly his willingness to accept western air support, he should prejudice India's negotiations for assistance with the expansion of the Indian Air Force to a point where India, and India alone, could provide the deterrent to further Chinese aggression.

The air defence mission left India at the end of February. The next three months witnessed a sustained Indian diplomatic offensive in

[1] *Times*, 19 Feb. 1963.   [2] *Hindu*, 22 Feb. 1963.   [3] Ibid.
[4] When, in subsequent debate, Congress M.P.s asked how the government proposed to deal with the short-term threat if they had ruled out the 'air umbrella' scheme, Nehru refused to be drawn into a detailed discussion. Mrs Lakshmi Menon, minister of state in the ministry of external affairs, was reported to have informed the standing committee of the Congress parliamentary party, however, that, while there was no formal agreement, India 'naturally expected friendly countries to come to her aid with their air power', in the event of a Chinese air offensive. *Hindu*, 22 Feb. 1963.

Washington, London, Ottawa, and Canberra. Early in March, Mr B. Patnaik, chief minister of Orissa, visited Washington, ostensibly on state business, but also with a personal brief from Nehru to discuss Indian rearmament plans with the Kennedy administration and to lobby support for India among the members of the US Congress. In April Mr T. T. Krishnamachari, the minister for defence coordination, visited Australia while a delegation of officials headed by Mr S. Bhootalingam, secretary of the department of economic and defence coordination, was sent to Washington to prepare the way for a later ministerial visit and to place before the state and defence departments the Indian evaluation of her defence production and import requirements.[1]

In part, these missions reflected the government's growing awareness of the need to improve India's image in the West. More immediately they were concerned with the level of Western arms aid. When the defence minister, Y. B. Chavan, finally announced the government's defence programme on 8 April, the full weakness of India's negotiating position was revealed. The Indian army was to be doubled in strength within two years; five new mountain divisions were to be raised, trained, and equipped immediately; six new ordnance factories were to be established, and the air force was to be modernized and expanded along the lines already announced by the prime minister. Of this four-point programme only the recruiting could be carried out without substantial external assistance.

For the time being, however, neither the British nor American government could be rushed into making a specific commitment on long-term military aid to India. At the end of the Bhootalingam mission to Washington the *Hindu* noted,

during the last ten days the talks between the United States and Indian experts have been more of a monologue than a dialogue. The Indian experts have been explaining their proposals and the Americans have been listening. If there were any differences in the approach to certain aspects of India's defence requirements, they were obviously not bridged.[2]

In fact, two major points divided the two sides. First, the Indian shopping list for military equipment was regarded by the western powers as grossly inflated in terms of what they might be prepared to supply and what India could usefully absorb. Second, as we have already noted, the US was unwilling to announce a programme of long-term military support for India so long as the Indo-Pakistan talks over Kashmir were still in progress. 'We do believe that it is very important to the security of the subcontinent that India and Pakistan should resolve problems between them so that they can present a solid front to any aggression to the subcontinent', Dean Rusk told a press conference on 9 March. 'I would in no

[1] *Hindu*, 31 Mar. 1963.   [2] *Hindu*, 29 Apr. 1963.

sense qualify our aid purposes by this word "condition". But I would say that from the point of view of the two countries in the subcontinent a condition of security is agreement between themselves.'[1]

(c) Kashmir interlude: the Pakistan reaction, April–May 1963

The fact that the Kashmir problem continued to engage the attention of the western powers was a source of constant irritation to India. Despite assurances to the contrary, it was widely believed that Britain and the United States intended to make their arms aid conditional on an Indo-Pakistan settlement in which India would be expected to make the major concessions. By the time the American secretary of state, Dean Rusk, and the British commonwealth secretary, Duncan Sandys, visited Delhi after the Karachi meeting of the CENTO Council at the end of April there had already been five fruitless rounds of ministerial discussions on the Kashmir problem and it was apparent that the two sides were as far apart as ever. When, the previous November, Nehru and Ayub Khan had agreed to negotiate over Kashmir there had seemed for a time to be some hope of success. But the talks had merely proved the occasion for mutual recrimination and they became increasingly unpopular in both India and Pakistan as time went on. Indeed it was reported that after the fifth round, which was held in Karachi on 22–23 April, a complete breakdown was averted only by the intervention of the British high commissioner and the American ambassador, who persuaded Mr Bhutto, the Pakistan foreign minister, to agree to one further round to be held in Delhi in May, by which time western, Indian, and Pakistan leaders would have had further opportunity for direct consultation.[2]

What kind of accommodation the western powers thought possible at this stage is unclear. For the Indians, the announcement on 26 November 1962, on the eve of the first round of talks in Rawalpindi, that Pakistan and China had agreed to demarcate the boundary between 'Azad Kashmir'[3] and China, had 'removed at once an assumption which lay behind the urgency for Indo-Pakistan negotiations, viz. a possible joint stance for the two countries vis-à-vis China'.[4] Pakistan's further action in

---

[1] Hindu, 10 Mar. 1963. Robert McNamara, the US defence secretary, was even more forthright in a testimony before the House of Representatives foreign affairs committee at the beginning of April: 'Military requirements and India's capacity to assimilate additional assistance are being evaluated within the Defence Department in the context of security measures for the entire continent of Asia. . . . Political and economic factors including India's efforts to help herself and reduce the vulnerability of the subcontinent by contributing to the resolution of Indo-Pakistan differences will be given due consideration in arriving at a final recommendation to the President.' Cited in Ibid., 9 Apr. 1963.

[2] Times and Dawn, 29 Apr. 1963.

[3] The Pakistani name, meaning free Kashmir, for that part of the state on their side of the 1948 ceasefire line.

[4] Sisir Gupta, Kashmir—a study in India-Pakistan relations (London, 1966), p. 353.

signing a border agreement on 2 March, which apportioned parts of 'Azad Kashmir' to the Sinkiang province of China, finally killed what little interest the Indians had ever had in the talks. 'The aggressor', the Indian representative at the UN protested to the Security Council, 'had not only assumed ownership of the part he unlawfully occupied by invasion, but has traded in the sovereignty of Indian territory, in collusion with China, to the detriment of the territorial integrity and the security of India.'[1] Yet it is doubtful whether India had ever contemplated any concession likely to elicit a positive response from Pakistan. At root Pakistan's claim to Kashmir rested on the state's Muslim majority, and on a deep sense of historical injustice that the state had been allowed to pass under Indian sovereignty in the first place. While India was prepared, under pressure and reluctantly, to partition Kashmir more or less on the lines of the existing ceasefire line, she rejected completely the wider claim pressed by Pakistan on religious grounds. 'This was', Nehru told the Lok Sabha, 'a vicious communal approach repugnant to the entire spirit animating our national struggle for independence, and contrary to our constitution and to our whole attitude to the problem of relationship between the state and the individual.'[2]

Pakistan's attitude to the talks proved equally intransigent. While many Indians continued to suspect the western powers of attempting to make arms aid conditional on a Kashmir settlement, in the Pakistani view it was their failure to do so which wrecked any hope of a negotiated settlement. India's steadfast refusal to consider either a plebiscite or a partition of the state of Jammu and Kashmir which even remotely approached Pakistan's minimum demands, was taken as proof that India was not genuinely interested in a settlement and was only anxious to keep the talks going until the US Congress had approved the necessary appropriations for a major military assistance programme.[3]

Pakistan's disenchantment with its western allies, and the reappraisal of Pakistani foreign policy which this occasioned, were not caused merely by the western reaction to the Sino-Indian war. The trend in the United States, from the late 1950s onwards, towards an acceptance of neutrality and the heavy concentration of American aid on India which this allowed had the inevitable effect of loosening Pakistan's allegiance to the western powers. Moreover, even when Pakistan's relations with the Soviet Union had been at their most hostile, they were still correct if not cordial.[4] Indeed, the drift towards an open Sino-Pakistani accommodation, which

---

[1] *SCOR* Eighteenth Year, Supplement for Jan., Feb., and Mar., 1963, pp. 133–6.
[2] *Foreign Affairs Record* (Ministry of External Affairs, New Delhi), Aug. 1963, pp. 169–71.
[3] *Daily Telegraph*, 6 May 1963.
[4] G. W. Choudhury, *Pakistan's Relations with India 1947–1966* (London, 1968), p. 274. Mr Choudhury's book contains a useful survey of Indo-Pakistan relations as viewed from Pakistan.

so alarmed Washington in 1963, can, in fact, be traced to the beginning of 1961 when the Pakistan foreign minister had revealed, prematurely as it turned out, that the Chinese had agreed in principle to demarcate the Sino-Pakistan border.[1] The western decision to aid India militarily in November 1962, thus blurring still further the distinction between western support for its allies and for neutral powers, undoubtedly hastened the process of adjustment. This distinction was of vital importance to Pakistan, since her membership of CENTO and SEATO had from the outset been motivated as much, if not more, by a desire to protect herself against a military imbalance within the subcontinent, in which Pakistan was the weaker party, as by the desire to make a contribution to 'free world' security. The western decision to arm India, which would inevitably increase the imbalance, touched the Pakistan government at its most sensitive point, particularly as President Ayub Khan contended that he had been given an explicit assurance by President Kennedy during his visit to Washington in 1961 that Pakistan would be consulted before any future decision on arms aid to India.[2]

The Pakistanis, moreover, made no secret of their belief that fears of a full-scale Chinese invasion across the Himalayas were no more than a figment of Indian and American imaginations, and that Indian rearmament on the scale proposed would be directed primarily against themselves not the Chinese.[3] Only a settlement of the Kashmir dispute, which the Pakistanis had always regarded as the central issue of Indo-Pakistan relations, could help Pakistan overcome the acute sense of insecurity and betrayal which India's new military relationship with the western powers had provoked. At the same time the reluctance of the western powers, particularly the United States, to jeopardize their new *entente* with India by making arms aid explicitly conditional on a Kashmir settlement (it was not, in any case, the kind of condition they could have maintained in the event of a second Chinese attack) and their refusal to participate directly in the talks[4] made Pakistan's leaders sceptical as to their outcome from the start. Following the Nassau agreement on western

---

[1] Ibid.

[2] Mohammad Ayub Khan, *Friends not masters: a political autobiography* (London, 1967), p. 138.

[3] See for instance the article by Ayub Khan in *Foreign Affairs*, Jan. 1964; 'Even in the unlikely event of a recrudescence of border fighting between China and India, India could not, considering the mountain terrain, deploy more than three to four divisions against the Chinese. One may justifiably ask, then, why India is doubling the size of her standing army to twenty-two divisions. Even allowing for the necessary reserves, what are these divisions aimed against? The fact of the matter is that, taking advantage of the favourable western response to her demand for arms, India is planning to raise two armies, one with which to face China and the other to use against Pakistan and her other smaller neighbours in pursuance of her expansionist objectives. It should also be noted that any army meant for China would by the nature of things be so positioned as to be able to wheel round swiftly to attack East Pakistan. Thus both the armies pose a grave threat to this country.'

[4] Mohammad Ayub Khan, p. 152.

arms aid, Ayub Khan summed up these Pakistani fears in a letter written on 2 January to Harold Macmillan:

> The extent of the military assistance which Britain and the United States have decided to extend to India for the present without making it contingent on a Kashmir settlement, gives us cause for great concern. The Nassau decision based on the assessment of your military experts, may seem, in the context of your global strategy to be the minimum aid necessary to enable India to defend itself from an attack through NEFA and Ladakh. We on the other hand find it hard to believe that any invasion of the sub-continent is likely to occur from these directions and consequently the quantum of military support for India, quantitative as well as qualitative, which you will be extending is fraught with serious consequences to the maintenance of the present ratio of military strength in the subcontinent and hence to the security of Pakistan.[1]

The detailed course of the Indo-Pakistan talks need not detain us here.[2] It is sufficient to note that as they progressed they confirmed the worst fears of both sides. And as public opinion in both countries hardened against any compromise solution, it became apparent that whatever leverage the Chinese invasion had given the western powers with the Indian government, it was not sufficient to overcome the legacy of mutual suspicion and fear that had plagued Indo-Pakistan relations since the partition of India in 1947, or even to deflect the two states more than momentarily from the tragic course which was to lead inexorably to war in 1965.

Yet while the complexity of the Kashmir problem, and the intransigence of both disputants, finally defeated them, the western powers were acutely aware of the illogicality of continuing to arm both sides with ultimately no control over the use to which the arms would be put.[3] They were now faced with a situation in which there was no clear way of reconciling support for Pakistan under existing regional security arrangements with support for India in the context of the United States' global policy of containing China. The more they armed India against China, moreover, the faster they weakened their influence with Pakistan and confirmed the Pakistani government in its policy of seeking an accommodation with China. 'If the main concern of the Christian West is the containment of Chinese communism,' *Dawn* observed in an editorial which summed up the Pakistani case, 'the main concern of Muslim Pakistan is the containment of militarist and militant Hinduism.'[4] The

---

[1] Mohammad Ayub Khan, p. 151.

[2] For a detailed account of these talks see Gupta, *Kashmir*, pp. 325–61.

[3] When the decision was taken in 1954 to provide Pakistan with military assistance, the US Government had assured India 'that if our aid to any country, including Pakistan, was misused and directed against another in aggression, the United States would undertake immediately . . . appropriate action both within and without the United Nations to thwart such aggression'. In a State Department release on 17 Nov. 1962, from which the above quotation is taken, Pakistan was given a similar assurance with respect to US military aid to India.

[4] *Dawn*, 26 Apr. 1963.

Rusk–Sandys mission to Karachi and Delhi made one final bid to bring the two sides together, but the breakdown of the Indo-Pakistan talks, while it could be delayed, could not be avoided. The result was to face the western powers with a choice between India and Pakistan, which for both historical and political reasons, they found virtually impossible to make. Instead they tried to blur the issue still further, thus pleasing neither India nor Pakistan.

Indian frustration at the continued reluctance of the western powers to commit themselves on the question of long-term military assistance, found a natural target in the British commonwealth secretary, Duncan Sandys, who was widely believed in India to be using his influence with the Kennedy administration to delay a final decision pending a new Anglo-American initiative over Kashmir.[1] The evidence does not, in fact, support this theory, although it is probably true that the British, whose attitude to Communist China was always more relaxed than that of the Americans, were more reluctant to abandon altogether their Kashmir initiative. Nehru himself remained deeply suspicious of Sandys, and, if the Indian press is to be believed, a serious breach in Indo-British relations over the Kashmir issue was only prevented by the personal intervention of Lord Mountbatten, who was in India on a farewell visit as chief of the British defence staff.[2] In any event, after meeting Sandys and Mountbatten on 2 May, Nehru informed the press that while he had been given an assurance that there was no connection between continued arms aid and a Kashmir settlement, he had been only 'partly satisfied' with his meeting, presumably because he had failed to obtain the firm commitment on military aid for which he had hoped.[3]

Indian suspicions about western intentions continued despite the assurances. A leader in the *Hindu* summed up the general attitude. 'Not for the first time in our history Pakistan is allowed to hold a veto over our destiny at a vital period.'[4] This was, of course, an extreme view and one which the western leaders went to some lengths to refute. As Sandys said in Bombay,

It has been suggested, that we in Britain have a condition that there would be no military aid unless the Kashmir problem was settled. It has even been suggested that we have withdrawn that condition. The truth is that we have never made that condition and therefore we have not withdrawn it.[5]

In retrospect it seems clear that both the United States and Britain had concluded that the basis for a Kashmir settlement did not exist and that there was little to be gained from pressing the issue further. They proposed

---

[1] *Hindu*, 2, 3 May 1963; *Guardian*, 1 May 1963.
[2] The timing of Lord Mountbatten's visit was doubtless not wholly coincidental. As the last British viceroy of India, Mountbatten had won and retained Nehru's friendship and respect.
[3] *Hindu*, 3 May 1963.   [4] Ibid., 5 May 1963.   [5] Ibid., 6 May 1963.

further official talks and third-party mediation but these suggestions seemed to be designed as much to ease the western powers out of their earlier position on Kashmir and to allow India and Pakistan to bring the discussions to an honourable close, as in any serious hope of effecting a settlement. At all events, while both governments were initially reported as having reacted favourably to the proposal for third-party mediation,[1] nothing in the end came of it, and the talks were brought to a close after a final fruitless meeting in New Delhi on 16 May.

From the Indian point of view the western backdown over Kashmir constituted a diplomatic victory. Nehru's statement to the Lok Sabha on 7 May reflected the 'face-saving' formula that had emerged from his talks with the British and American statesmen. On the one hand, he was able to report that while the western powers considered that an Indo-Pakistan settlement was desirable in the interests of subcontinental security, they would not make this a condition of further arms aid. On the other hand, he reaffirmed India's determination 'despite setbacks and difficulties, to continue our efforts to resolve our differences and to promote friendly and cooperative relations with Pakistan'.[2] Similarly, at their Birch Grove meeting seven weeks later, Kennedy and Macmillan announced their continued willingness to help in the resolution of Indo-Pakistan differences, and also confirmed 'their policy of continuing to help India by providing further military aid to strengthen her defences against the threat of renewed Chinese Communist attack',[3] and, in fact, committed themselves to provide a further $60m. worth of military equipment.

(d) *Indian rearmament, May–November 1963*

Nevertheless, the western attitude to India's rearmament programme was perceptibly cooler after the breakdown of the Kashmir talks than it had been at the beginning of the year.[4] While the Indians hoped that, with the Kashmir issue out of the way, T. T. Krishnamachari's visit to the western capitals in May and June would bring the arms negotiations to a point of political decision,[5] in the event he returned home virtually empty-handed. Moreover, as he admitted at a press conference in London on 31 May, the negotiations were not going to result in a single dramatic commitment (the Indians had been talking in terms of £536m. over a three-year period) but instead western assistance would be tailored to

---

[1] *NY Times*, 7 May 1963; *Dawn*, 9 May 1963.   [2] *Hindu*, 8 May 1963.
[3] For text of joint communique, see *Documents, 1963*, pp. 41–2.
[4] Cf. the report in the *NY Times* (5 May 1963) that a guide figure of the likely cost of long-term military aid to India had already been sent to Congress. 'The Kashmir issue', according to the state department source quoted in this article, 'would still have an important bearing on further arms aid to India . . . if the issue remained in an unsatisfactory state the result would undoubtedly be less aid than if the two countries should reach agreement.'
[5] *Hindu*, 17 May 1963.

meet Indian requirements as and when they arose, an arrangement which necessitated further technical negotiations on the Indian defence plan.[1] Although President Kennedy had impressed on Mr Krishnamachari his personal commitment to Indian defence,[2] there was no disguising Indian disappointment at the outcome of this mission. 'Though Mr. Krishnamachari argued his brief as well as anyone could possibly have done,' the *Hindu* noted with regret, 'he apparently has not been able to persuade either Washington or London to agree with the Indian assessment of the magnitude of the Chinese menace with the result that the assistance which may be expected from these quarters is likely to fall short of our requirements.'[3]

The failure of the Kashmir talks probably also decided the fate of the Indian attempt to persuade the Kennedy regime to supply the Indian air force with its own squadrons of supersonic aircraft, to match the two squadrons of F-104s which had been given to Pakistan in 1962. In any case, in the absence of a coherent defence strategy for the subcontinent as a whole, a unilateral and informal western guarantee to India would provide as effective a deterrent to China and would certainly be politically less troublesome for the West. Soon after Mr Krishnamachari's return to Delhi it was reported in the Indian press that the United States had revived some variant of the earlier 'air umbrella' proposal suitably amended. Nehru, however, still hesitated to commit himself to a line which both his own left-wing opposition, and India's critics in the Afro-Asian world, could so easily represent as a major departure from non-alignment. On 21 June he parried questions in the Lok Sabha about the possibility that the government would agree to hold joint manœuvres with the western powers. While he admitted that India was to receive radar and other communications equipment from the West, 'there was', he said, 'absolutely no question of foreign troops being based or operating from Indian territory'.[4] Despite detailed reports of the new proposal in the Indian press, Nehru would give no further indication of his position. Meanwhile, in a characteristic gesture, the Indian government had reactivated the issue of Soviet arms supplies, and on 16 July a technical mission under the leadership of Mr S. Bhootalingam was dispatched to prospect for arms in Moscow and Prague. While Indian officials

[1] Details of the plan, which provided for a standing army of 825,000 men and an air force of 45 squadrons, were only finally released to the Indian parliament by the defence minister, Y. B. Chavan, on 25 September 1964. For a discussion of the Indian defence plan, which had to be reformulated in 1965 after the suspension of US aid during the Indo-Pakistan war, see K. Subrahmanyam, 'Planning and Defence', in Paul Streeton and Michael Lipton, eds., *The crisis of Indian planning* (London, 1968), pp. 351–77.

[2] After seeing President Kennedy on 21 May, Mr Krishnamachari told the press: 'I am carrying back to my country the assurance that we have powerful friends here. This visit was a morale booster even if we were not promised millions of dollars.' *Hindu*, 22 May 1963.

[3] Ibid., 3 June 1963.   [4] Ibid., 22 June 1963.

emphasized that there would be no duplication in the equipment sought from East and West, 'for the moment', as one Indian observer noted, 'the Mission's mere presence in Moscow is useful as evidence that something of non-alignment lingers on, even if it is only willingness to seek weapons in all quarters outside China'.[1]

The western plan was announced simultaneously in Washington, London, and New Delhi on 22 July. Under the air defence agreement, the Americans were to supply mobile radar units to provide a warning system along the Himalayan border, which would be replaced at a later date by permanent installations. The air forces of India, the United States, Britain, and Australia would hold periodic exercises to test the new equipment in operation. All three governments emphasized that the agreement did not involve them in either the responsibilities or the obligations of a formal alliance, although behind the bureaucratic language there was little doubt as to its real purpose. In Washington, the state department announced that in the event of a second Chinese attack:

the United States had agreed, pursuant to the present agreement, to consult with the Government of India regarding possible measures to strengthen Indian air defences in the light of the situation existing at the time.[2]

In London, the commonwealth secretary, Mr Sandys, replied to a parliamentary question along similar lines:

It is clearly understood between the Government of India and Her Majesty's Government that the visits of a RAF Squadron will not constitute any prior commitment to come to the aid of India in the event of a renewed attack by China. In accordance with normal Commonwealth understandings the British Government would, in this event, immediately consult with the Government of India.[3]

In Delhi, the ministry of external affairs' release, after emphasizing that the government of India retained sole responsibility for India's air defence, concentrated on the contribution which the agreement would make to the training of the Indian air force:

As an important part of the training of the IAF personnel in this sophisticated radar and communications equipment, it has been agreed by the Governments of the United States and the United Kingdom that high performance fighter aircraft . . . may visit India temporarily and participate in joint training exercises with the Indian Air Force, under overall IAF aegis, to help in testing the equipment and in enabling the IAF personnel to master its use. These exercises will also provide an opportunity to IAF squadrons to practise alongside fighter aircraft from the United States and the United Kingdom from which they will gain valuable experience regarding the latest techniques of air defence.[4]

[1] Hindu, 17 July 1963.   [2] American Foreign Policy: Current Documents, 1963, p. 768.
[3] 681, HC Deb., c. 139, 22 July 1963.   [4] Hindu, 23 July 1968.

International reactions to the agreement ran on predictable lines. In Pakistan it confirmed the government's fears of isolation and desertion by the West. The agreement, it was felt, would inevitably heighten tension between India and Pakistan and might lead to border violations. Earlier, following the Birch Grove communique on western arms aid to India, Pakistan was reported to have withdrawn her agreement to third-party mediation in the Kashmir dispute on the grounds that this had been contingent on a moratorium on such aid,[1] and shortly afterwards the Pakistan foreign minister, Mr Bhutto, defiantly told the National Assembly of Pakistan that any attack by India would 'involve the largest state in Asia'.[2] In Moscow, however, the agreement was greeted with no more than token alarm. On 26 July the Indian ambassador to the USSR, Mr T. N. Kaul, delivered a note to the Soviet government which apparently described the background to the air defence agreement and gave an assurance that India would not abandon its traditional policy of non-alignment.[3] The following day, the official organ of the Soviet ministry of defence, the *Red Star*, warned India that the US and the UK were attempting to force her into the NATO-SEATO complex, a course which it claimed would have dire consequences for the peace and security of South East Asia as well as for India itself.[4] But even if the Soviet authorities were perturbed at the turn of events in India, they can hardly have been surprised by them, and there were certainly no signs that they intended doing anything about it.

Exercise Shiksha (the name given to the joint air exercises) took place without incident, though with varying reports as to its success, during the first three weeks of November.[5] In retrospect it seems a less significant turning point in Indian foreign policy than, judging by Nehru's vacillation and his contrived attempt to fit the agreement into the existing structure of India's foreign policy, he had evidently feared at the time. From the Indian point of view, the danger of the 'air umbrella' scheme had always been that it would make explicit India's *de facto* alignment with the West, undermining on the one hand what many Indians regarded as their special relationship with Moscow, and on the other further exposing the government to left-wing criticism at home. Such fears proved unfounded. In Moscow, the quarrel with Peking was by now too far advanced for the Russians to be seriously perturbed by India's defensive arrangements, even if it had not yet reached the point where Moscow would be prepared openly to contribute, on a major scale, to an Indian rearmament programme directed against China.

[1] Ibid., 17 July 1963.   [2] *Dawn*, 18 July 1963.
[3] *Hindu*, 27 July 1963.   [4] Reported in ibid., 29 July 1963.
[5] Ibid., 10 Nov. 1963; *Sunday Times*, 10 Nov. 1963; *The Times*, 20 Nov. 1963. The doubts arose from the fact that a significant proportion of the mock bomb attacks succeeded in penetrating the radar screen and avoiding interception.

Within India, also, once it became clear that the government could not obtain an independent air defence system, which would provide immediate protection against Chinese air attacks, effective domestic opposition to the agreement melted away. Moreover, Nehru was able to protect himself from left-wing criticism by taking a strong line on another controversial aspect of Indo-American relations which threatened to cut across Indian non-alignment. On 19 July, three days before the announcement of the air defence agreement, a deal had been concluded with the Indian ministry of broadcasting under which the Americans were to provide a medium wave transmitter to be used jointly by All India Radio and Voice of America for its broadcasts to South East Asia. Whether the government's hesitation over the air defence agreement was directly related to the criticism provoked by the VOA deal, as some western observers concluded,[1] it was clearly the more expendable arrangement. At Nehru's insistence—he later claimed to have been ignorant of its implications—an attempt was made to renegotiate and when this failed, the project was abandoned.[2]

A further domestic furore was sparked off in mid-December when the US chief of staff, General Maxwell Taylor, visited India and Pakistan to test opinion on a proposal that the Seventh Fleet should assume additional responsibilities in the Indian ocean as a further deterrent to Chinese expansionism.[3] Although they started from different premises, for once the Indian and Pakistan positions were broadly in line. Nehru was hardly in a position to oppose the plan outright but he was certainly not enthusiastic; Ayub Khan on the other hand warned General Taylor that the proposal could only add to the instability of the entire South Asian region.[4] In the defence field, therefore, the year ended much as it had begun. In the last resort the western powers were committed to supporting India even at the cost of estranging Pakistan. Yet partly because they were also committed to the support of Pakistan, and partly because their material assistance had not measured up to India's original expectations, all the latent ambiguities and uncertainties on both sides of the relationship were as much in evidence as ever.

(e) *India's foreign economic relations*

The debate between India and the western powers over the Indian rearmament programme took place against a background of uncertainty

---

[1] *Daily Telegraph*, 22 July 1963.   [2] *Hindu*, 4 Sept. 1963

[3] Ibid., 17, 18, 20 Dec. 1963. In reply to opposition questions in the Lok Sabha on 19 Dec., Nehru refused to see the prospective arrival of American ships as a new bulwark against Chinese expansionism. 'They are doing this', he said, 'for the obvious reason of letting people know they are there.' India had not been consulted, but since the seas were open, there was no reason, he suggested, why they should have been.

[4] Mohammad Ayub Khan, p. 152.

about the state of the Indian economy and the future of India's economic development plans. India's dependence on the West for defence was, in fact, only part of an over-all pattern of economic dependence on the outside world, particularly the United States, which had increased steadily in step with the growing complexity of India's development programme and the consequent shortage of foreign exchange with which to finance both new investment and the recurring needs of Indian industry.

We have already noted that the view was widely held in India and the West that the future of Indian democracy rested as much on the country's economic progress as on her capacity to defend her frontiers. This belief lay behind President Kennedy's approach to Asian politics. The American aid programme, not only to India but to developing countries in general, had been built up in the late 1950s on the assumption of a direct relationship between economic growth and both political stability and democratic government. Although, in its essentials, he had inherited this doctrine from his predecessors, it was Kennedy, and his advisers, who had refined and projected it as the basis of American policy in the Third World. The legacy of the Dulles era, they believed, had done much to damage America's image amongst the non-aligned states and in so doing had blurred the real distinction between national independence and totalitarian servitude. Chester Bowles explained the administration's new approach shortly before he took up his appointment as ambassador to India in July 1963. The purpose of the aid programme, he said, was not to create client states, subservient to America. 'Rather the aid program's objective has been to help to establish independent countries able and willing to stand on their own feet and prepared to defend what they believe to be their interests—interests that by and large coincide with our own.'[1] India, as the world's largest democracy and the recipient of the largest US aid programme, was the country where this policy was undergoing its most crucial test. In the long run, the fact that India was now more amenable to American plans for containing Chinese expanionism would be of no avail unless it was also possible to demonstrate the superiority of India's political and economic system.

American doctrine on foreign aid had been carried over, although the arguments were seldom made explicit, into the Aid India Consortium, which had been set up in 1960 under the auspices of the World Bank, but effectively under United States leadership, to concert the western aid effort to India.[2] The Chinese invasion had brought India the immediate and unqualified sympathy of the West, and while the main burden of assisting Indian rearmament had fallen on the United States and Britain, Canada, Australia, and several European states had also provided emergency assistance, on a smaller scale, during and immediately after the

[1] *DSB*, 17 June 1963, p. 941.   [2] Cf. *Survey, 1959–1960*, pp. 244–5 and *1961*, pp. 435–6.

fighting. It might have been expected, therefore, that in the economic field, the West would have made a similar gesture by increasing support for India's economic development programme. Unfortunately, however, there were few signs in 1963 of a common strategy between India and the western powers to meet the economic challenge posed by the Chinese attack. If anything, indications, at the turn of the year, suggested a growing disenchantment in the West with foreign aid in general. There were several reasons for this development, most of which were only indirectly, if at all, related to the Indian situation. Both the United States and Britain faced their own balance of payments troubles, which inevitably affected their approach to India's economic problems. In West Germany, where the government favoured a commercial approach to foreign aid, there was growing restiveness amongst businessmen at the restrictions which developing countries, including India, placed upon overseas investment. And although the French veto on British entry into the Common Market meant that India and other Commonwealth countries would continue to receive in the trade field the benefit of Commonwealth preference, the veto gave rise to renewed speculation about the growth of European protectionism, a development which was unlikely to be accompanied by a more generous approach to foreign aid. But while these causes of western disenchantment were general, the succession of Indian economic crises together with the country's enormous appetite for foreign capital which grew rather than diminished as industrialization proceeded, undoubtedly contributed to the prevailing pessimism.

India's economic problems were already formidable before the Chinese invasion made them still worse. The principal objectives of the Third Five Year Plan had been a 5 per cent over-all annual growth rate and, the target on which ultimately all else depended, the achievement of 'self sufficiency' in the production of food grains. By 1963, however, it was already clear that neither of these objectives could be reached. As noted earlier, the Indian Planning Commission estimated in November 1963 that the actual growth rate had been 2.5 per cent, half the projected rate, while far from achieving 'self sufficiency' in cereal production, imports of food grains rose steadily each year and would have placed an intolerable burden on the balance of payments had not most of them been obtained on soft terms from the United States under Public Law 480.[1]

As it was, the chronic weakness of the Indian balance of payments set narrow limits to India's economic progress. This was not, of course, a new development. From the beginning of the Second Five Year Plan in 1956, when India began to import capital equipment on a massive scale

[1] Public Law 480 provided the legal authority for US assistance to India and other developing countries of commodities, mostly foodstuffs, for payment in local currencies.

in a drive to secure the country's industrial base, Indian finance ministers had grown adept at managing the economy on a very low level of reserves. To do so, however, it had been necessary to create, and then progressively to extend, a stringent system of import restrictions and other economic controls. Indeed, by 1962 private industry had already had its import allocations cut to a point where many firms were forced to curtail production for lack of imported raw materials. To these perennial problems was now added a crisis of confidence in Indian industry, which was precipitated if not actually caused, by the Chinese invasion, and which in turn inevitably affected foreign confidence in the Indian economy.

The mood of impending breakdown could be clearly discerned in the behaviour of the Indian stock markets. Between October 1962 and January 1963 the prices of all the leading equity issues fell by around 30 per cent. The government did what it could to restore confidence, assuring investors that the need to expand production was now greater than ever (as indeed it was) and that, in consequence, industrial profits could be expected to increase.[1] But the year had opened with a foreign exchange crisis which was acute, even by Indian standards, and a crisis of confidence which reflected business fears about the new constraints under which they would have to operate. In a desperate attempt to tap India's most notorious source of hidden wealth, the finance minister, Morarji Desai, introduced new gold rules on 10 January, under which the possession of virtually all gold except personal ornaments was prohibited. But apart from an immediate wave of protest from Indian goldsmiths and a temporary fall in the prices quoted on the unofficial gold markets, there was little evidence that such measures would prove effective. The government's difficulties were compounded by the fact that one of the few actions which could have eased the economic strains of rearmament, namely a sharp reduction of expenditure under the Third Plan, had already been rejected. Thus, with the inevitable prospect of another round of import cuts and a huge increase in defence expenditure, and consequently higher taxation to pay for it, it was not surprising that the government's efforts to restore confidence lacked conviction.

In general, western opinion did not dissent from the official Indian view on the importance of maintaining the momentum of India's economic development. Indeed, when measured against India's 'needs', the Third Plan was certainly not over-ambitious. The pressure of population growth, at more than 2 per cent a year, was now so relentless, that even had it been possible to achieve all the targets adopted in the Plan, the improvement in living standards for the great mass of the people would still have been insignificant. While there was little argument over the objectives of Indian policy, there was considerable scepticism amongst the

[1] *Far Eastern Economic Review*, 17 Jan. 1963.

western powers about Indian planning methods and the priority which should be accorded to new investment under the Third Plan. Even before the Chinese invasion it was clear that the main obstacle to economic growth in India lay in the under-utilization of existing industrial capacity rather than in the need for new investment. Whether or not the World Bank actually proposed a reduction in new public sector investment, opinion within the Consortium was clearly in favour of some adjustment, which, by easing the strain on the foreign exchange reserves, would allow the government to be more liberal in the allocation of import licences to private sector firms.[1] Without action of this kind, or alternatively a much larger increase in foreign aid than seemed likely, India would be driven, by force of circumstances, to choose between large-scale rearmament and a major economic development effort.

It was, of course, precisely this dilemma which Nehru most wished to avoid. In the end, as with the rearmament programme, the limits on Plan expenditure were imposed from outside, as a result of the annual negotiations between the United States and the other members of the Aid India Consortium. Meanwhile, the government sought to establish its own credibility, at home and abroad, by tailoring economic policy to meet the new situation. On 28 February Morarji Desai introduced a budget which surpassed all forecasts in its severity. As expected there was no reduction of expenditure under the Plan and a massive increase in the allocation for defence, accounting for nearly half the total budgeted expenditure of £1,530m. To cover the anticipated revenue deficit of over £340m., the finance minister introduced a wide range of new taxes, both direct and indirect. Although the tax burden fell heavily on the business community, particularly with the new super profits tax, it fell heavier still on the middle and lower classes, all of whom faced a sharp levy on kerosene, the main urban cooking fuel, and many of whom found themselves subject, for the first time, to direct taxation in the form of a compulsory deposit scheme.[2]

Having thus clearly demonstrated their determination to uphold a 'business as usual' policy by economic sacrifices, the government turned its attention to winning support for this policy abroad. This was to prove an uphill task. While the budget was, for the most part, well received by the western press as evidence of India's determination to put her economic house in order, doubts were expressed about whether the imposition of additional burdens on the private sector of Indian industry was the best method of going about it, and at the preliminary meeting of the Consortium, in Washington in April, the leader of the Indian delegation, L. K. Jha, faced criticism of the government's import and industrial licensing

[1] See, for example, *Hindu*, 2 June 1963; *Financial Times*, 4 June 1963.
[2] *Hindu*, 9 Mar. 1963.

system for private sector firms[1] and discrimination in favour of public sector enterprises. However, another obstacle to India's economic growth was the aid policies of the western powers, as a result both of their marked preference for 'project' aid rather than for financing 'maintenance' imports, and of the commercial terms which some of them still attached to assistance.[2]

For the Indians the outcome of the Washington meeting was a disappointment, not least because it emphasized their excessive dependence on the United States at a time when the American aid programme was under domestic attack, and when it was uncertain that the Americans would be able to influence the other members of the Consortium as effectively as in the past. Although it was known that the US administration was prepared to waive its working rule of 'matching' the contributions of the other members, the 'burden sharing' device adopted two years previously in response to the US balance of payments crisis,[3] it was rumoured that Britain intended reducing her contribution to accommodate the £21m. of military aid which she had already pledged at Nassau, and that the other members were likely to follow suit.

In the event, the outcome of the ministerial pledging meeting, which was held in Paris on 4–5 June, was not quite so depressing as expected. Not only was the British pledge maintained at the previous year's level, but the British government announced its intention of introducing more generous aid terms, providing the other members of the Consortium did the same, a condition which was subsequently withdrawn.[4] Moreover, although the total committed fell to $915m., it was clear that the United States had been able to bring some pressure to bear on the other members of the Consortium. The final communique stressed both that a substantial proportion of the new aid should be untied (the only form of aid that could provide immediate relief to the balance of payments) and that the terms on which aid was offered should be softer than in the past.[5]

A month of intense diplomatic activity followed the Paris meeting. The Indian finance minister visited Tokyo in an attempt to persuade the Japanese to raise their contribution, and the Americans kept up their pressure on other members, particularly the West Germans who had made the largest cuts in their pledge, to do the same.[6] After several delays, the Consortium met again in Washington on 7 August and succeeded in raising the total to $1,052m., a figure still well below the original Indian

[1] Ibid., 27 Apr., 2 May 1963.
[2] With these practices in mind, L. K. Jha accompanied his request for $1,250m. for the third year of the Third Five Year Plan with an urgent appeal that a higher proportion of aid should be untied. But although this appeal was reasonable and had the backing of the World Bank and the American and British delegations, it apparently aroused little sympathy amongst the European Consortium members. [3] *Hindu*, 21 Apr. 1963.
[4] *Guardian*, 6 June 1963.   [5] *Hindu*, 7 June 1963.   [6] Ibid., 4, 5, 8, 25 July 1963.

request, but one with which, in the circumstances, the Indians could be satisfied.[1]

The successful outcome of the aid negotiations came too late to have much effect on the strains in India's relationship with the United States which had by now appeared in the economic as in the defence field. It was paradoxical that while it was American diplomacy which had been largely responsible for increasing the level of Consortium aid, and the Kennedy regime which, of all western governments, was most strongly committed in support of India, it was also in the United States that disenchantment with foreign aid in general, to India in particular, was most marked. It was an unfortunate blow to Kennedy's vision of a new Indo-American special relationship that, in a year when the struggle between President and Congress over the passage of the Aid Bill reached a new level of ferocity, Indian planning and Indian socialism, both of which aroused deep-rooted antipathies in Congress, should have become issues in the debate.

The trouble arose from an earlier Indian request for American assistance for the construction of a fourth public sector steel works at Bokaro in eastern India. The original request, which had been put to the Eisenhower administration, had been enthusiastically adopted by President Kennedy and his advisers. For the new frontiersmen, indeed, the Bokaro project had a special appeal: by 1962 India had become the largest single recipient of American economic assistance, yet it was widely held that the American aid programme had made a much smaller impact than the Russian counterpart, achieved at only about a sixth of the cost. One explanation of this anomaly was the lack of a single 'prestige' project with which the Americans could be identified in the way that the Russian, West German, and British governments were identified with the three public sector steel plants built with their assistance at Bhilai, Rourkela, and Durgapur. American support for Bokaro would go a long way, or so it was hoped, to overcome this handicap. More generally, the Kennedy regime had made an issue, in its policies towards the Third World, of moving away from the dogmatism which had characterized US foreign policy in the 1950s. Having demonstrated its willingness to support India militarily despite India's continued adherence to non-alignment, there could be no better demonstration of the *new empiricism* than an agreement, efficiently carried through, to construct a public sector steel works for India, whose commitment to non-alignment and socialism had imposed a continuous strain on Indo-American relations during the eight years of Republican rule.[2]

---

[1] *Financial Times*, 8 Aug. 1963; *Hindu*, 9, 17 Aug. 1963.
[2] This paragraph is based on the account of Kennedy's Third World policy in Schlesinger, pp. 485–6.

The project ran into immediate trouble, however, with the US Congress, and, in the end, had to be sacrificed to retain Congressional backing for the Aid Bill as a whole. 'The Committee to Strengthen the Security of the Free World' under the chairmanship of General Lucius Clay set up in December 1962 published its report on aid on 20 March. Although it endorsed, with certain qualifications, continued US aid to India, its general conclusion pointed to the future reduction of aid commitments. Of more immediate significance, however, were the Committee's recommendations on the question of aid to state-owned industrial enterprises:

We believe the U.S. should not aid a foreign government in projects establishing government owned industrial and commercial enterprises which compete with existing private endeavours. While we realise that in aiding foreign countries we cannot insist upon the establishment of our own economic system despite its remarkable success and progress, we should not extend aid which is inconsistent with our beliefs, democratic tradition, and knowledge of economic organization and consequences. Moreover, the observation of countless instances of politically orientated, heavily subsidized and carefully protected state enterprises in less developed countries makes us gravely doubt the value of such undertakings in the economic life of these nations.[1]

Whether or not this section of the report was drafted specifically with Bokaro in mind, its implications for the Indian project were ominous. An American 'feasibility' report, which was allegedly favourable to the project itself, had already given rise to one controversy over management. Both the West German and British built steel mills, though not the Russian mill, had met with a succession of labour and management problems, reported in the Indian press in a way which did not reflect to the credit of the West German and British governments. The United States government was determined to avoid these difficulties by persuading the Indians to accept a 'turnkey' contract, under which a United States firm would construct the steel works and then run it until production reached 100 per cent capacity and the mill could be handed over to the Indian government as a going concern.[2] Such an arrangement was far from ideal from the Indian point of view, and it certainly would have been strongly criticized by left-wing factions in the Congress party. But it was, in principle,

[1] Report to the President of the United States for the Committee to Strengthen the Security of the Free World, *The Scope and Distribution of United States Military-Economic Programs* (Department of State, Washington, D.C., 20 Mar. 1963), pp. 5–6.

[2] See, for instance, the statement by the American ambassador, J. K. Galbraith. 'On the question of what best serves our policy, and assuming feasibility and funds, there is no question in my mind as to the right, responsible, and practical cause. That is to have an American firm build the plant on behalf of the Indian Government and then run it for a considerable period of time. This will give the US a chance to show what we can do. It will assure the Indian Government of an efficient low cost source of steel. By this procedure we will not arouse suspicions, now happily stilled, that we are seeking to mould Indian economic policy in our own image. It did everyone a disservice. We should not feel impelled to repeat our mistakes.' *Hindu*, 13 Apr. 1963.

negotiable. The Clay Committee report, however, raised a more fundamental issue when it implied that the United States should withhold aid
for the project unless it could be operated under private enterprise. Even
if feasible, this would have involved a direct reversal of the Government of
India's 1956 'Industrial Development Policy', which had designated
steel as a public sector industry.

In the face of Congressional opposition, the US administration faced a
new dilemma. It was clear that if they were to press too hard for a
favourable decision on Bokaro, they might endanger not only this project
but the Aid Bill as a whole. On 9 April, David Bell, the new head of AID,
informed the House foreign affairs committee that he would not be
bound by Clay's anti-public sector recommendations,[1] a view which was
strongly supported by Ambassador Galbraith in New Delhi.[2] However,
when the US feasibility study was released to the public on 27 April it
was simultaneously announced by AID that the administration had
decided to postpone indefinitely its reply to the Indian Bokaro request.
The reasons given—that more information was required on the availability of manpower, raw materials, and power supplies—while not irrelevant, were not wholly convincing.[3] It seemed, in short, as the *New
York Times* noted, that the Clay report had successfully aroused three
strong Congressional prejudices, 'dislike of Socialism, dislike of India and
dislike of foreign aid'.[4]

Indian reactions to the AID announcement were cautious. The
government were aware that the US administration in general supported
the project—on 7 May President Kennedy had expressed his own support[5]
—and still hoped that Congress could be won round. The minister of
industry reassured the Lok Sabha that, from the government's point of
view 'Bokaro is an urgent necessity and we have taken a final decision
that the plant will be in the public sector. I hope that realizing this our
American friends will communicate to us very early their final decision
regarding this project.'[6] Short of actually reversing the industrial develop-

---

[1] *Financial Times*, 11 Apr. 1963.

[2] Galbraith summed up the administration's frustration at Congressional opposition to the
Bokaro project in a letter written to Schlesinger in Aug. 1963: 'The simple truth is this, and we
cannot repeat it too often; if our case opposes capitalism to communism, as Clay would have it
and as capitalism is regarded in this part of the world, we can hardly win. If our case opposes
the widest possible choice of free development to communism we can hardly lose. That, sirs,
is it.' Cited in Schlesinger, p. 486.

[3] *NY Times*, 28 Apr. 1963.   [4] Ibid., 4 May 1963.

[5] The President expressed his views at his press conference on 8 May in the following exchange:
Q. Mr President, in view of the Clay Report, do you think the Bokaro steel mill project in
India should be rejected on grounds of public versus private?
A. No. There is such a need for steel that it is going to be unfulfilled and providing it is an
efficient project, I would think we could assist if it meets what the economy of India requires . . .
Now the Congress may have other views but I think it would be a great mistake not to build it.
India needs that steel. *Public Papers, 1963*, p. 377.   [6] *Hindu*, 4 May 1963.

ment policy, the government was clearly anxious, however, to demonstrate that it was prepared to be flexible in negotiation. At the end of May the Indians agreed to set up a company separate from Hindustan Steel, the state-owned corporation which operated the other three public sector steel plants, in order to ease the negotiation of a special management contract with an American firm.[1] They also made it clear, in response to prompting from AID in Washington, that they were not opposed in principle to private investment, on a minority basis, in the new enterprise, even though, as a practical proposition, private participation was unlikely until the mill was in full production and could show a return on the capital invested.[2]

At the same time, the Indian government supported by some prominent Indian industrialists, attempted to educate the American public about its role in the country's economic development, and the relationship between economic growth and the security of southern Asia. Speaking in New York on 24 May, Mr J. R. D. Tata, the head of the Tata Iron and Steel Corporation, confirmed that the Indian private steel industry was in favour of the project:

> The simple fact is that we need more steel and we need it quickly. There is neither time nor sufficient private capital available to develop expanded production soon enough . . . I am convinced that once the American people and Congress understand the economic facts of the matter, opposition to the Bokaro project will diminish. If it is accepted that a strong viable economy in India is important to the non-communist world, and that steel is essential for such development, it will be seen that there is no alternative to Bokaro.[3]

It was symptomatic of the extent to which American public concern for India had weakened since the heady days of the Chinese invasion, that such arguments made little impact. Congress continued to oppose the Bokaro project, while the administration attempted to temporize by suggesting the need for a second technical report, a proposal which the Indian minister, Mr Subramanian, reportedly refused to accept without a prior US commitment to finance the steel mill.[4] The argument simmered on throughout the summer without producing any new developments. By mid-August, however, the Indians had evidently concluded that they would have to look elsewhere for aid, and on 13 August Mr Subramanian made a statement in the Rajha Sabha, the Indian upper house, in which he declared with more spirit than supporting evidence, that the government would 'begin the project within the Third Plan, irrespective of American aid' and that it was already examining alternative sources of assistance.[5]

[1] Ibid., 21 May 1963.   [2] Ibid., 25, 26 May, 10 June 1963.
[3] NY Times, 25 May 1963.   [4] Hindu, 25 June 1963.   [5] Ibid., 14 Aug. 1963.

The final debacle came on 22 August, when the House of Representatives approved an amendment to the Foreign Aid Bill forbidding any expenditure on Bokaro during the 1963/4 fiscal year.[1] To the extent that the Kennedy administration had regarded Bokaro as a test case for their new aid policy, this defeat in Congress reflected a deeper crisis, the significance of which extended beyond the Bokaro decision itself. In any event, the Indians were unwilling to wait another year in the hope that the Congressional veto might be lifted in 1964. At the end of August, Nehru wrote to President Kennedy offering to withdraw the Indian request for assistance, an offer which was received with a mixture of relief and regret in Washington and which Kennedy accepted in a letter which Chester Bowles delivered to Nehru on 5 September.[2] Almost immediately, in a manner which recalled the Aswan Dam affair, seven years previously, there were reports of Soviet interest in the Bokaro project. For the time being, the Indians seemed anxious to avoid further controversy. On 11 September Mr Subramanian explained the Indian decision to withdraw its request in a statement which aptly summed up the ambiguity of India's relations with the United States. In withdrawing the request, he told the Lok Sabha,

I should like to emphasize that we are deeply appreciative of the efforts made by the U.S. administration, and indeed by President Kennedy himself, to help us. I should also like to make it clear beyond doubt that this withdrawal is being made with a view to avoiding any further embarrassment to the advisers of both countries in the long term interests of Indo-American friendship and cooperation, and also with a view to not losing time on a project which we consider an urgent necessity.[3]

At the end of the year India's relations with the United States and with the West generally, in both economic and defence fields, had not undergone the major improvement that had seemed possible at the start. As the Chinese danger receded, the former pattern reasserted itself on both sides of the relationship. On the Indian side, Nehru's powers, at the end of his long career, were visibly diminished and he appeared, at least to many western observers, to have neither the inclination nor the energy to undertake the radical reorientation of Indian policy which the Chinese invasion had rendered necessary. But if Nehru appeared more anxious to return to the *status quo ante* than to advertise India's new understanding with the western powers, the fault was not entirely, or even perhaps primarily, his alone. The western powers, also, hesitated to commit themselves whole-heartedly to the Indian cause. Partly this was because, in the last resort, they did not have to; as the year progressed, and the

---

[1] *NY Times*, 4 Sept. 1963.
[2] Ibid., 5 Sept. 1963; *Hindu*, 7 Sept. 1963.
[3] *Hindu*, 12 Sept. 1963.

Chinese did not renew their attack, it seemed increasingly likely that the invasion had been both limited in its original purpose, and that the clear demonstration of western support for India which it had provoked, was itself a sufficient deterrent. But it was also because, as the Bokaro incident had shown, public opinion in the United States did not fully understand, let alone share, the administration's views of the role of foreign aid in America's foreign policy in the Third World. And what was true of the United States, held broadly for the western powers as a whole. In general terms, their friendship for India was not in doubt, but with opinion in most countries running strongly against any increase in foreign aid, there was no real prospect of the West mounting a substantial rescue operation on behalf of Indian democracy as an outpost against China.

Yet reassertion of the ambiguity of India's relations with the western powers did not, in fact, signal a return to the *status quo ante*. Western military and economic assistance might fall short of what the Indian government considered necessary, but it was still sufficient to persuade the Pakistan government that, having been taken for granted for so long, they were being betrayed by the West. This sense of betrayal, in turn, convinced Pakistan's leaders of the rightness (and righteousness) of their *entente* with China and the Soviet Union. It thus set in train a reorientation of Pakistan's foreign policy, characterized on the one hand by an accommodation with China, and on the other by increased suspicions of Indian motives and an increased determination to withstand Indian military pressure, feelings which were reproduced, in full measure, on the Indian side. There followed a period of intense bitterness in Indo-Pakistan relations, leading eventually to war between the two states in 1965, a war which not only left the conflict itself unresolved, but further undermined the position of the western powers in the Indian sub-continent.

CHAPTER V

MALAYSIA, INDONESIA, AND THE PHILIPPINES: PRELUDE TO CONFRONTATION

(a) *Introduction*

INDONESIA's long campaign against the Netherlands over West Irian was finally crowned with success when the temporary UN administration withdrew on 1 May 1963 and the territory was formally absorbed into the Indonesian Republic.[1] A little over two weeks previously, on 12 April, the first armed attack across the Indonesian border with Sarawak[2] indicated the next target of Sukarno's foreign policy. The Indonesian government did not commit itself irrevocably to the policy of 'confrontation' with Malaysia, of which Sarawak was to form a part, until shortly before the new Federation was proclaimed on 16 September. But by this time it would have been difficult, if not impossible, for Sukarno to abandon a policy which had not only proved successful against the Dutch in West Irian but which provided one of the few issues on which the two major political forces in Indonesia, the army and the communist party (PKI) were united.

At first sight the Malaysian dispute had much in common with the 'confrontation' between Indonesia and the Netherlands, and there is a sense in which it could properly be regarded as a continuation of this dispute on the Indonesian side. Both the techniques employed by Indonesia—a combination of anti-colonial propaganda, military threat, infiltration, and subversion—and what the Indonesians regarded as the real enemy, namely the entire system of western imperialism, were the same.

At its most straightforward, Indonesia's 'confrontation' with the Dutch had been a typical colonial dispute between a European power and a colonial nationalist movement; it was, in Sukarno's terminology, an open struggle between the 'Old Established Forces', the perpetrators of colonialism, and Indonesia, the leading representative of the 'New Emerging Forces,' to whom the colonialists were implacably opposed. For the Indonesians, the Malaysian case was merely one of substituting the British for the Dutch. 'We consider Malaysia an encirclement of the Indonesian

---

[1] For a full account of the Indonesian acquisition of West New Guinea, see *Survey, 1962,* Chapter IX.

[2] The attack took place at Tebedu, a small town in the Serian district of Sarawak, three miles from the border.

Republic', Sukarno told a conference of national front committees in February 1963, 'Malaysia is the product of the brain and efforts of neo-colonialism . . . Malaysia is to protect the safety of tin for the imperialists, Malaysia is to protect rubber for the imperialists, and Malaysia is to protect oil for the imperialists. For this reason we are determinedly opposed, without any reservation, against Malaysia.'[1]

At the same time, the differences between the two disputes were more striking than the similarities. In West New Guinea, the conflict had arisen out of a specific territorial claim; in Malaysia, the issue was the manner of decolonization. Moreover, in the context of world politics, the final settlement of West Irian probably owed as much to the support the Indonesians received from the United States as to their own efforts. American calculations had clearly reflected the conviction that it was more important to accommodate Indonesian ambitions, however expansionist, in the interest of creating a potential bulwark against Chinese expansionism, than to attempt to satisfy either Dutch pride or the nationalist demands of the indigenous peoples of West New Guinea.[2]

The creation of Malaysia, on the other hand, provoked a conflict of more varied dimensions. It is true that American concern to strengthen the non-communist elements in Indonesia led the Kennedy regime to view the Malaysian experiment with more reserve than their British allies, who had a major stake in its success. But since, as the Malay and Singapore prime ministers repeatedly emphasized, the containment of communism was one of their principle objectives, and since the British made it clear that they intended to honour their defence agreement with Malaya to help repel Indonesian infiltration, the Americans had little choice but to welcome the new federation.[3] They also hoped to divert Indonesian energies from foreign policy adventures to the urgent task of economic reconstruction,[4] while at the same time encouraging the development of a system of South East Asian co-operation.

The creation of Malaysia, however, was not viewed primarily as an exercise in world stability by any of the other powers involved. For the British, its formation provided a convenient means of easing themselves out of the North Borneo territories, which seemed unlikely to face a viable future as independent states, and of solving the problem of Singapore, without either handing the island to the communists or surrendering the

[1] George Modelski, ed., *The new emerging forces: documents on the ideology of Indonesian foreign policy* (Canberra, 1963), p. 75.

[2] *Survey, 1962*, pp. 396–402. See also Schlesinger, *A thousand days*, pp. 425–7; and Hilsman, *To move a nation*, pp. 371–81.

[3] Replying to a question concerning threats to the peace in South East Asia at his news conference on 14 Feb., President Kennedy said that 'We have supported the Malaysian Confederation and it's under pressure from several areas. But I'm hopeful it will sustain itself, because it's the best hope of security for that very vital part of the world.' *Public Papers, 1963*, p. 180.

[4] Below, pp. 146–9.

British military base there. For Indonesia, it was, above all, Britain's continued military presence in the area which lent credibility to the theory of 'neo-colonialist encirclement'. But from mid-1962 Malaysia was also opposed by the Philippines, despite an alliance with Britain and the United States in SEATO, as a result of the revival of an old Filipino claim to North Borneo.[1] From its inception, therefore, Malaysia was opposed by its two regional neighbours in a dispute which brought them into direct conflict not only with Britain but, by extension, with Australia and New Zealand who feared any further concessions to the principle of Indonesian hegemony in South East Asia.

For Malaya and Singapore the proposed federation represented a serious attempt to solve the intractable problem of Singapore's relationship with the mainland, a problem which stemmed in essence not from Britain's continuing presence but from the delicate and potentially explosive communal relationship between the predominantly Malay community of Malaya and the predominantly Chinese community in Singapore.[2] By the summer of 1963 both Lee Kuan Yew and Tunku Abdul Rahman, the prime ministers of Singapore and Malaya, agreed on the paramount importance of achieving federation quickly, lest internal opposition should make this impossible. This sense of urgency led to a cavalier attitude by both premiers towards their counterparts in Indonesia and the Philippines.

(b) *The origins of Malaysia, May 1961–January 1962*

Whether the initiative to create a new federation of Malaysia came from the British or Malay government has still to be determined.[3] There is no doubt, however, that it was the speech delivered by the Malay prime minister, Tunku Abdul Rahman, on 27 May 1961 to the Foreign Correspondents' Association of South East Asia, that formally set the process in motion. Reversing his traditional opposition to the idea of a merger with Singapore,[4] the Tunku announced that Malaya 'should have

---

[1] Below, pp. 138–46.

[2] For the fullest account of Singapore-Malay relations in the making of Malaysia, see Milton E. Osborne, *Singapore and Malaysia* (South East Asia programme, Department of Asian Studies, *Data Paper: No. 53*, Cornell University, Ithaca, New York, July 1964).

[3] For its part, Singapore had been pressing for a merger with Malaya since the People's Action Party (PAP) had assumed office in 1959. Circumstantial evidence, however, suggests that Britain took a leading part in framing the Malaysian plan, at least to the extent of proposing the inclusion of the Borneo territories as a device for redressing the racial balance following Singapore's merger with Malaya. The commonwealth secretary, Duncan Sandys, visited Singapore and Kuala Lumpur between 13 and 15 Jan. 1961, ostensibly to discuss the situation in Laos, and he was preceded by John Profumo, minister for war, and followed in mid-February by the chief of the British defence staff, Lord Mountbatten. *Straits Times*, 11, 12, 17 Jan. and 14 Feb. 1961.

[4] As late as 30 Jan. 1961, following Sandys' visit, the Tunku reiterated his belief that the idea of a merger was premature. He was not, he explained, opposed to the Chinese in Singapore, but was opposed to the China-orientated Chinese there. *Straits Times*, 31 Jan. 1961. Cited in Osborne, p. 13.

an understanding with Britain and the peoples of the territories of Singapore, North Borneo, Brunei and Sarawak. It is premature for me to say
how this closer understanding can be brought about but it is inevitable
that we should look ahead to this objective . . .'[1]

It was not the idea of a greater Malaysia itself which was so remarkable.
Different variations of the same idea had captured the imaginations of
both Malay and Indonesian nationalists in the past, and the concept had
been encouraged by the occupying Japanese forces during the Second
World War. But in the postwar period, the different experience of
decolonization in Malaya and Indonesia, the long Malayan emergency,
and Malay fears of political instability in Singapore, removed the question
of federation from the area of political debate.[2] It re-emerged between
1958 and 1963, as a result, partly, of Lee Kuan Yew's advocacy of the
principle of merger within Singapore, partly through skilful Singapore
diplomacy in relations with the mainland, and partly by the gradual
realization by the Malayan Alliance Party government that, if Singapore
was granted full independence, it was likely to go communist, a contingency that would inevitably undermine Malay's own security. In
the calculations of both Malay and Singapore leaders 1963 was the critical
year, since the 1958 constitution, under which the city state of Singapore
had acquired semi-independence, was due to expire and the arrangements
under which the island's internal security had been handled by the Singapore Internal Security Council, consisting of representatives of Malaya,
Singapore, and the UK, would automatically lapse.

Geographical proximity and the pattern of trade built up during the
colonial period almost inevitably dictated some association between the
two territories.[3]

The main obstacles to this association lay, as we have already noted, in
the racial balance between them: whereas the Malays, although the
largest single community in the federation, comprised just under 50 per
cent of the population with the Chinese in second place with 37 per cent,
the population of Singapore was 75 per cent Chinese and only 13.6 per
cent Malay.[4] In addition, in the politics of Singapore, the communist
party exercised a strong attraction for the Chinese communalists, one
result of which was that both political debate and competition for political
office was conducted in the rhetoric of anti-colonialism and radical
socialism. Once in office, Singapore's leaders generally found this rhetoric

[1] *Malaysia*, No. 2, Department of Information, Federation of Malaya (Apr. 1962), p. 6.
[2] Gordon P. Means, 'Malaysia—A New Federation in South-East Asia', *Pacific Affairs*, vol. 36,
No. 2, summer 1963, p. 138.
[3] In addition for some years Singapore and Malaya had been integrated, in a physical sense,
by the Johore Causeway; the merging of the two territories was also reinforced by the increasing
reliance placed on water supplied from Johore. Osborne, p. 1.
[4] Means, p. 140.

inconsistent with the constraints imposed upon them by the environment in which they had to operate, above all by their dependence on the continued British presence to provide employment and revenue. Yet the British presence was no more than a palliative; conditions on the island, with its high birth rate, inadequate housing and welfare services, and chronic unemployment, were such that no government could long escape pressure from the left even if it had assumed office with left-wing support.[1] By the same token, however, the inherent radicalism of Singapore's politics, and fear lest the island's turbulence should spread to the mainland, merely reinforced Malayan reluctance to concede a merger with Singapore, which, by upsetting the communal balance, might undermine Malay political hegemony.

From its foundation in 1954, the People's Action Party of Singapore (PAP) had pursued a policy of independence through a merger with the existing Malayan Federation. It was only when the party won a sweeping victory in the 1959 elections, however, that the PAP leadership had a chance of promoting their policy by direct negotiation with Kuala Lumpur.[2] They pursued their goal on three fronts. Culturally, they attempted to convince the Malayans, through extensive propaganda, that Singapore was set upon creating a genuine Malay spirit, and hence to allay suspicions of the island's orientation towards China; politically, they co-operated with the British and Malay governments in the Internal Security Committee in the hope of convincing the federal leaders that they were not open to communist influence, and economically they attempted—at this stage unsuccessfully—to alleviate Singapore's economic problems (arising partly from over-population and partly from the relative decline of the island's traditional role as an entrepôt for South East Asia), by negotiating a common market with Malaya.[3]

But despite the constant stream of ministerial visits across the causeway, there were few signs of progress towards merger between 1959 and the Tunku's sudden conversion in May 1961. Ironically, the PAP's election platform, comprising a militant anti-colonial and anti-British line, which had secured its success at the polls, at first militated against merger, since

[1] For a discussion of Singapore politics pre-1959 see Osborne, pp. 1–8.
[2] Ibid., pp. 8–9.
[3] In 1960 the central executive committee of the PAP published a policy statement under the title 'The Fixed Policy Objectives of Our Party' opposing independence prior to merger on the grounds that on its own Singapore would not be viable militarily or economically, and that 'An independent Singapore once established, even for an interim period, will create a situation whereby vested interests, based on Chinese appeals, will become permanent. For once independence is achieved in this island city, 75 per cent of whose population is Chinese, the logical consequence would be that the Chinese chauvinist sentiments which are at present being muted and slowly dissolved because of the objective of independence through merger, will openly and aggressively come to the fore.' Quoted in Lee Kuan Yew, The battle for merger (Singapore, 1963), pp. 169–70.

it reinforced Malay suspicions of Singapore radicalism. It was only when the traditional pattern of the island's politics reasserted itself, and the government's failure to live up to its pre-election promises in housing and social welfare resulted in a loss of popular support, that the dangers of an independent Singapore under a more radical administration began to register on the federal government. The return to radical politics began with the challenge to the PAP leadership, and subsequent expulsion from the party in July 1960, of the minister of national development, Ong Eng Guan.[1] Ong resigned from the Legislative Assembly in December 1960 to force a by-election in his constituency of Hong Lim. In the election campaign he attacked the government for its domestic failures and its subservience to the British and United States governments, while the PAP concentrated on the issue of a merger with Malaya.[2] The result (in April 1961), was a landslide victory for Ong. While this probably reflected his personal popularity rather than wide support for the issues on which he had campaigned, it nevertheless posed a direct challenge from the left, the implications of which were probably decisive in bringing about the Tunku's dramatic *volte-face*.

While the Malayan government now recognized the dangers, they were still disinclined to upset the federation in favour of the Chinese, whose loyalty they held to be suspect.[3] A way round this impasse was found by extending the merger to include not only Singapore but the British administered territories of Borneo as well.[4] Although the Chinese would still be the largest single community in the enlarged federation, the Malay and other non-indigenous people would outnumber them. Within a broader framework, moreover, the special position of the Malays, already recognized in the constitution of the Federation, would, it was hoped, raise fewer problems than in a direct merger with Singapore alone.

At the time of the Tunku's 'Malaysia' speech there was no agreed programme of decolonization for the Borneo territories. By comparison

[1] Ong Eng Guan had been mayor of Singapore in 1957–9. For a detailed account of his open challenge at the PAP Party Conference in June 1960, see Osborne, pp. 10–11.

[2] Cf. Lew Kuan Yew's comment during one rally in the campaign, 'We are not playing to a Singapore audience but we have to play to a Pan-Malay audience', *Straits Times*, 31 Mar. 1961.

[3] On 4 May 1961 the Tunku stated that Singapore could not be accommodated within the Federation until the people were loyal to Malaya as a whole; ibid., 5 May 1961.

[4] The idea of some kind of association between the Borneo territories was not new. Their administrative consolidation, through a common judiciary, civil aviation authority, and other unified government services had already been undertaken by the colonial authorities, who were also reported to be steering the three territories in the direction of a customs union (see for example a dispatch by Robert Turnbull in the *NY Times*, 7 May 1961). At the same time there is no evidence to suggest that the colonial authorities in the area were planning to bring these territories to independence in 1963 by federation with Malaya. In Singapore, on the other hand, Dr Toh Chin Cheye, the PAP party chairman, referred to the possibility of a wider federation at a New Year rally on 1 Jan. 1961, perhaps in an attempt to breathe new life into the negotiations with the Federal government; *Straits Times*, 2 Jan. 1961.

with Malaya and Singapore, all three territories were constitutionally backward.[1] Sarawak, the most advanced of the three, had held its first indirect elections to the legislature in 1959; in Brunei similar elections were planned for 1962, while there were no political parties in North Borneo at all.[2] Inevitably, therefore, attention was initially focused on the British reactions to the Malaysian proposal. These were at first ambivalent. Although the prime minister, Harold Macmillan, welcomed the proposal as deserving the widest discussion in all the territories concerned, the British authorities in North Borneo and Sarawak, who were in touch with local opinion, were initially more sceptical. This became clear after a meeting summoned by Lord Selkirk, the British commissioner-general for South East Asia, on 26 June 1961, at which the governors of North Borneo and Sarawak and the high commissioner in Brunei discussed the implications of the Malaysian proposals for British policy. The issue was not over the principle of the Malaysian Federation itself, which was accepted by the colonial authorities and by most politically conscious elements in the territories; it was over priorities. The governors concluded that given the relative economic and political backwardness of the three territories, a closer economic union of their own was an essential first step if they were to be in a position to do business with Malaya and Singapore on equal terms.[3]

First reactions to the Malaysia plan amply justified the cautious attitude of the authorities. Upset by the patronizing tone adopted by the Tunku during a goodwill tour to Sarawak and Borneo in July,[4] three leading political figures from the territories met at Jesselton in North Borneo to concert their views. In a joint statement, Donald Stevens, president of North Borneo's Kadazan and founder of the territory's first political party, Ong Kee Hui, chairman of the Sarawak United People's Party (SUPP), and Inche Am Azahari, president of the Party Rakyat of Brunei, announced the formation of a united front to oppose the 'Mighty Malaysia Plan' on the grounds that so far as the wishes of those concerned could be ascertained 'any plan in accordance with the pronouncements made by Tunku Abdul Rahman in Brunei and Sarawak would be totally unacceptable to the people of the three territories'.[5]

This setback to the Malaysian proposal was shortlived. From the point of view of the PAP government in Singapore it was crucial that, having

[1] For a useful survey of the constitutional arrangements of the Malaysian Federation, see T. E. Smith, *The background to Malaysia* (Oxford, Sept. 1963).

[2] The first political party, the United National Kadazan Organization of North Borneo, was founded in July 1961, largely as a response to the Malaysian proposal.

[3] The idea of a Borneo federation had been explored in a series of conferences after it had been advanced by the governors of North Borneo and Sarawak in 1958. See T. E. Smith, 'Proposals for Malaysia', *World Today*, May 1962, p. 195.

[4] At one point, for instance, he was reported as saying that there was really no difference in race or interest between the Malays and the Daiaks of Sarawak; *Straits Times*, 24 July 1961.

[5] Ibid., 10 July 1961.

manœuvred the Tunku so far, the plan should not be torpedoed at the outset by a misunderstanding with the Borneo territories. Thus when the Commonwealth Parliamentary Association met in Singapore at the end of July, the Singapore government deliberately set out to win round the Borneo delegates.[1] Their efforts were evidently successful; at any rate agreement was reached on a resolution put forward by Donald Stevens, one of its members, to form a 'Malaysia Solidarity Consultative Committee' to collect views and make proposals for the creation of a Malaysian federation.[2]

The stage was now set for negotiations on the economic and political arrangements for the new federation. As time went on, the question of the inclusion of the Borneo territories, and of the degree of popular support in the territories for Malaysia, emerged as a major issue. But at the outset, while some indication of the support of the territories was regarded as a necessary preliminary if the negotiations were to proceed with some expectation of success, Malaysia was conceived primarily as a solution to the problem of Singapore. It was the political situation on the island which very largely determined the way in which the Malayan, Singapore, and British governments handled the issue not only in direct negotiations amongst themselves but in the wider context of South East Asian politics.

In their appreciation of this problem the question of timing was paramount. The drift to the left which had been reflected in the Singapore Hong Lim by-election in April continued unabated after the Tunku's Malaysia speech. Consequently the success of the Malaysian experiment would depend on arresting this drift before the government's prestige, and the policies to which it was committed, suffered still further. As it was, some weakening of the PAP's position in Singapore was probably inevitable since the radical wing of the PAP drew much of its strength from the Malayan communist party, which opposed the government's merger plan.[3] The main issue at stake concerned responsibility for internal security. The Internal Security Committee's working arrangement under which a deadlock between the two Singapore and two British members was always likely to be resolved in favour of the British side by the Malayan representative, had been accepted by Lee Kuan Yew in 1959 because he realized it would be the minimum acceptable price for any progress

[1] For example Lee Kuan Yew expressed concern for their interests, while the Singapore government offered several Malaysian scholarships for students from North Borneo to study at Singapore University, training for Sarawak radio operators, and a scheme for training civil servants from the three territories within the Singapore Civil Service: ibid., 22, 27 July 1961, cited in Osborne, p. 65.

[2] Subsequently the SUPP reverted to its opposition to Malaysia; but at the time all three parties from the Borneo territories agreed to participate.

[3] For the background to communist participation in the PAP, see Justus M. Van der Kroef, *Communism in Malaysia and Singapore; a contemporary survey* (The Hague, 1967), pp. 33–56; also Osborne, pp. 16–23.

towards independence and union with Malaya. For the communists and their sympathizers within the PAP ranks the only condition on which they might accept Federal control over security was if the merger was achieved with a common electoral role on a one-man-one-vote basis, a condition which would have given the Chinese the commanding position in the central government. There was never any prospect of a negotiation on this basis, so that a split in the PAP ranks was an almost inevitable precondition of the merger itself. In fact when the Tunku and Lee Kuan Yew met in mid-August 1961 to draw up the preliminary agreement, it was already clear that not only would security, along with defence and foreign policy, remain with the central government, but that the price for Singapore retaining special responsibilities over labour and education policy, and a high proportion of its revenues—about 75 per cent—to cover these responsibilities, would be fewer seats in the Federal House of Representatives than its population would otherwise have warranted.[1]

In the event, the split in the PAP ranks came even before the terms of the preliminary agreement were published. The occasion was the Anson by-election in July 1961 in which the contestants were David Marshall, a former chief minister, for the Workers' Party and the president of the Singapore Trades Union Council. The campaign focused on the question of the proposed merger, with Marshall opposing the PAP policy of 'Independence through Merger' with a call for 'Independence before Merger'. Marshall won the by-election[2]; but it was the support he received from a group of six dissident PAP assemblymen, rather than his own victory, which was significant in the struggle for Malaysia.

This group consisted of six pro-communist trade union leaders, all of whom had been detained in a purge of the trade unions in 1956. At that time the PAP had campaigned for their release, with a view to maintaining a united front against the British. They were finally released after the PAP's electoral success in 1959, and five of them were subsequently appointed to political secretaryships within the government.[3] Although the dissident group had withheld their support from Ong Eng Guan in the Hong Lim April by-election, their support of Marshall precipitated the split; within a week of the Anson election, thirteen PAP assemblymen had crossed the floor to join the opposition, reducing the government's majority in the assembly to two seats. The formation, on

---

[1] For the text of the official communique issued after Lee Kuan Yew's meeting with Tunku Abdul Rahman, see Lee Kuan Yew, Appendix II, p. 116; and for the preliminary details of the agreement see *Memorandum setting out the heads of agreement for a merger between the Federation of Malaya and Singapore* (Cmnd. 33, 1961).

[2] Marshall defeated his PAP opponent by a majority of 546 votes.

[3] However, they were first persuaded to sign a statement endorsing the non-communist aims and objectives of the PAP. For the text, and Lee's comments on it, see Lee Kuan Yew, Appendix IX and pp. 20–5.

26 July 1961, of the Barisan Socialis, a new party on the extreme left, marked the end of the PAP united front.

For the PAP leadership the emergence of the Barisan posed a major threat: they had to compete for popular support in the certain knowledge that the Barisan would exploit the same techniques—the appeal to anti-colonialism and anti-British sentiment—on which the PAP had relied in the past. The existence of this powerful opposition made them extremely vulnerable on the terms under which the merger would be negotiated. Nevertheless, despite demands that the government should resign, Lee not only refused to give way (although he did finally agree to submit the merger proposal to a referendum),[1] but embarked on a vigorous counter attack designed to explain the implications of the merger to the people.[2]

If the PAP split, in the context of Singapore's domestic politics, threatened the merger plan, it probably had the reverse effect on the course of the negotiations with Malaya. After their meeting on 24 August 1961, and the publication of the heads of agreement, the Tunku and Lee Kuan Yew set up a joint working party to go into the political and financial implications of the plan.[3] Negotiation of the economic arrangements was to prove difficult and led to tension between the two countries in 1963. At the time, however, the heads of agreement established not only the broad political outline of Malaysia, but so improved relations between Singapore and the mainland that at a second meeting in September the two prime ministers agreed to bring about 'the integration of the two territories and its peoples in or before June 1963'.[4]

This agreement in principle on the timetable paved the way for an approach to the British government on the two external issues which would have to be settled before the merger could come into effect: the future of the Singapore military base and the participation of the Borneo territories in the federation. Since defence was a federal responsibility, it fell to the Tunku to take up with the British authorities the question of Britain's future commitments in the area. Once again, however, the initial impetus came from Singapore where British vacillation about the base was adding to Lee Kuan Yew's domestic difficulties. While no political party was opposed to the merger as such, the Barisan Socialis attacked the PAP persistently for its refusal to press for full proportional representation in the federal parliament.[5] The Barisan's representation of the merger as

---

[1] *Times*, 23 Sept. 1961.

[2] In particular, Lee gave a series of twelve radio talks in which he defended the PAP's policy on merger and exposed the former role of the communists in the PAP and their aims and objectives. These talks were subsequently published by the Singapore government as *The battle for merger*.

[3] *Straits Times*, 25 Aug. 1961.   [4] Ibid., 17 Sept. 1961.

[5] At its inaugural meeting, the chairman, Lim Chin Siong, committed the Barisan to complete union or full internal self-rule by 1963; *Straits Times*, 18 Sept. 1961.

an offer of second-class citizenship was almost bound to attract Chinese communal support. It was galling to Lee, therefore, to meet British hesitation on an issue which primarily concerned Malaysia's future international posture, and was consequently of secondary importance, in his view, to the internal struggle between communists and democratic socialists in Singapore, the result of which would probably decide the fate not only of Malaysia but of the future of communism in the area. At the close of his second meeting with the Tunku, Lee forced the issue into the open with characteristic dexterity by telling the press that the British were effectively assisting the Singapore communists. 'For the time being', he said, 'the biggest obstruction comes from the British, but in the long run it will come from the Communists.'[1] In a clearly calculated indiscretion he also threatened to generate heat by playing on Chinese xenophobia in Singapore if the British continued to 'squat on their bases'.[2]

The problem that arose was not over the continued British presence in Singapore as this was accepted as necessary even by the extreme left,[3] but over the status of the British base in the Malaysian federation. So long as Britain retained control over Singapore's defence and foreign affairs, the military bases could be, and were, used at the discretion of the British government as the depot on which Britain's commitment to the South East Asia Treaty Organization (SEATO) was based. While British forces were also stationed in Malaya under the 1957 defence treaty, and while the Alliance government was nothing if not anti-communist, Malaya was not a member of SEATO. She believed not only that her bilateral treaty with Britain provided adequately for Malayan defence, but that she had the right to prevent the deployment of Malayan-based troops for SEATO purposes.[4] There was, therefore, a potential conflict of interest between Britain and Malaya.

Despite the economic significance of the base, it had traditionally been a target for left-wing agitation in Singapore. Consequently Lee was probably content that the Tunku should negotiate direct with London over the question of its status. He was concerned, however, lest the

[1] Sunday Times, 1 Oct. 1961.
[2] Sunday Times (Singapore), 1 Oct. 1961.
[3] At a trade union meeting on 9 Oct. 1961, for instance, S. Woodhull, a leader of the Barisan, declared his party's support for the bases, referring to them as a 'blood transfusion' into the economy. Financial Times, 10 Oct. 1961.
[4] In fact, the interpretation of the 1957 Treaty on this point is ambiguous. Thus while Article VIII provides that if Britain wants the troops to be used elsewhere it 'shall obtain the prior agreement of the Government of Malaya before committing the UK forces to active operations involving the use of bases in Malaya', it also states that 'this shall not affect the right of the Government of the UK to withdraw forces from Malaya', a stipulation which technically would have allowed the withdrawal of troops from Malaya to Singapore for SEATO purposes. It was this technical loophole, which an extension of the defence treaty to Singapore would finally close, which reportedly provided the grounds for British hesitation in transferring sovereignty over the bases, OFNS, 11 Oct. 1961.

British should attempt to retain their sovereign rights, a position which the Malayans regarded as unacceptable, and so delay the merger to his party's disadvantage. He put his position succinctly on 30 September, 'If Singapore goes into the Federation the bases on the island will cease to be SEATO bases unless the Federation of Malaysia goes into the Treaty Organisation. But this is out of the question.'[1]

A way round the impasse did not emerge at once, although there seemed to be an assumption in Singapore, Kuala Lumpur, and London that a way round would have to be found. In a debate in the Malayan House of Representatives on 16 October the Tunku revealed that he had indicated earlier to the British that while he wished them to stay in Singapore he could not accept the continued use of the bases for SEATO purposes, and that, until there was an agreement on this, direct talks would be fruitless.[2] Whether he was impressed by the Tunku's intransigence, or had already devised a formula which could satisfy both sides, the British prime minister responded with a message that Britain welcomed the concept of Malaysia and wanted direct talks 'so that we could best work together in the attainment of this plan'.[3]

The Tunku visited London between 17 and 23 November 1961. From the Malayan point of view the outcome was a success on two counts. First, agreement was reached on the terms under which the British would continue to occupy their Singapore base. This involved, in fact, no more than an extension of the existing defence agreement between Britain and Malaya to cover the other territories of Malaysia, with the proviso that the Federation would allow the British government to retain its bases in Singapore 'for the purposes of assisting in the defence of Malaysia, and for Commonwealth defence and for the preservation of peace in South-East Asia'.[4] On the face of it, this was, as the British press recognized, the existing arrangement. Without reference to SEATO it preserved the substance of the British claim, namely the right to use the Singapore base for operations not necessarily concerned solely with the defence of Malaysia itself.[5] Admittedly the Tunku reacted quickly to correct this interpretation,[6] but the flexibility of the formula had much to

[1] At the same time he added a tacit threat of the kind which he was to apply often during the negotiations, 'if, because of British obstinacy, the merger is frustrated we will have to be a little difficult'. *Times*, 2 Oct. 1961.

[2] *Straits Times*, 17 Oct. 1961.   [3] Ibid.

[4] *Federation of Malaysia: joint statement by the Governments of the United Kingdom and the Federation of Malaya* (Cmnd. 1563, 1961).

[5] *Times*; *Guardian*, 23 Nov. 1961.

[6] In an interview on 23 Nov. 1961 the Tunku insisted that the agreement represented an extension, and only an extension, of the 1957 defence agreement. Without explaining why the Singapore base had been singled out for special mention he pointed out that Article III of the 1957 Treaty already provided the British with base facilities to meet the same purpose, i.e. Malayan, Commonwealth, and international defence obligations. 'We made it clear that Singapore was not to be regarded as a SEATO base and were given an assurance by the British

recommend it from all points of view. At any rate, after the London agreement, the future status of the British in Singapore was not an issue in the internal struggle over the creation of Malaysia.

The second major accomplishment of the London talks was the agreement to appoint a Commission (comprising two Malayan and two British representatives under a British chairman) 'to ascertain the views of the peoples of North Borneo and Sarawak' before a final decision was taken on Malaysia itself.[1] There had already been preliminary talks within the Malaysia Solidarity Consultative Committee on the terms under which the Borneo territories would be merged with the new federation, and the colonial authorities had attempted to publicize, in simple terms, its advantages. There were certain inherent difficulties in this task, since despite the existence of proto-nationalist movements and parties, areas of the territories were so remote as to be virtually inaccessible, and only about a quarter of their population, predominantly the Chinese elements, were literate.[2] There remained, therefore, a genuine doubt both as to the wisdom and to the practicality of speeding up their constitutional development sufficiently to allow them to merge with the Malaysian Federation at its inception in 1963.

At the London talks the Malayans had insisted that a merger with Singapore would only be possible providing the Borneo territories joined at the same time. The alternative, in the Malayan view, was for the British to ride out Singapore objections and to retain sovereignty over both the Borneo territories and Singapore itself. But while ideally the Malayan government might have preferred such a course, they accepted that by 1963 it would no longer be a practical possibility. As a member of the Tunku's staff explained during the talks:

> The Malayan Government is aware, however, that communism can only be contained if these territories are joined with Malaya to present a common bulwark against Communism. The establishment of the Federation of Malaysia, therefore, is the key to the problem and this must be done in the quickest possible time if Britain is to avoid having to deal with a demand for complete independence when the island's constitutional arrangements are due for review in mid-1963. This is no time for wrangling.[3]

That Malaya's preoccupation with the dangers of communist infiltration, and the urgent need to create a framework within which the

government that Singapore had never been regarded as such . . . The British government also conceded that although they had the right to use the base freely for the purposes of the agreement, they had no right to transfer its control to any other government or treaty organisation.' *Straits Times*, 24 Nov. 1961.

[1] Cmnd. 1563.
[2] Francis L. Starner,' Malaysia and the North Borneo Territories', *Asian Survey*, vol. iii, No. 11, pp. 527–8.
[3] *Straits Times*, 27 Nov. 1961.

danger could be combated, was, in its essentials, accepted by the British is reflected in the Commission's terms of reference which implicitly required it to find in favour of Malaysia, effectively ruling out any discussion of alternatives.[1]

Thus the London talks secured the acceptance of the Malaysia concept by all the major parties involved, the strong presumption being that it would come into being in 1963, providing the PAP government in Singapore could maintain its authority in the face of the challenge from the extreme left. The following year, 1962, witnessed a consolidation of the project within the area and a shift in the main focus of attention from the internal lines of conflict to the external challenges with which the new federation would be faced.

(c) *The origins of Malaysia, February–December 1962*

In February 1962 the preliminary discussions within the Malaysia Consultative Committee resulted in a memorandum according general agreement on the establishment of Malaysia and the lines along which the special interests of the Borneo territories should be safeguarded.[2] Given the political backwardness of these territories, it was not surprising that there emerged a proliferation of political parties, mostly founded along narrow communal and sectarian lines, reflecting attempts by different communities to define their interests in such matters as the role of Islam and the Malay language in the new federation, and to safeguard themselves against an over-rapid influx of migrant labour.[3] Nevertheless, after this initial period of fragmentation there emerged, in both Sarawak and North Borneo, pro-Malaysian alliances. Their formation was encouraged by Malay politicians depicting the Alliance Party as the centre of three communal parties in the existing Malayan Federation, and also by the spectre of Indonesian and Communist infiltration which was to become a major issue after the Brunei revolt in December 1962. As a result of these developments, by the time the Cobbold Commission Report was published in August, only the SUPP, which had originally endorsed the agreement to negotiate on Malaysia, had reverted to a position of opposition, a reflection of the party's dominance by radical Chinese elements in Sarawak

[1] Moreover the speed with which the Commission's report was drawn up—its chairman, Lord Cobbold, and the others were appointed in Jan. 1962, they started work in February and their report was submitted in June—also suggests that alternatives were not seriously entertained. The terms of reference were as follows: 'Having regard to the expressed agreement of the governments of the United Kingdom and the Federation of Malaya that the inclusion of North Borneo and Sarawak (together with other territories) in the proposed Federation of Malaysia is a desirable aim in the interests of the peoples of the territories concerned—(a) to ascertain the views of the peoples of North Borneo and Sarawak on this question; and (b) in the light of their assessment of these views to make recommendations.' *Report of the Commission of Enquiry, North Borneo and Sarawak, 1962* (Cmnd. 1794).

[2] For the text of the committee's memorandum, see ibid., Appendix F, pp. 98–105.

[3] Means, pp. 145–50.

and also, if Lee Kuan Yew and the Sarawak Alliance Party are to be believed, as a direct result of communist infiltration.

Because of the high rate of illiteracy in the territories and of the inaccessibility of a significant proportion of the population, the Cobbold Commission Report was, on the author's admission, both tentative and impressionistic. The Commission as a whole, however, endorsed the Chairman's opinion that:

About one-third of the population in each territory strongly favours early realisation of Malaysia without too much concern about terms and conditions. Another third, many of them favourable to the Malaysia project, ask, with varying degress of emphasis, for conditions and safeguards varying in nature and extent: the warmth of support among this category would be markedly influenced by a firm expression of opinion by Governments that the detailed arrangements eventually agreed upon are in the best interests of the territories. The remaining third is divided between those who insist on independence before Malaysia is considered and those who would strongly prefer to see British rule continue for some years to come.[1]

But while the Commission's members were unanimous in recommending Malaysia as the best prospect for stability and prosperity for the Borneo territories, the British and Malayan members divided on the crucial question of timing. The British favoured an early decision in principle with a phased programme of implementation, while the Malayan members argued that, given wide support for Malaysia in the territories, 'their relative inexperience in working a system of government within the framework of the Federation should not, in our view, be an insurmountable factor'.[2]

In the second half of July 1962 there was a further round of negotiations in London between the Tunku, Lee Kuan Yew, and the British government. The two sides divided, as the members of the Cobbold Commission had divided, on the necessity for a transitional period. The Malayans remained adamant against any delay in the transfer of executive and legislative authority for the territories. Indeed, the Tunku claimed that the talks nearly broke down on this issue.[3] In the end a formula was devised which, while substantially giving the Malayans what they wanted, also provided for a reasonably orderly transfer of power. The joint Anglo-Malayan Agreement was signed on 1 August 1962 and published simultaneously with the Cobbold Report. In it the two sides recorded their agreement both with Lord Cobbold's main recommendations and that Malaysia should be brought into being by 31 August 1963. To meet

[1] Cmnd. 1794, pp. 41–2. The Commission also agreed that a 'vocally and politically active hard core', around one-fifth in Sarawak and rather less in North Borneo, would remain opposed to Malaysia unless independence and self-government preceded it.

[2] Ibid., p. 62.   [3] *Times*, 2 Aug. 1962.

British objections that the pace was being forced, it was also agreed that there would be 'after the transfer of sovereignty, a transition period, during which a number of federal constitutional powers will be delegated temporarily to State Governments'.[1] Following the conference an Inter-Governmental Committee[2] was set up under Lord Lansdowne, the British secretary of state for the colonies, to work out the constitutional arrangements for the territories. In September the Legislative Council of North Borneo and the Council Negri of Sarawak passed resolutions endorsing the Anglo-Malayan Agreement,[3] and by the end of February 1963, when the Committee published its report, the technical problems stemming from the territories' backwardness had been resolved.[4]

Meanwhile, with Britain fully committed to federation, everything turned on the political struggle between Lee Kuan Yew's government and the Barisan Socialis in Singapore.[5] The struggle centred on the preparation for the referendum to which Lee had agreed in the autumn of 1961, even though constitutionally the result would have no legal effect and would certainly not be considered binding by Malaya.[6] In concentrating their attacks not on the issue of the merger itself, but on the form of merger proposed (in particular the unequal citizenship provisions) the extreme left exerted a strong appeal for mass Chinese communalist support. In pressing for a 'genuine merger' the Barisan argued for Singapore's incorporation in the Federation on the same basis as Malacca and Penang —the two non-Malay states included in the 1948 Federation of Malaya.[7] But while this proposal had strong attractions for the Chinese in Singapore and on the mainland who would benefit by being able to combine their strength, the federal government, even had they been prepared to accept it, could never have agreed to waive the citizenship regulations for

[1] Joint public statement issued by the British and Malayan governments on 1 Aug. 1962. For the full text, delivered on the British side by Duncan Sandys, secretary of state for commonwealth relations, see Nicholas Mansergh, ed., *Documents and speeches on Commonwealth affairs, 1952–1962* (Oxford, 1963), pp. 211–12.

[2] Consisting of members of the British, Malayan, North Borneo, and Sarawak governments.

[3] See *Malaysia—report of the inter-governmental committee, 1962* (Federation of Malaya, 1962).

[4] The terms worked out for the territories were quite generous, particularly when compared with those envisaged for Singapore. For example, North Borneo was to have sixteen seats in the House of Representatives and Sarawak twenty-four, compared with fifteen for Singapore. Both states would exercise immigration and deportation control even against Malaysian citizens; English was to remain the official language; non-Muslim religions were to receive special protection and both states would receive a guaranteed proportion of federal revenue through a system of ear-marked taxes and guaranteed sums for economic development. See Means, p. 149.

[5] The most difficult inter-governmental negotiations, on the economic and financial aspects of the merger, did not come to a head until the following year.

[6] The Tunku made one notable intervention in the referendum debate. During a visit to Singapore in Mar. 1962 he stated that in the event of difficulties Malaya would close the causeway and that 'if the extremists and opposition parties want to create trouble and cause bloodshed after merger then it is better that we do not have merger'. *Straits Times*, 26 Mar. 1962.

[7] *Straits Times*, 30 Aug. 1961.

non-Malayans which were much more restricted in the Malayan than in the Singapore constitution. The end result of the Barisan proposal would have thus been a drastic reduction in the number of Singapore citizens with voting rights—certainly not what they intended.[1]

While the PAP took every opportunity to exploit this weakness in their opponents' case, their own position in the Legislative Assembly was precarious,[2] a fact which no doubt influenced their determination to control both the manner and timing of the referendum—and the choices to be offered to the voters. Lee Kuan Yew argued that since there was no disagreement between the parties about the desirability of merger itself, the choice should be between different kinds of merger. Moreover, since the Barisan was, in the government view, a communist front organization, it followed that their objections to the 'citizenship' proposals were merely a cover for their real object which was to prevent the extension to Singapore of security arrangements which would limit their own activities. Lee supported this argument by alleging collusion between the Barisan and the Indonesian communist party, the PKI, which had already declared its unequivocal opposition to Malaysia.[3]

Under the Singapore National Referendum Bill which, despite relentless opposition from the Barisan, was passed by the Legislative Assembly on 7 July by 26 votes to 18, the electorate was to be offered three choices. The first was a merger on the terms agreed between Singapore and Malaya in November 1961 (Alternative A); the second, merger on the basis of the position occupied in the Federation of Malaya by Malacca and Penang (Alternative B), and the third a merger in terms no less favourable than those under negotiation for the Borneo territories, which at this stage had still not been announced (Alternative C). Having failed to prevent the passage of the bill, the Barisan, together with other left splinter parties set up a Council for Joint Action to take the referendum issue before the UN Committee on Colonialism. While this action of itself did not noticeably affect the course of events,[4] it provided the first clear sign of the tactics that the left was henceforth to adopt, namely: concerted action in all the territories of the proposed federation and a

[1] Osborne, p. 20.
[2] At the beginning of July, the government lost its over-all majority in the Assembly with the defection, in opposition to the way in which the referendum was being presented to the electorate, of Mrs Hoe Puay Choo. This reduced PAP strength to 25 against the combined opposition strength of 26. *Times*, 4 July 1962.
[3] Osborne, p. 25.
[4] The UN Committee met to consider the referendum on 27 July 1962. The Council for Joint Action was represented by Dr Lee Siew Chow and Mr Woodhull, who petitioned for a UN observer and an alternative choice. . . . 'A genuine merger of Singapore with the Federation of Malaya, with Singapore entering the Federation as the twelfth state and all its citizens automatically becoming Federal citizens on the merger date.' Lee Kuan Yew, en route for the London conference, also addressed the Committee. No action resulted. *Times*, 28 July 1962.

direct appeal for wider Afro-Asian support against 'a sell-out to neo-colonialism'.

The Singapore referendum was held on 1 September 1962. Despite efforts by the Barisan to persuade the electorate to spoil their ballot papers, the results confirmed that the left had for the time being lost the initiative to the PAP. These were as follows: Alternative A 397,626 (71·1 per cent), Alternative B 9,422 (1·7 per cent), Alternative C 7,911 (1·4 per cent), Blank votes 144,077 (25·8 per cent).

Under the terms of the referendum bill the blank votes were regarded by the government as additional votes for Alternative A (because 'the undecided voter is willing to let the government decide'[1]) and on this basis the government was able to claim that its policies had been endorsed by over 90 per cent of the electorate.[2] Lee Kuan Yew did not conceal his satisfaction with the way things had gone. 'Faced with the clear verdict of the people,' he said, 'the Communists and pro-Communists would be wise to accept the will of the people as expressed by free democratic vote. The people of Malaya and the Borneo territories now know that the overwhelming majority of the people of Singapore are good citizens, who, given a fair deal, want to become part of a united Malaysian nation.'[3] There was still room enough for argument about what would constitute this fair deal, but the results of the referendum undoubtedly buttressed Lee's hold on the political situation. Despite their immediate denunciation of the referendum, and a clear warning that 'in our future struggle the people in Singapore must think on the Pan-Malayan basis'[4] the Barisan was inevitably forced to reconsider its strategy. Within Singapore, the government victory was followed by a period of relative political calm.

(d) *External challenge and response*

(i) *The Brunei revolt*

By this time other challenges to the Malaysia concept had shifted the focus from Singapore to the Borneo territories and beyond. Both the Philippines and Indonesia, while they had yet to join forces in opposing Malaysia, had already shown signs of misgiving.

Towards the end of 1962 relations between Indonesia and Malaya began to deteriorate sharply. Reacting to a statement by Dr Ali Sastroamidjojo, a former Indonesian prime minister, that Indonesia would not remain indifferent to a Federation of Greater Malaysia, the Tunku issued a warning to Indonesia on 25 September to 'keep your hands out of our affairs',[5] a statement which in turn produced an official, though equivocal,

---

[1] Means, p. 145.
[2] The Barisan claimed many voters had been intimidated into casting their votes for Alternative A. See the report in *Straits Times*, 3 Sept. 1962.
[3] *Times*, 3 Sept. 1962.   [4] *Straits Times*, 14 Sept. 1962.   [5] *Times*, 26 Sept. 1962.

rejoinder from Dr Subandrio, the Indonesian foreign minister, who insisted that the Tunku had created 'an imaginary conflict. . . . We have not made any territorial claims on Malaysia but because we have a common frontier with the territories involved, it is only natural that we should not remain indifferent to it.' More specifically, he was reported as saying that if a military base was established in Sarawak, Brunei, or North Borneo after these territories had entered the Malaysian state, Indonesia would have to take 'counteraction', and if an American base were to be established, 'we shall then arrange for a Soviet base in our part of Borneo'.[1]

Despite such exchanges it is doubtful whether conflict between the two states was inevitable at this stage. That it became so was probably due more to the revolt in the sultanate of Brunei than to any other factor. Economically, historically, ethnically, and perhaps above all geo-graphically—the sultanate is surrounded on three sides by Sarawak—there was a strong case for incorporating Brunei in Malaysia. But because the territory had been a British protectorate but never a colony its in-clusion raised special problems. The Sultan had from the start claimed the right to negotiate as an independent power with Britain and Malaya.

There were differences between Brunei and the other Borneo territories. Not only did Brunei's oil industry raise problems concerning the future disposal of the oil revenue, but the towns to which the oil industry had given rise had fostered a radically orientated Malay community, in sharp contrast to the conservative Malay communities of the Federation; it was in the towns that the Party Rakyat, the most important political party in the territory, had built up its strength.

Political opposition to Malaysia developed faster in Brunei than in Sarawak or North Borneo. In July 1962, after the Sultan had accepted, in principle, the possibility of Brunei joining Malaysia, the deputy state secretary issued a warning that a small 'but treacherous' section of the population was attempting to incite feeling against the Sultan on the Malaysian question.[2] In political terms, opposition to Malaysia was already well established. From its registration in 1956, the Party Rakyat had built itself up to a position where, in August 1962, it won almost all the seats at the first popular elections to district councils, and, since these acted as the electoral college for the Brunei Legislative Council, all six-teen indirectly elected seats in that Council.[3] It is true that the government, which held seventeen non-elected seats, retained over-all control. But since the Party Rakyat had from the start opposed Malaysia, proposing instead that the British government should return the Borneo territories to the Sultan of Brunei and should establish a Democratic Borneo Federation

---

[1] *Straits Times*, 26, 27 Sept. 1962.   [2] *Straits Times*, 31 July 1962.
[3] For useful background on the political developments in Brunei prior to the revolt see T. E. Smith, 'The Brunei Revolt: Background and Consequences', *World Today*, Apr. 1963.

with the Sultan as its constitutional head,[1] an open clash between government and the Party was always a possibility.

The clash eventually came—there had been rumours of its preparation for several months—at the end of the year. The organizing genius behind the revolt was the half-Malay, half-Arab leader of the Rakyat, H. M. Azahari.[2] A veteran of the Indonesian campaign for independence, Azahari and his few associates had long dreamed of restoring the Brunei sultanate over the neighbouring territories of North Borneo and Sarawak. To this end, he formed an alliance with the Chinese-dominated SUPP in Sarawak (conveniently ignoring the fact that much of his support in Brunei arose from his exploitation of Malay hostility towards the Chinese business community), and with the Pasok Momugun organization of North Borneo. The purpose of this triangular alliance was to petition the UN Committee on Colonialism[3] and press for an independent federation of North Kalimantan (North Borneo) under the constitutional headship of the Sultan of Brunei.

At the same time Azahari also established close links with the Philippine and Indonesian governments, reputedly obtaining from the former an assurance that they would drop their claim to North Borneo if the federation was formed[4] and from the latter financial and material assistance including the setting up of a base at Malinau in Indonesian Borneo to train the nucleus of the so-called *Tentera Nasional Kalimantan Utara* (North Borneo National Army). Finally, or so the Malay and Singapore governments subsequently alleged, he was in close touch with opposition elements in Malaya and Singapore, including the Malayan Party Rakyat and the Barisan Socialis.

The revolt began during the night of 7 December. At dawn, on 8 December, a force of about one thousand attacked oil installations at Seria and in the Kuala Belait district of Brunei. In Manila Azahari announced first that 'the Sultan is in our hands and supports the revolution' and later that the capitals of Sarawak and North Borneo were besieged. He also proclaimed the Sultan head of the new *Kalimantan Utara* state and named himself as premier. In fact, the Sultan declared a state of emergency and denounced the radicals as traitors. He immediately requested and was granted military assistance from Britain. With the aid of British Gurkha troops, flown in from Singapore, and local irregulars, the rebellion was crushed within a few days. With very minor exceptions, the revolt had not spread as planned to North Borneo and Sarawak. While it continued to oppose Malaysia, the SUPP had denounced the revolt.

[1] T. E. Smith, 'Proposals for Malaysia', *World Today*, May 1962.

[2] For a more detailed discussion of Azahari's role in the revolt see Means, pp. 150–3; also Justus M. Van der Kroef, 'Indonesia, Malaya and the North Borneo crisis', *Asian Survey*, vol. iii, No. IV, Apr. 1963.

[3] *Straits Times*, 24 Sept. 1962.   [4] Ibid., 23 Nov. 1962.

But if the rebellion was a fiasco, its impact on the preparations for Malaysia was far-reaching. The collapse of the revolt was not immediately followed, as might have been expected, by a firm decision by the Sultan of Brunei to enter the Federation. Indeed he finally decided to remain outside, partly because of the difficulty in negotiating an acceptable distribution of Brunei's oil revenues,[1] and partly, it was rumoured, because he was sensitive over his own status within the Federation hierarchy.[2] Many Brunei Malays had supported the rebellion in the genuine belief that they were acting on behalf of the Sultan rather than against him. Hence the government could not immediately reverse its policy since it was partly out of respect for the Party Rakyat's opposition to Malaysia that the Sultan had gone slow in his negotiations with Kuala Lumpur. While the banning of the Party after the revolt removed the source of the conspiracy, it also left a political vacuum.[3]

In the Borneo territories, however, the immediate effect of the revolt was to weaken those elements opposing Malaysia: it brought home the threat of communist infiltration, particularly from Indonesia, and encouraged individual governments, like those of Singapore and Malaya itself, to tighten their own security. Evidence that the Indonesian PKI was actively involved in supplying and training the Brunei rebels convinced the Malayan government that all opposition to Malaysia was communist-inspired (which even in Brunei it certainly was not) and reinforced the Tunku's determination to stick to the Malaysian timetable, whether or not Brunei was to be included. Paradoxically, it was the revolt in Brunei, the only one of the six territories which chose to opt out of Malaysia, that transformed a relatively straight-forward exercise in decolonization into a major issue of South East Asian politics.

(ii) *The Philippines and Malaysia: the North Borneo claim*

Although it was clear, after the Brunei revolt, that the main external threat to Malaysia would arise from Indonesian pressure on the Borneo territories, and that the Indonesians had a convenient instrument to hand in the so-called North Borneo National Army, Azahari's choice of Manila rather than Djakarta as a base underlined Malaya's isolation in South East Asia. It also aggravated relations between Manila and Kuala

[1] The negotiations finally broke down at the end of June after the federal government had offered to allow Brunei to retain control of its oil revenues for a transitional period of ten years. The Sultan demanded that these revenues should remain with Brunei perpetually. *Straits Times*, 24 June 1963.

[2] R. S. Milne, 'Malaysia', *Asian Survey*, vol. iv, No. 2, Feb. 1964, p. 695. The office of the titular head of the Malayan Federation is rotated amongst the hereditary rulers of the Malay states. The Cobbold Commission encountered similar feelings in Sarawak and North Borneo that their rulers should be eligible for this post but noted that 'we see no way of meeting it without undue disturbance to the existing arrangements in Malaya'. (Cmnd. 1794), p. 43.

[3] *Straits Times*, 28 Dec. 1962.

Lumpur which had already deteriorated, despite the fact that, as recently as 1961, the Philippines, Malaya, and Thailand had set up the Association of South East Asia (ASA) to facilitate economic and political co-operation. The issue between the two governments arose out of the sudden Filipino revival, in mid-1962, of a virtually forgotten claim to North Borneo (Sabah).[1] Previous to this date the claim had been known to only a handful of Filipino politicians, and had played no part in either Philippine domestic politics or in relations with Malaya. Its presentation not only brought co-operation within the ASA to a halt but was to dominate all aspects of Malay-Philippine relations for the next three years.

It is not clear why the Filipinos lent their support, even unofficially, to Azahari as there was potentially a direct conflict of interest between their claim to North Borneo and the professed aim of the Party Rakyat to establish a federation under the Sultan of Brunei. The most probable explanation is that by the end of 1962 Manila was so affronted by the total lack of response which their claim had elicited from either London or Kuala Lumpur, that they reacted sympathetically to Azahari on the principle of 'the enemy of my enemy is my friend', calculating that without some upheaval in the area, nothing could stop Malaysia coming into being according to plan.[2]

The Philippine claim had been announced on 21 June 1962 by President Macapagal, one of the few who possessed a detailed knowledge of the subject.[3] The claim derived from an agreement in 1878 under which the Sultan of Sulu had ceded to Baron von Overbeck, agent of the British firm of Dent Brothers, territory in North Borneo extending from Jesselton on the west coast to the Sibuco River in the east. Ten years later, the British North Borneo Company, successors to Dent Brothers, concluded an

---

[1] For a useful analysis of the origins and developments of the Philippine claim to North Borneo see Bernard K. Gordon, *The dimensions of conflict in South-East Asia* (New Jersey, 1966), pp. 9–41.

[2] Azahari himself was also expert at playing on the susceptibilities of his two allies, appealing to the Indonesians on the basis of anti-colonialism and radical nationalism and to the anti-communism of the Philippines. For example, in a speech in Manila on 22 Nov. 1962 he suggested that far from creating a bastion against communism, the creation of Malaysia would lead in no time to its domination by the Chinese; that the creation of a Borneo Federation would protect the territories themselves against communist infiltration and that it would protect the Philippine rear from the same threat. But the underlying conflict of interest remained and it is significant that at no time did the government of the Philippines confirm, as Azahari claimed, that they had agreed to waive their claim in favour of a united Borneo. *Straits Times*, 22–23 Nov. 1962.

[3] *Malaya-Philippine Relations* (Kuala Lumpur, 1967), p. 22. Later in Jan. 1963 Macapagal claimed that his own interest in North Borneo went back to 1946–7 and had even been encouraged by US officials. This was an apparent reference to Francis Benton-Harrison, the American governor-general of the Philippines between 1913 and 1920. In 1946, Harrison, who was no longer an American official, was appointed an adviser to the Philippine government and was reported as having advised them that the British assumption of sovereignty over North Borneo and Sarawak constituted an act of aggression against the Philippines. *Times*, 4 Jan. 1963.

agreement with the British government under which the territory became a protectorate of the British Crown, a status which it enjoyed until 1946 when the company gave up its rights and North Borneo became a British colony. As legal successors to the Sultan of Sulu the Philippine government claimed that no transfer of sovereignty had ever taken place. In part the claim arose out of conflicting interpretations of the original agreement: the Malay word *padjak* is translated in the official British version as 'grant and cede' and in the Philippine version as 'lease', for which an annual payment was stipulated in the treaty.[1] But in essence the Philippine case rested on the contention that no transfer of sovereignty had, or indeed could have, taken place since Baron de Overbeck was neither himself a sovereign nor represented any sovereign entity. All subsequent transactions over the status of Borneo were, in the Philippine view, void.[2]

There was at first no response from London to Manila's presentation of this legal case, the British government refusing to discuss the claim either with the Sultan's direct heirs or with the Philippine's government. This was partly because the claim apparently did not rouse any popular feeling in the Philippines and moreover, the attorney, Nicosia Osmena, who acted for the Sultan's heirs, and who was probably responsible for bringing the matter to the government's attention, was widely believed to be more interested in a cash settlement than in the issue of sovereignty itself.[3] Furthermore, Manila was not wholly consistent in pressing its claim. According to the treaty of 1878, for example, the southernmost limit of the Sultan's domains lay on the Sibuco River, now in Indonesia, to whom the Philippines had made no protest, while part of Borneo had been ceded to the British by the Sultan of Brunei to whose territories Manila had no legal claim.

The British attitude none the less failed to take account of domestic pressure on the Philippine government to adopt a more nationalistic and anti-western position, and a specifically Asian identity. This pressure had been developing for some time, and was encouraged in 1962 by a fresh wave of anti-Americanism sparked off by the delay of the US Congress in appropriating $73 million due to the Philippines in payment of war damage claims.[4] What was regarded in Manila as British high-handedness in refusing to discuss the claim may well have confirmed Macapagal in his determination to stand firm, as a demonstration to the

[1] Gordon, pp. 12–15.

[2] Ibid., p. 12. For a detailed historical analysis of the claim see also K. G. Tregonning, 'The Claim for North Borneo by the Philippines', *Australian Outlook*, vol. 16, No. 3, Dec. 1962.

[3] Questioning the nature of the transfer in this way was a tactic which the Sultans of Sulu had periodically employed in the past whenever they needed to raise money; ibid., p. 19.

[4] The claims were finally settled under US Public Law 88–94 which Congress passed at the end of July 1963. For the text of the Department of State communique see *D.S.B.*, 19 Aug. 1963, p. 301.

western powers (Britain as well as the United States was allied to the Philippines in SEATO), that Filipino support could not always be taken for granted. One immediate result of his stand was a rapprochement between Manila and Djakarta to which the mutual sympathy for Azahari's rebellion in Brunei no doubt also contributed.

If by allowing Azahari to operate from Manila (although without official support) Macapagal intended to demonstrate his independence of action, and thus force Britain and the United States to take him seriously, it was a measure of his success that at the end of 1962 the British government finally yielded to the Philippine request for bilateral talks.[1] But the formula devised by the British to accommodate the talks slurred over the central issue—the North Borneo claim itself. The emphasis was placed, instead, on the 'security and stability' of South East Asia in which, as members of SEATO, both states shared a common interest. In a joint statement issued on 31 December 1962 both governments admitted that 'recent developments had made such conversations in the spirit of the Manila treaty and the Pacific Charter highly desirable'.[2] But while the British move was clearly intended to forestall more active anti-Malaysia co-operation between the Philippines and Indonesia,[3] there was no sign that either state was prepared to move from its established position.[4]

The Anglo-Philippine talks took place between 24 January and 1 February 1963 in London, the two sides being led by Emmanuel Pelaez, the Philippine vice-president, and Lord Home, the British foreign secretary. But while they were officially described as taking place in a 'frank and friendly atmosphere', as predicted by the British, Philippine, and Malayan press, it proved impossible, in practice, to separate the issues of regional defence against communist subversion, which the British were prepared to discuss, from the North Borneo claim which they were not. Thus while agreement was reached on certain co-operative measures 'in the prevention

[1] The original request, made at the time of Macapagal's speech in June 1962, was specifically related to the North Borneo claim and had been ignored by the British government until August 1962, by which time Britain and Malaya had agreed in principle on the creation of Malaysia In their reply, the British apparently had not ruled out the possibility of talks but had pointed out that the Philippine government had still not rebutted the official view of the status of North Borneo, i.e., that it was a British protectorate. *Times*, 1 Jan. 1963.   [2] *Times*, 1 Jan. 1963.

[3] The joint statement was the outcome of discussions between President Macapagal and John Pilcher, British ambassador in Manila, who was reported to have received an assurance from the Philippine government that they were not supporting the rebels in North Borneo. The British used this in an attempt to obtain a similar assurance from the Indonesian government. Ibid.

[4] Thus while the British were prepared for co-operation providing the two issues of defence and the Borneo claim were kept separate, the Philippine government insisted on linking them Following the joint statement of 21 December Macapagal stated publicly that there would be no change in the Philippine position, adding that 'the Philippine claim to North Borneo was initiated not only on the basis of legal rights but also as a matter of national interest. This claim does not only involve a legal claim but also the security of our country.' *Straits Times*, 4 Jan. 1963.

of piracy and armed raids and on problems of smuggling and illegal immigration in the region',[1] there was no meeting-point on the best means of securing the future political stability of the Borneo territories. The British side stood firm in their defence of the Malaysian project, while the Philippines countered with a proposal for a Confederation of Malay States, and continued to oppose the inclusion of North Borneo in Malaysia. Any hope that they would agree to drop their North Borneo claim in return for a reiteration of British determination to uphold the stability of the region against Communist infiltration was shattered by the Philippine president. In a state of the nation address delivered in Manila while the London talks were still proceeding, Macapagal emphasized his own deep opposition to the incorporation of North Borneo in Malaysia. The legal aspects apart, he based his argument on two grounds, first, that if Malaysia fell to the communists, 'a Communist territory . . . immediately at the southern frontier of the Philippines . . . [would] pose a grave and intolerable threat to our country', and second, because 'it can be expected that Indonesia will not accept the authority of Malaya over these territories'.[2]

But if Macapagal was determined to match British intransigence, the same considerations which had kept the Philippines within the western camp (economic and military dependence on the United States and fears of Communist subversion) now prompted him to take up a mediatory position between Indonesia and Malaya. In the same speech he announced an initiative which was presumably intended to provide an 'Asian' solution to the problem which all could accept, even if the Philippines had to surrender its claim. It had already been reported that Manila wanted a summit conference of the heads of state of Malaya, the Philippines, Indonesia, and Thailand to discuss regional problems.[3] Macapagal now emphasized that the Philippines accepted the principle of self-determination for North Borneo and proposed that the issue should be tested through a United Nations referendum in which the people would be asked whether they wished to be independent, part of the Philippines, or 'placed under another state'.[4]

By the beginning of 1963 it was already clear that the government in Manila stood in need of a means to reconcile Philippine fears of communist subversion with a nationalist demand for an active foreign policy. What was not yet clear was that, as a party to the dispute over Malaysia, the Philippine government was inevitably handicapped as a mediator between Indonesia and Malaya, a role which, in other respects, might have given Macapagal his best opportunity for resolving this dilemma.

[1] Anglo-Philippine talks, official communique. For full text see *Documents, 1963*, pp. 344–5.
[2] *Times*, 29 Jan. 1963.   [3] *NY Times*, 22 Jan. 1963.
[4] *Times*, 29 Jan. 1963.

(iii) *Indonesia and Malaysia: the approach to 'confrontation'*

The Philippine initiatives for a UN referendum and a summit conference matured slowly. This was partly because the Malayans were determined that their agreement to participate in regional talks should not be made conditional on prior agreement to delay the creation of Malaysia,[1] and partly because of the need for preparatory consultations to define detailed objectives of the talks.[2] Perhaps the main reason for the delay, however, was the crystallization of Indonesian opposition to Malaysia. Indonesia's policy of confrontation, like Azahari's revolt in Brunei, was founded, in the last analysis, on premises quite incompatible with Filipino claims to Borneo. But in the short run it was in Sukarno's interest to widen the anti-Malaysia front to include Manila.

To understand the events which led ultimately to the severance of diplomatic relations between Djakarta and Kuala Lumpur in September 1963, two preliminary points must be made. First, as noted earlier, confrontation was not, at the beginning of 1963, inevitable. Officially, Indonesia had no territorial ambitions beyond West New Guinea, a position which had been confirmed before the United Nations by Dr Subandrio, the Indonesian foreign minister, at the end of 1961:

We are not only disclaiming the territories outside the former Netherlands East Indies . . . but . . . when Malaya told us of its intentions to merge with the three [*sic*] British Crown colonies of Sarawak, Brunei and British North Borneo as one Federation, we told them that we had no objections and that we wished them success with this merger so that everyone might live in peace and freedom.[3]

While in the conflict between the Old Established and the New Emerging Forces, on which President Sukarno based his foreign policy, confrontation with Malaysia was regarded as a natural extension to Indonesia's successful confrontation with the Dutch, in substance, if not in style, it was quite different: against the Dutch, Indonesia had advanced a territorial claim; Indonesia's interest in Malaysia on the other hand was ostensibly merely ideological. 'Confrontation' in this case constituted a direct intervention in the internal affairs of a neighbouring state. In diplomatic terms this had the important consequence that Sukarno was not able to depend on Afro-Asian support as he had done in opposing the Dutch.

But while the decision to oppose Malaysia by all means short of outright war was taken in response to specific stimuli which presented themselves

[1] *Straits Times*, 20 Feb. 1963.
[2] The immediate outcome of the Philippine initiative was a tripartite meeting between Vice-President Palaez, Dr Subandrio, the Indonesian foreign minister and Tun Razak, deputy prime minister of Malaya, during the ECAFE meeting in Manila in March. But little appears to have been accomplished at this meeting.
[3] *GAOR*, 16th Session, 1058th plenary meeting.

in early 1963 and which were not present before this, the ground was none the less well prepared both in terms of Indonesia's domestic politics and of the officially suppressed but powerful element of irredentism in Indonesian foreign policy. The second point to be made, therefore, is that the Indonesian leadership was both willing and eager to engage in confrontation when the opportunity offered.

In the domestic context, 'confrontation' was a policy to which both the PKI and the army—Sukarno's twin supports—could rally.[1] Both thrived in conditions of crisis. The PKI, the world's third largest communist party, had been the first Indonesian organization publicly to condemn Malaysia, branding the proposed federation as a form of neo-colonialism in December 1961. (This stand was adopted by Moscow and Peking although there is no evidence that it was inspired from either capital.) The army, while not publicly committed against Malaysia, stood to gain from any policy which diverted the government's attention from the much needed programme of economic reform, since in such a programme the swollen army budget presented an obvious target for drastic reduction.[2] At this time, moreover, a reordering of priorities to accommodate economic reform was being pressed on Sukarno by members of his government as well as by the United States. The Indonesian military had hitherto been able to justify the size of their establishment by reference to 'confrontation' with the Dutch and their vital role in maintaining internal security. However, the successful suppression of the Darul Islam rebel movement in West Java in 1962 created a situation 'unprecedented since independence, in which civil security prevailed throughout the country'.[3] This and the subsequent solution of the West Irian affair posed a direct threat to the army's political position. But if, therefore, the army had a stake in confrontation, it was probably also to the advantage of President Sukarno himself. As one observer suggested, 'with a foreign crisis, the various balanced pieces of the governing coalition can stay together with a common goal; while if domestic problems, such as economic deterioration were tackled, there would be strong clashes of interest within the coalition'.[4]

Externally, Indonesia's confrontation with Malaysia derived from the same irredentism which inspired the campaign for West Irian.[5] While Indonesia never formally claimed any territories in the new federation

---

[1] For a useful discussion of shifts in the relative standing of the PKI and the Indonesian army in Indonesia's domestic politics see Herbert Feith, 'President Sukarno, the Army and the Communists; the Triangle changes shape', *Asian Survey*, vol. iv, No. 8, Aug. 1964, pp. 969–80.

[2] There was, for example, talk at the beginning of 1963 of a reduction of 47 per cent in the military budget as well as large-scale demobilization. See Donald Hindley, 'Indonesia's Confrontation with Malaysia: A search for motives', *Asian Survey*, vol. iv, No. 6, June 1964, p. 910.

[3] Feith, p. 969.   [4] Hindley, 'Indonesia's Confrontation', p. 909.

[5] *Survey, 1962*, pp. 377–8. For a detailed discussion of the origins of expansionism in Indonesian foreign policy see also Gordon, pp. 79–87.

there is no doubt that many in the Indonesian leadership had dreams of a 'Greater Indonesia', to be achieved through the return of various 'lost' territories including the Malayan peninsula. Most prominent amongst the advocates of Indonesian expansionism, until his death in October 1962, was Muhammid Yamin, a deputy first minister and minister of information. Yamin had formulated his vision as early as 1945 and had continued to insist that Indonesia was the rightful heir to the eight groups of islands which had formed the prehistoric empire of Nusantara.[1] Although he was primarily an Indonesian nationalist, Yamin also believed that Indonesia's security would be threatened by an independent Malaya commanding the neck of the Indonesian archipelago.

To separate Malaya from the rest of Indonesia amounts to deliberately weakening from the outset the position . . . of Indonesia in her international relations. On the other hand to unite Malaya to Indonesia will mean strengthening our position and completing an entity to accord with our national aspirations and consistent with the interests of geo-politics of air, land and sea.[2]

Yamin's thesis was substantially endorsed by Sukarno when, with Japanese backing, he set up the Investigating Committee for Preparation of Indonesia's Independence (BPKI) in 1945. 'Indonesia will not become strong and secure', he said during the BPKI debate on the territorial limits of the new Republic, 'unless the whole Straits of Malacca is in our hands. If only the west coast of the Straits of Malacca, it will mean a threat to our security.'[3] Although it was finally the Japanese who ruled on the question of Indonesia's boundaries, and although Sukarno accepted independence at their hands for the former Dutch East Indies alone, it is also significant that within the BPKI forty-five out of sixty-six members voted for an independent Indonesia that would include all of what eventually became Malaysia.[4]

It is impossible to establish a direct link between the formulation of the 'Greater Indonesia' thesis in 1945 and the promulgation of confrontation with Malaysia in 1963. Yet the latter policy inevitably recalls the former. During the long confrontation with the Dutch, the Indonesians had built up their armed forces, with substantial assistance from the Soviet Union, to a point where they were the leading indigenous military power in the area, a position which fell short of hegemony largely by virtue of the military presence which Britain and the United States continued to

[1] Viz., the Malay peninsula, the islands of Sumatra, Kalimantan (Borneo), Java, the South-Eastern islands, the islands of Sulawesi, Moluccas, and West Irian.

[2] Muhammid Yamin, 'A Legal and Historical View of Indonesian Sovereignty over the Ages', *Dewan Nasional* (Djakarta), Sept. 1958, p. 6.

[3] 'The territory of the Indonesians' state: discussions in the meeting of the Investigating Committee for Indonesian Independence', extracted and translated from the book, *Naskahi Persiapan Undang—Undang Dasar, 1945* (Kuala Lumpur, 1964), p. 21, cited in Gordon, p. 84.

[4] Ibid., p. 85.

maintain in South East Asia.[1] It is not surprising therefore, that Djakarta opposed so strongly the British and American bases, nor that the Indonesians demanded, as of right, mutual consultation in any change in the political *status quo* in South East Asia. Moreover, while Indonesia's foreign policy rested on unsatisfied irredentist claims, the active support which the British and Americans allegedly rendered to the Sumatra Separatist Movement in 1958, using Malaya, Singapore, and North Borneo as bases from which to supply the rebels, had created a deep-rooted suspicion not only of the Western powers but of Malaya itself, which, although not a member of SEATO, was linked by a bilateral defence treaty with Britain. In this context, then, in Indonesian eyes, Sukarno's theory of Indonesia's 'encirclement' seemed plausible.[2]

In Indonesia as in the Philippines, it was Azahari's rebellion in Brunei which provided the occasion for the crystallization of opposition to Malaysia. In the months preceding his revolt, Azahari established contact with the left-wing parties in Singapore and Malaya and through them with the PKI in Indonesia; for their part the Indonesians had established a base at Malinau in Indonesian Borneo to train the so-called North Borneo National Army. This unofficial assistance was followed during the revolt by an official proclamation of support for the rebels. Although Sukarno never recognized Azahari as the legitimate government of Brunei, in February 1963 he declared Indonesia's opposition to Malaysia,[3] linking the Indonesian position directly to the Borneo question, adding, 'We sympathize with the struggle of the people of North Kalimantan. This we do not hide. We sympathise with the struggle for the liberation of North Kalimantan because it is a matter of principle to us.'[4]

(e) *Malaysia in international and regional diplomacy*

(i) *United States–Indonesian relations*

Matters of principle did not prevent Sukarno from toying with the idea of a negotiated settlement over Malaysia. In the spring of 1963 he was involved in exploratory talks with the Philippines and Malaya aimed at finding a regional solution to their differences. Although he denounced any idea of talks on Malaysia prior to the independence of the Borneo territories in a May-day speech,[5] in April Indonesia had been

---

[1] For a useful discussion of foreign assistance to Indonesia see Donald Hindley, 'Foreign Aid to Indonesia and its Political Implications', *Pacific Affairs*, Summer 1963, pp. 108–9.

[2] Hindley, 'Indonesia's Confrontation', p. 909.

[3] The government gave its first indication of opposition to Malaysia on 11 Feb. 1963 when Subandrio stated that the Tunku 'has always been hostile to Indonesia'. *Straits Times*, 12 Feb. 1963.

[4] Modelski, p. 75.

[5] Viz., 'The stand of the Indonesian Republic . . . the stand of Bung Karno . . . is to give freedom to Kalimantan Utera. After Kalimantan Utera has its independence, after it has its freedom, let us hold talks.' Cited in Gordon, p. 99.

represented in Manila at a sub-ministerial meeting called to prepare for a subsequent foreign ministers' meeting on the subject.[1]

While it is impossible to do more than speculate on what persuaded Sukarno to reverse his stand, or rather to operate on two separate and contradictory levels, it is known that Indonesia was, at this time, under heavy pressure from the US government to embark upon a programme of economic stabilization and reconstruction, one result of which, the Americans hoped, would be to deflect Indonesian energies from a prolonged and wasteful campaign against Malaysia.[2] Although, as we have seen, President Kennedy had declared his support for Malaysia, the US administration remained acutely aware of Indonesia's potential, a factor which singled out the Indonesian government as a natural focal point around which a group of Asian states might coalesce to balance Chinese power and contain Chinese expansion in South East Asia. At the same time the US government, especially Congress, were suspicious of Sukarno and apprehensive about the influence of the PKI on his government. For similar reasons to those that led to American mediation in West Irian, the Kennedy regime was anxious that its policy towards Malaysia should neither weaken the non-communist forces in Indonesia nor deflect the government from economic reforms. By the beginning of 1963, Sukarno's lack of interest in economic policy, the crippling burden of defence expenditure,[3] and the political strength of the PKI in opposing any programme of economic co-operation with the 'Imperialists', had combined to bring the Indonesian economy to a point of virtual collapse.[4] For the United States, this situation posed a dilemma: while in economic terms, they were unwilling to throw good money after bad, politically, economic aid was one of the few remaining instruments of influence available. It was presumably with this in mind that they attempted to give a new direction to their economic relations with Indonesia. Negotiations with the World Bank and the IMF over the 1961 Eight-Year development plan, for which Indonesia had requested $5 billion in development aid, had proved difficult because of Indonesian reluctance to undertake the recommended economic stabilization programme. An American aid mission appointed in 1962 was more successful: it concluded that the Indonesian plan was feasible, that foreign aid over five years of between $325 and $390m. would be required, and that, providing Indonesia

---

[1] For the text of the joint final communique see *Malaya-Philippine relations*, Appendix V.

[2] For a detailed account of US policy towards Indonesia by one of those responsible for its formulation, see Hilsman, pp. 367–409.

[3] Indonesia's debt to the Soviet Union alone, arising from the purchase of combat aircraft, warships, and munitions, probably amounted to $1 billion. *NY Times*, 5 Apr. 1963.

[4] For example, there were few industries operating at more than 50 per cent capacity, while in Java less than half the island's trucks and buses were on the roads for want of spare parts. The result was a period of chronic inflation unprecedented in Indonesia's history. Hilsman, p. 384.

embarked on the stabilization programme, the United States would provide between $200 and $285m. It was, therefore, from a seemingly strong bargaining position that the US sought to implement its policy of deflecting Indonesian energies into constructive channels.

The first signs that the Indonesian leadership was contemplating a serious attack on the country's economic problems in fulfilment of this bargain were not reassuring. At the beginning of March, Sukarno instructed a government committee to prepare recommendations for economic and financial reform by the middle of the month. But not only was the committee to include D. N. Aidit, PKI chairman,[1] when, finally, Sukarno announced an emergency economic programme at the end of March, he emphasized measures which the government must take to evolve 'a nationalist democratic economy' free from 'feudalistic and imperialist influence', including a ban on the repatriation of profits by foreign firms and the appointment of a 'selective Consultative Committee' which would first reorganize and subsequently take charge of all industry.[2] Indeed, Sukarno seemed to indicate that the primary purpose of the new policy was to make the Indonesian economy independent of outside powers. In contrast to the early years of independence when the economy had remained largely under foreign control, Sukarno suggested that the government was now able 'to conceive and organise the construction of its own Indonesian economy'.[3] Only if 'self-help' measures failed to produce the required results within two years would it be necessary for Indonesia to look abroad for credit.

Despite the revolutionary style, the short-term measures for economic stabilization—stockpiling of rice, raw materials, and spare parts, and incentives to encourage both import substitution and exports—suggested that IMF and US pressure were beginning to yield results. At the end of May the government announced a set of further measures, including the lifting of price controls on a number of essential commodities and public services, designed to combat inflation and check the declining value of the Indonesian rupiah.[4]

For Indonesian foreign policy, however, the results were ambiguous. Although they had previously endorsed Sukarno's economic declaration, the PKI reacted strongly against the new measures,[5] accusing the government of giving in to 'Imperialist pressure'.[6] In retrospect there seems little doubt that domestic opposition was partly responsible for Sukarno's

---

[1] *Straits Times*, 5 Mar. 1963.   [2] Ibid., 30 Mar. 1963.   [3] Ibid.

[4] The official exchange rate of the Indonesian rupiah had been pegged at 45 to the US dollar. In May 1963, however, the black market rate was reported at more than 1,100 to the dollar, falling after the introduction of the government measures to about 900. *NY Times*, 28 June 1963.

[5] Opposition was particularly vehement against the rise in the charges for public services: bus fares were doubled, rail fares trebled, and post and telegraph quadrupled.

[6] *Straits Times*, 11, 17 June 1963.

decision to drop the policy of conciliation with the United States, the World Bank, and the IMF, and to adopt a policy of confrontation with Malaysia, even at the cost of foregoing Western aid. At the time, however, it appeared that he was prepared to risk opposition at home in a genuine attempt to reach an accommodation abroad. While the immediate issue arose out of negotiations between the Indonesian government and a group of Western oil companies, the acceptance of American good offices appears to have played a part also in Sukarno's attempt to reach an understanding with the Malaysian prime minister.

Sukarno agreed to meet Wilson Wyatt, President Kennedy's representative, in Tokyo after the oil companies had informed the US government that they would rather cease operations than submit to an Indonesian demand for a profit-sharing agreement involving 60:40 split between the companies and the government calculated on the basis of posted rather than realized prices.[1] Had the oil companies carried out their threat, this would have had a serious effect, both on the stabilization programme and on Indonesia's already precarious relationship with the Western powers. The settlement achieved in Tokyo seemed to vindicate US policy. Although both sides made concessions, the oil companies obtained substantially what they wanted, while, for the time being, Sukarno seemed genuinely grateful for American intervention and receptive to American ideas.[2]

(ii) *Regional diplomacy, May–July 1963*

As further evidence of the new Indonesian attitude, Sukarno invited the Tunku to join him in Tokyo for a private meeting immediately after the conclusion of the oil talks. Although this proposal appears to have been made spontaneously, it had been pressed on him by the American, Australian, and Philippine governments. And in fact it was made possible by the success of the meeting of deputy foreign ministers, referred to above,[3] which had already cleared the air between Indonesia, the Philippines,

---

[1] The three companies involved were Caltex, Shell, and Stanvac. The negotiations followed the Indonesian announcement in 1960 that oil was henceforth to be regarded as 'wealth which is controlled by the state', a decision which transferred the companies into contractors working for the government. Apart from the disagreement over profits, there were other differences over the basis of taxation and the prices to be paid by the Indonesian government for the companies' marketing facilities. For a full discussion of the US-Indonesian oil negotiations, see Hilsman, pp. 385-9.

[2] The oil companies accepted both the 60:40 split in profits and an Indonesian proposal for phased payments for company assets, while the Indonesians accepted that the profit split should be made on the basis of actual not posted prices, and that tax should be paid before and not after the division.

[3] This meeting itself was prompted by the diplomatic efforts of the Australian foreign minister, Sir Garfield Barwick, who had used the opportunity of the ECAFE meeting in March to give public support both for Malaysia and for Macapagal's efforts at conciliation between Malaya and Indonesia. *OFNS*, 17 May 1963.

and Malaya and created the climate necessary for constructive diplomacy. While the official communique issued after this Manila meeting had made no specific mention of Malaysia, the Malayans had agreed, in principle, to a summit between the three heads of state. The three foreign ministers, however, were to meet first for a 'general exchange of views on common problems and an explanation of how each country is endeavouring to solve them as well as a consideration of arrangements by which the three countries can achieve closer co-operation towards their solution'.[1] Despite Indonesian vacillation, following the announcement that the Malaysian agreement was to be concluded in London at the end of June,[2] the diplomatic momentum was maintained.[3] When Sukarno had a brief meeting with President Macapagal in Manila at the end of May, he confirmed that Dr Subandrio would attend the foreign ministers' meeting in the second week of June and that he himself would attend the subsequent summit meeting 'to thrash out outstanding problems'.[4]

Against this background, the Indonesian and Malayan leaders met on 31 May in the house of Mr Ohira, the Japanese foreign minister. The success of this meeting was as welcome as it was unexpected. Not only did the two leaders agree to settle all differences between them in the spirit of the 1959 Treaty of Friendship between Malaya and Indonesia, but, as an immediate proof of this commitment, they agreed 'to refrain from making any acrimonious attacks and disparaging references to each other'.[5] The meeting had the immediate effect of creating an aura of optimism and gave rise to speculation about a possible framework for future regional co-operation. Neither leader appeared, however, to have fundamentally revised his previous attitude. On his return from Tokyo, the Tunku appeared to be optimistic about the future, although he reiterated that, in response to repeated requests, he had insisted that he neither could nor would delay the establishment of Malaysia beyond 31 August.[6] On the Indonesian side, the Tokyo meeting was regarded as successful in so far as it had secured from Malaya an explicit recognition that the Malaysian proposal was not merely a domestic issue, but this did not imply, as Dr Subandrio quickly made clear, that Indonesia had dropped its opposition in principle to the whole project.[7]

Despite such intimations the atmosphere was further improved when the foreign ministers met between 2 and 11 June in what appeared to be a genuine spirit of compromise. Although both Dr Subandrio and Tun Abdul Razak were initially reported as sceptical about the Philippine

[1] *Straits Times*, 18 Apr. 1963.   [2] Ibid., 19 Apr. 1963.
[3] *NY Times*, 18 May 1963.   [4] *Straits Times*, 24 May 1963.
[5] For the full text of the communique issued after the Tokyo meeting see *Documents, 1963*, p. 345.
[6] At the same time the Tunku also announced that the Malaysian defence build-up was to continue. *Straits Times*, 6 June 1963.
[7] Ibid.

proposal for a confederation of Malay states,[1] it was this formula on which they eventually agreed. In the Manila Accord, the document containing the foreign ministers' recommendations to their respective heads of governments, they agreed on the establishment of machinery for regular inter-governmental consultation 'at all levels to deal with matters of mutual interest and concern consistent with the national, regional, and international responsibilities and obligations of each country without prejudice to its sovereignty and independence'.[2] In contrast with the earlier atmosphere of hostility, when the possibilities of a summit conference had seemed little more than a pious hope, the change now seemed, as the *Straits Times* commented, so complete and the success of the foreign ministers' conference so fundamental, that failure at the summit was unthinkable.[3]

However, what was agreed, but omitted, from the official communique gave ample scope for varied interpretation and future misunderstanding. It was subsequently revealed, for instance, that Indonesia and the Philippines had agreed to 'welcome the formation of Malaysia, provided the support of the people of the Borneo territories is ascertained by an independent and impartial authority, the secretary-general of the United Nations or his representative'.[4] This formulation left unanswered the two most important questions: the method by which opinion in the Borneo territories was to be tested and the timing of the inquiry. Moreover on the Malayan side, it was also contingent, as Tun Razak pointed out, on Britain's prior approval.[5]

In Kuala Lumpur and Singapore the Manila conference was regarded as a triumph for Razak's diplomacy, the official view being that there was now no external objection to the establishment of Malaysia according to schedule on 31 August.[6] In Indonesia, on the other hand, the government adopted a different interpretation.[7] Whether as a result of a genuine misunderstanding, or, as has been suggested, as part of a deliberate policy of alternating periods of pressure and negotiation, Dr Subandrio promptly announced on his return from Manila that he had secured

---

[1] *NY Times*, 9 June 1963.

[2] For the full text of the Manila Accord see *Documents, 1963*, pp. 350–2.

[3] *Straits Times*, 13 June 1963.

[4] The Manila Accord, Article 10. The official communique had not referred in detail to this part of the Accord which was only released later in the year by the Philippine government.

[5] *Straits Times*, 15 June 1963.

[6] This interpretation was confirmed on 13 June by both Tun Razak and Lee Kuan Yew. The latter, however, qualified his support for the 'confederation' agreement with a statement that if this meant that Singapore was to be absorbed into an unknown entity 'then we must reserve our position', a statement which was at once a reflection of Lee's anxiety to avoid any delays in the creation of Malaysia and of his desire to allay popular suspicion that the agreement would establish an anti-Chinese alliance amongst the three Malay states. *Straits Times*, 14, 18 June 1963.

[7] Cf. Gordon, p. 100.

agreement for a referendum to be held in the Borneo territories before the merger date.[1]

Amongst the political parties in Borneo, this proposal was only taken up by the SUPP in Sarawak,[2] but the federal government's rival interpretation was used by the Indonesians as an excuse for renewed hostility towards Malaysia. Only two weeks before the projected summit, Dr Subandrio issued a warning that active confrontation would be resumed if the Borneo territories were 'forced into Malaysia without their agreement in accordance with the principle of self-determination'.[3] And on the following day, Sukarno himself declared in a speech to the West Java War College that confrontation was necessary 'to maintain our security'.[4]

(iii) *Singapore and Malayan diplomacy*

The most serious issue arose over timing. This was not new, but it was now brought into the open. While Sukarno's injured pride at not being consulted had been partly assuaged by the Tokyo and Manila meetings, at no point had the Tunku conceded the possibility of delaying the merger in response to external pressure from either Indonesia or the Philippines. It was probably not fear of appeasing either Philippine irredentism or Indonesian expansionism which made the Tunku intractable but the fact that any change in the timetable would have prejudiced the negotiations between Malaya and Singapore, on the success of which, it was believed, the viability of the new federation would rest.

The problem here was partly constitutional. If the merger was to take place as proposed on 31 August, then the detailed arrangements would have to be settled and approved by the British government by the beginning of July to allow time for the appropriate procedures to be applied in Britain and the Malaysian territories. These dates also acquired a deeper significance as a result of the way they were used by both sides in the negotiations over the economic arrangements for Malaysia. Having surrendered, in the interests of merger, Singapore's claim to the control of internal security and an independent foreign policy, it was all the more important, in terms of Singapore's domestic politics, that Lee Kuan Yew should drive a hard bargain in the financial negotiations. In the course of the negotiations, moreover, it had become clear—there had already been one breakdown in April 1963—that the fixing of specific

---

[1] *Straits Times*, 14 June 1963.
[2] Ibid. Pro-Malaysia political leaders in the territories reacted differently. Donald Stevens, first minister designate of North Borneo, argued that there was no need for a referendum since in the state's first general elections, held in Dec. 1962, the Five Party Pro-Malaysia Alliance had won 86·5 per cent of the vote. *NY Times*, 16 June 1963. The Pro-Malaysia Sarawak Alliance at first conceded that it would be logical to hold a referendum after Malaysia had been established but subsequently stated its opposition. *Straits Times*, 14 June 1963.
[3] *Straits Times*, 11 July 1963.   [4] Ibid., 12 July 1963.

deadlines was a useful device for securing a last-minute compromise. It worked to the advantage of both sides. Although the Tunku might threaten to bring Malaysia into being without Singapore,[1] this would leave unresolved the fundamental internal security problem to which the Malaysian proposal had originally been addressed. On the other hand, given the volatile nature of Singapore public opinion, a failure to reach a satisfactory agreement could have proved disastrous to the PAP, which had staked its reputation against the Barisan Socialis on the success of the merger.[2]

Although there was, therefore, a common sense of purpose on both sides of the causeway, relations had deteriorated under the strain of the financial negotiations from the cordiality which had prevailed during the political negotiations the previous year. By the third week of June, the date originally fixed for finalization of the merger plan in London, the two sides had reached deadlock. The difficulties arose over questions of financial control and the creation of a Malaysian common market.[3] Because the postwar economic development of Singapore had been different from that of the Federation, and because a higher proportion of Singapore's revenues were devoted to social services, the Singapore government insisted on retaining in full its revenue-raising power and proposed to pay a lump sum to the Federal government to meet its share of Federal expenses. This proposal was rejected by the Federal finance minister, Tan Siew Sin, on the grounds that the centre should have 'at least ultimate control on what is eventually regarded as Federal Revenue'.[4] Again, as a result of differences in economic development, the Singapore government attached far greater importance than Malaya to the creation of a common market. Singapore insisted that the arrangements should form part of the constitution while the Federal government agreed in principle to the common market proposal but was prepared to delay its detailed negotiation until later.

A succession of ultimata between 20 and 24 June failed to produce a solution on three outstanding issues. First, there was a disagreement about the amount of tax which Singapore was to provide, 40 per cent as demanded by the Federation, or 39 per cent tied to an undertaking to establish the common market, as offered by Singapore. Second, the common market itself remained in dispute.[5] Third, there was an unresolved

[1] Ibid., 21 June 1963.

[2] In the context of Malaysian-Indonesian relations, for example, there was little doubt that it was internal pressure of this kind which led Lee Kuan Yew, in 1963, to switch from his previous soft line towards Indonesia to an openly hostile one, and to his noticeable lack of enthusiasm for the Maphilindo proposal. Cf. Osborne, pp. 68–70.

[3] For a full analysis of the Singapore-Malayan financial negotiations see ibid., pp. 50–61.

[4] *Straits Times*, 5 Mar. 1963.

[5] The common market plan had originally been drawn up, at the request of the Malayan government, by a World Bank team under the economist Jacques Rueff. The Rueff Report was

controversy between Lee Kuan Yew and Tan Siew Sin, who alleged that the Singapore government (although not Lee personally) had agreed to make a grant of $50m. (£5·8m.) towards the economic development of the Borneo territories. Singapore refused to make this grant part of the merger settlement and proposed instead to make available loans to the value of $150m. (£17·5m).[1]

Faced with the deadlock, the Tunku was forced to resort to British mediation. The final agreement was, therefore, the outcome of a series of meetings in London between the British commonwealth secretary, Duncan Sandys, and the Malayan and Singapore delegations led by Tun Abdul Razak (the Tunku having delayed his own departure for London) and Lee Kuan Yew. Although Lee subsequently insisted that he had only finally agreed to settle out of personal regard for the Tunku, it was clear that it was a combination of the logic of the situation, neither side being prepared to risk failure, and Duncan Sandys' idiosyncratic working methods—on several occasions he kept the delegates up all night—that finally secured agreement on 5 July.

The text of the Malaysia agreement, covering all aspects of the merger,[2] was signed at Marlborough House at midnight on 8 July. While, on the economic arrangements, both sides made concessions, the terms were still relatively favourable to Singapore. Thus, while the city state agreed to pay 40 per cent of its national income from taxes to the federal government, this provision was made subject to a periodic review by an independent body, while, in deference to Singapore's wishes, the details of the common market were spelt out in a special annex to the agreement.[3] A compromise was also reached with respect to Singapore's contribution to the development of the Borneo territories, whereby she agreed to loan $150m. over fifteen years with a five-year interest-free period for the first $100m.

(iv) Regional diplomacy, July–September 1963

The signing of the Malaysia agreement freed the Tunku from a major constraint on his diplomatic efforts, namely, the need to forestall any change in the internal balance of power, particularly in Singapore. Consequently it also left him free to concentrate on the task of reconciling Indonesia and the Philippines to the new Federation. That this was likely to prove difficult had already been demonstrated by Indonesia's

finally published in July. Prior to publication, however, its findings were endorsed by the Singapore government, particularly a recommendation that within the common market, industry should be located on economic rather than political criteria, which they believed to be necessary to offset the gradual but inevitable erosion of Singapore's entrepôt trade. It was believed that it was this aspect of the report that was least welcome to Kuala Lumpur.

[1] *Times*, 28 June 1963.   [2] *Documents, 1963*, pp. 352–60.   [3] Ibid.

reversion to a position of open hostility. Not only had Djakarta inter-preted the foreign ministers' agreement as committing Malaya to referen-dum in the Borneo territories before the creation of Malaysia, but by signing the agreement in London, the Tunku had, or so Sukarno alleged, gone back on his own word at Tokyo.[1] Initially, the Indonesians reacted to the Malaysia agreement by renewing their verbal and propaganda attacks although Sukarno threatened that if Malaya maintained its negative attitude towards the referendum proposal, he would revive a policy of military confrontation in support of rebel activity in Sarawak and North Borneo.[2]

A campaign to conciliate Djakarta was now apparent. When Tun Abdul Razak defended the Malaysia agreement on 16 July he pointed out that the Federation would not come into being until it had been ratified by all the governments concerned. He continued:

> There is, therefore, still time before 31 August for the United Nations Secretary General or his representative to ascertain the wishes of the peoples of North Borneo and Sarawak in accordance with the agreement reached in Manila . . . The Federal government had already taken action to inform the UN Secretary General and the British government so that once the summit conference has approved the recommendation it will be possible to ensure that this part of the agreement can be proceeded with immediately.[3]

There was no immediate response to this statement from Djakarta. Indeed, despite an appeal from President Macapagal, which drew an immediately favourable reply from the Tunku, Sukarno announced that he was still undecided on whether to attend the summit.[4] And when a few days later, at an anti-Malaysia rally, he announced his decision to attend, he was going, he explained, 'to continue Indonesia's confrontation policy towards Malaysia' and 'to make Malaysia fail'.[5]

The background to the Manila summit (30 July–5 August) could scarcely have been less auspicious. Yet the immediate outcome once again seemed a triumph for good sense and moderation. Before leaving Kuala Lumpur, the Tunku reiterated that he would not yield to Indo-nesian pressure for a referendum in the Borneo territories.[6] But it seemed that, in other respects, he was prepared to make substantial concessions. The framework for a compromise was provided by the foreign ministers' recommendations (the Manila Accord): the three leaders agreed to tackle the immediate problem of the Borneo territories through an appeal

[1] *NY Times*, 16 July 1963.   [2] Ibid.   [3] *Straits Times*, 16 July 1963.
[4] Ibid., 19 July 1963. At the same time, after a meeting with the Indonesian defence minister, General Nasution, it was reported that Sukarno had ordered 'the strengthening of everything relating to defence'. Responding to this challenge, the Tunku declared his willingness to use arms if necessary to defend Malaysia, if anyone, including Indonesia, threatened its integrity. *Straits Times, Japan Times*, 23 July 1963.
[5] Ibid., 28 July 1963.   [6] *Daily Telegraph, NY Times*, 30 July 1963.

to the United Nations secretary-general, U Thant, and the long-term question of regional co-operation through the adoption of President Macapagal's proposal for a confederation of Malay states. In addition to countersigning the Manila Accord, however, the summit produced two further documents—the Manila Declaration and the Joint Statement—which expanded its recommendations in several directions.[1]

On the central issue of the Borneo territories, the outcome seemed to vindicate Sukarno's pressure tactics prior to the conference. For not only did the heads of state endorse the recommendation for an appeal to the secretary-general but in their joint statement it was formally conceded that this should be done 'prior to the establishment of the Federation of Malaysia', a provision which led the Tunku to agree to a few days' delay.

In other respects also the Tunku (and for that matter President Macapagal) seemed prepared to make formal concessions in return for an accommodation with Sukarno. The drafting of the conference documents unmistakably bore his imprint. There were, for example, several references to the Bandung declaration of 1955,[2] and also to the spirit of Afro-Asian solidarity which had allegedly emerged from it. The three leaders agreed that their states would co-operate as 'New Emerging Forces' while even Macapagal's confederation plan was endowed with an Indonesian-style acronym: 'Maphilindo'. Of more potential significance, Sukarno succeeded in obtaining an admission from Malaya and the Philippines that:

. . . foreign bases—temporary in nature—should not be allowed to be used directly or indirectly to subvert the national independence of any of the three countries. In accordance with the principle enunciated in the Bandung declaration the three countries will abstain from the use of arrangements of collective defence to serve the particular interests of any of the big powers.[3]

As a result of his concessions the Tunku found himself out of favour in both London and Singapore. The British government, indeed, was at first opposed to any delay, partly because they considered a referendum unnecessary but partly also because an appeal to the UN would breach a long-standing principle of British colonial policy, namely not to allow the United Nations to send commissions of inquiry or hold referenda in British territories.[4] Still, the British were in no position to press opposition which would have forfeited international sympathy for Malaysia and provided Sukarno with a justification for stepping up Indonesian confrontation. In the event the Tunku was vindicated, for, after consultation with U Thant,[5] Sukarno dropped his demand for a referendum and accepted that the secretary-general should scrutinize the results of the

---

[1] For the full text of the three documents see *Documents, 1963*, pp. 347–52.
[2] Text in *Documents, 1955*, pp. 429–38.
[3] *Tripartite Summit Meeting—Joint Statement*, Para. 11.
[4] *Times*, 2 Aug. 1963.   [5] Ibid., *Guardian* and *Japan Times*, 3 Aug. 1963.

recent North Borneo and Sarawak elections, a procedure which left little doubt that the result, as the elections themselves, would be favourable to Malaysia.[1] But, for the Singapore government, the result was not the issue; committed to a general election at the end of September they feared the consequences of delay on their domestic political position. Presumably with this in mind, Lee Kuan Yew announced on 5 August that since Singapore was not a party to the Manila agreements, so far as he was concerned the merger would go forward as planned on 31 August.[2]

The immediate result of the PAP stand was to reinforce Britain's dislike of the Manila agreements. Both governments apparently now believed that any delay would create uncertainty and provide opposition groups in Singapore and Borneo with an opportunity for agitation. Thus, even when he had finally agreed to a UN inquiry,[3] Duncan Sandys insisted that Britain's agreement was contingent on the immediate dispatch of the secretary-general's representatives and the minimum possible delay in the submission of their report.[4]

(v) *The secretary-general's inquiry in North Borneo and Sarawak*

If, to some Western diplomats, the Manila agreements appeared to constitute a 'South East Asian Munich',[5] they were no more popular amongst the Indonesian communists and their sympathizers who felt that Sukarno had brought home nothing but words. Whether as a result of this criticism, or because Sukarno personally had never reconciled himself to Malaysia, the rapprochement achieved at Manila suffered the same fate as all previous attempts at reconciliation. In assessing responsibility for the ensuing crisis, it is impossible to know precisely where the blame rests. For while Sukarno appeared anxious to resume confrontation, it is also true that the British authorities were adamant against any steps which might be construed as appeasing Indonesian expansionism.

[1] In assessing the wishes of the Borneo peoples the secretary-general was asked to take into consideration:
1. 'The recent elections in Sabbah and Sarawak', nevertheless further examining, verifying, and satisfying himself as to whether
    a Malaysia was a major issue if not the main issue;
    b electoral registers were properly compiled;
    c elections were free and there was no coercion; and
    d voters were properly polled and properly counted.
2. The wishes of those who being qualified to vote would have exercised their right of self-determination in the recent elections had it not been for their detention for political activities, imprisonment for political offences or absence from Sabbah or Sarawak. *Joint Statement*, 5 Aug. 1963, Paragraph 4.
[2] *Straits Times*, 6 Aug. 1963.
[3] Despite the political difficulty of opposing a personal request from the Tunku, British objections were withdrawn only after it had been made clear that the secretary-general would conduct the inquiry in his personal capacity and that he would not be answerable to the General Assembly. *Daily Telegraph*, 12 Aug. 1963.
[4] Ibid.   [5] *Guardian*, 7 Aug. 1963.

And given Indonesian sensitivity, it might have been realized, perhaps, that what was intended by Whitehall as firmness would be viewed in Djakarta as provocation.[1]

In the event, the procedures and timing of the secretary-general's investigation provided Djakarta with an immediate target for renewed pressure. In deference to the British and Malayan desire for speed, U Thant announced on 12 August the names of the secretariat's team and its immediate departure for Borneo.[2] Although an Indonesian foreign office spokesman indicated that the team was acceptable,[3] the tide of anti-Malaysian feeling was now flowing fast, and the government made no visible attempt to check anti-Malaysian demonstrations, sponsored by both left-wing organizations and the army. Soon after the arrival of the UN team in Sarawak, moreover, it became clear that the government had no intention of accepting a report in favour of Malaysia.

The pretext for the approaching Indonesian *volte-face* was provided by a dispute over the number and status of the observers who were to accompany the UN team. In conceding the Malayan request to allow the secretary-general to test opinion, the British had made no secret of their belief that this should not delay the foundation of Malaysia. Their anxiety was understandable: in Sarawak, the SUPP defied a government ban on all demonstrations to mount a strong Chinese protest against the Federation to coincide with the arrival of the UN mission on 16 August; in Borneo, British troops were already in action repelling guerrilla infiltration from across the Indonesian border.[4] It was perhaps not surprising therefore, that Britain and the governments of the two territories regarded with scepticism an Indonesian request for an observer team of 'not less than thirty persons' in response to a British offer which would have allowed Malaya, Indonesia, and the Philippines one observer each on the secretary-general's team.[5] Djakarta's request for a larger number of observers, promptly echoed by Manila, was regarded in London as a crude attempt to influence the work of the mission and turned down on these grounds.[6]

[1] For example, in mid-August it was announced that nine British warships would visit Borneo ports, ostensibly in connection with the Malaysian celebrations, but in fact throughout the period of the secretary-general's inquiry. *Straits Times*, 15 Aug. 1963.

[2] The team was led by an American, Laurence Michelmore. The other members were Georges Janacek (Czechoslovakia), George Howard (Argentina), Neville Kanakakaratne (Ceylon), Kenneth Dadzie (Ghana), Irshad Baqai (Pakistan), Abel Dajamri (Jordan), Jasushi Akashi (Japan), José Machado (Brazil). *Times*, 13 Aug. 1963.

[3] Ibid., 14 Aug. 1963.

[4] Ibid., 17 and 20 Aug. 1963.

[5] This offer was subsequently increased to two after U Thant had explained that in the interests of speed the UN team would be split to allow it to operate in both territories simultaneously.

[6] Responding to the Indonesian request, which was directed to the British government by the Malayan federal authorities, an official British announcement stated that 'if the other two governments concerned were to demand teams of similar size this would create the absurd

Whether the British authorities were wise in their handling of this issue is open to question. By resisting pressure over the observer question, which was not of itself of much intrinsic importance, they undoubtedly made it easier for the two opposing governments to repudiate the secretary-general's report when it eventually announced, as expected, in favour of Malaysia. This was certainly the view held in Washington. Throughout the crisis the Americans urged the need to make tactical concessions to Sukarno in order to put him 'on the spot' should he subsequently attempt to revive confrontation. That this view did not prevail in London was no doubt due partly, as the Americans believed, to Duncan Sandys' intransigence, but it was also due to the situation in North Borneo and Sarawak, where the governments of both territories protested strongly against Sukarno's delaying tactics, as did Lee Kuan Yew in Singapore.[1]

The deadlock over observers was finally resolved after discussions at the UN between U Thant and Britain and the British now offered to issue visas for four observers from each country, each of these to be accompanied by a clerical assistant.[2] That this offer represented the limit to which the British were prepared to go was emphasized by the departure for Malaya of Duncan Sandys. His visit had the immediate, and presumably intended, effect of stiffening Malayan resistance to further concessions. After a preliminary meeting on 23 August at which the Tunku tried to persuade the political leaders of the Borneo territories that it was worth paying the price of a few days' delay to achieve external security, a second meeting between the five Malaysian leaders, at which Duncan Sandys was also present, settled on a new date—in mid-September—for the inauguration of Malaysia.[3] This announcement, which inevitably appeared to prejudge the secretary-general's report[4] effectively rendered redundant the British concession on observers, even though it was eventually accepted by both the Philippine and Indonesian governments.[5]

All hope of a regional solution to the Malaysia problem was now lost. In Indonesian eyes, the new hard line which Malaysian leaders had adopted, with the full support of the British government, confirmed the neo-colonial nature of the Malaysian experiment. From the pronouncement of the new Malaysia date the crisis deepened along tragically

situation in which 90 persons would be engaged in watching the work of nine representatives of the secretary-general. This would obviously be unacceptable.' Quoted in *Straits Times*, 20 Aug. 1963.

[1] *Times, Straits Times*, 24 Aug. 1963.   [2] Ibid.
[3] *NY Times*, 24 Aug.; *Straits Times*, 25 Aug. 1963.
[4] Commenting on the announcement of 16 Sept. as the new Malaysia Day, the *Manila Times* suggested that the Tunku had given in to British pressure to repudiate the Manila agreements. The result would inevitably be, the paper suggested, confrontation not only between Indonesia and Malaya but between the Philindo group of the now dormant Maphilindo and the British. Cited in *Straits Times*, 6 Sept. 1963.
[5] *Daily Telegraph*, 28 Aug.; *Times*, 29 Aug. 1963.

predictable lines. The next day, on 28 August, the official Indonesian news agency announced that the government observed the right to determine its attitude to the secretary-general's report on the grounds that 'British technical difficulties' had prevented Indonesia from sending observers. On 3 September Djakarta filed a strong protest against the announcement of 16 September as Malaysia Day which it described as a 'reckless and premature decision . . . a unilateral act contravening the letter and spirit of the Manila agreements'.[1] Finally on 5 September, only four days after Indonesian and Philippine observers had taken up their posts, Sukarno himself publicly denounced not only the inquiry but the United Nations which he described as obsolete 'because it does not reflect the spirit of the new emerging forces of which Indonesia is the pioneer'.[2]

The secretary-general's report was not finally published until 14 September.[3] Well before this date, however, it was known that the UN survey team had found in favour of Malaysia.[4] In his statement U Thant castigated Britain both for her failure to grant more promptly the necessary facilities for the observers, and for concurring with the premature announcement of the new inaugural date for the Federation, a decision which, he suggested, 'led to misunderstanding and confusion and even resentment amongst other parties to the Manila Agreements which could have been avoided if the date could have been fixed after my conclusions had been reached and made known'. Nevertheless he found there to be 'no doubt about the wishes of a sizeable majority of these peoples to join in the Federation of Malaysia', and he ruled, accordingly, in favour of the new federation.

(vi) Conclusion

Thus ended the Malayan attempt to placate Indonesian and Philippine opposition. The mutual antagonisms engendered during the previous two and a half years were to dominate the first three months of Malaysia's existence as an independent state. For Indonesia, the formal inauguration of the new state on 16 September finally removed the possibility of exacting further concessions from either the Federal government or Britain, and while her position was complicated by her membership in SEATO, there was no reason to expect that the Philippines would accept the *fait accompli* without protest. Both states withheld recognition and recalled their ambassadors for consultation.[5] By adopting this approach, they may have hoped—they referred to the possibility of recognition at a later date—

[1] *Straits Times*, 6 Sept. 1963.   [2] Ibid.
[3] For the text of the secretary-general's letter, which was sent to the foreign ministers of Malaya, the Philippines, and Indonesia see *Documents, 1963*, pp. 360–4.
[4] The Philippine and Indonesian representatives at the UN objected formally to U Thant before the publication of his report. *Times*, 14 Sept. 1963.
[5] *Straits Times*, 16 Sept. 1963.

to reopen the Borneo question in the General Assembly of the United Nations. But after an emergency meeting of the cabinet on 17 September, the new Malaysian government took the initiative and severed relations with both countries.

These symbolic actions were the signal for the onset of a full-scale 'confrontation' between Indonesia and Malaysia which was to occupy them for the next three years. By contrast, the conflict between Malaysia and the Philippines, while it continued to aggravate the situation, faded into relative insignificance.

The process of escalation was marked by a series of civil disorders. In Kuala Lumpur a crowd of a thousand demonstrators attacked the Indonesian Embassy, tore down the Indonesian emblem and trampled it in the dust.[1] Reactions in Djakarta were more savage but of the same kind. Mobs of Indonesian youths attacked first the Malaysian embassy and then the British, breaking down doors and windows and overturning and setting alight the British ambassador's car.[2] An official British protest produced a statement of mild regret from the Indonesian government but while deploring the violence and promising action against those responsible, they added their appreciation of 'the militant attitude of various groups of our society, and the fact that our people have shown indignation about the formation of Malaysia, which is not in accordance with the Manila summit conference'.[3]

Worse was to follow. On 17 September left-wing trade unionists took over the industrial installations of Shell Oil, British-American Tobacco, and Unilever, together with other smaller British firms.[4] During a Djakarta riot the next day the British embassy was ransacked and burnt to the ground.[5] The Indonesian leadership was now faced with a breakdown of law and order and a threat to its own authority. Sukarno appeared to have become a prisoner as much of his rhetorical ability to arouse a crowd to a high pitch of enthusiasm or anger as of the extremists in the PKI and the army. Yet it was too late to back down from the policy which was directly responsible for the crisis. The only alternative, which the government adopted, was to channel public animosity directly on to Malaysia while taking a tough line on the maintenance of law and order. On 18 September martial law was declared in Djakarta and two days later the government announced that they had taken over all British concerns in Indonesia, ostensibly to insure the continuance of production

[1] *Straits Times*, 17 Sept. 1963.
[2] *Times*, 17 Sept. 1963. This demonstration was the occasion of a celebrated, and somewhat provocative, gesture of defiance by the British assistant military attaché, Major Roderick Walker, who, defying insults and stones, marched up and down outside the Embassy playing the bagpipes.
[3] Ibid., 18 Sept. 1963.   [4] *Guardian*, 18 Sept. 1963.
[5] *Daily Telegraph*, 19 Sept. 1963.

but no doubt also to obtain diplomatic leverage in bargaining with Britain over Malaysia.[1]

The stance adopted by Djakarta over the next two weeks was along these lines. The government took immediate steps to strengthen the military position on the Borneo and Sarawak borders, and the defence minister announced that Indonesia not only would not prevent volunteers joining local guerrillas in the Borneo territories but would 'help and train the youth of North Borneo'.[2] The government's firm reaction to mob violence suggested that they were being pushed faster than they wanted. Not only did British protests produce an assurance that Indonesia would guarantee the safety of British subjects and British property, and that further violence would not be condoned,[3] but the new government-sponsored National Front 'Crush Malaysia Action Command' made clear that its main task was to combat destructive rioting and mob violence.[4]

Although the Indonesians were aware of the need for restraint, the situation rapidly forced them to a point of no return. On 22 September Sukarno announced that he was breaking off economic and trade relations with Malaysia, an action which, while harmful to both sides, was likely to cause more damage to the Indonesian than to the Malaysian economy since a substantial proportion of Indonesia's foreign exchange was earned through trade with the free port of Singapore.[5] Moreover, despite their guarantees, the Indonesians made no attempt to conceal their basic hostility to the British. British personnel, most of whom were evacuated to avoid further harassment, were buzzed by Indonesian aircraft as they were waiting to embark for Singapore; the British ambassador was unable to obtain an interview with any major government figure for over a week after the riots, and the government refused to respond to repeated British requests for clarification about the future status of British investments.[6] On 25 September Sukarno addressed an anti-Malaysian rally in Djakarta and reiterated his determination to 'crush Malaysia' unless the UN mission to Borneo was reconvened to reassess the wishes of the North Kalimantan people in line with the 'procedures agreed upon in Manila'.[7]

---

[1] Although the Indonesians insisted that their intention was not the nationalization of British assets (valued at about £150 million), they refused to clarify on what conditions they would be returned, or whether compensation would be paid if they were not. *Times*, 21 Sept. 1963. Eventually on 26 Nov. 1964 President Sukarno announced that all British enterprises in Indonesia were to be put under full Indonesian control and management.

[2] In the week following the inauguration of Malaysia, the Indonesians dispatched a unit of 'combat-ready' parachute troops to reinforce the 12th military command on the Borneo border and a detachment from their marine corps to reinforce those in Sarawak. *Times*, 26 Sept.; *NY Times*, 30 Sept. 1963.

[3] *NY Times*, 20 Sept. 1963.   [4] Ibid., 23 Sept. 1963.

[5] *Observer*, 22 Sept.; *Times*, 24 Sept. 1963. Amongst the measures announced to put the trade ban into effect, the two most important were the ban on oil and natural gas shipments to Malaysia and the decision to redirect tin concentrates for smelting from Malaya to Europe.

[6] *Guardian*, 25 Sept. 1963.   [7] 'Crush Malaysia' cited in Modelski, p. 85.

There was, of course, no prospect that such action would be taken. The immediate result of the Djakarta riots had been to convince the British and Malaysian governments of the possibility of major Indonesian aggression. On 18 September the Tunku announced that the Federation had been put in a 'state of preparedness'. Army reservists were called up and the territorial army expanded; simultaneously the British government confirmed its commitment to help with the defence of Malaysian independence and territorial integrity.[1] The Tunku still preferred to play down the military aspect of confrontation; he was reported, for example, to have opposed a cabinet proposal for general mobilization. But with the turn of events he was widely criticized for appeasing Sukarno at Manila. Whatever his views, there was now no question of a Malaysian initiative to reopen diplomatic relations with Indonesia or the Philippines.[2]

The position of the Philippine government in the new situation was difficult. Their attitude towards Malaysia was dictated not so much by the failure of the UN mission to endorse the Philippine claim to North Borneo, as by the fact that, by serving as a pretext for Indonesian confrontation, the mission had put paid to any hope of establishing the 'Maphilindo' confederation. Had such a confederation of Malay states existed, along the lines envisaged by President Macapagal, then the Borneo claim would probably have lost its significance in Filipino politics, but without it Manila was deprived of any practical hope of acquiring North Borneo. More important, there was no opportunity for an active role in regional politics, and thus to acquire the Asian identity which the government sought. It was then more from a sense of frustration than conviction, that the Philippines maintained their common front with Indonesia after the creation of Malaysia.

During the opening session of the 18th UN General Assembly both Indonesia and the Philippines publicly expressed their reservations about the findings of the secretary-general's Borneo mission. But when it became clear that the majority of states, including the majority of Afro-Asian states, approved of Malaysia, the Philippine government had to decide whether to accept the *fait accompli* or to join Indonesia in a general indictment of the UN. In the light of this new situation, the Indonesian and Philippine positions once more began to diverge. While Indonesian-Malaysian relations continued to deteriorate, the defence build-up of each side leading inevitably at the end of September to an outbreak of border

[1] *Guardian*, 19 Sept. 1963.
[2] Commenting on the prospects for another meeting with Macapagal and Sukarno, the Tunku said at a press conference on 18 Sept.: 'What is the use? I went to Tokyo and spoke with them, and the result was confrontation. I went to Manila and spoke with them and the result was a withdrawal of ambassadors. What is the use? It is a waste of time and money when we know they will not abide by the decisions taken by conferences.' Ibid.

clashes on the Sarawak and Borneo borders,[1] the Philippines seemed anxious to find some formula which would allow them, without losing face, to restore relations with Kuala Lumpur.

However, Manila's Malaysian policy was so closely entwined with that of Indonesia it proved impossible during 1963 to find a way of repairing Malaysian-Philippine relations outside a general reconciliation, which looked increasingly unlikely.[2] None the less various approaches were tried. The most promising seemed to be mediation by Thailand, with which both Malaya and the Philippines had been linked in the Association of South East Asia (ASA). But while the good offices of the Thai foreign minister, Tun Thanat Khoman, were apparently successful in narrowing the ground between the two governments,[3] nothing concrete had been achieved by the end of the year. A further attempt, also on a Thai initiative, to use the occasion of the Colombo Plan conference in Bangkok to stage a foreign ministers meeting also proved abortive. The Malaysian government refused to attend unless Indonesia and the Philippines took the initiative in renewing diplomatic relations and Indonesia withdrew its troops from the Indonesian-Sarawak border.[4] Nevertheless, this meeting took place, without Malaysia, during the third week of November. The official communique announced that the three countries had agreed 'to exert all possible efforts not to exacerbate further the tense situation already existing in the area', which they rightly regarded as a necessary preliminary to formal negotiations.[5] But the meeting had no visible impact on the situation. Indeed, all the evidence now suggested that the pace of confrontation was to be hotted up: there were reports of a continuing military build-up by the regular Indonesian army (TNI) at Batu Tiba, a garrison on the border with North Borneo, while in the south repeated hit-and-run raids led some observers to believe that the Indonesians were softening up the area prior to a concerted attempt to cut Sarawak in two at its narrowest point.[6] Meanwhile, Dr Subandrio chose the occasion of his return from Bangkok to launch a savage attack on Malaysia which he claimed was totally dependent on Britain.

For their part, the Malaysians not only appeared uninterested in any diplomatic initiatives but were clearly preparing for a protracted campaign. Their military build-up continued. By the end of the year there

---

[1] *NYHT, Sunday Times*, 30 Sept. 1963. This state of affairs persisted for the rest of the year, although it was kept under control by the presence of British and Gurkha troops.

[2] Speaking at a political rally on 4 Oct. 1963 the Tunku stated that 'if the Philippines offers to renew diplomatic relations with Malaysia, we are ready to accept'. But he added that Malaysia would never sign an agreement with Indonesia so long as Communists retained their influence in the government because 'nothing can be achieved and we can never be secure with them'. *NYHT* 6 Oct. 1963.

[3] *Straits Times*, 17 Nov. 1963.   [4] *Times*, 24 Oct. 1963.

[5] *Straits Times*, 18 Nov.; *NY Times*, 19 Nov. 1963.

[6] See the dispatch by Clare Hollingworth, *Guardian*, 18 Nov. 1963.

were 2,400 regular Malayan troops in the Borneo territories. In addition the British had committed 7,000 troops, mostly Gurkhas, to the area in compliance with their commitment under the defence treaty.[1] The Malaysian government announced on 17 November a registration scheme for all adult males as a preliminary to the possible introduction of conscription[2] and, to counter the economic threat posed by confrontation, a programme of economic support for Singapore, the territory which would suffer most from the Indonesian boycott.[3]

By the end of the year, however, it was clear that neither side was prepared for an open conflict. Any settlement would consequently have to come about as a result of changes in the internal situation of either Indonesia or Malaysia. The strategy of patient but determined resistance, which the Malaysian measures envisaged, was eventually to bring its reward when confrontation was formally ended on 11 August 1966 after a prolonged crisis in Indonesia which led to the political demise of the PKI and the overthrow of Sukarno by the army. Indonesian policy, on the other hand, led to the country's isolation at a time when, contrary to official protestations, diplomatic and economic support from outside was more necessary than ever. For although the effects of severing trade relations with Malaya and Singapore were partly offset by trade agreements with the Soviet Union and China,[4] and although in the short-run the Indonesian economy showed its usual resilience, relations with the Soviet Union were already strained as a result of Indonesia's failure to pay for past shipments of armaments, while anti-Chinese sentiment in Indonesia (which Sukarno had not hesitated to exploit in opposition to Malaysia) set limits to any alignment with Peking. In the end, cutting off major Western resources of economic and financial support strained Sukarno's credibility as a political leader.

By basing his policy on the image of Malaysia as a neo-colonialist outpost whose major purpose was to allow Britain (as the local representative of the Old Established Forces) to 'encircle' Indonesia, Sukarno effectively transformed these fears into a self-fulfilling prophecy. The major result of 'confrontation' was to reverse the trend, of which ASA and

[1] In addition the British ground troops were backed up by naval and air support providing both coastal and inland air patrols and reconnaissance. See *Economist*, 14 Dec. 1963, p. 1153.

[2] *Sunday Times*, 1 Dec. 1963.

[3] It was, for example, estimated that as a result of confrontation Singapore would lose about 9 per cent of its existing revenue. In this situation there was an obvious danger of a deterioration in the island's internal security position since any economic hardship would inevitably be used by the Barisan Socialis to lure the island's workers from their allegiance to the PAP. Ibid.

[4] In November, for instance, for reasons which may or may not have related to Malaysia, the Soviet Union suspended its normal iron ore purchases from Malaya and signed an agreement providing for increased Indonesian supplies during 1964. Earlier at the end of October an Indonesian trade mission had visited China with the stated purpose of replacing 'lost trade'. *Financial Times*, 29 Oct.; 27 Nov. 1963.

Maphilindo were examples, towards an Asian diplomatic community, from which the influence of outside powers might be gradually excluded. After the September riots the British terminated such aid as they provided to Indonesia.[1] Under the terms of the bilateral defence treaty, moreover, the British were committed to active intervention in combating Indonesian guerrilla activity in Borneo. And while they were no doubt alarmed at having taken on such an open-ended commitment at a time when the British presence east of Suez was emerging as an important issue in British politics, it was clear that they had no intention of reneging on it.[2]

Confrontation forced the United States administration to close ranks with the British. The Kennedy regime was still committed to the analysis of the Indonesian situation on which American support for the stabilization programme had been based.[3] Indeed they regarded the disastrous events between 15 and 21 September as being primarily the result of Britain's handling of the Malaysian crisis. Not without justification they felt that the British had presented Sukarno with an opportunity for political gain which he was unlikely to let pass, and their immediate intention was to offer a 'political opportunity in the opposite direction' through the medium of a projected Presidential visit to the Far East.[4] This possibility was frustrated by President Kennedy's assassination.

American policy towards Indonesia and Malaysia was coloured by Washington's overriding preoccupation with the Chinese threat to Asia; it was designed to provide the maximum encouragement to the 'nationalist' as distinct from 'Communist' elements in the Indonesian élite. The success of the policy depended on the one hand on Congress leaving the administration with maximum flexibility to deal with specific situations as they arose, and on the other on an enlarged foreign aid programme. However, in Indonesia, as elsewhere, Kennedy's attempt to win support for a programme which would allow him to underwrite the 'new nationalism' backfired; the Clay Committee, whose report was published in March, delivered what amounted to a public rebuke to Indonesia for its economic and political adventurism.[5] In July, Congressman Broomfield

[1] They also later persuaded two British companies with contracts for the construction of an Indonesian air control system to suspend operations. These companies, Dakar Radar and Fairing Aviation, both of which were fully indemnified by the British government, had been under contract with the Indonesian government since 1959; *Times*, 18 Dec. 1963.

[2] *Economist*, 24 Dec. 1963, p. 1155.

[3] Above, pp. 146–9.   [4] Hilsman, p. 405.

[5] On Indonesia, the Committee reported: 'Because of its population, resources, and geographic position it is of special concern to the free world. However, we do not see how external assistance can be granted to this nation by free world countries unless it puts its internal house in order, provides fair treatment to foreign creditors and enterprises, and refrains from international adventures. If it follows this path, as we hope it will, it deserves the support of free world aid sources.' 'The Scope and Distribution of United States Military and Economic Assistance Programmes', *Report to the President of the United States from the Committee to Strengthen the Security of the Free World* (Department of State, Washington DC, 20 Mar. 1963).

succeeded in carrying an amendment to the Aid Bill under which military aid was to be suspended altogether and economic aid was to require special Presidential authority. When the stabilization programme was halted following the severing of economic relations with Malaysia, the US suspended all new military and economic aid to Indonesia. But despite British and Malaysian pressure, the US refused to suspend aid 'in the pipeline'.

Partly as a result of the settlement of the West Irian affair, and partly of the deterioration of British trade with Indonesia, there was a revival of Indonesian-Dutch trade in 1963. But the reversal of US policy on aid was adopted by others in the West. One result of the IMF and US backing of the stabilization programme had been to set in train discussions amongst other major aid donors within the Development Assistance Committee of the OECD. Once the Americans withdrew their support, however, these allied efforts inevitably collapsed also. By the end of the year even France, which on most issues involving the Third World was reluctant to follow an Anglo-Saxon lead, had responded to a Malaysian request and imposed an embargo on all arms sales to Indonesia. The effect of the West's military embargo was probably of more symbolic than real importance but the economic consequences of 'confrontation', were more serious. In what is surely one of the most revealing statements of the relationship of domestic priorities to foreign policy, Dr Subandrio told a group of visiting Philippine veterans,

President Sukarno is now trying to revive the iron spirit of the people to give them confidence. We need technical knowledge but first the man must be revived. . . . We are neglecting our wealth purposely because we are concentrating on nation-building. Because of the natural wealth of Indonesia, we can afford not to give priority to economic problems.[1]

The subsequent history of Indonesia was to demonstrate the weakness of such arguments. But at the end of 1963, the PKI, the army, and the Indonesian public had all enthusiastically embraced 'confrontation', irrespective of its consequences and in the short-run at least, the impact of this policy on the Malaysian Federation was the creation of a sense of solidarity.

[1] *Straits Times*, 5 Dec. 1963.

CHAPTER VI

VIETNAM

(a) *The course of the war*

IN South Vietnam the year 1963 began with a battle: at Ap-Bac, a hamlet on the edge of the Plain of Reeds in Dinh-Tuong province, 1,200 government troops supported by helicopters suffered serious casualties, including the loss of eight helicopters and three American dead, when they were attacked by Communist guerrillas on 2 and 3 January. The battle was to become famous amongst supporters of the National Front for the Liberation of South Vietnam, thanks to the 'emulation campaigns' named after it in March and November. But it had more than merely a propaganda significance, for it followed the creation by the Communists of special teams to deal with the helicopters introduced into the war by the Americans the previous year, and was the first proof that helicopters are not invincible in guerrilla warfare.[1] This encouragement was of the greatest importance to the Communists in a year when it was necessary for them to increase the scale of their operations if they were not to be defeated by the new policies adopted by the Saigon government, with American support, during 1962.

The story of the war in 1963 was indeed that of a gradual increase in the scale of Communist activity, with little significant change of tactics on the part of the government and their American advisers. Reporting on developments during the first seven months of the year, David Halberstam of the *NY Times* drew attention to a number of indications of the new Communist effort.[2] First, there was a marked increase in their supplies of weapons, which appeared to have been brought in from outside and not merely captured from their opponents. Secondly the number of guerrilla battalions was increased from nineteen to twenty-one, whilst the average size of battalion rose from 150–200 men to around 400. And thirdly, the Communist forces showed a greater willingness to stand and fight than had been the case in the previous year, when their tendency to flee from any large force had brought false optimism to many American officers. These new developments were reflected in a number of engagements during the first half of the year. Some of the heaviest fighting was in the Ca-Mau peninsula, where government forces suffered serious losses on 5 February, 29 March, and 24 April: it was an area in which the

[1] *NY Times*, 3, 4 Jan. 1963. Le Hong Linh, *Ap-Bac, major victories of the South Vietnamese patriotic forces 1963–4* (Hanoi, 1965).
[2] *NY Times*, 15 Aug. 1963.

Communists had maintained a strong position since 1945. There was also further fighting in Dinh-Tuong province, notably in June, and engagements were reported in Vinh-Binh, Vinh-Long, and Kien-Phong provinces.[1] All these provinces were in the Mekong Delta region, and it was clearly an object of Communist strategy to bring that region more firmly into the struggle during 1963. There was also serious fighting in Quang-Ngai province in March and April, and on one occasion Communist troops actually entered Quang-Ngai town.[2] Another serious attack occurred in April in the vicinity of Kontum, in the Central Highlands.[3] In July and August there were some government and American successes: for example on the 20 July the unit which had suffered so badly at Ap-Bac avenged itself by killing 58 guerrillas at Quan-Long (Dinh-Tuong province); and in the Ca-Mau area American forces sprang a trap to kill 90 guerrillas early in August.[4] There were also a number of occasions when T-28 air strikes saved the situation for government forces on the ground. Nevertheless the Communists continued to make progress in overrunning outposts and hamlets, one of their more spectacular successes in the summer being the government decision to abandon a base at Rang-Rang, in War Zone D north of Saigon, which had once been a showplace for foreign visitors.[5]

The strategy of the Saigon government and its American advisers during this period was focused upon two programmes: that of the 'strategic hamlets', which owed its inspiration, though not much of its detailed execution, to British methods in the Malayan Emergency; and that of the 'special forces', in which American forces sought to win over potentially pro-Communist Vietnamese and give them military training in 'special' camps. The strategic hamlet programme had been launched in April 1962; it involved, in many cases, the resettlement of peasants from dispersed farms in more compact villages which could be defended against Communist infiltration; in some cases, however, it may have involved less of a physical change and merely a change of name. Official statistics of October 1963 showed that there were 9,000 strategic hamlets, out of a total of 11,864 hamlets in South Vietnam, and that about 70 per cent of the population were living in settlements called strategic hamlets. However, an investigation following the overthrow of Ngo Dinh Diem in November was said to have revealed that only 10 per cent of the strategic hamlets were properly defendable.[6] Inevitably the strategic hamlets became a target for Communist attack, and a number of incidents—notably those in Quang-Ngai province in March and April—were directed

---

[1] *Times*, 7 Feb., 15 June; *NYHT*, 30 Mar., 25 Apr., 25 May; *Guardian*, 1 July 1963.
[2] *NYHT*, 18 Apr. 1963.   [3] *Times*, 29 Apr. 1963.
[4] *NY Times*, 22 July, 7 Aug. 1963.   [5] Ibid., 27 July 1963.
[6] Nghiem Dang, *Viet-Nam, politics and public administration* (Honolulu, 1966), p. 159.

against them. On 19 August the showplace hamlet of Ben-Tuong (in Binh-Duong province, 30 miles north of Saigon) was razed to the ground.[1] David Halberstam's report observed that the government had hoped to use the resettlement method to establish a completely secure area in Vinh-Long province by mid-August; instead, by that time, the Communists had over 30 combat hamlets of their own in the area. The special forces camps were also Communist targets, but it was not until November that they had enough military capacity for a frontal attack on one of them to succeed. Another aspect of the government's policy was the 'open arms' programme, which was inaugurated by President Diem on 16 April: he offered a virtual amnesty to pro-Communist forces who surrendered, with the exception of 'hard-core' cadres. In his address to the National Assembly on 7 October, the President claimed that over 10,000 people had surrendered during the first six months of the programme, a figure which it was impossible to verify, but could well have been accurate.[2]

One major question about the war concerned the nature and extent of North Vietnamese involvement. The official United States view on this question was expressed in a White Paper issued in February 1965: namely that the principal cause of the war was 'aggression from the north'.[3] The aggression was not, however, by any means overt, and throughout 1963 the Hanoi government continued to deny its involvement. An important contribution to debate on this question was later made by Douglas Pike in a book about the National Liberation Front, in which he shows that during this year the relationship between the Front and Hanoi changed a great deal. Whilst not denying an original connection between the Front and the Democratic Republic of Vietnam, nor that there had been some infiltration from the North in earlier years, Pike found evidence amongst captured documents that 'in early 1963 well-known old-line Communist cadres of the Viet-Minh days, who had gone North, appeared for the first time at the provincial level, and in August and September at the village level'.[4] He was of the opinion that the increasing military development of the Front's forces was accompanied by increasing political control by the Vietnam Workers Party in Hanoi. In itself a southern organization, the Front probably came under firmer control from the North after the creation of the 'Central Office for South Vietnam' sometime in 1962.

[1] *NY Times*, 21 Aug. 1963.   [2] *Times*, 17 Apr., 8 Oct. 1963.
[3] *Aggression from the north, the record of North Vietnam's campaign to conquer South Vietnam*, US Department of State (Washington DC, 27 Feb. 1965). The report gave the total of 'confirmed infiltrators' from North to South Vietnam in 1963 as 4,200 compared with 5,400 in 1962 and at least 4,400 in 1964. The report gives biographical details of some of those who infiltrated in 1963, mostly natives of south central Vietnam. It also deals with the use by the infiltrators of weapons made in China.
[4] Douglas Pike, *Viet Cong, the organisation and techniques of the National Front of South Vietnam* (Cambridge, Mass., 1966), p. 117.

Douglas Pike also commented on the changing character of the war, and noted very significant developments in September and October. Early in September two generals of the Democratic Republic of Vietnam held a 'military conference', probably just over the Cambodian border opposite the Darlac plateau; its apparent purpose was to reorganize the Front's military units. This was followed in October by a 'series of two-week special training courses throughout the liberated area at which guerrilla units received re-training in conventional small-military-unit tactics, anti-aircraft defenses and techniques of sabotage'.[1] The effect of these developments was soon felt in the field: the number of 'incidents' initiated by the Communists increased from 500 in September to 1,200 in October, and to nearly 3,000 in November.[2] An important step from the Communist point of view was the battle of Hiep-Hoa, one of several initiated to commemorate the anniversary of the insurrection of 23 November 1940, in which an American special forces camp twenty miles west of Saigon had been overrun.[3] There was a particularly sharp increase of activity in the weeks following the *coup d'état* which removed Ngo Dinh Diem from power, and which caused considerable disruption in the provinces owing to changes in personnel, judged to be politically necessary but inevitably harmful militarily. In view of the way that Communist strategy and tactics had been developing throughout the year, however, it would probably be incorrect to ascribe the increase in activity in November entirely to the political crisis of the summer and autumn in Saigon.

(b) *The Buddhist crisis*

The National Front for the Liberation of South Vietnam was not the only source of opposition to the government of President Ngo Dinh Diem during 1963. From May until his overthrow by the *coup d'état* of 1 November, he was challenged by a revolt of Buddhist monks and laymen which became a focus for non-Communist opposition to his regime. The Buddhist revolt began with an incident at Hué on 8 May, the anniversary of the Buddha's birth and enlightenment (calculated according to the lunar calendar).[4] It was customary to hold special ceremonies and processions on that day, and to bedeck Buddhist temples with flags and bunting. Although the public use of any flag other than the National Flag was prohibited under a regulation of 1950, the regulation had often been broken, even in Hué, on the occasion of the celebrations to mark the

---

[1] Ibid., p. 162.   [2] *Sunday Times*, 23 Feb. 1964; and Pike, p. 164.
[3] Le Hong Linh, pp. 35–43; *Times*, 25 Nov. 1963.
[4] No contemporary press report of the incident can be relied on, owing to the Saigon government's reluctance to allow journalists to inquire closely into it; but see the subsequent eyewitness account of Erich Wulff, *Observer*, 18 Aug. 1963; also D. J. Duncanson, *Government and revolution in Vietnam* (Oxford, 1968), p. 329.

jubilee of Archbishop Ngo Dinh Thuc in April 1963. However, on 6 May, the government circulated an order that in future this regulation should be enforced. By that time, the flags were already up at Hué and the Buddhists naturally protested against the order to take them down. The disagreement might well have caused a serious incident itself, but it appears to have been settled to the partial satisfaction of the Buddhists before the day of celebrations dawned; on the other hand, it contributed to the mood of unrest which pervaded Hué on 8 May. The actual incident arose from another cause. The senior monk of the Tu-Dam temple in Hué, Thich Tri-Quang, was due to broadcast a sermon in the evening, but refused to hand in a text for censorship until he was due to go on the air; as a result the director of the radio station cancelled the broadcast. A crowd gathered outside the radio station, whereupon the provincial authorities brought in troops to disperse it. In the mêlée which followed at least eight people died, including some children. The Buddhists alleged that they were killed when the troops opened fire and the crowd stampeded; the official version of the incident (put out by the government in Saigon) was that a Communist agent had thrown a grenade into the crowd. The United States Consulate in Hué informed the Embassy in Saigon that it believed the Buddhist version to be substantially correct.

Out of this incident there developed a formal Buddhist protest and the submission of five 'aspirations' to the government: (i) the ban on religious flags should be lifted; (ii) there should be the same legal status for Buddhists as for Catholics, the existing law being that Catholicism was a religion and Buddhism merely an association; (iii) there should be freedom for Buddhists to preach their religion; (iv) compensation should be given to the victims of the riot on 8 May, there being sixty injured as well as the dead; and (v) the officials responsible for the deaths and injuries on that day should be punished.[1] The demands were supported by the first of what was to become a long series of hunger strikes by monks and nuns in their temples at Hué, and later in the month by a series of meetings in Hué of Buddhists from various parts of the country. On the 30 May a much wider protest began in support of the Buddhist demands. At Hué a thousand monks and nuns began a protest fast, and in Saigon itself there was a demonstration of several hundred monks in front of the National Assembly. The following day, President Diem received a delegation of Buddhists and promised in vague terms to consider the five 'aspirations'. A few days later, he replaced the mayor and the government delegate at Hué, but this did not prevent a further demonstration by Buddhist students, some of whom were injured when they were dispersed by troops using tear-gas.[2] The crisis had barely begun.

---

[1] John Mecklin, *Mission in torment* (New York, 1965), pp. 154–5.
[2] *Observer*, 18 Aug. 1963; *Times*, 4 June 1963.

The most spectacular event of the crisis occurred on 11 June, when Saigon and the world were shocked by the news that an elderly monk, Thich Quang-Duc, had burnt himself alive in one of the main streets of the Vietnamese capital.[1] His remains were taken to lie in state at the principal Buddhist temple in Saigon, the Xa-Loi, and became an object of devotion and pilgrimage. The event made such a great impact that the government felt it had no choice but to take the Buddhist demands more seriously, and a conference was arranged. From 14 to 16 June there was a series of meetings between three ministers (led by Vice-President Nguyen Ngoc Tho) and three monks (led by Thich Thien-Minh) which issued a formal agreement, signed by the President himself and by the senior Buddhist monk, Thich Tinh-Kiet.[2] It laid down specific conditions for the flying of the Buddhist flag (usually with the national flag as well), and also put forward new arrangements for religious associations, which would have to be submitted to the National Assembly; it appointed a committee to investigate complaints of arrest; it promised freedom to propagate the Buddhist religion; and it promised the punishment of officials responsible for the incident at Hué, if any were found guilty on investigation. The day the agreement was signed nevertheless saw further demonstrations in Saigon, resulting in scores of arrests and the report of at least one death.[3] Meanwhile, there were indications that the willingness of President Diem to make concessions to the monks was not shared by his brother, Counsellor Ngo Dinh Nhu, nor by the influential Madame Nhu, who on 8 June alleged in a speech that the Buddhist movement had been infiltrated by Communists. She and her husband continued to take that line throughout the summer and autumn.

The crisis which began in this dramatic way was to prove important not only in terms of Vietnamese internal politics, but even more because of its impact upon public opinion in the United States and throughout the world. The Buddhist leaders were well aware of the need to impress foreigners, especially Americans, and took great pains to establish good relations with foreign press representatives in Saigon. Finding that Buddhist monks were accusing a Catholic president of religious persecution, Western commentators inevitably began counting heads, and reached the conclusion that whilst only about 10 per cent of the population of South Vietnam was Christian, at least 70 per cent was Buddhist. These figures, however, were very easily misunderstood. In a Christian context it is readily assumed that a profession of faith implies membership of a Church. In Vietnam, this was indeed true of those who said they

[1] The scene was witnessed and photographed by a single Western newsman; see M. W. Browne, *The new face of war* (London, 1965), pp. 175–81.
[2] The text of the agreement is printed in *American foreign policy: current documents, 1963*, pp. 856–9.
[3] *NYHT*, 17 June 1963.

were Catholics; but it was not the case that all those who described themselves as Buddhists were similarly held together by a single religious community or Church. Traditional Vietnamese religion had three elements: Confucianism, which was the ethic of the scholarly élite rather than a popular religious faith; ancestor worship, practised well-nigh universally, within each individual family or clan; and a variety of beliefs (including various forms of Buddhism and Taoism) whose adepts belonged to their own different sects rather than to a single nationwide Church. The sectarian character of Vietnamese religion continued into the twentieth century, and no single sect embraced all the various movements which arose during the Vietnamese religious revival that began in the 1920s.[1] In the Mekong Delta area, and to the north of Saigon, two of the most important sects were the Cao-Dai and the Hao-Hao sects, neither of which played any important part in the Buddhist movement of 1963; the latter movement was indeed largely confined to Saigon and the provinces of central Vietnam.

The Buddhists themselves were not united into a single sect: although they attempted to form a 'Unified Buddhist Church' towards the end of the year, during the summer of 1963 their activities were directed by an 'Inter-Sect Committee' with its headquarters at the Xa-Loi pagoda. Nor did the various sects share all the same beliefs. There was a considerable difference between the 'militants', who came mostly from central Vietnam and whose beliefs centred on the *Lotus Sutra* (almost the only Buddhist text, incidentally, which sanctions self-immolation), and the more 'moderate' Amidists whose principal temple was the Xa-Loi and who were mostly natives of the more southerly provinces. The leader of the former group was Thich Tri-Quang; the most prominent figure among the latter was Mai Tho Truyen. Additional mention may be made of the group of Tongkingese Buddhists who were refugees in Saigon, led by Thich Tam-Chau. These were the three most important groups, but they were by no means the only sects calling themselves Buddhist at this time. Moreover, it was only the monks and a minority of active laymen who had any formal attachment to a particular sect; most of the ordinary Vietnamese who called themselves Buddhist were so only in the more vague sense of venerating the Buddha image wherever they found it, and perhaps endeavouring to keep the Buddhist precepts (including fast-days) in their own homes. The achievement of the 'militant' or 'Lotus' Buddhists in 1963 was that they succeeded in uniting the followers of Mai Tho Truyen and those of Thich Tam-Chau into a single alliance, led by themselves, which was ready to oppose as vigorously as possible the regime of President Diem; an alliance which broke up soon after the

[1] On the character of Vietnamese religion and its sects, see Ralph Smith, *Viet-Nam and the West* (London, 1968), pp. 70–83.

regime had been overthrown. But few, if any, Western observers ap-
preciated the complexity of sectarian differences which lay behind that
alliance: they saw only 'the Buddhists'.

The United States Embassy was bound to view with some concern the
increasing evidence of Buddhist opposition to the President and his family
during the first half of June. American officials had already come to the
conclusion that the Buddhists were right and the government wrong in
their reporting of the incident at Hué. In the temporary absence of the
ambassador, the American chargé d'affaires paid a number of visits to the
Palace in the hope of persuading the President to reach a compromise
with the Buddhists so as to reduce the tension and avoid further trouble.[1]
The agreement reached on 16 June did perhaps reduce the tension for a
few weeks, but it was very far from a solution to the problem. Moreover,
as time went on, attempts by the government to hinder American press-
men from reporting further Buddhist incidents led to their complete
alienation and encouraged them to write very favourably about the
Buddhists and their aspirations.[2]

In July the government risked disapproval from other quarters by its
decision to bring to trial a number of people who had long before been
charged with complicity in the attempted coup of November 1960,
together with others who had signed the famous 'Caravelle Manifesto'
of April 1960, demanding that the government make liberal reforms. On
7 July thirteen army officers were sentenced to terms of imprisonment, and
from 9 to 12 July there was a trial of thirty-four civilians, including Dr
Phan Quang Dan, Phan Huy Quat, Tran Van Huong, Tran Van Do, and
Nguyen Luu Vien.[3] Many of these were sentenced to imprisonment. In
the meantime, on 8 July the famous novelist and politician Nguyen
Tuong Tam (whose literary name was Nhat Linh) committed suicide
before he could be brought to trial. Amongst the liberal 'bourgeoisie'
of Saigon this event probably had just as significant an impact as the
self-immolation of Quang-Duc.[4] The trial and the death of Nhat Linh
were probably an important reason why, when the second phase of the
Buddhist revolt began at the end of July, it began to be transformed from a
merely sectarian opposition movement seeking specifically religious concessions into a more widely supported political movement bent on the
destruction of the regime. It is important, nevertheless, to recognize that
this was essentially a movement of the cities and towns, and in the Mekong
Delta not even of the towns. Whatever the secret relationship (if any)
between Thich Tri-Quang and the Communists, the Buddhist movement

[1] NY Times, 15 June 1963.
[2] Mecklin, pp. 172–3, 177.
[3] NY Times, 8 July 1963; Times, 13 July 1963; Tu-Do, 13 July 1963.
[4] NY Times, 9 July 1963.

was not a strategic or tactical extension of the campaign being waged by the National Liberation Front in the countryside.

On 30 July there were new Buddhist protests in four cities, including Saigon, and on 5 August there occurred at Phan-Thiet the second self-immolation of a Buddhist monk.[1] The first half of August saw a growing number of Buddhist demonstrations, and three more immolations (at Hué and at Ninh-Hoa), which produced a very serious crisis by the middle of the month. All this culminated on 18 August in a demonstration by 15,000 Buddhists at the Xa-Loi temple. Three days later, in the early hours of 21 August, government forces raided a large number of temples, including the Xa-Loi in Saigon and the Tu-Dam in Hué. Several hundred monks, nuns, and laymen were arrested, and for the time being this source of opposition to the regime was silenced. At the same time the government declared a state of siege and appointed General Ton That Dinh (commander of the Vietnamese Army's Third Corps area) to be military governor of Saigon.[2] At first it appeared that the Army had taken control, but it soon became clear that the man responsible for the move and whose power was greatly increased by it was the President's brother, Counsellor Nhu. It was even being rumoured by the 26th that the latter intended to take over the presidency himself.

Vietnamese reaction to the 'pagoda-raids' was one of disapproval in many quarters. The foreign minister, Vu Van Mau, not only offered his resignation (which was rejected), but shaved his head in the style of a Buddhist monk and announced his intention to proceed on a pilgrimage to India. His address on the 24th to the students of the faculty of law at Saigon University, of which he had formerly been Dean, undoubtedly encouraged the student unrest on that day and the next. On the 25th there was a student demonstration near the central market in Saigon, and a girl was killed when it was broken up by riot police. Many students, especially in the law faculty, were arrested before they had time to join the demonstrations: it was subsequently admitted that 1,380 students had been arrested, in addition to the 845 Buddhists imprisoned on 21 August.[3] All universities and schools were closed until further notice on the 25th, but schools were mostly allowed to reopen on 4 September. During the last days of August Saigon was untroubled by riots, but there were rumours of an impending military coup.

The first few days of September were calmer, but on the 7th and 9th there were several demonstrations by pupils in secondary schools, and on the 10th a number of schools were occupied by troops. It was not until

[1] *NY Times*, 31 July, 6 Aug. 1963. Most events of the Buddhist crisis are covered in detail by this newspaper.

[2] *American foreign policy: current documents, 1963*, pp. 862–3.

[3] At a press conference given by General Ton That Dinh, *Guardian*, 30 Aug. 1963.

16 September that the state of siege of 21 August was lifted and things began to return to something like normal in Saigon.

An important diplomatic event which occurred in late summer was a statement by President de Gaulle to the French council of ministers on 29 August, that France would like to see Vietnam develop 'in internal peace and unity and in harmony with her neighbours', and that France would extend her 'cordial co-operation' to Vietnam in such circumstances.[1] The statement was interpreted to mean that France would wish to see a unified and neutral Vietnam and reports of secret contacts between Paris and Hanoi suggested that the French president was taking some action to bring this about.[2] In September there were rumours of secret contacts between Counsellor Nhu and Hanoi, in which the French again were said to have played an important part. For the first time since 1956, the French were taking an initiative in the affairs of their former colony. But before anything could come of it, President Diem and Counsellor Nhu had fallen from power and the situation had once again radically changed. President de Gaulle alarmed some of Saigon's French nationals by hesitating to recognize the new Military Revolutionary Council in November, but he finally did so before the month was out.[3]

Another diplomatic development which arose out of the Buddhist crisis but was cut short by the November coup, was the involvement of a United Nations investigation team. As early as 18 May the Buddhist leaders in Hué had sent a letter of appeal to the secretary-general of the United Nations.[4] On 31 August U Thant wrote to President Diem expressing concern at the situation regarding the Buddhists of Vietnam; but for the time being he had to be satisfied with a reply from the Vietnamese president, dated 5 September, to the effect that the crisis had been resolved.[5] Nevertheless there were moves to place the question on the agenda of the UN General Assembly, due to meet in October. On 4 October, therefore, Dr Buu Hoi, who had been appointed South Vietnamese observer at the UN, wrote to the president of the Assembly inviting him to send a fact-finding mission to Vietnam. This was agreed, and the mission arrived in Saigon on 24 October. It had started its investigation when the regime was overthrown. On 3 November the mission returned to New York.[6]

(c) *United States policy*

Although the policies adopted in South Vietnam were formally those of the government in Saigon, it was no secret that many of the most

[1] *American foreign policy: current documents, 1963,* p. 869.   [2] *Observer,* 1 Sept. 1963.
[3] *Le Monde,* 13 Nov. 1963.   [4] *NY Times,* 19 May 1963.
[5] *American foreign policy: current documents, 1963,* pp. 869–72.
[6] United Nations Fact-Finding Mission to South Viet-Nam, *Report on the violation of human rights in South Viet-Nam,* UN Document A 5360 (New York, 1963).

important decisions were taken by the United States. In addition to its normal diplomatic presence and a CIA station, the United States was also represented in Saigon by a military advisory group (MAAG) and by an AID mission. In Washington, policy towards Vietnam was the concern of a group of officials which included members of the Pentagon administration, the office of the Joint Chiefs of Staff, the State Department, and the National Security staff of the White House. With the publication of the *Pentagon papers* in 1971, it became possible to obtain greater insight into the complexities of American decision-making on Vietnam, even though in some respects the documents which were published still conceal as much as they reveal.[1] In particular there has been controversy over the extent to which they conceal a lack of continuity between the policies of President Kennedy and those of President Johnson at the end of 1963.

The central concern of the United States was with the war, and the need to defend South Vietnam as a separate state with an anti-Communist regime. That had been the purpose of their intervention in 1954–5, rather than the maintenance of any particular government or set of institutions. At the same time Vietnam was seen in the context of global international relations, in which there was some easing of tension between the superpowers by the summer of 1963. The question of the degree of American commitment to Vietnam remained an issue throughout the administration of J. F. Kennedy, and he refused to be drawn into making an open-ended commitment despite the pressure on him from some of his officials to do so. On the other hand, amongst officials more specifically concerned with policy in Vietnam, there were differences of opinion regarding tactics which came to a head in the summer and autumn of 1963. For the joint chiefs of staff Vietnam was becoming increasingly a military problem, even though the 11,000 American forces in Vietnam at the beginning of the year were special forces rather than regular combat units. 'Counter-insurgency' was a new problem calling for new military techniques, which would need to combine the 'covert action' methods of the CIA with the lessons to be learnt from studying revolutionary guerrilla warfare. Most of those who approached the problem in this way were not concerned about forms of government in Saigon, or with the popularity or otherwise of particular political leaders. They merely wanted stability, and tended to prefer the existing regime of Ngo Dinh Diem to the uncertainties that might arise from any decision to

---

[1] *The Pentagon papers: the defense department history of United States decision-making on Vietnam.* 'The Senator Gravel Edition', Beacon Press, Boston, 1971: 4 vols. A fifth volume of critical essays was added in 1972. There are two other editions of the papers: an official one in twelve volumes, published by the Government Printing Office, Washington; and an abridged version with articles of commentary, published by the *New York Times* staff. References are to the Senator Gravel Edition, so-called from the fact that it was he who read the papers into the record of Congress.

overthrow him. During the debates of the summer months, it was the Pentagon which tended to insist on giving Diem one more chance. Those who saw Vietnam as a political and diplomatic problem, however, tended towards the opposite view: that the war could only be won by a leader with genuine popular support in Vietnam, which Diem was rapidly losing. This school of thought, especially strong in the State Department, was behind the efforts to put pressure on Diem throughout the years 1961–3; and when pressure failed to produce reforms, it favoured his removal by a *coup d'état*.

The debates in Washington about Vietnam must be seen against the background of a desire by President Kennedy and Secretary of Defence McNamara to prevent the military aspect from getting out of hand. They had resisted proposals to send combat units to Laos in the spring of 1961, and to Vietnam in 1962. In July 1962, immediately following the Geneva agreement on Laos, Secretary of Defence McNamara had decided at a conference in Honolulu to concentrate on a policy of training and equipping the South Vietnamese Army and phasing out the American military presence as rapidly as possible.[1] He saw the end of 1965 as a deadline for this process, and on that assumption ordered the preparation by the military commanders of a 'Comprehensive Plan for South Vietnam'. It was this plan which was eventually forwarded to the joint chiefs of staff, from the Pacific Command in Honolulu, on 19 January 1963, and by them to the secretary of defence on 7 March.[2] It proposed some increase of American personnel in 1964, then a gradual phasing down to 1,500 men by 1968. But proposals for specific military actions were already creating pressure for more rather than fewer Americans in Vietnam, and by April one has the impression of a behind-the-scenes struggle by McNamara to prevent force-levels from rising beyond those envisaged in the 'Comprehensive Plan'. At a further meeting in Honolulu on 6 May, he made criticisms of the Plan and insisted on accelerating the pace at which Vietnamese forces were trained and Americans withdrawn. He also insisted on a decision in principle that 1,000 men should be withdrawn from Vietnam by the end of 1963.[3] In the next few days he gave directions for plans to be made on that basis.

In these circumstances, it was natural that attention should focus on the question whether the Diem government in Saigon provided adequate basis for a policy of 'Vietnamization' at this stage. Precisely at the moment when this question was being asked, the Buddhist crisis broke out at Hué. Unfortunately the *Pentagon papers* tell us very little about decision-making during late May and June, but a few clues suggest that while President Kennedy's attention was being absorbed by his visit to Europe, some of his middle-level advisers in Washington were devoting theirs to the problem

---

[1] *Pentagon papers*, ii, pp. 175–6.   [2] Ibid., pp. 177–9.   [3] Ibid., pp. 180–1.

of Laos and were working out some kind of plan for new action there.[1] In late June, whilst he was visiting Ireland, the President confirmed a decision that Frederick Nolting, ambassador in Saigon, would be succeeded by Henry Cabot Lodge in September.[2] The background to this decision remains obscure, but it should be noted that an American reporter, Robert Shaplen, was later to write that the first plot to overthrow Ngo Dinh Diem was being hatched as early as July, under the aegis of Tran Kim Tuyen, a key figure in Ngo Dinh Diem's intelligence organization.[3] The possibility of a coup was discussed at a White House meeting on 4 July.[4]

Ambassador Nolting was absent from Saigon during the height of the first Buddhist crisis in June, and action there was left in the hands of William Truehart his deputy. In early July Ambassador Nolting was in Washington and argued the case for continuing to support Diem; and as a result he was allowed to return to Saigon and make one last effort to repair American relations with the Vietnamese president. His final period in Saigon, from 11 July to 15 August, brought no solution to the problem, however, and by mid-August American–Saigon relations were worse than ever. It is not impossible that an American-supported coup was planned for the interval between Nolting's final departure on 15 August and the intended arrival of Ambassador Lodge on 26 August. A secret meeting of Vietnamese generals on the 18th led to a request to Diem to implement martial law, which would have increased the army's control over Saigon.[5] But any plans of this kind were foiled by Ngo Dinh Nhu's swift use of his own special forces to occupy the Buddhist pagodas and arrest the militant monks. The *Pentagon papers* suggest that this was a wholly unexpected turn of events, which produced a sudden crisis in Washington. Ambassador Lodge flew immediately from Honolulu to Saigon, but there was little he could do to rescue the situation. After ten days of apparent uncertainty about how to deal with Nhu's own 'coup', it would appear that on 31 August the Americans decided to abandon any thought of overthrowing Diem and Nhu for the time being.[6] This left the ambassador in a difficult position, finding it almost impossible to establish a working relationship with Ngo Dinh Diem, and it was natural that he should continue to favour a coup, if a new opportunity arose. American military leaders on the other hand favoured a serious attempt to renew good relations with Diem.

At this point, in early September, Washington also became concerned about the war situation and the possible effect upon it of the continuing

[1] *Pentagon papers*, ii, pp. 230, 726. On the president's visit to Europe, see pp. 16–17.
[2] Ibid., p. 230.
[3] Robert Shaplen, *The lost revolution* (New York, 1965), pp. 197 ff.
[4] *Pentagon papers*, ii, pp. 727–8: text of Memorandum of meeting.
[5] Ibid., pp. 232–3.   [6] Ibid., pp. 233–40; 734–43.

political crisis in Saigon. By way of taking stock, President Kennedy
sent a two-man mission to inquire into the situation in Vietnam, consisting of Major-General Victor Krulak (US Marines) and the state
department's Joseph Mendenhall.[1] Their report to the national security
council on 10 September occasioned President Kennedy's famous remark:
'You two did visit the same country, didn't you?' General Krulak was
optimistic about the progress of the war, and whilst admitting that the
Communists were still strong in the Mekong Delta, felt that current
policies would eventually be successful. He argued that the political
crisis was not affecting the war, and that Vietnamese officers might dislike Nhu but were not eager to take risks in order to remove him.
Mendenhall was, on the contrary, pessimistic about the possibility of
winning the war if Diem and Nhu remained in power, and saw dangers of
a religious war between Buddhists and Catholics. It was on this occasion
too that a USOM official confirmed the pessimistic view of the rural
situation which David Halberstam's newspaper reports had revealed in
August. But the conflict of opinion went on, and was not finally resolved
until October.

In the meantime, during the first week in September McNamara
approved a plan for the withdrawal of 1,000 men from Vietnam by the
year's end, which he had determined upon in May. But it is clear from
the terms of the plan and his comments that the joint chiefs of staff
wanted to water down his decision. In effect they planned to increase the
number of men to 16,732 by October, before reducing it to 15,732 at
the end of December.[2] There are indications, indeed, that the joint
chiefs of staff were thinking in a quite contrary direction by this time.
Between May and early September they had prepared what was to become
known as OPLAN 34-63, which amounted to the first specific proposals
for covert action against North Vietnam. Although the military leaders
approved it on 9 September and forwarded it to McNamara, it would
appear that he did not act upon it and that it remained inoperative until
late November.[3]

In order to gain a clearer picture of the situation within Vietnam, it
was decided to send a high-level mission there, and as a result McNamara
and General Maxwell Taylor, chairman of the joint chiefs of staff,
visited Saigon from 23 September to 2 October. On their return, they
expressed some reservations about Diem, but on the question of the war
they were optimistic. A White House statement on 2 October recorded
their judgement that the war could be brought to a successful conclusion
and 'the major part of the United States military task can be completed by
the end of 1965'.[4] It was decided to proceed with the token withdrawal of

[1] Ibid., pp. 234-5.   [2] Ibid., pp. 168-9, 182-3.   [3] *Pentagon papers*, iii, 141, 150-1.
[4] US Department of State, *American foreign policy: current documents, 1963*, pp. 874-5.

1,000 men by the end of 1963. At the same time, it appears to have been decided in early October to go ahead with plans for a military coup; thus began the train of events leading up to the actual coup of 1 November. But at all points thereafter, the United States government denied any participation in the coup and insisted that it was entirely the responsibility of the Vietnamese army.

The fall of Ngo Dinh Diem had profound consequences for political stability in Saigon, and led to a situation where the United States could no longer apply the policy of winning the war by training and equipping the Vietnamese army. Diem had been at least an effective centre of power, upon which the Americans could build a policy of that kind. Once he had gone, no single leader was able to emerge with the same authority and Saigon politics became an arena for the rivalries of perhaps half a dozen officers over the next two years. However, it has also been argued that equally important consequences for Vietnam followed from the death of President Kennedy on 23 November. The *Pentagon papers* imply a large measure of continuity between the Kennedy and Johnson periods. But if one reads carefully the record of what happened, it becomes apparent that a new kind of policy was being followed as early as the end of November. The token withdrawal decision was carried through, but it no longer had the significance originally intended by McNamara: the Comprehensive Plan of January was now dead.

The key document in the setting of a new course would appear to be National Security Action Memorandum 273, approved by President Johnson on 26 November; it is referred to and partially quoted in the *Pentagon papers*, but no full text has been published.[1] Quotations from it and references to it indicate that it contained at least two new departures. First, a direct quotation in the Pentagon studies shows that there was now an emphasis on the situation in South Vietnam as an 'externally directed and supported conspiracy', whose defeat was the 'central objective' of American policy. Secondly, it is noted at one point that this Memorandum 'authorized planning for specific covert operations, graduated in intensity, against the DRV'.[2] In other words, the plans worked out by the joint chiefs of staff earlier in the year now became operative, and as a direct result General Krulak went ahead with the more detailed planning which was set forth in his Report of 2 January 1964.[3]

There is some indication that these matters had been discussed at a further Honolulu Conference on 20 November, attended by Dean Rusk, McNamara, and the whole South Vietnam team from Saigon, before

---

[1] For an analysis of the references to this Memorandum and an attempt to reconstruct its contents, see *Pentagon papers*, v, pp. 240–7.

[2] *Pentagon papers*, iii, pp. 117, 141.   [3] Ibid., pp. 118.

President Kennedy's death. It is therefore impossible to say with complete certainty that the new policy departures would not have occurred if the President had lived. What is clear is that the second half of November did see a major turning-point in United States policy towards Vietnam, and that this was indeed the point of departure for many of the debates and decisions of 1964. In particular, a situation which in January had been seen as primarily a question of defeating counter-insurgency within South Vietnam was now regarded increasingly as a matter of persuading North Vietnam to abandon its 'aggression' against the South. At the same time the official optimism about the war which had persisted until October was now giving way to pessimism, especially about the situation in the Mekong Delta. On 19–20 December there was yet a further visit to Saigon by the secretary of defence, accompanied by General Krulak, John McCone (the director of central intelligence) and others. On his return, McNamara admitted that there had been some deterioration in the situation since the change of government in Saigon and that the position was now serious. This recognition was accompanied, however, by a growing determination to take any action that seemed necessary. On the last day of the year the United States commitment to South Vietnam was reaffirmed in a letter from President Johnson to the chairman of the Military Revolutionary Council, General Duong Van Minh.[1]

(d) *The overthrow of Diem and Nhu*

It is evident from the *Pentagon papers* that shortly after McNamara and General Taylor returned to Washington, there was a renewal of secret contacts between Generals Duong Van Minh and Tran Van Don and an officer of the CIA.[2] The record insists that it was on Vietnamese initiative. As a result, the American embassy in Saigon once more began to take seriously the possibility of a military coup. Although Washington was not immediately convinced of the practicability of a successful coup and was very anxious that there be no appearance of United States involvement in a failure, events gradually moved towards the overthrow of the Diem regime. An important step was taken towards that end on 18 October, when General Harkins informed the Vietnamese president that American financial support for the 'special force' of Colonel Le Quang Tung would be discontinued.[3] This force, originally financed by the United States to prosecute unconventional warfare against the Communists, was known to be personally loyal to Counsellor Nhu. It had

[1] *American foreign policy: current documents, 1963*, pp. 883–5.
[2] *The Pentagon papers*, pp. 213–15.
[3] Ibid., p. 179. This move had been anticipated by the report of McNamara and General Taylor on 2 October. Cf. also David Halberstam, *The making of a quagmire* (London, 1965), p. 265.

been moved into the capital at the height of the August crisis and its continued presence there was a major obstacle to any coup by the regular army. Despite the removal of funds it remained in Saigon until the end of October.

A new factor in American calculations during the latter part of October was the receipt of intelligence reports that the tempo of Communist military activity was increasing. A state department report on the war, dated 22 October, noted 'an unfavourable shift in the military balance' since July.[1] By 24 October Ambassador Lodge had made it clear to the generals that the United States would not thwart a coup. General Harkins, despite some reservations which he communicated to Washington as late as the 30th, agreed not to stand in the way.[2] Continuing doubts in the minds of some members of the national security council in Washington did not lead to any firm reversal of the decision of Ambassador Lodge to support a coup, and by 31 October the attempt was under way.

The events of the coup, which took place on 1–2 November, indicate the great complexity of the situation. The most detailed account is once again that of David Halberstam of the *NY Times*.[3] The key to the complexity was the fact that Counsellor Nhu was himself seeking to pull off a counter-coup to deceive and defeat the generals whom he knew to be plotting against him. General Dinh was considered unpredictable by both sides, and even after he had thrown in his lot with the coup generals, he was still being wooed by President Diem and Counsellor Nhu. Thus in the last days of October General Dinh was able to persuade Diem to give him authority to move troops into the capital, on the grounds that a show of force would be to the advantage of the government. He even convinced Colonel Tung of the need to withdraw the 'special force' lest the Americans became worried by the large number of troops in the city. As a result, when the coup leaders began to move their own forces into Saigon on the morning of 1 November, Diem anticipated troop movements and saw no cause for alarm until it was too late. When Vietnamese marines seized the police headquarters and the radio station, the Palace was unable to make contact with General Dinh, and the generals had gained the initiative. Colonel Tung was arrested, and almost all other principal commanders in and around the capital agreed to join in the coup. During the course of the afternoon and evening, it became clear that, apart from the presidential guard, the president and his entourage had no military support within the capital. They still hoped that the Seventh Division (whose headquarters were at My-Tho, south-west of Saigon) might come to their rescue, but in fact General Dinh had taken steps to neutralize it. The nearest support was at Can-Tho, in the western Mekong Delta, where General Huynh Van Cao was commander of the

[1] *The Pentagon papers*, p. 180.   [2] Ibid., pp. 180–4, 217–31.
[3] *NY Times*, 7 Nov. 1963; Halberstam, pp. 288–98.

Fourth Corps area; but there was no chance of his coming to the president's aid in time. While troops were pounding the barracks of the presidential guard, and others were surrounding the palace itself, the president and his brother left by a secret exit and proceeded to a house in Cholon. An assault on the palace in the early hours of 2 November was successful after a two-hour battle, but its principal occupants were gone. The president and his brother were finally arrested by one of the coup plotters at about 9.30 a.m., and shortly afterwards were killed on the way to the General Staff headquarters. By mid-day on 2 November it was clear that the coup had succeeded. There followed a period of great rejoicing in the streets of Saigon, whilst large numbers of people who had been held prisoner by the regime were released, including those sentenced at the trials in July.

On the afternoon of 1 November the new Military Revolutionary Council headed by General Duong Van Minh issued its first proclamation, justifying its action in overthrowing the government and calling on the people for support; it was signed by fourteen generals and eight other officers.[1] On 4 November the names of a provisional government were announced; the new cabinet was headed by the former vice-president, Nguyen Ngoc Tho (now named prime minister), and included three generals.[2] The new government was able to consolidate its power in those parts of the country not controlled by the Communists, and in Hué they arrested another brother of the late president, Ngo Dinh Can, after he had been refused asylum at the US consulate.[3] Although not holding any formal office, he had been undoubtedly the most powerful man in central Vietnam during the past nine years. In due course he was brought to trial, sentenced, and finally executed on 10 May 1964.

The provisional government remained in power from the beginning of November until 30 January 1964, when it was itself overthrown by a further coup, directed by Major General Nguyen Khanh. The new regime was soon recognized by the United States and other nations, and inherited the support which the American administration had afforded to President Diem before the Buddhist crisis began. US aid was resumed, and it was hoped in Washington that the war would now be prosecuted with vigour. Meanwhile, the Buddhists, whose leaders had been released from prison, set about the task of creating a new organization which would enable them to take advantage of the position of influence they had won for themselves in South Vietnamese politics. Early in January 1964 some of them joined together to form what came to be known in English as the 'United Buddhist Church' of Vietnam. They, the army, and the communists, three by no means compatible forces, were the beneficiaries of the events of 1963.

[1] *American foreign policy: current documents, 1963*, p. 878; *Documents, 1963*, pp. 378–9.
[2] *Times*, 5 Nov. 1963.   [3] *Times*, 6 Nov. 1963.

(e) *North Vietnam*

The year 1963 was one in which the ruling Vietnam Workers' Party in Hanoi was obliged to take difficult but important decisions in the face of a rapidly changing world situation. In the development of its policy towards the South, the year was probably the most decisive of the decade. The chief spokesman of the party during 1963, and probably the most powerful member of its political bureau (apart from President Ho Chi Minh) was its first secretary, Le Duan. But an important role in policy-making was probably also played by Truong Chinh, by now president of the national assembly, who was commonly believed by outsiders to be Le Duan's chief rival in the party hierarchy. General Vo Nguyen Giap, head of the army, seems to have played a more subdued role during 1963. At the beginning of the year, the party line was still essentially that which had been enunciated by Le Duan in his report to the third congress of the party in September 1960.[1] It comprised three related policies: socialist transformation and construction in North Vietnam, including the first steps towards establishing heavy industry with Soviet and Chinese aid; support for the 'national democratic revolution' in South Vietnam; and emphasis on the importance of solidarity within the world communist movement, in which the Soviet Union was recognized as the clear leader. This recognition was indeed confirmed as late as January 1963, with the reception in Hanoi not only of a high-level Soviet party mission, but also of President Novotny of Czechoslovakia.

By the spring of 1963 fresh thought and new policies were called for. Within the Communist world relations between the Soviet Union and China had come near to breaking-point, and Vietnamese efforts to promote unity throughout 1962 had been of no avail.[2] On the economic front, not only had 1962 been a disappointing year, but there was a serious possibility that Vietnam might not be able to rely indefinitely on both Russian and Chinese aid, and for political reasons might have to side with China. Moreover, increased American aid to President Ngo Dinh Diem in the South, although in the long-run less decisive than Washington expected, meant that the struggle there would now be a long and difficult one, requiring perhaps many years of sacrifice and a much more active role on the part of Hanoi than was envisaged in 1960.

The first signs of a shift in policy are to be found in a speech made by Le Duan on 13 March, to commemorate the 80th anniversary of Marx's death.[3] He presented an analysis of the world class struggle which sided

---

[1] *Third National Congress of the Viet-Nam Workers' Party* (Hanoi, 1960), vol. i, pp. 23–213.

[2] K. Chen, 'North Viet-Nam in the Sino-Soviet Dispute, 1962–64', *Asian Survey*, iv, no. 9, Sept. 1964, pp. 1023–36.

[3] Le Duan, 'Hold High the Revolutionary Banner of Creative Marxism', *On some present international problems* (Hanoi, 1964), pp. 57–122. Cf. *Nhan Dan*, editorial, 14 Mar. 1963, broadcast by VNA. *SWB*, FE/1200/C2/1–3.

with China's view that that struggle must be primarily political and not merely economic, and ended with an attack on Yugoslav revisionism. His appeal to the spirit of the Moscow statement of the 1960 meeting of communist parties reflected a continuing Vietnamese desire to heal the breach between Moscow and Peking; but the general tone of the speech veered towards China. Two months later (10–16 May) Chinese approval of the new Vietnamese attitude was reflected in President Liu Shao-chi's state visit to Hanoi. The joint communique of Presidents Liu and Ho, issued at the end of the visit, reiterated the desire for Communist unity but also repeated the attack on Yugoslavia and 'modern revisionism'.[1] When, in July, the Moscow conference between Soviet and Chinese communists broke down, followed immediately by the initialling of the partial Test-Ban Treaty (25 July), the Vietnam Workers' Party very soon made up its mind to give its wholehearted support to China.[2] In doing so, the Vietnamese leaders were well aware that the decision would involve sacrifices. In May the party's central committee had considered the economic implications of the new situation. In a speech on 18 May Le Duan placed new emphasis on the need for self-reliance and careful use of resources, and admitted that the country had, at an earlier stage, imported consumer goods, 'some of which were not badly needed'.[3] The speech suggested an attempt to anticipate a reduction, even a cessation, of Soviet and East European aid. In the event, this was what happened in the autumn of 1963.

For the North Vietnamese leaders, the central consideration underlying these decisions and statements was the situation in the South. Documents captured by Americans seemed to suggest that by April 1963 the National Liberation Front was becoming reconciled to the need for a new policy, and recognized that there would be a long struggle ahead.[4] The same impression is gained from an article in the Vietnam Workers' Party journal *Hoc Tap* for April 1963, which warned that the struggle would be 'long drawn-out, arduous and complicated'. It also noted that Southern bourgeoisie and intellectuals needed to be drawn more fully into the struggle.[5] A document captured in Long-An province, dated May 1963, emphasized that the Front would respect the rights of rich peasants and even landowners who did not co-operate with the Diem regime, whilst in June there were signs of a campaign to win over South Vietnamese teachers to the Front's cause.[6] In keeping with the new attitude towards the war, the National Liberation Front established its own Foreign

[1] *SWB* FE/1252/C1/1–7, for the text as broadcast by NCNA, 16 May 1963.
[2] Chen, for references to *Nhan-Dan* and *Hoc-Tap* articles on this theme, Aug.–Nov. 1963.
[3] Le Duan, 'Enthusiastically to March Forward to fulfil the First Five Year Plan', *On the Socialist revolution in Viet-Nam*, ii (Hanoi, 1965), pp. 171–212.
[4] Pike, p. 160.
[5] *Observer Foreign News Service*, 24 Apr. 1963.   [6] Pike, p. 277.

Relations Commission in 1963, which made every effort to win over world public opinion to the anti-American view.[1]

As relations between Moscow and Peking became more tense, the Vietnamese Communist leaders became increasingly committed to the war. That, more than ideological considerations, may have decided them in favour of supporting the Chinese view. On 21 July a massive demonstration was held in Hanoi to protest against American aggression in the South, and to demand complete withdrawal of American forces.[2] In the July issue of *Hoc Tap*, an article by General Nguyen Chi Thanh contradicted any suggestion that the North might develop separately from the South.[3] He argued that 'the building of a strong and prosperous North Viet-Nam and the carrying out of the revolution by the people of the South are closely related . . . the building of the North cannot by itself supply a solution to the internal contradictions of South Vietnamese society'. *Hoc Tap* in September carried an article entitled 'Men and Weapons' which insisted on the ability of the Southerners to withstand American weaponry despite its vast superiority.[4] It was in this context that the change in the character of the war on the ground, noted above, began to take place during September and October.[5]

Thus by the autumn of 1963 a coherent new policy was emerging in North Vietnam. There are signs that in November, after the fall of President Ngo Dinh Diem, the Soviet Union may have hoped for some kind of neutrality for the two halves of Vietnam.[6] The position of Hanoi was that the South might be neutralized but certainly not the North, although this was not publicly declared until February 1964. In December 1963 the ninth plenary session of the party's third central committee met to discuss the whole question of Vietnamese policy towards the international situation. It ended by passing a resolution, formally proposed by Truong Chinh but elaborated upon by Le Duan, which reiterated the line already taken since August: alignment with China, accompanied by pious hopes for eventual Communist unity. The offensive strategy in the South was likewise reaffirmed.[7] Since the communique of this meeting was not published until 20 January 1964, perhaps there was still an element in the party opposed to this line. It may be that the issue was only finally resolved by the special political conference presided over by President Ho Chi Minh in March 1964.[8] But to all intents and purposes, by the beginning of 1964 the die was cast.

[1] Pike, pp. 315–16.   [2] H.N.A., 21 July 1963.
[3] Translated in *Vietnamese Studies*, no. 1, 'South Vietnam 1964' (Hanoi, 1964), pp. 14–23.
[4] Translated in *On the problem of war and peace* (Hanoi, 1964), pp. 95–118.
[5] See above p. 170.
[6] Chen, *Asian survey*, Sept. 1964, p. 1033, citing *NY Times*, 5, 10 Nov. 1963.
[7] Le Duan, *On some present international problems*, pp. 123–83; *SWB*, FE/1459/C/1–4, reporting VNA broadcast of 20 Jan. 1964.   [8] *SWB*, FE/1518/C/1–11.

PART III

THE MIDDLE EAST

CHAPTER VII

THE END OF ARAB UNITY

(a) *The failure of the Ba'th*

To analyse the course of international politics in the Arab Middle East, two points need to be emphasized. The first is that for much of the time the Arab Middle East forms a self-contained system. Although at first sight a number of states in the area seem involved in a patron–client relationship with one or more of the major world powers, their responsiveness to the state of relations between their various patrons is very limited and, contrariwise, the degree of influence and control exercisable by their patrons appears equally inhibited. The one external factor to which they are all responsive is external only in the sense that it is completely differentiated from them culturally and is excluded from all their councils and other politico-social links. This is the permanent outsider, envisaged by them as antagonist, threat and tool of the outside, non-Arab world, the state of Israel.

Writers on classical Arab concepts of international law have long insisted that this phenomenon of self-containment is paralleled by the division of the world, found in all four of the classic schools of Arabic writing on the subject, into the abode of Islam (i.e. of peace) and the abode of discord or war, the *dar al-Islam* and the *dar al-Harb*.[1] In classic times a united Islamic *umma*, the word so inadequately and confusingly translated into 'nation' (just as *ummaya* becomes 'nationalism'), faced a divided external world.[2] The nineteenth- and twentieth-century experience of the Arabic world reversed this situation and internalized much of the attention of the politically active segment of Arabic society; so that whereas in classical Arabic history the ruler overbore internal opposition as a preparation for dealing with the advance of Islam, in twentieth-century Arab politics success in dealing with the external world was a necessary preparation to success in coping with the strains within the *dar al-Islam*.

This then becomes the second point essential to the understanding of inter-Arab politics. To translate these into Western terms and to construe them as being concerned with a struggle for mastery or leadership in a movement for Arabic unity is to misconstrue Arabic rhetoric twice over,

---

[1] Chapter II, p. 38, footnote 1 above.

[2] Sylvia G. Haim, 'Islam and the theory of Arab nationalism', in Walter Z. Laqueur, *The Middle East in transition* (London, 1958); id., 'Islam and Arab nationalism', *Welt des Islams*, iii, pp. 201 ff.

once as Arabic and once as rhetoric. Arab politics in the 1950s and 1960s, especially in 1963, were concerned not with unity but with legitimacy. Plans for union never envisaged the disappearance of the individual regimes engaged in the negotiations into a larger union, involving their demotion to the level of local government offices. Their aim was to confer legitimacy on the regimes involved.

In these struggles the Arab monarchies felt only a limited involvement. The Imam of the Yemen until his overthrow, the ruler of Saudi Arabia, and the sheikhly families of the Gulf states were certainly aware that the hereditary basis of their legitimacy was not accepted by states such as Iraq, Syria, or Egypt, or by those who felt excluded by lack of family origins from the power they felt should belong to them. They were also aware that such dissidents traditionally appealed to some higher and broader concepts of Islam itself or of the Islamic *umma* to challenge the claims to power of a ruler deemed inefficient or corrupt. In practice, however, they felt themselves more vulnerable to discord from within their own sheikhly families rather than from partisans of Arab unity, or from dissidence among those whose tribal loyalties or membership of a dissident Islamic sect made them *ab initio* uncommitted towards a particular ruler's claims to legitimacy. The moderate exception to this rule was King Hussein of Jordan. By family, his claims to legitimacy rested on his descent from the Sharifian family of Mecca, descendants of the Prophet Mohammed, and his grandfather's successful annexation of Transjordania amidst the collapse of the Ottoman Empire. That same grandfather had, however, lost his life after having extended his rule over the Palestinian Arabs of the West Bank in 1948-9. To the Bedu of the deserts, Hussein's legitimacy was unquestioned. To the Arabs of the Transjordanian cities and villages it rested on his ability to rule. To the Palestinian refugees, especially to their Christian communities, it was alien and unwelcome and was accepted only so long as it could be confidently asserted.

Among the remaining Arab states, Egypt was the exception, as she had been throughout the long period of Ottoman rule and decline. Dependence on the Nile, cosmopolitanism in the cities, the insulating effects of rule successively by the Mamelukes, the Khedivial family, and the British, and the existence of a non-Arab Pharaonic tradition of greatness embodied for all to see in the massive monuments of ancient Egypt, gave Egyptians, even before the rise of Colonel Nasser, a sense of uniqueness within the Arab world. By 1963 Nasser had successfully established his legitimacy in the Arab world on the basis of his victories not against Israel but against the 'imperialists' of the *dar al-Harb*. Since the cultural, economic, and political resources of Egypt so greatly outweighed those of the other Arab states, the approval of President Nasser became one of the most sought-after sources of legitimacy throughout the Arab world, especially among those whose circumstances led them to challenge the claims to legitimacy of the local holders of power. This ability to confer legitimacy upon those he chose to support was not entirely welcome to the leaders of other factions in the Arabic world. To the Saudi Arabian royal house, steeped in the fundamentalism of the Wahabi sect of Islam, it was a permanent affront. It was equally unwelcome to successive rulers in Iraq and Syria. Most of all, it was an affront to the various sections of the party of the Arabic Socialist Renaissance, the Ba'th, established in Syria, Iraq, the Lebanon and, as long as King Hussein did not feel strong enough to suppress them, in Jordan.

The Ba'th party saw itself as the living embodiment of Arab unity. It preached, in the words of a French observer[1]:

une ideologie nationaliste, intégrale et totale: la définition du nationalisme Arabe est le centre de gravité de toute la doctrine du parti. Ce nationalisme Arabe repose sur l'existence de la nation Arabe, entité éternelle, provisoirement morcelée en diverse contrées soumises à la domination de l'impérialisme et des classes réactionnaires, féodalité et haute bourgeoisie pactisant avec lui. Liberer la nation arabe de la domination etrangére, faire disparaître les frontières artificielles et iniques qui mutilent la nation arabe, supprimer les classes exploiteuses et corrompues, abattre les barrières entre les classes sociales, tels sont les buts suprêmes du parti . . .

To this 'unity' which 'existed before the appearance of Western imperialism and will continue to exist after its liquidation', the ideologists of the Ba'th were in the process of contributing firstly a secular historical view of the Arab nation, the *umma*, and secondly a Marxist interpretation of its internal weaknesses. Whereas the Wahabi fundamentalist regarded the weakness of the Islamic *umma* faced with the West to be the result of Islam's departure from a strict literal interpretation of the *Quran* and the *Shari'a*, the Ba'thi intellectual regarded the weakness of the secular Arabic *umma* towards the West as a consequence of treachery to the *umma* practised by monarchs, sheikhly families, and merchants seeking to enrich or advance themselves.

The advantage of this interpretation is its adaptability to the circumstances of the different Arab countries. In Jordan it was hostile to King Hussein and the old Transjordanian families and their adherents on whose loyalty the Jordanian government rested. In Iraq it appealed to the younger officers (mainly Sunni Moslems, incidentally) who were challenging the older families of Baghdad and Basra, as against the divisions introduced by Shi'ite and Kurdish families and their partisans and adherents. In Syria it appealed especially to the non-Sunni minorities, Christians, Druses, Alawites, and Ismailis and to the families from the

---

[1] Jean-Pierre Viennot, 'Le Ba'th entre la theorie et la pratique', *Orient*, No. 30, 1964, p. 14.

lesser cities, Latakia, Homs, Hama, and the provinces resenting the domination of Damascenes and families from Aleppo. In this adaptability, however, lay the seeds of disaster for any attempt to get the national sections of the party to function together on a supra-national level.

The search for legitimacy to justify the exercise of sovereign power was particularly acute in Syria where a sense of regional cohesion was notably lacking. The old Ba'th, it will be remembered, had stampeded Syria into union with Egypt in 1958. The experience of Egyptian national self-consciousness had alienated all levels of Syrian society and led to a break-up in the Union which had re-established for a time the rule of the old Damascus and Aleppo families and their supporters in the army leadership. The subsequent propaganda war with Egypt had led at the Shtura meeting of the Arab League in August 1962 to a complete break between the Syrian and Egyptian governments. The political balance in Syria had shifted under Egyptian attack towards the centre and left, the Khaled al-Azm cabinet which took office in September 1962 being based on a coalition between the major political parties represented in the constituent assembly elected at the beginning of 1962 and representing the traditional political leadership throughout the country. Three members of the Ba'th party were included in the cabinet; the principal opposition came from those who had achieved power and status during the period of union with Egypt, a point underlined that autumn when the Syrian government sought to dissolve the leadership of the various labour unions set up during the period of union, and from the extreme orthodox Sunni Moslems of the Moslem Brotherhood.

The Ba'th party as represented by Akram Hourani had, however, been undergoing major changes behind his back since the destruction of the union and the initial dissolution of the Ba'th as being too closely involved in its establishment. The old Ba'th had been divided between partisans of Hourani (himself a Sunni) and Michel Aflaq (a Christian), both of them Damascenes. When the Ba'th was permitted to recommence political activities in 1962, the appeal by the old cadres for a party reorganization under their leadership was rejected by the provincial members who had entered the party during the period of union with Egypt, especially those from the Alawi and Ismaili areas around Latakia and from the new cadres in the north of Syria. These *Qutriyyun* (Regionalists) were paralleled in the army by the establishment, especially among those Syrian army officers who had served in Egypt during the period of union, of the so-called Military Committee, three of whose leaders, Mohammed Umran, Salah Jadid, and Hafiz al-Asad, were also Alawis. Aflaq in the meantime was engaged in challenging Hourani's leadership among the old Ba'th cadres. The introduction of a heavily Marxist element among the new members by a group from Homs, Hama, and Latakia, refugees from the disastrous ambivalence of the Arab Communist fringe, largely escaped his notice.

This ferment from below within the Ba'th party was matched by a continuation of agitation by President Nasser's supporters in Aleppo and Damascus. This reached a peak in January 1963. The Syrian cabinet decided to close the border with the Lebanon, after the Egyptian military attaché in Beirut had defected to them with evidence of Egyptian support for the organizers. On 4 February a number of Lebanese were arrested on the frontier on allegations of smuggling arms into Syria and conspiracy to assassinate the premier. Support from the Ba'th and Islamic Union members of the cabinet gradually melted away as a result of conflict within their ranks. Aflaq's supporters refused to join the now doomed cabinet.

The final knell for the Syrian government was struck on 8 February 1963 when a conspiracy of officers from the Iraqi wing of the Ba'th party overthrew Colonel Qasim's regime in Iraq. Qasim himself was given a summary trial and executed. A major purge was launched against the Iraqi communist party. The National Committee of the Revolutionary Council almost immediately took steps to end Iraq's feud with Egypt, dispatching a delegation on 22 February to attend the Egyptian Independence Day celebrations. After talks with President Nasser the delegation returned to Baghdad to announce that a basis had been found for effective co-operation between the United Arab Republic and Iraq in such a way as to lead to the realization of unity in the Arab nation.

Khaled al-Azm, the Syrian premier, had been desperately trying to improve relations with Qasim. In the aftermath of the latter's overthrow he turned for economic aid to the Soviet and Chinese authorities. At the same time he decided on one final purge of the Syrian high command of its dissident officers. The army leadership and Michel Aflaq were, however, ahead of him. Aflaq, who had foreknowledge of the coup in Baghdad, took a delegation of his supporters to Baghdad just before the Iraqi delegation left for Cairo. For Aflaq the support of the Ba'th in Iraq was his ace of trumps against Akram Hourani. The Iraqi coup swung the remaining senior officers in the Syrian army towards the Nasserite and Ba'thi officers. If there was to be a fresh round of talks on Arab union as Aflaq's links with the Iraqi Ba'th and the latter's overtures to President Nasser suggested, they had no choice. On 8 March a military coup led by three colonels of the Damascus garrison arrested President Kudsi, Akram Hourani, and other prominent leaders; Khaled al-Azm took asylum in the Turkish embassy.

Faced, as they saw it, with the necessity of a new coup, the senior officers of the Syrian army had begun to close their ranks. Since April 1962 they had adopted the Egyptian device of a Military Defence Council to which

all senior officers had belonged. In addition to the officers of the Military
Committee so-called there were factions of pre-unionist Ba'thi officers,
moderate supporters of union with Egypt, outright Nasserites as well as
personal factions such as those led by Zahr ed-Din and the Damascene
officers led by Nahlawi. It was the latter faction which had been responsible
for the 1961 break-up of the UAR and the abortive coup of 28 March
1962. The Homs garrison had also revolted then. It was as a result of
these coups that the Military Defence Council had been established and
Nahlawi and his principal followers exiled. Other attempts, made by
unionist officers such as Hamad Ubaid and Luayy al-Atasi, in Homs
and Aleppo, had been pacified by the Military Defence Council without
difficulty.

The 8 March 1963 coup was managed by a coalition of unionists,
Nasserites, and Ba'thi officers, though the Nasserites withdrew at the last
moment. They felt the need, however, for a new civilian government, and
they made their approach therefore to Salah ad-Din al-Bitar, a prominent
Ba'thi politician who leant more towards Aflaq than Hourani. Parallel
with Bitar's cabinet they set up a National Committee of the Revolutionary
Council of ten officers, one Ba'thi, one Druse, two Alawite leaders from
the Military Committee, Luayy al-Atasi from Homs and his co-unionist,
Ziyad al-Hariri, from Hama, three Nasserite officers, and one independent.
The cabinet was equally a coalition of Ba'th, Unionist, and various splinter
groups. More importantly its composition, only six from Damascus and
Aleppo and seventeen from the rest of Syria, demonstrated the collapse of
the former domination of Syrian politics by those two cities.

On 10 March three extremely significant events took place. Demonstrations organized by the extreme Nasserites in Damascus and Aleppo
were put down by military action. Thirteen leading Syrian supporters of
President Nasser were refused permission to return to Syria from exile.
And an Iraqi delegation led by Ali Salih al-Sa'di, the deputy premier,
and Shabib, the Iraqi foreign minister, arrived in Damascus with proposals
for a joint military command and a joint political leadership and, a most
significant demonstration of the need they felt for legitimacy and security,
a proposal that a joint statement, to which the governments of Egypt,
Algeria, and the Yemen should also be signatories, should be adopted
giving the armies of these powers the right to enter each other's territories when they were exposed to the threat of external intervention or
internal subversion supported from abroad.

The Nasserite riots shook the Ba'this very badly; it made their entry
into tripartite unity talks with Egypt inevitable. But it also threatened
them with direct pressure from Cairo during the talks. The experience
began to open the rifts between the younger union and post-union members
and the older pre-union leaders. The latter felt that only support from

President Nasser could legitimize the separate role they desired Syria to hold. The vision of a tripartite union dominated by the Ba'th still tempted them. The younger members saw that union with Egypt would mean dominance by a Sunni majority and that they would have to share power within Syria with an organization larger and more efficient than their own. The establishment on 13 March of a new Syrian regional command of the Ba'thi Party showed this dichotomy. The Military Committee, three Alawites and two Ismailis, was formally recognized by Michel Aflaq as having exclusive and autonomous control over the military section of the party.

The immediate reactions of Cairo radio to the suppression of the Nasserite demonstrations showed that President Nasser was well aware of the implications. The 'unity talks' that followed made three other points about his attitude clear. Firstly, he was well aware that what he had to confer upon the new Syrian government was legitimization. Secondly, he was well aware that his command of the big city mobs in Aleppo and Damascus gave him a very potent weapon of pressure upon the Syrian negotiators. Thirdly, he had no intention of entering a coalition of Syria, Iraq, and Egypt which would be dominated by the Ba'th.

These unity talks fall into three stages. The first from 14 to 16 March was tripartite in character. The second from 19 to 20 March consisted of five bilateral talks between Aflaq and al-Bitar for Syria and President Nasser. This was followed by a third round of tripartite talks from 6 to 17 April and ended with the signature of an agreement on a tripartite political union.[1]

The talks were ostensibly tripartite in their first and third stages. But the Iraqi delegation played very much second fiddle to that from Syria and the principal theme discussed at the bulk of the meetings was not the ostensible subject, negotiations for a tripartite union, but the main issues, past and present, between Nasser and the Ba'th. That this was at President Nasser's initiative can be seen both from the membership of the Syrian delegation at the various talks and from the alleged transcripts of the talks later broadcast on Cairo radio. The Syrian delegation at the

[1] The Egyptian record of the talks was published later. See *SWB*, ME/1283/E/1–11, 25 June 1963; ME/1285/E/1–19, 27 June 1963; ME/1286/E/1–8, 28 June 1963; ME/1292/E/1–12, 5 July 1963; ME/1295/E/1–13, 9 July 1963; ME/1297/E/1–16, 11 July 1963; ME/1298/E/1–19, 12 July 1963; ME/1303/E/1–15, 17 July 1963; ME/1304/E/1–18, 19 July 1963; ME/1305/E/1–14, 20 July 1963; ME/1306/E/1–15, 22 July 1963; ME/1307/E/1–20, 23 July 1963; ME/1308/E/1–14, 24 July 1963; ME/1309/E/1–14, 25 July 1963; ME/1310/E/1–15, 26 July 1963; ME/1311/E/1–17, 27 July 1963; ME/1312/E/1–11, 29 July 1963; ME/1313/E/1–15, 30 July 1963; ME/1314/E/1–14, 31 July 1963; ME/1318/E/1–20, 6 Aug. 1963; ME/1321/E/1–34, 9 Aug. 1963; ME/1324/E/1–28, 13 Aug. 1963; ME/1326/E/1–19, 15 Aug. 1963; ME/1330/E/1–32, 20 Aug. 1963; ME/1333/E/1–40, 23 Aug. 1963; ME/1336/E/1–24, 27 Aug. 1963; ME/1339/E/1–33, 30 Aug. 1963; ME/1343/E/1–20, 4 Sept. 1963; ME/1350/E/1–22, 12 Sept. 1963; ME/1357/E/1–23, 20 Sept. 1963, and *Arab political documents, 1963*, pp. 75–218.

first round of talks included only one member of the Ba'th, Abdul Karim Zuhur, an ex-Marxist, who was minister of finance. The others included General Kutayni, General Hariri, Major Muhareb, and Major Shair, of whom only Shair, a Druse, was to join the Ba'th later.

In his opening remarks Nasser threw down the gauntlet,

I do indeed welcome union with Syria and Iraq—and I mean a union, not a secession in the form of a union. . . . We are at the beginning of relations with Iraq and we have no problems between us, but we have five years of experience with Syria and there are certain matters we must review. . . . A spirit of regionalism exists both here in Egypt and in Syria and it would be a mistake to ignore this factor.

Another question is that we must be fully conscious of what we are doing. Are we being asked to unite with the Ba'th party or with Syria? If the Ba'th party is ruling Syria and we are being asked to unite with it, then I am not prepared to continue these discussions. Union with Syria would be welcome but to union with the Ba'th my answer would be, 'No, thank you.'

The role of Hourani and Salah ad-Din al-Bitar in the break-up of the UAR he regarded as particularly treacherous. But he put his finger on the Syrian motives at once when he asked:

What then is being asked? Is it a union or a federation? An actual or a ritual union? Do you ask for a union to be implemented forthwith or for a postponed union?

And he got his reply against on the first day when Zuhur said:

The complete Syrian–Egyptian union was not successful and is, in my opinion, impracticable at this stage in Arab history. . . .

We do not wish a formal union which might restore us to the previous 1958 ideas of union: economic and military agreements, a unified command and so on. Thus what is asked for is a federated union.

Nasser's distrust of the Ba'th's ideas of union came out most strongly when he remarked:

We do not wish to be caught between the hammer and the anvil of a Ba'thist Syria and a Ba'thist Iraq. . . . A union in which there are two Ba'thist votes against the U.A.R.'s one . . . is for us unfortunately out of the question. . . . I cannot link the U.A.R. in a union with the Ba'th alone. . . . If there are eleven Ba'thists in your Council, it means that we can no longer discuss a union . . .

The Iraqis remained onlookers in this discussion intervening only in some anger when Nasser proposed a two-stage union to begin either with a bilateral union of Egypt and Syria or with one between Syria and Iraq. Ali Salih al-Sa'di, leader of the Iraqi delegation, and a leading member of the Iraqi wing of the Ba'th, described this as 'detrimental to the Arab cause' and 'unacceptable'. And it was as-Sa'di who first suggested that

Nasser seek out the leaders of the Syrian Ba'th and settle the differences between them.

The second round of talks, from 19 to 21 March, was thus confined to the Egyptian and Syrian delegations, the latter now strengthened by the arrival of Salah ad-Din al-Bitar and Michel Aflaq of the Ba'th and General Luayy al-Atasi, president of the Syrian Revolutionary Council. Their presence indicates the enormous importance the various elements in the Syrian coalition attached to a successful outcome of the talks.

Nasser's tactics in these talks show that he was determined to legitimize the new government in Syria only if it was prepared to share power with his partisans in Syria and follow forms of organization which would give him control over Syrian political life. His partisans, it was already clear, could call out the 'masses' (Nasserite parlance for the urban mobs of the larger Syrian cities). In this they had, at the moment, the edge over the other political groupings in Syria.

This was something that neither the Syrian officers of the Revolutionary Council nor the political members of the Ba'th could allow. For the 'regionalists' (*Qutriyyun*) this would mark a return to the domination of Syrian politics by Damascus and Aleppo. For the Druse, Ismaili, and Alawite members of the NCRC, the Military Committee, and of the Ba'th it would mean a return to Sunni dominance. For the Marxist revolutionary element it aroused fears of dominance by an Egyptian-controlled bureaucracy. If Nasser had been adequately informed of the true state of power within the Ba'th he might have played his hand differently. He remained, however, obsessed with the past role of Hourani, Aflaq, and Bitar, all men who still felt a need for the legitimacy his support alone could confer, and who hoped for an Arab union in which Ba'thi ideology would gradually come to dominate. His refusal to meet them halfway and to provide the legitimacy they desired marked them out for political destruction; the beneficiaries, however, were not his own supporters on the NCRC, Kutayni, Muhareb, or General Mohammed as-Sufi, but the independent Sunni, Brigadier Amin al-Hafiz, and the Alawite, Colonel Salah Jadid.

Nasser showed his hand most clearly during the third stage of the talks which opened in Cairo on 6 April. The draft constitution under discussion provided for a parliament of two houses, a Federal Assembly in which each country would be equally represented and a National Assembly with representation proportional to population. There would, in addition, be a president, premier, and cabinet and a 'council of leadership' either in the form of a committee of the Federal Assembly or as a Presidential Council. The final solution, a dominant president, who was also C. in C., an appointed premier and cabinet responsible to the National Assembly, and with powers to veto legislation and dissolve parliament, was a victory for Nasser all along the line. During the period of transition, five months to the proclamation of the union and twenty before the constitution should take effect, a Presidential Council formed on the basis of equality between the three countries was to rule the union. These transitional requirements represented a compromise between the Iraqi delegation and President Nasser.[1] It was a compromise that the Ba'th in both countries insisted upon, else, they argued, immediate elections would return the old politicians, the 'secessionists', to power. But the period of transition was to be used, they hoped, not merely to make the Ba'th a mass party but also to break the power of the Nasserites in Syria.

Preliminary skirmishing with Nasser's supporters in Syria began almost immediately after the March coup. Prominent Nasserites in exile in Egypt had been denied permission to return to Syria. After the second round of talks in Cairo, Luayy al-Atasi and Bitar attacked the Syrian Nasserites, in speeches echoing the theme of similar attacks in *al-Ba'th*, the Ba'thist newspaper, provoking Haikal to violent counter-attack in *al-Ahram*. His attacks were followed by pro-Nasser demonstrations in Damascus and Aleppo, which were put down by the Ba'thi minister of the interior, Brigadier Amin al-Hafiz. Disagreements with the Nasserite ministers were temporarily patched up and two of them, Nihad al-Qasim and Hari al-Hindi, were appointed members of the Syrian delegation to the third round of talks at Cairo. But the patch-up was purely temporary, and the announcement of the agreement on a federal union made it clear that Nasser had submitted to Ba'thi demands and had for the time being conferred upon them the legitimacy they desired.

This recognition was not to last long. But it gave the Ba'thi officers and politicians the chance greatly to strengthen their position. Disturbances in the army and disagreement between junior Ba'thi and Nasserite officers led to a dismissal of the minister of defence, Mohammed as-Sufi, and of General Kutayni on allegations that a coup was being planned. They carried with them the all-important group of moderate officers around Generals Hariri and Atasi. Thus when the various non-Ba'thi and nationalist groupings in the cabinet began to press for an increase in their share of cabinet seats in accordance with the spirit of the Cairo agreements, the purge of their military supporters left them no option but to resign. Their resignation brought down the cabinet. And after a two-day attempt by a moderate non-Ba'thi, Sami al-Jundi, to form a cabinet, in which Sami Drubi, the Ba'thi minister of education, acted as an intermediary between President Nasser, the NCRC, and the non-Ba'thi groups, a new cabinet was formed by al-Bitar with six Ba'this and six reliable pro-Ba'thi independents. These manœuvres were accompanied by more rioting in Damascus and Aleppo which Brigadier Hafiz dealt with efficiently, to be rewarded with the position of deputy premier in the new

[1] For the Declaration of Union see *Documents, 1963*, pp. 291–315.

cabinet. General Hariri became minister of defence. The move of
General Haddad to the sinecure Ministry of Planning left the vital post of
director of officers' affairs to Salah Jadid.

The cabinet changes in Syria were paralleled by a similar purge in
Iraq. Brigadier Bakr's cabinet resigned and Bakr formed a new cabinet
in which the Nasserite element was entirely eliminated. A purge with
arrests and executions of the Nasserite element in the army followed. To
maintain unity, the Iraqi government then instituted a violent campaign
against the Iraqi communist party, with a number of mass executions.
The campaign broke the hold of the Iraqi communists on the Baghdad
mob, and practically eliminated the riot as an element in Iraqi politics.
At the same time, Bakr moved against the supporters of Michel Aflaq
within the Iraqi Ba'th.

This dual defeat of the elements on which President Nasser most relied
was followed by a period of increasing tension in Egypt's relations with
Iraq and Syria. The Ba'th in Syria followed Iraq's example in recruiting
a National Guard of a paramilitary character. At the same time they took
strong measures to provide themselves with a broader base. The party
embarked on indiscriminate recruiting at all levels, doing its best to win
over from the Nasserite camp the student organizations and such labour
unions as existed. In the course of this five-fold expansion of the party
membership, the minority elements and the regionalists greatly increased
their hold on the party machinery. The supporters of Michel Aflaq, who
had seen the whole post-coup era as his chance to outmanœuvre Akram
Hourani and to capture the leadership of the whole party for himself, were
themselves outmanœuvred by a group led by Hamid al-Shufi, a Druse,
and Ahmed Abu Salih, a Sunni lawyer from Aleppo, allies of the Military
Committee.

The weakening of Aflaq and Bitar's position showed first of all in June
1963 when General Hariri was forced out of office, and General Amin al-
Hafiz, as he now was, took over the vacant portfolio of defence. The
National Guard was mobilized and Hariri, having rejected the post of
military attaché in Washington, thought it wise to accept a similar post in
Paris.

The advance of the Ba'thi officers to power in Syria was accompanied
by a steady stream of gestures designed to establish their claim to be true
Arab socialists. The nationalization of the banks had just preceded the
fall of the first Bitar government and the resignation of the Nasserite
ministers. The crisis with General Hariri was accompanied by the
promulgation of a new agrarian law severely limiting landownership and
making peasant purchase of land much easier.

These developments were watched by the Egyptians with increasing
hostility. The new Bitar cabinet of May 1963 was dismissed by Cairo radio

as an unjustified blow to the union, and the Voice of the Arab Nation, an 'unofficial' nationalist propagandist radio broadcasting from Cairo, became the vehicle for Cairo's attacks on the Ba'th agents in Syria. The Damascus radio and press retaliated in kind, and relations steadily deteriorated until on 18 July General Luayy al-Atasi led a delegation to Alexandria to try to break the deadlock in implementing the April agreement.

That same day, presumably with Egyptian encouragement, the Nasserite elements in Damascus attempted a *coup d'état*. Some two thousand troops and civilian elements were involved, led by Colonel Jasim Alwan. The coup was only suppressed after severe and bloody fighting with many hundreds of casualties. Colonel Alwan and the Nasserite members of the first Bitar cabinet managed to escape into exile. But twenty of the leaders were immediately executed—a not abnormal procedure by Iraqi standards but a completely new and horrifying element in Syrian practice. Luayy al-Atasi resigned in protest and the presidency of the NCRC and the position of commander-in-chief of the Army passed to General Hafiz.

The suppression of the coup and the exile or execution of his adherents deprived President Nasser of any remaining hopes he might have had of events in Syria moving in his direction. In a speech of 22 July[1] he denounced the April agreement as impossible to maintain with a regime he described as Fascist, 'non-unionist and non-socialist', and 'secessionist, inhumane and immoral'. 'We cannot', he said, 'presume to unite under the shadow of scaffolds, blood baths and collective massacres.' General Hafiz was denounced as the 'shedder of blood'. He followed these denunciations with a second speech, delivered on 28 July at the University of Alexandria, damning the Ba'thists as the party of irreligion and heresy, and less than genuine Arabs. His attack on Michel Aflaq, however, showed how very far he was from appreciating the real shift in power in Syria, a picture which was confirmed by the records of the March and April conferences which were broadcast continuously on Cairo radio.

On 4 August the third Bitar cabinet was announced in Damascus. It lived up to Nasser's denunciation by consisting entirely of Ba'this and 'independent Unionists'. It included two Druses, representatives of the Ismaili and Alawite communities, a Syrian Kurd, and a Greek Orthodox among its members. The orthodox Sunni Moslem upper middle class families of Damascus and Aleppo, merchants, bankers, middlemen, with their political tails of client traders, owners of small-scale workshops with their employees, apprentices, relatives, etc., who had provided the basis of the moderate traditional Syrian political 'parties' were totally excluded from power. The Egyptian denunciations struck particularly strong echoes among their number and faced the new regime with the problem of legitimacy all the stronger.

[1] American University of Beirut, *Arab political documents, 1963* (Beirut, 1964), pp. 332–3.

To cope with this problem the new Syrian cabinet embarked on a double course. Hafiz and Bitar, heads respectively of the military and civilian sides of the government (and both, incidentally, Sunni Moslems), began a programme of receiving delegations from all over Syria. At the same time, both at the party and the government level, the Ba'th leadership turned towards Iraq.

The Iraqis had been powerless spectators at this exacerbation of relations between their two would-be partners in the union. So far as the Ba'thi element in the Iraqi government was concerned, their sympathies were naturally with their Syrian confreres. President Arif, conservative in his religion, an orthodox Sunni, an old Nasserite whose enthusiasm for socialism was a good deal less than absolute, did his best in visits to Cairo and Damascus in August 1963 to mediate between the two capitals, but in vain. On his return from Damascus the establishment of joint Syrian–Iraqi committees to speed up co-operation in the field of defence and to open the way to complete economic co-operation was announced.[1] This was followed on 28 September by an announcement from the Sixth National Congress of the Ba'th party meeting in Damascus that Syria and Iraq were to form a popular Socialist democratic state.[2] The formation of a supreme Iraqi–Syrian Defence Council was announced on 8 October, by a treaty of military union.[3] The Iraqi minister of defence, General Salih Mahdi Ammash, was appointed commander-in-chief of the combined armies of the two countries with headquarters in Damascus. And a Syrian brigade was sent to Iraq to participate in operations against the Kurdish insurgents.[4]

This movement towards the establishment of a Ba'thi-dominated state of the Fertile Crescent represented the resurrection of a threat to Egypt which had first materialized with Nuri es-Said and the Hashemite dynasties of Iraq and Jordan, and which had done more than anything else to involve Egypt in the mainstream of pan-Arab politics in the 1940s. It seemed, however, that President Nasser was powerless to prevent it. That it failed to materialize was due to the combination of three factors, the ineptness of the Ba'thi leadership in Iraq, changes in the balance of power within the Syrian wing of the party, and the differing nature of the social composition of the party and the role it played in the very different societies of Syria and Iraq. As has been pointed out above, the Ba'th in Syria represented a coalition between a variety of groups, of which 'regionalists', Marxists, and members of the minority sects, Alawites, Druses, Ismailis, and others were the most important. The younger university-educated sons of established families tended to be Nasserite rather than Ba'thi in their politics. The minorities were

---

[1] Ibid., pp. 370–1. [2] Ibid., pp. 381–4.
[3] *Documents, 1963*, p. 315. [4] See below, pp. 206–12.

particularly well established in the officer corps, and had been so even in the days of the French occupation.

In Iraq, by contrast, the Ba'th was much more the party of the Sunni Moslem 'have-nots' in the cities. Its organization was essentially conspiratorial, an absolute necessity both under Nuri es-Said and the Qasim regime. Although it certainly enjoyed the support of elements in the officer corps, it preferred to rest its support on the paramilitary force, the National Guard, with which it could dominate and turn to its purposes the urban mob in Baghdad and the other cities. But the existence of the National Guard raised eventually the twin questions of its control and of competition with the armed forces. The officer corps, especially the senior commanders, were inevitably alarmed and alienated, especially as they had their hands full with the control of the Kurdish risings.

In Syria the drive towards a Ba'thi state raised in its strongest form the question of the leadership of the party. It has already been pointed out that at the outset of the Syrian Ba'thi regime, after the coup of March 1963, the party leadership was divided between adherents of Akram Hourani and of Michel Aflaq, the two ideologues of the party most involved in the union of 1958–62 and its break-up. In the manœuvres of March–May 1963 Hourani came off very much worse; and he was indeed among the so-called 'secessionists' arrested in May 1963 and indicted in August as part of the Bitar cabinet's campaign to demonstrate its Arab orthodoxy. But the Ba'thi drive to acquire mass support to balance that enjoyed by their Nasserite rivals had the effect of converting Aflaq's supporters, in turn, into a minority within the party. The party apparatus fell into the hands of Hamid al-Shufi, a Druse, and Ahmed Abu Salih, a Sunni lawyer from Aleppo, who allied themselves with the members of the Military Committee.

This emerged very strongly with the conference of the Syrian regional wing in September. All eight seats on the so-called Regional Command of the party were won by Aflaq's rivals, Shufi becoming secretary, and three officers, one from the Military Committee, being among his colleagues.[1] The majority of the eighteen Syrian delegates elected to the sixth national [i.e. pan-Arab] congress of the Ba'th which met in Damascus in October was equally controlled by Aflaq's rivals. The Iraqi delegation was equally divided, the main rivalry being between the moderate faction led by Hazim Jawad and Talih Shabib, who were in the minority, and the more radical faction led by Ali Salih al-Sa'di, the organizer and controller of the Iraqi National Guard. The radicals were not quite ready to force Aflaq out of the position of secretary-general to

[1] Nur ad-Din al-Atasi (from Homs), Khalid al-Hakim, Mahmud Naufal, Ahmed Abu Salih (Aleppo), Colonel Hamad Ubaid (a Druse), Colonel Hafiz al-Asad (an Alawite, member of the Military Committee), Captain Muhammed Rabah at-Tawil.

the party, as he still enjoyed the support of the Lebanese and Jordanian delegates and an enormous prestige. But he could not prevent the congress from calling for written self-criticism from 'those Comrades responsible for' the party's policy in Syria from the mid-1950s until 1963 or imposing on itself a series of resolutions which, despite numerous amendments, in effect relegated Arab unity to a secondary position to the need for a socialist revolution and the 'liquidation of exploitation', especially by the 'national bourgeoisie' and its petty bourgeois allies. 'Popular Democracy', conceived as a para-Leninist alliance of workers, peasants, petty bourgeois, and revolutionary intellectuals under the leadership of the 'revolutionary vanguard' operating according to the principles of 'democratic centralism', was to be the central goal of the party.

The resolutions of the conference[1] represented a rather muddled attempt to adapt these new ideological 'Points of Departure' with the realities of the Syrian scene and the comparative weakness of the Ba'th party. Nevertheless the proceedings of the congress as a whole represent a determined attempt to put forward a version of Arab revolutionary nationalism which would, by its secular nature, destroy the threat to the Syrian minorities which Nasser's religious conservatism represented and at the same time appeal to the desire of the politically conscious 'have nots' in Arab society to support an Arab ideology that promised them power.

If Aflaq survived the congress, Bitar did not, nor did his Iraqi allies or rivals. On 12 November, Bitar resigned and General Hafiz became premier. Salah Jadid, the Alawite founder of the Military Committee became chief of staff. Mohammed Umran, the principal Alawite rival to Hafiz, became deputy premier. More regionalist members of the radical wing of the party were added to the cabinet.

The moderate minority in the Iraqi delegation appear to have returned home conscious for the first time of the very serious differences between the Syrian faction and themselves and determined to break al-Sa'di's strength and the support he enjoyed from the Syrian radicals. On 11 November they forced the election of a new Regional Command, and bundled al-Sa'di and his principal ally, the secretary of the Iraqi regional wing, into a plane for Madrid. The National Guard then broke into violent disorder between factions of al-Sa'di and the moderates, and some of al-Sa'di's supporters even attacked the military. The National Command of the party was summoned from Damascus at the instance of the Iraqi minister of defence, the Regional Command was dissolved, and the moderates Shabib and Jawad induced to go into exile in Beirut. All of this took place at the party level without any meeting of the Iraqi NCRC, the supreme constitutional authority in Iraq and the embodiment of the

[1] *Arab political documents, 1963*, pp. 438-44.

army leadership, although the effects of the party action were the removal of four leading cabinet members from office.

This, more than anything else, prompted President Arif into action. On 18 November he took full emergency powers in the name of the NCRC, dissolved the National Guard, and appointed the chief of staff, General Tahir Yahya, as prime minister. The Air Force commander, Brigadier Takriti, became minister of defence. General Ahmad Hasan al-Bakr, the former premier and one of the five Iraqi members of the Ba'th National Command, became deputy premier. But the new regime, it soon became clear, was in no way Ba'thist in sympathy. Arif himself was a pan-Arab nationalist and a supporter of President Nasser.

With this, the Syrian bid to make Ba'thist doctrine an alternative focus for Arab nationalist aspirations virtually collapsed. Syria once again was isolated within the Arab world. Damascus and Baghdad were embroiled in a vicious propaganda battle. The Syrian extremists even turned in their folly on Hafiz and the military committee. With this, however, they went too far. The new Syrian regional congress meeting in February 1964 saw an alliance between the military committee and Aflaq's faction. A new Syrian regional command of seven military and eight civilians, dominated by General Hafiz, was elected. And the seventh National Congress meeting on 12 February 1964 was flooded with obedient delegates from some fictitious branches (there were even five delegates from Yugoslavia!). The ultra-leftists were expelled from the new National Command, and the Shufi faction, deprived of its leader, dismissed from the regional secretary-generalship, collapsed. The minority element was stronger than ever (the six Syrian members of the National Command in February 1964 were all from different minority groups; of the twelve members of the Regional Command, three were Alawis, two were Druses, two Ismailis); but the defeat of the extremists had already been demonstrated. The regime had to proceed shortly thereafter to the violent suppression of Sunni Moslem discontent in Banyas, Homs, and Hama. Bitar made a comeback as premier of a new Syrian cabinet in May 1964. But the course of Syrian politics thereafter was to reveal the continuing problem to which the lack of any recognized source of legitimacy gave rise.

(b) *Iraq and the Kurdish problem*

Nowhere was the question of legitimacy more of an embarrassment to the political regime than in Iraq. Reference has already been made to the fragmented state of Iraqi politics, the Arab population being divided so deeply between Sunni and Shi'ite. The position was, however, even more complicated by the existence in the northern third of Iraq of a race whose very existence made a nonsense of the idea of Iraq being part of the Arab nation. The Kurdish nationalist movement has been dealt with

before in the pages of the *Survey of international affairs*.[1] In Iraq it comprised
an uneasy alliance between the tribal adherents of Mulla Mustafa Barzani,
a brilliant guerrilla leader, and the intellectuals of the Kurdish Democratic
Party. Barzani had a long record as a leader of Kurdish nationalist up-
risings. He had led the 1945 uprising in Iraq, served with the so-called
Kurdish republic of Mahabad in Iran in 1946[2] and, on its suppression, had
taken refuge in the Soviet Union, where the rank of general had been conferred upon him. It was with Soviet assistance that he had returned to
Iraq in 1958 after the overthrow of the monarchy.

Despite this apparent record of pan-Kurdish revolutionary activity,
Mulla Mustafa Barzani was essentially concerned with the Kurds of
Iraq alone, among whom his tribe was the largest and wealthiest. He was,
in fact, much more indispensable to the intellectuals of the KDP than
they to him. His prestige, his powers of leadership among the tribes, his
international connections were of immense advantage to them. The confinement of his ambitions to Iraq made him *persona grata* to the Turks and
Iranians as well as to the Soviets, each of which, remembering their own
Kurdish minorities, might have looked at him askance. His twelve years
of exile in the Soviet Union had immunized him against any tendencies
towards social change he might otherwise have been expected to enter-
tain. He leaned, in fact, heavily towards the maintenance of the traditional
organs of Kurdish society in which, by virtue of his blood, his birth, his
ability, and experience, he was the recognized leader.

The KDP, by contrast, lacked any outstanding leader, preferring a
collegiate direction, with a political bureau of six members and a central
committee of twenty-one. Its aspirations, like its history, were pan-
Kurdish, the KDP of Iraq being the surviving wing of an organization
founded in Iran in 1945, itself the heir to a succession of organizations
mainly clandestine, whose overt activities could only manifest themselves
among Kurdish exiles in Cairo or Paris. Its members were urbanized,
detribalized, professionally educated intellectuals and its organization
correspondingly rigidly structured, with an agreed 'party line' and
ideology. Essentially it was a nationalist quasi-conspiratorial political
organization of the didactic, reformist left.

On his return to Iraq in 1958, Barzani had initially supported the
regime of Qasim; his efforts were mainly devoted to securing the leadership within the tribes. Frequent inter-tribal clashes and the murder of
a former Kurdish member of the Iraqi national assembly marked his path
to success. As Qasim came for a time heavily under the influence of the

[1] *Survey of international affairs, 1939–1946, The Middle East in the war*, pp. 156, 466–7; *Survey,
The Middle East, 1945–1950*, pp. 62, 72, 83, 147; *Survey, 1961*, pp. 518, 545; *Survey, 1962*, p. 478.
[2] On the Kurdish republic of Mahabad see William Eagleton, *The Kurdish republic of 1946*
(London, 1963).

Iraqi Communist Party, so their efforts were concentrated against the urban Kurdish populations and the KDP. The Mosul massacres in 1961 were directed against KDP claims on the surrounding oilfields as Kurdish rather than Arab property. The Kurdish alarm and fury at the massacres led directly to the rising of the Kurdish tribes under Barzani's leadership in December 1961. A Kurdish 'government' was established for a time in the mountain town of Amadija. Iraqi reluctance to commit ground forces in the inhospitable mountain terrain led to an ill-judged attempt to control the rising by aerial bombardment of Kurdish townships and villages and the imposition of a blockade of the mountains. The effect of this was to drive the wobblers and neutrals into Barzani's camp. Armed groups came together into the *Lachkari Shawreshgari Kurd* (Kurdish Revolutionary Army) whose strength was speedily augmented by Kurdish deserters and prisoners of Kurdish origin from the Iraqi army. Offers of amnesties, as in March 1962 and January 1963, were met by counter-demands for genuine Kurdish autonomy within an Iraq governed by constitution not by military fiat.

The KDP took a little time to recover from the initial suppression of the rising of September 1961 and to define their attitude to Barzani's leadership. But the success of the LSK drove their more adventurous members into the hills to join its ranks. From volunteering to the sporadic proselytization of KDP doctrines, to the establishment of KDP political 'advisers' at the shoulder of the LSK unit commanders and the attempt to carry through agrarian reform in areas under Kurdish control were logical developments limited by the difficulty of imposing ideas of urban intellectual origin upon land-hungry devotees of the practice of peasant proprietorship. By January 1963 the Barzani forces had brought about the virtual collapse of Iraqi defences in Northern Iraq.

The military coup d'état by Ba'thist officers of 8 February 1963 followed the normal traditions of such coups in proffering the 'hand of friendship' to the Kurdish people. A Kurdish officer, Brigadier Fu'ad Arif, became minister of state, and Hasim Jawad, one of the leading members of the National Committee of the Revolutionary Council, was quoted on Baghdad radio as alleging that the Kurdish issue had been fabricated by the Qasim regime in order to undermine Iraqi unity.[1] Not to be outdone, the Barzanists in north Iraq were quoted as talking of the brotherhood of Kurds and Arabs; more seriously their message spoke of the 'realization of autonomy within true Iraqi unity', a theme echoed in a message from KDP members in Baghdad who spoke of 'just self-government within the beloved Iraqi people'. This last message bore Brigadier Fu'ad Arif's name.

The Ba'thist officers of the new regime began by recognizing the 'nationalist rights of the Kurdish people on the basis of decentralization'

[1] *SWB*, ME 1175/A/1, 15 Feb. 1963.

in an NCRC statement of 9 February 1963. 'Co-operation among Arabs, Kurds and other nationalities' the statement said, constituted the basis of Iraq's unity.[1] A law of amnesty was announced.[2] And a special committee was set up to draw up the broad lines of 'decentralization'. This, so Ali Salih al-Sa'di, the new deputy premier, said in an interview on Damascus radio, in no way implied Kurdish secession. The new local administration would not handle foreign policy; nor would they deal with economic or defence matters.[3] The blockade of the Kurdish-held areas was lifted on 18 March.

These new developments contained within themselves the seeds of future disagreement. In the first place, the NCRC's ideology with its heavy emphasis on the organic unity of the Arab people made it, in an Iraqi context, particularly hostile to 'divisionism' (shu'ubiyya), that is, the encouragement of non-Arab nationalism. It was, in their doctrine, an imperialist invention. The inclusion of various arabized Kurds such as Fu'ad Arif in the NCRC administration in comparatively subordinate positions was as far as they could be expected to go: and any sign of outside support for Kurdish aspirations was certain to awaken their suspicions.

In the second place, the NCRC found themselves faced with two Kurdish organizations, the KDP and the Barzanists. The principal Kurdish representative in the subsequent negotiations, Jalal al-Talabani, was of KDP origin though more than a little independently ambitious. Having decided to enlist the support of other Arab leaders, he visited Cairo and Algiers at the end of February 1963, action which gave him an international status he was quick to exploit and which the NCRC found impossible to reconcile ideologically with what to them were essentially discussions about local government reform. The temptation to play the KDP off against the Barzanists, and, after he had established residence abroad and began visiting Kurdish communities in Europe, denouncing al-Talabani for shu'ubiyya, was to prove too difficult to resist.

In the third place, the success of al-Talabani in Cairo and elsewhere in no way discouraged the Kurds, whether Barzanist or KDP, from interpreting decentralization as implying autonomy. In Algiers, Ben Bella publicly praised the Kurdish movements while in Cairo, according to Mohammed Haikal's later revelations in al-Ahram,[4] al-Talabani defined autonomy as 'involving an executive and a legislative council as in any state in India. We Kurds do not want or seek secession . . . all we are afraid of is that the fighting will begin again.' 'Autonomy' was the only basis on which any Kurd who hoped to retain any position of authority among his fellows would settle, whether within an independent Iraq, or an Iraq as a member

[1] Ibid., ME/1197/A/1–2, 12 Mar. 1963; Arab political documents, 1963, p. 8.
[2] SWB, ME/1198/i, 13 Mar. 1963.   [3] Ibid., ME/1199/A/3–5, 14 Mar. 1963.
[4] Cited in ibid., ME/1288/A 2–2, 1 July 1963.

of an Arab federation or a unified Arab state, depending on the development of Arab unity. The, at first sight, successful outcome of the talks in Cairo between Egypt, Syria, and Iraq only strengthened their determination on this point.

In the fourth place, the Communist reactions to the violent action taken by the NCRC against the Iraqi Communist Party switched at once from supporting action against the Kurds by Qasim to incitement of the Kurds not to accept the blandishments of the new regime. As early as 12 February an alleged statement by the Iraqi Communist leadership appealing to the Kurds not to support the regime was broadcast on East German radio.[1] After the arrest and execution of the secretary and the other members of the Central Committee of the Iraqi Communist Party by the NCRC, Radio Iran Courier, a Soviet-sponsored 'black radio' broadcasting (actually from Soviet Azerbaijan) in Persian, Arabic, and Kurdish, began a series of broadcasts designed to represent the Barzanists as hostile to the Ba'thist regime.[2] On 19 April,[3] for example, it alleged that the Iraqi government was discussing joint measures against the Kurds with the Turkish and Iranian governments. Similar warnings were issued on 13 May both by RIC, and the clandestine Turkish Communist radio,[4] while five days later the 'National Voice of Iran', another black radio less obviously identifiable with the Tudeh party, announced that Iraqi military operations against the Kurds had reopened[5] (a piece of clairvoyance to be confirmed by the events of 10 June).

The negotiations themselves are difficult to follow in detail. The critical period appears to have come during the Cairo unity talks. On 4 April al-Talabani was quoted by Reuters as saying that 'under special circumstances the Kurds were prepared to delegate questions of defence, foreign policy and financial affairs to the Iraqi Central Government'.[6] This corresponds very closely with the definition of decentralization by Ali Salih al-Sa'di quoted above. The Kurdish demands of 24 April[7] went, however, a long way further than this; while conceding citizenship of Iraq and no separatism they demanded a share of the revenues from the 'Kurdish' oilfields of Mosul and Kirkuk and that the 'Kurdish national armed forces' be stationed on Kurdish territory.

Under the circumstances, Hazim Jawad's remark, quoted by the Iraqi News Agency on 29 April, that having studied decentralization with a view to its implementation in practice, the national authorities of Iraq

[1] *SWB*, ME/1175/i, 15 Feb. 1963.
[2] *SWB*, ME/1215/A/6–7, 2 Apr. 1963; ME/1220/A/2, 8 Apr. 1963.
[3] *SWB*, ME/1230/D/1–2, 23 Apr. 1963.
[4] *SWB*, ME/1251/i, 17 May 1963.   [5] *SWB*, ME/1254/D/1–2, 21 May 1963.
[6] *SWB*, ME/1220/A/2, 8 Apr. 1963. See also the Memorandum of 8 April presented by the Kurdish members of the delegation in Cairo, *Arab political documents, 1963*, pp. 222–3.
[7] *Arab political documents, 1963*, pp. 248–51.

were not 'prepared to allow anything to happen which might shatter the united struggle of Arabs and Kurds', was understandable, if ominous.[1] Barzani, it emerged, was struck by the Iraqi failure to release Kurdish prisoners under the terms of the amnesty. Optimistic noises made by al-Talabani in mid-May did nothing to bridge the gap and on 10 June the NCRC issued a proclamation denouncing Barzani as a factionalist (*shu'ubiyuu*) and putting a price of 10,000 dinars on his head. Barzani, the proclamation alleged, wrongly claimed the right to represent all Kurds. He had supported the Qasim regime. His men had participated in the Mosul and Kirkuk massacres in 1959. He had showed 'friendliness to local Communists in their criminal and hostile policy towards the people'. He had a 'clear feudalist identity'. He had a 'relationship with imperialism and Zionist antagonism and their committing of crimes towards other Kurdish citizens'. His followers continued to exercise authority, fired on Iraqi troops and police, arrested Iraqi officials, attacked arms stores and seized arms, and incited Kurdish members of the army and the police to desert. 'As from today', the proclamation continued, it had been decided to clear the 'remnants of the Barzanis and their followers from the northern regions of Iraq.' The rebels were given 24 hours to surrender. The north of Iraq was to be considered as a war zone.[2]

The Iraqis scored a certain success for the time being in parading various other Kurdish feudal leaders, rival agas, to denounce Barzani. In October they even induced his brother to declare for the government. But although individual KDP personalities at first acceded to NCRC's propaganda, it took the KDP only six weeks to see that negotiation with the Ba'thist officers was impossible. At the end of June al-Talabani was already addressing groups of Communist Kurdish *émigrés* in Berlin (and receiving publicity for this over Radio Iran Courier). On 4 August an official KDP statement was issued accusing the NCRC of having gone back on its agreement and proclamation of 9 March and saying of its proposals for decentralization that 'no sincere or honourable Kurd can accept this cheap price for his struggle and bloodshed'.[3]

The Iraqi assault was no more successful under President Arif than that under Qasim had been. The date for final surrender was regularly advanced, regular victories and lifting of the blockade on selected areas were announced, mopping-up operations were said to be all that were left; but all in vain. A novelty was the arrival of Syrian troops in October to take part in the action against the Kurds, in consequence of the Treaty of Military Union of 8 October. President Arif's overthrow of the Ba'thi officers in mid-November and the appointment of the partisans of Bakr

[1] *SWB*, ME/1237/A/3-4, 1 May 1963.
[2] *SWB*, ME/1771/A/5-8, 11 June 1963. See also *Arab political documents, 1963*, pp. 285-90.
[3] *SWB*, ME/1319/A/6-7, 7 Aug. 1963.

and Air Force commander Takriti was made the occasion for new offers of amnesty and clemency.[1] But the Barzanis were by now immune to such diplomacy. Iraq retained its divided state, and the Kurds remained in control of their mountain fastnesses.

(c) *The Jordan waters crisis*

The future of the hopes, if any, President Nasser had pinned on the strength of the popular support his name could arouse in Syria and Iraq and the defeat of Ba'th hopes of an Arab union under their revamped revolutionary ideology had profound effects for the future of the Middle East and for the relations of its states with the outside world. These events implied the destruction of any possibility that the very strong consciousness of identity within diversity throughout the Arabic-speaking world including North Africa would find any political expression other than in its reactions to the external world. The *dar al-Islam* of the twentieth century could be defined only in terms of its relations with the *dar al-Harb* and by nothing else. The events of 1947–9 had provided its members with a permanent embodiment of that hostile external world, the world of imperialism, in their midst, the state of Israel. By that and by that alone could Arab states and governments now appeal for recognition and legitimization.

The intrusion into the various internecine Arab conflicts at the end of 1963 of the issue of the Jordan waters, and the rapid if temporary suppression of those conflicts at the Arab summit of January 1964 provides a more remarkable illustration of this development in that so much of the conflict stemmed from exactly these issues of legitimization discussed in the preceding sections.

The river Jordan provides the main, almost the only, source of water for Israel, Jordan, and the southern sections of Syria and the Lebanon. Its tributaries, the Hisbani, the Banias, and the Dan, with sources inside the Lebanon, Syria, and Israel met, under the demarcation lines of 1956, inside Israeli territory to form the river Jordan. From their juncture the Jordan flowed through Israeli territory down the Hulah Valley into Lake Tiberias. Emerging again at the south end of Lake Tiberias, it flowed for five miles through Israeli territory or through the then demilitarized zones to the point where it joined the river Yarmuk, which formed the Syrian–Jordanian frontier. For the next twenty miles it divided Israeli-held territory from that held by Jordan and then flowed for forty miles through Jordanian-held territory until it emptied itself in the Dead Sea. Of its total flow of 1,800 million cubic metres, about 77 per cent originated in Arab-held territories, 23 per cent in land held by Israel.

The idea of using the common sharing of the Jordan waters as a link

[1] *Arab political documents, 1963*, p. 486.

between the riparian states had been advanced in the 1950s by President Eisenhower's emissary, Johnston. In furtherance of his abortive project, Israeli engineers had embarked on a project to pump water from the Hulah Valley through pipelines to Israel's developing south, the Negev, but had stopped after Security Council protests. The need for water in the south had, however, remained unsatisfied. Early in 1958, Israel began allocation of funds for an alternative scheme to pump water from Lake Tiberias, 700 feet below sea level up to the top of the intervening range of hills, some 1,200 feet above sea-level where gravity flow would carry it through 150 miles of pipes to the Negev. The irrigation of the Negev would, it was hoped, provide for up to a million more settlers, would raise Israel's agrarian exports, and, above all, counter the increasing salinity of the existing water sources which was imperilling the land's fertility. The first phase was due to be finished in 1963. The plan involved the drawing off of 320 million cubic metres. The scheme had given rise to discussion in the Arab press of various proposals to interfere with the flow of the various tributaries of the Jordan which were in Arab-controlled territory. These schemes had been taken sufficiently seriously for Israel to issue a warning, embodied in a speech made on 17 February 1963 by Yigael Allon, the minister for labour, that any attempt of this kind would be considered as an act of aggression.[1]

For much of the summer the attention of the Arab states was taken up with the unity negotiations and their breakdown. The Jordan waters issue became acute, however, at the beginning of September. On 3 September Sayed Nofal, the assistant secretary-general of the Arab League, sounded the warning[2] and it was reported that the Arab League Council would meet on 9 September to consider ways of blocking the Israeli plan. Neither this report nor a subsequent report that the Council of Arab Defence Ministers would meet to study the situation had any chance of realization given the current state of inter-Arab relations. Characteristically it was Syria through Salah al-Bitar who turned the issue into the support of Syrian claims for legitimacy by challenging the other Arab states to support her. Syria, he said, would prevent the diversion by all the means at her disposal, even if she were compelled to act alone. But Syria would not remain alone since the Iraqi army would help her.

This somewhat fustian bombast (the Iraqi army at the time had their hands full with the Kurds and, as noted above, a Syrian brigade was shortly to be sent to their assistance) was echoed at the time of the signature of the Syrian-Iraqi military treaty. In a statement of 28 October 1963 the two governments threatened the use of force to counter the diversion of the Jordan waters.[3] These remarks were taken at little value in Cairo.

[1] *Daily Telegraph*, 18 Feb. 1963. [2] *Dawn*, 4 Sept. 1963.
[3] *Daily Telegraph*, 29 Oct. 1963.

The view in Egyptian military circles was that none of the Arab armies was militarily prepared to deal with Israel, least of all the Syrian army after all the purges and counter-purges of the previous three years. Something, however, had to be done to counter the burden of Syrian propaganda which grew increasingly hysterical as the Syrians felt increasingly isolated. At the end of October, therefore, President Nasser convened a meeting of Arab chiefs of staff in Cairo. The meeting, which took place eventually on 7 December, was attended by representatives of Egypt, Syria, Iraq, Jordan, the Lebanon, Saudi Arabia, Kuwait, the Yemen, Algeria, and Libya. There was a joint Syrian-Iraqi delegation as, despite the total breakdown of Iraqi-Syrian relations after President Arif's coup of 18 November, the joint military command established by the treaty of 28 October was still in being. The mood among the delegates initially tended towards military action as demanded by Syria, as the only alternative, presumably, to the disastrous loss of prestige (with all its political implications) that inaction would involve. But Ali Sabri, the Egyptian premier, dealt with such aspirations very firmly. While Marshal Amer, the Egyptian commander-in-chief, told the opening session that some action must be taken to prevent the catastrophe,[1] Sabri told them that President Kennedy had made it clear before his death that if any attack was made on Israel over the Jordan waters issue, Israel would have American support. The Arabs, said Sabri, could not under present circumstances count on Soviet support. The military should therefore be realistic and not mix propaganda with military planning.

This cold dose of political realism would have been adequate if left as it was. But the Egyptian propaganda apparatus was unfortunately no more responsible to Sabri than the generals. Allegations that the governments of Jordan, Syria, and Saudi Arabia were hoping to embroil Egypt with Israel so that they might 'stab her in the back' may only have been intended to justify Egyptian inaction to her own people. But they provoked violent reactions in Syria, Jordan, and in the Lebanese press. The worst offence was caused by an article in *Rose al-Yusuf*'s issue of 17 December 1963, which was denounced by Hussein ibn-Nasser, the Jordanian premier, as 'an insult' and drove *al-Ba'th* to compare President Nasser to Marshal Pétain.

On 23 December, therefore, in a speech at Port Said which it is difficult not to see as a highly successful attempt to regain the initiative, President Nasser called for a meeting of Arab kings and heads of state.[2] He made it fairly clear that in his view force could not be used at that time. But he, characteristically, laid even more emphasis on his determination that whatever might occur at the conference, it would all be in the open; 'we will not say one thing behind closed doors and another thing outside'.

[1] *NY Times*, 8 Dec. 1963.   [2] *Documents, 1963*, pp. 315–21.

War against Israel was he said a political matter, not to be decided by the
Army chiefs of staff or at a purely military level.

The conference was attended by virtually every Arab ruler of note.[1]
President Nasser gave a particularly cordial welcome, followed by private
conference, to King Hussein, to Ben Bella, and to President Arif. General
Hafiz got a polite handshake, no more; even though he stayed an entire
day in the hope of a private meeting. The Saudi acceptance of the invitation came very late. King Sa'ud was in fact in very ill health. He had to be
supported while disembarking at Cairo airport. An indication of Sa'ud's
feelings was given by the fact that the first off his plane was a Saudi guard
with sub-machine gun at the ready.

President Nasser's behaviour at the conference itself was a little difficult
to reconcile with the promises of openness given in his speech of 23
December. His opening speech was embarked upon in the mistaken
apprehension that he was speaking in a closed session. After a few sentences he stopped, alerted by a tap on the shoulder from Marshal Amer
to the fact that the proceedings were being televised. There were a few
seconds, seemingly interminable. Then the hall was cleared.

The burden of his speech was the impossibility of action. Arab political
feuds should be buried, a united Arab military command set up. The
Jordan's waters should be diverted before they reached Israeli territory.
Only long-term preparations could deal with Israel. But the details are
less important in themselves than for the tactical skill with which President
Nasser employed them. In the settlement of Moroccan–Algerian differences, the initiation of Saudi–Yemeni talks, the granting of Iraqi
recognition to the government of Kuwait, and the restoration of diplomatic
relations between Egypt and Jordan ('reconciliation by mass production'
in the headlines phrase of *L'Orient* of Beirut), Amin al-Hafiz, the Syrian
leader, found himself totally isolated. His denunciation of the 'psychosis of
fear', which paralysed Arab states face to face with Israel, and his declaration that Syria was ready to fight with or without her Arab brothers were
effectively put in their place by the other speeches. A Jordanian proposal
for regular meetings every six months was accepted. And Nasser's two
proposals, a unified Arab command and a technical commission to discuss
the diversion of Jordan waters, were accepted.[2] Marshal Amer became
head of the unified command, and a £15m. subsidy for arms purchases
was raised for Syria, Jordan, and the Lebanon to be paid from the oil
revenues of Kuwait, Saudi Arabia, and Iraq. Arab foreign ministers

[1] Ibrahim Abboud (Sudan), Abdullah al-Salim as-Sabah (Kuwait), President Arif (Iraq),
Premier Rashid Karami (the Lebanon), Mohammed Ben Bella (Algeria), Prince Hassan ar-Rida
al-Sennussi (Libya), King Hassan (Morocco), President Habib Bourguiba (Tunis), Abdullah
as-Sallal (the Yemen), King Sa'ud (Saudi Arabia), King Hussein (Jordan), General al-Hafiz
(Syria).

[2] For the final statement of the Conference see *Documents, 1963*, pp. 321–2.

embarked on a series of travels to agitate against Israeli exploitation of the
Jordan waters; and Hafiz was forced to return to Damascus to face the
denunciations of Shufi's supporters for unnecessary concessions and for
missing the chance of using the Jordan waters issue to push the Arabs into
war with Israel and of exposing 'to the masses' the regimes which were
really hostile to the Arab revolution and conspired 'with imperialism in the
Arab homeland'.

Israel had become the sole yardstick by which Arab regimes could
claim legitimacy and authenticity. The subsequent defeat of Shufi's
faction, although this by no means marked the end of the Ba'th's flirtation
with an Arabized version of Marxism (rather the contrary), put Hafiz's
regime in a less vulnerable position. But the Ba'th's accusations made it
virtually impossible for any Arab regime to seek to compromise on the
issue of Israel. Even though Palestinians complained bitterly that 'the war
they have been promising us for fifteen years has been put off to the Greek
Kalends',[1] the issue of Israel had been injected into the domestic politics
of every Arab state.

The Jordan waters crisis itself fizzled away. Israel began pumping
water from Lake Tiberias to Tel Aviv on 5 May 1964 as a test. By the
summer of that year the Kinneret–Negev pipeline was delivering half a
million cubic metres of water a day. The Arab technical commission
duly discussed projects to divert the waters of the Hisbani within Lebanon
into the river Litani and those of the Banias into the river Yarmuk, but
the difficulty of defending the workings, once embarked upon, against
Israeli attack rendered these plans futile. The only project put into effect
was the diversion of some of the river Yarmuk's waters from the Mukheiba
dam along the East Ghor canal, a project of great economic benefit to
Jordan and already under consideration. Jordan now found the Arab
states committed to paying the bulk of the costs. The work was undertaken by an Egyptian company to symbolize the new spirit of co-operation.

The events of 1963 put an end to any hopes that might have remained of
the Arab *umma* taking on a territorial-political shape. Unity within the
Arab world would continue to be an ideal; but it had, perforce, to remain
a unity of purpose and spirit rather than a union of states. United military
commands and the like remained the only quasi-institutional ways of expressing that unity; and lacking common military training, practice, arms
supplies, staff colleges, command structures, and the like, these military
commands remained metaphysical exercises at the same exalted level. More
seriously the Arab world remained divided between those who attempted
to transfer the *umma* into a secular revolutionary Marxist ideology and those
who were content to accept traditional Islamic forms of rule whether by
monarch or self-appointed military usurpers of the role of monarchy.

[1] *Le Monde*, 19/20 Jan. 1964.

CHAPTER VIII

THE YEMEN REVOLUTION AND THE
SAUDI–EGYPTIAN CONFLICT

'A MEASURE of the magnitude and pervasiveness of the impact of modernity upon Africa and Asia', wrote an American political scientist in 1960, 'is the surprisingly few traditional polities that remain. Perhaps Yemen is the closest approximation of a purely traditional system, but the outside world knows very little about the character of its regime.'[1] Both the nature of the Yemen's political system and the world's ignorance of it were largely due to the policies of the country's ruler, the Imam Ahmad ibn Yahya, who, by a remarkable combination of political skill and sheer ruthlessness, had apparently succeeded in insulating his domain from the political and social ferment which characterized the Arab world in the 1950s.

At home, Ahmad's chief aim was to remain in power; abroad, it was to drive the British out of south Arabia, which he considered to be properly a part of the Yemen. Both aims led him, after 1955, into a strange flirtation with President Nasser of Egypt and the Communist bloc. His pro-Egyptian policy culminated, in March 1958, in his decision to join the union between Egypt and Syria while at the same time preserving complete autonomy for the Yemen, and his reliance upon economic and military aid from the Communist world prompted a full-dress statement of American concern from CIA chief, Allen Dulles, in April. Ahmad's honeymoon with Nasser ended after he had published a poem attacking Arab socialism at the end of 1961, and from then on he was the object of a violent propaganda campaign organized from Cairo. In the circumstances, it was surprising that he should continue to favour his son, Muhammad al-Badr, as his successor, for the latter had been an enthusiastic supporter of the pro-Egyptian policy and was reputedly imbued with radical ideas. Nevertheless, when Ahmad died peacefully in his sleep on the night of 18/19 September 1962, it was Muhammad who succeeded him.[2]

The new Imam's first actions certainly seemed to bear out his progressive reputation. 'We shall introduce new regulations to secure for the

[1] James S. Coleman in Gabriel A. Almond and James S. Coleman, eds., *The politics of the developing areas* (Princeton, 1960), p. 575.

[2] For the Imam Ahmad's Yemen, see Harold Ingrams, *The Yemen* (London, 1963), especially Chapters 6, 7, and 8; J. Heyworth-Dunne, 'Témoignage sur le Yemen', *Orient*, No. 31, 1964, pp. 20–73; and Manfred W. Wenner, *Modern Yemen, 1918–1966* (Baltimore, 1967), especially Chapters 5 and 7.

citizens their rights in conformity with those of the modern world', he announced in his first speech from the throne on the day after Ahmad's death.[1] And words were soon followed by deeds. On 21 September an amnesty was granted to all political offenders and the system whereby Yemeni tribes had to give hostages to the Imam to ensure their loyalty and good behaviour was abolished. Four days later more royal decrees announced the establishment of a new advisory council for the Imam, half of whose members were to be elected, and promised the setting up of elected municipal councils.[2]

It is impossible to say how far Muhammad's reforms would have gone, or what effect they would have had upon the Yemen, for on 27 September the radio of the capital city of San'a announced that the Imamic regime had been overthrown by a group of 'free officers' acting under the orders of the supreme army command and that a 'Yemeni Arab Republic' had been established in its place. The Imam Muhammad was said to be dead, buried beneath the ruins of his palace, which had been shelled by the revolutionaries.[3] The leader of the revolution appeared to be the new Imam's erstwhile friend and chief-of-staff, Colonel Abdullah as-Sallal, for it was he who was named by San'a radio as president of the Revolutionary Council and subsequently prime minister and commander-in-chief as well. The new regime promised far-reaching political and social reforms and proclaimed its belief in Arab nationalism and non-alignment, its opposition to 'imperialism and foreign interference in all forms', and its desire 'to establish stronger bonds with the liberal Arab states for the sake of realising Arab unity'.[4]

It soon became clear, however, that the supporters of the Imamate had no intention of giving up without a fight. On 27 September, the day the coup was announced, Amman radio broadcast a statement from the Yemeni legation in Bonn which declared that the organizers of the coup were facing 'strong resistance' from some tribes and that certain key towns, including the old administrative capital of Ta'izz and the port of Hudaydah, had expressed their opposition to 'the mutineers'.[5] On 30 September the Yemeni legation in Amman announced that:

H.R.H. the Amir Sayf al-Islam al-Hasan[6] has arrived in Yemen and has been installed as legitimate Imam of the country by the masses of the people. He has thus become the new Commander of the Faithful and the legitimate king of Yemen. The legation affirms that the recent mutiny movement has nothing to do with the people. The liquidation of this movement will take place shortly.[7]

The new Imam promptly issued a statement announcing the formation of

[1] *SWB*, ME/1053/A/1–2.   [2] Ibid., ME/1055/A/9–10; ME/1056/A/5–6.
[3] Ibid., ME/1060/A/6–7.   [4] Ibid., ME/1061/A/2–3.   [5] Ibid., ME/1060/A/9.
[6] Muhammad's uncle and hitherto Yemeni representative at the United Nations.
[7] *SWB*, ME/1062/A/8.

'people's commands' in various parts of the country, together with his intention of 'putting an end to the mutiny and arresting Sallal and his mob government'.[1] The revolutionary high command's order of 4 October cancelling all army leave shows that these threats were taken seriously.[2]

The Imam's supporters—or royalists as we shall henceforth call them, as opposed to the revolutionary republicans—received a tremendous boost to their morale when it was revealed that Muhammad had not after all been killed on the night of 26 September. Reports that he had survived the shelling of his palace began to circulate early in October,[3] and on the 15th Amman radio broadcast what purported to be the text of a telegram from him to King Hussein of Jordan.[4] Two days later the Jordanians reported that Hasan had relinquished the title of Imam to his nephew, the legitimate holder.[5] While eventually admitting that Muhammad had escaped from San'a, Sallal (now president of the Republic) now claimed that he had died of wounds in Saudi Arabia.[6] The issue was not finally resolved until 11 November, when Muhammad showed that he was indeed alive and well by holding a press conference for a group of Western and Arab journalists 'somewhere in north-west Yemen'.[7]

The civil war which was fast developing in the Yemen fed upon age-old divisions within the country. One of the most important was the religious split between Zaydi and Shafi'i Moslems. As well as being the temporal ruler of the Yemen, the Imam was the spiritual leader of the Zaydi sect, which had been founded by the first Imam in the ninth century A.D. Shi'ite Zaydis, therefore, tended to support the royalists, while the Sunni Shafi'is rallied to the Republic.[8]

More important than the internal divisions, however—and much more sinister—was the fact that both sides were receiving help from abroad. On the royalist side, as we have seen, Amman radio began broadcasting reports hostile to the revolution almost from the moment it occurred. Initially it was claimed that Jordanian support for the Imam meant no more than favouring him as opposed to Sallal, but on 8 October the texts of messages exchanged between Hasan and Hussein which were broadcast went much further. In his message Hasan claimed that he was the legitimate Imam[9] and that he controlled 'most parts of the Yemen, except for a few towns'. He asked for Hussein's support for his delegation and representatives at the United Nations and elsewhere. In his reply Hussein not only expressed the hope that Hasan would destroy the rebels, but added, 'you have all our support in all the fields'.[10] Exactly what form

[1] Ibid.   [2] Ibid., ME/1066/A/3.   [3] Ibid., ME/1064/A/4; *Times*, 4 Oct. 1962.
[4] *SWB*, ME/1075/A/4.   [5] Ibid., ME/1078/A/2.
[6] Ibid., ME/1086/A/1.   [7] *Times*; *NY Times*, 12 Nov. 1962.
[8] This was not of course a hard and fast rule. Sallal, for example, was a Zaydi.
[9] This was before it was known with certainty that Muhammad was still alive.
[10] *SWB*, ME/1070/A2.

this 'support' took is hard to say. Hussein himself gave one indication when he told a group of Swiss journalists at the beginning of November that a part of the former Jordanian military delegation in San'a, totalling some sixty officers, was now at the Imam's headquarters.[1]

Saudi Arabia maintained a discreet radio silence concerning events in the Yemen until 10 October. This was done, it was claimed, in order to avoid interference in the country's internal affairs.[2] But the silence was a cloak for activities which can only be described under the heading of that very interference which the Saudis claimed to be eschewing. Another of the Imam Muhammad's uncles, Prince 'Abd ar-Rahman ibn Yahya, provided a very full account of how the Saudi government helped to organize royalist resistance to the Sallal regime from the very outset.[3] He had arrived in Aden on 27 September to take up the post of minister of health in his nephew's government, but was prevented from flying on to San'a that morning because there was not enough room for his party on the plane. It was only when he returned to his hotel that he heard about the previous night's coup. 'We stayed in Aden and I telephoned to New York to my brother Hassan', he recounted. '... Prince Hassan set out at once and a few days later we flew to meet him in Jeddah.... From there we went to Riyadh, to see King Sa'ud and Crown Prince Faisal, and then we continued to Najran.' From Najran, which is in Saudi Arabia, the royalists drew up their plans to reconquer the Yemen. The Saudis gave Hasan a radio telephone, gold sovereigns and silver Maria Theresa dollars (for long the principal monetary medium of exchange in the Yemen), rifles and machine-guns. A force was sent to take over the northern city of Sa'da. It arrived there on 1 October, less than five days after the revolution.[4]

On the republican side, it has been argued that Egyptian intervention even antedated the coup, in that the latter was master-minded from Cairo. One scholar has published what purports to be a report from an Egyptian intelligence officer, dated 12 August 1961, which advocates the overthrow of the Imamate in much the way that it eventually occurred and which refers to Sallal as 'our friend'.[5] Moreover, the relentless propaganda campaign which Egypt had waged against the Imamate from the end of 1961 onwards was mainly conducted by men who were

[1] *NZZ*, 15 Nov. 1962.

[2] *SWB*, ME/1071/A/2–4.

[3] Dana Adams Schmidt, *Yemen: the unknown war* (London, 1968), pp. 61–4. Schmidt was the *NY Times* correspondent who covered the Yemen civil war and his book contains a great deal of information which was not published at the time.

[4] The Royalists were soon driven out of Sa'da.

[5] Stanko Guldescu, 'The Background of the Yemeni Revolution of 1962', *Dalhousie Review*, vol. 45, No. 1, 1965, pp. 68–9. Of course, this document, which Dr Guldescu says was obtained by Syrian security police at the time of the break-up of the UAR in Sept. 1961, may be a forgery. He does not say how or when it came into his hands.

to become ministers in Sallal's government.[1] On the other hand, John S. Badeau, US Ambassador in Cairo in 1962, recorded that

there is little evidence . . . to indicate that the U.A.R. directed the coup d'état. The revolt came from natural causes within Yemen, not from Egyptian machinations . . . [although] there is some reason to believe that revolutionary groups both within and outside Yemen may have expected Egyptian support if they mounted a potentially successful coup d'état.[2]

If Badeau's interpretation is the correct one, the republicans certainly obtained their Egyptian support promptly. Egypt was the first to recognize the Yemeni Arab Republic (YAR) and, in the telegram announcing this decision on 29 September, President Nasser told Sallal that 'we stand with the Yemeni people without hesitation and support their wish and legitimate right'.[3] At the beginning of October British military intelligence disclosed that an Egyptian aircraft carrying arms, ammunition, and military experts had flown from Luxor to the Yemen on 30 September. The flight was said to be one of a series which had been taking place over the previous few days. On this occasion the Egyptian president was said to have resisted pressure from some of his advisers for direct military intervention, but a few days later the same source revealed that the scale of Egyptian military assistance was increasing sharply. At least three warships had been observed unloading men and equipment at Hudaydah, including tanks, mortar bombs, and grenades, and two aircraft, piloted by Egyptians, were said to have machine-gunned tribesmen in the Sa'da area.[4] On 19 October President Sallal admitted that 'large striking forces have arrived to protect our country against every criminal aggressor',[5] and, a couple of months later, President Nasser himself declared that he had sent 2,000 Egyptian troops and two aircraft to the Yemen between 5 and 16 October.[6]

The Egyptian leader claimed that his decision had been prompted by Saudi intervention on behalf of the royalists, as evidenced by the defection to the UAR on 2 October of three Saudi pilots who had been flying arms and ammunition to the royalist forces.[7] It is true that the Saudis, and possibly the Jordanians too, did send help to the royalists before the Egyptians dispatched ground forces to the Yemen, but if the British intelligence reports quoted above are to be believed, Nasser had been sending equipment and advisers before then, so that there cannot be very much in it when it comes to deciding who technically intervened first. Moreover, in spite of the daily accusations broadcast by Cairo radio, no independent observer ever turned up any 'hard' evidence that Saudi or Jordanian

[1] Ingrams, pp. 124–6.
[2] John S. Badeau, *The American approach to the Arab world* (New York, 1968), p. 127.
[3] *NY Times*, 30 Sept. 1962.   [4] *Times*, 2, 3 Oct. 1962.   [5] *SWB*, ME/1079/A/1.
[6] Ibid., ME/1133/A/4.   [7] Ibid., ME/1064/A/2–3; ME/1068/A/11–12.

regular forces fought on the royalist side.[1] Saudi and Jordanian help for the royalists, although important and perhaps even crucial to their survival, seems to have been exclusively confined to the provision of money, material, and propaganda. The Egyptians, on the other hand, not only supplied these same three commodities to the republicans, but a sizeable army as well.

Egyptian, Saudi, and Jordanian intervention in the Yemen cannot be understood without reference to the 'Arab cold war'[2] which had divided the Middle East at least since 1957–8. Originally a struggle between the 'revolutionary' and 'traditional' state of the Arab world, it had become rather more complicated as a result of General Qasim's early reversal to the traditional anti-Egyptian Iraqi role after the revolution of July 1958 and Syria's secession from the UAR in September 1961. But the core of the conflict remained the antithesis between revolutionary, republican, and socialist Egypt on the one hand, and traditional, monarchist, and conservative Saudi Arabia and Jordan on the other. Less than a month before the Yemeni revolution, this division had been underlined by the Ta'if agreement between King Sa'ud and King Hussein, which provided, among other things, for a joint Saudi-Jordanian military command and the co-ordination of foreign and economic policy, all very obviously with a view to the common threat from Egypt.[3]

The way in which the Yemeni situation fitted into this inter-Arab confrontation was brilliantly analysed by Arnold Hottinger, the Middle East correspondent of the *Neue Zürcher Zeitung*:[4]

Cairo sees in a revolutionary Yemen an ally against Saudi Arabia and hopes that the wave which began in San'a will also sweep away the kings of Riyadh and Amman. But the Nasser regime also sees its own 'revolution' and 'political philosophy' endorsed by the officers' revolution. Of late, it has been admitted that Syria's secession had aroused grave doubts. The victory of the 'reactionaries' over 'progress' on that occasion gave rise to many questions. People now believe that, in the San'a revolution, they have found an answer. 'Defeats may have occurred from time to time, but progress must come. It is as inevitable as the course of life itself.' Such is the text of Hasanayn Haikal's Friday political sermon,[5] from which it is possible to deduce the current thought of the U.A.R. leadership. It has thus recently been revealed how much the secession of Syria must have irritated and upset the ideology of the regime. For Ridyadh and Amman, therefore, the defence of the Imamate signifies not only self-defence,

---

[1] With the possible exception of the sixty or so officers of the Jordanian military mission referred to by King Hussein (see above, p. 220).

[2] The phrase is Malcolm Kerr's. See *The Arab cold war, 1958–64* (London, 1971).

[3] For the Ta'if agreement, see *Oriente Moderno*, vol. xlii, Nos. 8–9, 1962, pp. 647–8.

[4] 'Die arabische Reaktion auf den Umsturz in Jemen', *NZZ*, 20 Oct. 1962.

[5] Haykal wrote a weekly column for the Cairo newspaper *al-Ahram*. It appeared on Fridays and was generally reckoned to be an authoritative account of the Egyptian government's views on the questions with which it dealt.

but a simultaneous attack upon Cairo. Should the overthrown regime be restored to power, it would mean in the first place a blow against Nasser as far as the Arab kings are concerned. Thus Jordan and Saudi Arabia have sided unequivocally with the [royalists]. The propaganda and military help for [them] is thought of primarily as a weapon in the struggle against Nasser.

The attitudes of the other Arab countries also reflected the wider scenario of the 'Arab cold war', as Hottinger pointed out in the same article. Syria, for example, had recognized the YAR and even extended her credits, but this was in order to wean her away from Nasser's influence. This policy seemed to bring some results, for the republican foreign minister had reportedly assured the Syrians that his government would remain neutral in inter-Arab disputes. As the situation deteriorated, Syria took further steps to prevent Egyptian domination of the Yemen. Thus, on 6 November, she appealed to the heads of Arab states not involved in the conflict 'to hold urgent consultations among themselves ... with a view to making an honourable, unbiased attempt to save the shedding of blood in sister Yemen'.[1] But this attempt at mediation came to nothing.

What prompted the Syrian peace initiative was almost certainly the sharp increase in tension at the end of October and the beginning of November. On 30 October the YAR's deputy prime minister, Baydani, warned Saudi Arabia over San'a radio that 'if the Saudi aggression continues to defy and provoke Yemenis' feelings, we shall be compelled to take the battle inside Saudi territory, in accordance with the lawful right of self-defence'.[2] Then, on 3 November, Mecca radio reported that Egyptian aircraft, 'operating with the Yemeni mutineers', had carried out five raids against sites in Saudi territory at noon the previous day.[3] On 6 November the recently appointed Saudi prime minister, Crown Prince Faysal,[4] gave a press conference during which he announced that his government had broken off diplomatic relations with the UAR as a result of these attacks. When asked about Baydani's threat 'to take the battle inside Saudi territory', his reply was measured but firm. 'This depends on the battle they say they will move into our territory,' he said. 'If it is an armed one, then we will meet it with arms. But if it is a battle of words, then things will be different.'[5] He knew that he could count upon full support from Jordan, for the latter's government had already publicly declared that 'it stands by the sisterly kingdom of Saudi Arabia with all its potentialities and ... it regards the aggression against Saudi Arabia as direct aggression against Jordan'.[6]

[1] *Le Monde*, 8 Nov. 1962. [2] *SWB*, ME/1088/A4. [3] Ibid., ME/1091/A/1–2.
[4] Faysal had taken over the premiership from his brother, King Sa'ud, on 17 Oct. This was probably because it was felt that his firm hand would be needed to deal with the Yemeni situation.
[5] *SWB*, ME/1094/A/3–6. [6] Ibid., ME/1092/A/5.

These developments were paralleled by signs of increasing Egyptian influence in the YAR. From 26 to 29 October Field-Marshal 'Abd al-Hakim Amir, the commander-in-chief of the Egyptian armed forces and deputy president of the UAR, carried out what was reported to be an inspection trip to the Yemen. His visit was followed on 31 October by a cabinet reshuffle in San'a in which the allegedly pro-Egyptian elements, headed by Baydani, strengthened their influence, and it was rumoured that the two events were not unconnected.[1] On 10 November it was announced that a new five-year defence pact had been signed between the YAR and Egypt to replace the Jiddah Pact of 1955 between Egypt and Saudi Arabia, to which the Imam Ahmad had subsequently adhered and under the terms of which, somewhat ironically, the Egyptians had been helping the republicans to date.[2] By this time, the number of Egyptian troops in the Yemen had probably reached five figures.[3]

The civil war in the Yemen was not only of concern to the states of the Arab world, but also to external powers with interests in the Middle East, notably the USA and the UK. The former, as Badeau noted, had no interests in the Yemen as such. There was little investment and scarcely any trade. 'But there were American interests outside Yemen which could be affected by the outbreak of civil strife within that country. One of these concerned the petroleum resources at the head of the Persian Gulf . . .' This implied 'a cordial and continuing relation with the kingdom of Saudi Arabia' and, while there seemed to be no direct military threat to that country from the Yemeni civil war, 'revolt in Yemen and the Egyptian–Saudi confrontation . . . might nonetheless have imperilled the continued stability of Saudi Arabia. The danger lay in the possibility that the conflict would so shake the existing government that it would lose control or possibly be overturned by revolt.' Also, the USA was interested in the stability of Jordan. 'What was threatened was the uneasy equilibrium of the monarchy, which, if destroyed, could have led to a move for union with or domination by the U.A.R. Should this occur there was serious risk that Israel might respond with military action.'[4] As far as Jordan was concerned, these fears were by no means imaginary. The defection to Cairo in November of the commander-in-chief of the Jordanian air force, because of his disagreement with his government's policy towards the Yemen provided a revealing indication of just how precarious the situation in Jordan was.[5]

British interest in the situation in the Yemen stemmed mainly from a physical presence in the region immediately to the south and east of the

[1] SWB, ME/1087/A/4; Sunday Times, 4 Nov. 1962.
[2] SWB, ME/1097/A/2–3.
[3] In a dispatch in the Guardian, 30 Nov. 1962, David Holden put the number of Egyptian troops then in the Yemen at a minimum of 10,000.
[4] Badeau, pp. 132–4.   [5] SWB, ME/1099/A/7; ME/1101/A/3.

country, which was going through a particularly crucial phase at the very moment of the Yemeni revolution. In 1959 the British government had set up the 'Federation of Arab Amirates of the South', consisting of six states of the Western Aden Protectorate. By 1962 nine more states of the Western Protectorate had joined the Federation, which, while enjoying a considerable degree of autonomy in internal matters, was entirely dependent upon the UK for foreign affairs and defence. Under the terms of the treaty which set up the Federation, the British government was committed to prepare it for independence, but before this could be done, the vital question of its relationship to the Crown Colony of Aden had to be solved. On administrative and economic grounds, it was logical that Aden should itself become a member-state of the Federation. But this was not so easy in practice, partly because of the suspicion with which the sophisticated, urban Adeni ministers regarded the traditionalist sheikhs, sultans, and amirs of the Federation, but also because of the existence of a powerful radical Arab nationalist movement in the shape of the Aden Trade Union Congress and related People's Socialist Party (PSP). This movement, which relied heavily upon migrant Yemeni workers for its support, was totally opposed to the idea of Aden's joining the Federation, advocating union with the Yemen instead.[1]

In spite of these political difficulties the British government decided to press ahead with the integration of Aden into the Federation. An agreement along these lines was hammered out at a tripartite conference in London in the summer of 1962 between the British, the Federal leaders, and the Aden government. The Aden legislative council met on 24 September to consider the agreement, to the accompaniment of a general strike and counter-demonstrations organized by the Aden TUC and the PSP. On the 26th the council ratified the agreement. Twenty-four hours later came the news of the revolution in the Yemen.[2] As one observer noted,

The revolution in Yemen had a profound effect on the situation in Aden and the Federation. . . . The weakness of the policy of the People's Socialist Party . . . was that the rule of the Imam Ahmad was the most repressive and reactionary in the Arab world, so that, while they called for democratic rights in Aden, they were at the same time calling for union with a country where no civil rights were granted. A substantial part of the Yemeni population of Aden itself consisted of people who had for many years supported the . . . movement against the Imamate, and these would have been the last to submit

---

[1] A complicating factor was the fact that most of these Yemenis were disfranchised under Aden law. In protest, the Aden TUC called for a boycott of the 1959 election to the colony's legislative council, the result of which was that the council was elected on a 27 per cent vote and contained no direct representative of the radical point of view.

[2] For full details on Aden and the Federation, see Tom Little, *South Arabia: arena of conflict* (London, 1968), upon which this account relies heavily.

themselves again to its rule. It seemed that all was now changed. Yemen had put itself in the vanguard of the Arab national movement and had the support of the supreme leader, Nasser, and almost everyone in the Arab world. Opposition to the Aden government, the British and the federal plans was strengthened as a result.[1]

Indeed, the then Governor of Aden went so far as to record his belief that 'if the Yemeni revolution had come one day earlier, or the legislative council vote one day later, I feel pretty certain that the London agreement would never have obtained the support of a majority of local members'.[2]

The immediate issue facing both the US and British governments was whether or not to recognize the YAR. The Middle East experts in the state department were reported to be urging the Kennedy administration to recognize the Sallal regime as early as the beginning of October on the grounds that it was not beholden to Nasser, and that recognition would prevent further foreign intervention which was, of course, the United States' chief concern.[3]

The prospect of American recognition of the new Yemeni regime was profoundly disturbing to the British government. Ever since the disaster which had overtaken the British operation against Suez in November 1956 it had been axiomatic in Whitehall that British policy in the Middle East should, almost at all costs, be aligned with that of the USA. Voices were not lacking in the foreign office sympathetically disposed towards the new regime and arguing that, unless Britain recognized it and abandoned support of 'reactionary and rather outmoded regimes', Sallal's government, like so many other 'progressive' Arab regimes, would 'drift into violent revolutionary and anti-western positions'.[4] But the colonial office, the ministry of defence, and the prime minister himself remained adamantly opposed to recognition. Precautions were taken against a possible 'overspill' of Yemeni intervention in Aden. Any serious revolutionary trouble in Aden, any mass desertion of the British connection by local notables anxious to preserve themselves by backing the winner, would make the Aden base useless and destroy what was then regarded as the foundation of British authority in the Gulf. Sir Charles Johnson, the governor of Aden, called to London for consultation on 22 October, urged that recognition should be delayed as long as possible. The republican regime could not be described as being in *de facto* control of the Yemen. It was essential to give the royalists a chance and to make it clear to the rulers of the Aden protectorate that they had been given a chance. Time was needed, moreover, to get 'our friends to realize that recognition was

---

[1] Little, p. 94.
[2] Sir Charles Johnson, *The view from Steamer Point* (London, 1964), pp. 124–5.
[3] *NY Times*, 7 Oct. 1962.
[4] See Macmillan's letter to the Queen of 7 Oct. 1962 (Macmillan, p. 268).

unavoidable and give us at least a chance of getting on some working basis with the new republican Government'.[1] 'Recognition . . . before the completion of the merger process,' Sir Charles subsequently wrote, 'would have had a deeply unsettling effect in Aden and in the Federation. In both places it would have been interpreted as a humiliating retreat by the British government and as a sign that our influence in South Arabia was on the wane.'[2] The Federal government, too, was bitterly hostile to recognition. Sir Kennedy Trevaskis, the British official in charge of relations with the Federation under the governor, has argued that its reasons were less selfish than its critics maintained. 'In Fleet Street', he wrote,

it was readily assumed that, as miniscule Imams, the federal ministers had been influenced by nothing more than an aristocratic allergy to republicanism. In fact, they cared not a jot whether the Yemen's ruler was crowned with an Imamic turban or a republican forage cap. What concerned them was his disposition towards themselves. Here was a régime, they said, which denied their validity, had called for their destruction and was in close alliance with their most malevolent enemies—Egypt and the P.S.P. For the British government to recognize [this] regime . . . would be a gross betrayal of their trust for the conduct of the Federation's foreign affairs.[3]

To judge from hints dropped in a subsequent account by Julian Amery, who was then minister of aviation in the British government, in addition to there being pressure in favour of recognition from the USA, there was a division of opinion within the government. A great deal of the credit for the resolution of this division in the direction of non-recognition was owed, according to Mr Amery, to the activities of a back-bench Conservative MP, Colonel Neil McLean. McLean, he said, resolved to visit the Yemen at his own expense to find out what the situation was for himself and 'when he got out he sent a telegram through the Governor [of Aden] to friends in the government to say that at least half the country was in royalist hands and that it would be a disaster if we recognized the republic'. According to Amery, his telegram 'arrived at the same time as advice was being given to ministers to follow the American policy and recognize Sallal. On the strength of Colonel McLean's warning the whole thing was studied again; and to this day [20 October 1965] we have never recognized the republic in the Yemen.'[4]

Further impetus for what was to become the British government's

---

[1] Macmillan's diary entry of 22 Oct. 1962 (ibid., p. 269).
[2] Sir Charles Johnson, p. 151.
[3] Sir Kennedy Trevaskis, *Shades of amber* (London, 1968), p. 185.
[4] Amery gave this account when introducing a lecture by McLean to the Royal United Services Institution in London. See the Institution's *Journal*, Feb. 1966, p. 14. What must have been the gist of McLean's telegram to his friends in the government was published in an article in the *Daily Telegraph*, 6 Nov. 1962.

policy of non-recognition of, and barely disguised hostility towards, the Yemeni republican regime was provided by an aggressive speech by President Sallal on 9 November. He declared:

We have been waiting since the beginning of the revolution for ageing and tattered Britain to recognize us so that we can establish friendship with it. . . . But it has been conspiring against us and sending Jordanian and Saudi forces to our country. We have determined and we will always determine to strike at the aggressors. Brethren, if Britain is conspiring against us and massing forces to aggress against us, we also have friends, headed by the Soviet Union and the U.A.R. We shall ask them for aid to put an end to the imperialist attempts. . . . We call upon our brethren in the south to be in readiness to take part in the revolution and the battles which we are waging even with the Devil. . . . We call upon our brethren in the south to inform Britain that Yemen has given up its lethargy and intends to achieve a free and dignified life. We ask them to act in the south as their brothers in the north are acting.[1]

Accusations that Britain was actively supporting the Yemeni royalists abounded on Cairo and San'a radios at this time. There is no evidence to support these charges, although one cannot be nearly so sure about the activities of certain federal politicians, notably Sharif Husayn, the minister of the interior from the state of Bayhan on the eastern border of Yemen.[2] Nevertheless, when the Aden-Federation merger debate took place in the House of Commons on 13 November 1962, the British government made its sympathies abundantly clear. The commonwealth and colonial secretary, Duncan Sandys, argued that the controversy over whether Aden should join the Federation had been completely overshadowed by events in the Yemen. Referring to Sallal's speech, he said,

this serious new development has widened the whole issue and has lent urgency to our decision. The main issue is no longer whether or not there should be elections [in Aden] before merger.[3] The central issue now is whether Aden and the Federation should, by union with one another, be strengthened and consolidated in the face of open incitement to rebellion. The alternative is to yield to intimidation from within and without and to postpone the merger, which we know to be right, and thereby dispirit and discourage all those who believe in ordered progress in partnership with Britain. This is a course which we are not prepared to take.[4]

Winding up the debate for the government, the under-secretary of state, Nigel Fisher, expanded upon this point. If there were elections in

---

[1] *SWB*, ME/1097/A/1.

[2] After the British had left Aden and the Federation, Sharif Husayn was put on trial by the new People's Republic of South Yemen. One of the charges was that he had helped the royalists in the Yemeni civil war. See the report in *The Times*, 20 Feb. 1968.

[3] It was one of the Labour opposition's charges that the merger was being pushed through without proper consultation with the Adenis themselves as expressed by means of an election.

[4] 666 *HC Deb.*, cols. 250–1, 253.

Aden, he said, either the moderates or the PSP would win them. If the moderates won, the merger would go ahead but with a year's delay. If the PSP won, it would be 'totally unacceptable to Her Majesty's Government'. He later explained why. 'There can be no doubt', he said, 'that Brigadier Sallal and his government are very much under the influence of Colonel Nasser. . . . I do not regard Colonel Nasser as our greatest friend in the Middle East, and Her Majesty's Government would not be happy to see Aden Colony absorbed into a Yemen dominated from Cairo.'[1]

These were then the main considerations in London when, in the aftermath of the Cuban missile crisis, President Kennedy turned his attention towards the question of recognition. He was apparently receiving very positive recommendations from the state department in favour of recognition as the only way of obtaining a withdrawal of Egyptian forces from the Yemen; he was also very sensitive to the argument that it ill-befitted the man who had, in his inaugural, made a bold bid to align the United States with the forces of change and revolution outside the Sino-Soviet sphere, to back 'reactionary' against 'progressive' Arab regimes. Apparently warned of the way in which the pressures on Kennedy were developing, Macmillan made a strong appeal to him on 14 November to delay recognition. He addressed himself to the question of the danger to American interests in Saudi Arabia and to the British in Jordan and Aden, and to the disastrous effect on the 'whole Anglo-American position in the Gulf' if Aden was lost. Recognition and aid, Macmillan argued, should only be given in return for actions—the announcement of a precise programme for the withdrawal of Egyptian forces, including a time-table, and certain specific steps such as the withdrawal of the Egyptian air force. Disengagement could be supervised by UN observers.[2]

After several telephone conversations with Macmillan, Kennedy agreed to make an Egyptian commitment to withdraw and a declaration by Sallal accepting the normalization of, and friendly relations with, all neighbouring states, the precondition of recognition.[3] On 17 November, he sent a personal message to Nasser, Sallal, King Hussein, and Crown Prince Faysal in which he proposed that Egyptian troops withdraw from the Yemen, and the Saudis and Jordanians stop helping the royalists.[4] The text of the message went some way in the direction of Macmillan's suggested approach. It proposed, in order of precedence, an Egyptian statement expressing willingness to undertake reciprocal disengagement and an expeditious and phased removal of troops as Saudi and Jordanian

---

[1] Ibid., cols. 327–8.   [2] Macmillan, pp. 270–1.   [3] Ibid., pp. 272–3.
[4] *NY Times*, 27 Nov. 1962. For the text of his message to President Nasser see Mohammed Haikal, *Nasser: the Cairo documents* (London, 1972), pp. 196–7. It should be noted, on the issue of recognition, that no message was sent to the Imam Mohammed, to his publicly expressed chagrin. *SWB*, ME/1122/A/2–3.

troops were removed from the frontier and support for the royalist forces cut off, and a proclamation by the Yemen republican government that it intended to honour its international obligations, establish normal and friendly relations with its neighbours, and concentrate on domestic affairs. American recognition of the Yemen republican government would follow on receipt of these guarantees. Macmillan would no doubt have preferred something more concrete than declarations, mistrusting President Nasser as he did.

None of the replies to President Kennedy were encouraging. Nasser[1] accepted that clashes should be avoided, but defended his policy of rendering them inevitable unless Saudi Arabia abandoned its 'attempt to invade the Yemen from outside'. Faysal made it plain that he was not interested in disengagement until after a royalist victory, which he confidently predicted for the coming winter, while Sallal, who lacked Nasser's gift for plausibility, insisted upon a complete cessation of every form of hostile activity on the part of Saudi Arabia and Jordan, to be followed by a withdrawal of Egyptian troops in stages, thus ensuring a republican victory. Only King Hussein made a positive counter-proposal, which was that an impartial team of outside observers, possibly from the United Nations, should investigate the situation in the Yemen. The Yemeni people, he argued, should be given the right of self-determination, but added that this was dependent upon the departure of Egyptian troops and that he intended to go on recognizing, and presumably helping, the Imam until the Yemenis decided otherwise.[2]

In spite of the failure of its disengagement initiative and the obvious reservations of its British ally, the United States government recognized the YAR on 19 December 1962.[3] In an authoritative letter to Senator Hickenlooper of Iowa some seven months later, the assistant secretary of state for Near Eastern affairs, Phillips Talbot, justified recognition on four main grounds: YAR control of the apparatus of government; apparent popular support; YAR control of most of the country; and YAR willingness and capability to honour its international obligations.[4] The second and third of these reasons, which in turn determined the weight that could be put upon the first, were hardly demonstrable in the confused situation prevailing in the Yemen at the end of 1962, while the fourth rested upon nothing more than a declaration of intent by the YAR government. One must therefore suppose that the other reasons adduced

[1] For extracts see Haikal, p. 197.

[2] Faysal's reply is reported in *NY Times*, 30 Nov. 1962; the joint Egyptian–YAR reply in an article in *al-Ahram*, broadcast over Cairo radio on 28 Nov. 1962 (*SWB*, ME/1112/A/5–6); and King Hussein's reply in the *Daily Telegraph*, 11 Dec. 1962.

[3] For the text of the United States government's statement announcing recognition, see *Documents, 1963*, pp. 322–8.

[4] Ibid., pp. 332–4.

by Talbot in his letter to Senator Hickenlooper were of at least equal importance. 'We realized', he wrote,

that only by recognizing the regime could we play a useful role in preventing an escalation of the Yemen conflict causing even more foreign interference and placing in serious jeopardy major U.S. economic and security interests in the Arabian peninsula. Furthermore, our presence in Yemen—including an A.I.D. mission—could not have been continued for long without recognition. The A.I.D. mission was originally established in Yemen for the purpose of maintaining a beachhead of U.S. influence in the face of a sustained Communist interest and a growing Soviet presence.

Yet another reason is offered by Badeau, to the effect that recognition

would make it possible for the United States to care for British interests in Yemen and possibly to moderate the impact of republican enthusiasm on the already perturbed situation in Aden colony.[1]

In this connection, it is interesting to note that, in its announcement of recognition, the United States government expressed its gratification at the passage in the YAR declaration of intent which called upon Yemenis living in adjacent areas 'to respect law and order', and emphasized that the treaties which the YAR government had promised to honour included

the Treaty of San'a concluded with the British government in 1934 which provided for reciprocal guarantees that neither party should intervene in the affairs of the other across the existing international frontier dividing the Yemen from territory under British control.

Probing these additional reasons more deeply, however, it is hard to see how they provided any more justification for recognition than the four points already discussed. It is far from clear how recognition of one side in a civil war could be seen as a means of preventing escalation and increased foreign interference. Badeau suggests that the United States administration believed recognition of the YAR would strengthen the latter's position *vis-à-vis* Egypt.[2] But any such effect could only be purely marginal since the YAR was dependent upon the presence of Egyptian troops for her very survival. It was true that the Egyptian government had paralleled the YAR's declaration of intent with a statement of its own to the effect that it was prepared

to cease the armed clash on its part, and to begin gradually to withdraw its forces in Yemen, provided the Saudi and Jordanian forces which are jointly supporting the dethroned king in the border areas will withdraw and on condition that the Saudi, Jordanian, and foreign aid to the royalists is ended. . . .[3]

[1] Badeau, p. 138.
[2] Ibid., pp. 137–8. It is interesting to note that the royalists, apparently, were considered to have no position to strengthen, being totally dependent upon Saudi Arabia.
[3] *Documents, 1963*, pp. 331–2.

But just before this statement was broadcast, Cairo radio carried a long report of Field-Marshal Amir's latest visit to the Yemen, which concluded that 'the prevailing opinion at the high command is that there is a new round coming up in Yemen'.[1]

As for the desire to preserve American influence in the Yemen in the face of Communist encroachment, it should be pointed out that the AID mission to which Talbot referred was set up in 1959, at the height of the Imam Ahmad's flirtation with the eastern bloc. Although Communist countries were among the first to recognize the Sallal regime, there is no evidence to suggest that they were operating in the Yemen in late 1962 on anything like the same scale which they had been three years previously.

Nor was the American action really likely to be of much assistance to the British. US recognition of the YAR, which was followed by recognition by several other countries and by the seating of the republican delegation as the representatives of the Yemen at the UN,[2] was bound to enhance the prestige of Sallal's regime among the radicals in Aden and to encourage the former's ambitions. Moreover, the YAR had been careful to provide itself with a let-out in its declaration of intent, by stating that 'we hope to live in peace and harmony with our neighbours in so far as they share this hope'. It was, of course, always open to the YAR to cast doubts upon the motives of its neighbours.

The false premisses upon which American policy was based were revealed almost immediately. On 30 December 1962 Mecca radio announced that the town of Najran had been twice bombed by Egyptian Ilyushin aircraft and, on 3 January 1963, Prince Faysal announced general mobilization as a precautionary measure.[3] At the end of January, Field-Marshal Amir paid yet another visit to the Yemen, accompanied on this occasion by Anwar as-Sadat, a close confidant of President Nasser and minister responsible for relations with the Yemen. This visit was followed, in mid-February, by the launching of the so-called 'Ramadan offensive' in northern and eastern Yemen. This required more troops, and one American official claimed on 21 February that the number of Egyptian troops in the Yemen had risen from 12,000 to 20,000 in four to six weeks. Even this was not considered enough, and there were reports that Field-Marshal Amer was asking for 20,000 more.[4]

At the same time, relations between the YAR and Britain deteriorated rapidly. On 27 December President Sallal attacked 'Britain, that grey-haired old woman, the empire on which the sun has set', and claimed that 'the sons of the south are the sons of Yemen'.[5] This was followed by

[1] *SWB*, ME/1130/A/4–5.
[2] On 20 Dec. 1962.   [3] *SWB*, ME/1137/A/3, ME/1141/A/1–2.
[4] Ibid., ME/1164/A/7; Schmidt, pp. 164–5; Arnold Hottinger, 'Die militärische Lage in Jemen', *NZZ*, 7 Mar. 1963; *NY Times*, 22 Feb. 1963.
[5] *SWB*, ME/1135/A/1.

reports of Egyptian troop movements in the direction of the Yemen's frontier with the Western Protectorate, which in turn prompted precautionary measures on the part of the British and Federal forces.[1] There were renewed discussions as to whether anything would be gained by British recognition of the Sallal regime, but it was again decided to stall until the Federation of Aden was completed. And there was a renewed exchange of messages between Macmillan and Kennedy.[2] Amid increasing tension along the Yemen-Protectorate border, the YAR told the British diplomatic mission at Ta'izz, which was still technically accredited to the Imam, that if their government was not prepared to recognize the new regime, they had better leave. On 12 February 1963 the Foreign Office in London confirmed that it had received a formal note from the republican authorities requesting the closure of the British legation within seven days, a request which was complied with on the 16th.[3] The break in relations was followed by the worst border incident to date, when on 26 February, a force of some 300 republicans armed with mortars and machine-guns were driven out of Federal territory, which they had occupied some days previously, by British and Federal troops. The YAR promptly filed a complaint at the United Nations, while San'a radio exhorted the 'Arab people in the south' to 'strike' at the British. 'Burn the oil sites,' it proclaimed, 'burn the refineries; strike at these invaders; destroy their pride; strike with a bomb, with a stone, with bottles and with dynamite. . . . Burn them with fire, petrol and gas.'[4]

The United States was faced with a complete failure of its policy. Kennedy had continued to try to prevail on President Nasser, insisting that it was not in his power to force Prince Faysal or the British to recognize the Sallal regime. His powers of persuasion, he pointed out, availed little in the face of Egyptian bombing of Najran or Sallal's threats and bombast.[5] At the same time a White House 'task force' under Robert Komer was set up to deal with the Yemen.

Then by a number of public actions,[6] the US government emphasized its commitment to support the territorial integrity of Saudi Arabia and, on 8 March, conveyed a blunt warning to President Nasser that Egyptian bombing raids upon Saudi Arabia were jeopardizing relations between

---

[1] *Times*, 31 Dec. 1962. [2] Macmillan, pp. 276–7.

[3] *Times*, 2, 30, 31 Jan. 1963; 13, 16, 18 Feb. 1963.

[4] For the border incident, see *Documents, 1963*, pp. 323–5. For the San'a broadcast, see *SWB*, ME/1189/A/3–4. [5] Haikal, pp. 198–9.

[6] e.g., a protest on 3 Jan. 1963 against the Egyptian bombing of Najran, *DSB*, 21 Jan. 1963, pp. 90–1, the publication on 8 Jan. 1963 of the exchange of letters between President Kennedy and Prince Faysal in late autumn 1962 in which the former pledged, 'You may be assured of full US support for the maintenance of Saudi Arabian integrity' (*American foreign policy: current documents, 1962*, vii, 21, p. 783), the dispatch of a destroyer to Jiddah, the enlargement of the American military aid and advisory missions to Saudi Arabia, and joint US–Saudi paratroop exercises (*NY Times*, 9 Jan., 5 Feb. 1963).

the UAR and the United States and that, if these raids were followed by an invasion, the two countries would be on a 'collision course'.[1] Reports of major Egyptian reinforcements being sent to the Yemen accentuated American anxieties.[2] At the same time, a confidential mission to Saudi Arabia was undertaken by Ellsworth Bunker, who, armed with a National Security Council directive of 27 February 1963, brought with him a plan to send an American fighter squadron to protect Saudi Arabia against Egyptian air attack—code-named Operation 'Hard Surface'—in exchange for a Saudi pledge to stop all aid to the Yemeni royalists as the first step in a general settlement.[3]

American activity was paralleled by that of the United Nations, for immediately prior to Ellsworth Bunker's mission to Saudi Arabia, the secretary-general asked his deputy, Dr Ralph Bunche, 'to go to Yemen and the United Arab Republic . . . on a fact-finding mission primarily devoted to talking with the Presidents of Yemen and the United Arab Republic . . . with the purpose of ascertaining their views of the situation and what steps might be taken to ease tension and restore conditions to normal'.[4] It seems that Dr Bunche had originally intended to visit royalist Yemen and Saudi Arabia as well, but that the Egyptians put pressure on the YAR government to refuse to meet him unless he agreed not to contact the royalists. As the Saudis had already made it clear that they would not receive him unless he did talk to the royalists, this meant that his mission would almost inevitably gain a one-sided impression.[5]

Indeed, when Dr Bunche arrived in San'a at the beginning of March, the 'Ramadan offensive' was in full swing and he was taken on a victory tour of the eastern region of the country. The Egyptian–republican successes clearly impressed him and, to judge by remarks he made at press conferences in Aden and Cairo after leaving the Yemen, he was convinced that the republicans were in more or less complete control of the country. He even asserted that the YAR had a perfect right to call in Egyptian troops to help deal with the royalists and that, as far as he could tell, the Egyptians had not tried to interfere in Yemeni affairs.[6]

Dr Bunche's remarks may have partially accounted for the somewhat dusty reception which Bunker received in Riyadh on 6 and 7 March from

[1] *NY Times*, 8 Mar. 1963.

[2] According to British information there were 28,000 Egyptians (one-third of Egypt's active forces) in the Yemen in March (Macmillan, p. 276).

[3] For the background to the Bunker mission, see Edward Weintal and Charles Bartlett, *Facing the brink. A study of crisis diplomacy* (London, 1967), pp. 43–4. See also Schmidt, p. 193.

[4] 'Report of the Secretary-General to the Security Council concerning developments relating to Yemen', 29 Apr. 1963, *Documents, 1963*, pp. 325–7.

[5] *NZZ*, 7 Mar. 1963. The secretary-general was rather disingenuous about this point in his report, quoted above. He wrote: 'It was left open whether Mr Bunche would eventually go also to Saudi Arabia, but developments made this unnecessary.'

[6] *Guardian*, 5 Mar. 1963; *NZZ*, 6 Mar. 1963; *Le Monde*, 7 Mar. 1963.

Prince Faysal. 'If US government help and support is forthcoming only as a result of a condition imposed upon me', the latter is reported to have told Bunker, 'then all I can say is we cannot have it that way.'[1] But Bunker and the United States government refused to take no for an answer. Bunker returned to Saudi Arabia on 17 March and finally persuaded Faysal to agree 'in principle' to suspend all aid to the royalists in exchange for a simultaneous Egyptian withdrawal from the Yemen and the Operation 'Hard Surface' fighter squadron as a guarantee, although one account has it that he did not inform the Saudi prime minister of the somewhat restrictive conditions under which the squadron was to operate.[2] On 1 April Bunker saw President Nasser and put to him a detailed plan for mutual disengagement from the Yemen. This was apparently accepted and then cleared with Prince Faysal. The formal agreement, which involved the YAR as well as Egypt and Saudi Arabia, was announced in U Thant's report to the Security Council on 29 April.[3] Under its terms, Saudi Arabia agreed both to stop all aid to the royalists and to deny them the use of her territory in exchange for a rapid, phased withdrawal of all UAR forces in the Yemen. The UAR further agreed not to take reprisals against any royalists for actions taken prior to the beginning of disengagement, and to stop all raids on Saudi territory. A demilitarized zone, twenty kilometres in width, was to be established on each side of the northern frontier between Saudi Arabia and the Yemen. 'Impartial observers' would be stationed in this zone on both sides of the frontier to check that the terms of the disengagement agreement were being kept. In this connection, they would also have the task of travelling into Saudi Arabia to see that all aid to the royalists had in fact ceased, as well as to Yemeni sea and air ports to check upon the withdrawal of Egyptian forces and equipment.[4]

In view of the need for an observer mission, the secretary-general sent the Swedish Major-General Carl von Horn, who was at that time chief of the United Nations Truce Supervisory organization in Palestine,[5] on a brief tour of inspection to Egypt, the Yemen, and Saudi Arabia 'for the purpose of consulting with the appropriate authorities on details relating

[1] Weintal and Bartlett, pp. 45–8.
[2] Ibid., pp. 48–50; Schmidt, p. 194, who writes: 'The original instructions for "Operation Hard Surface" were that American planes would "attack and destroy" any intruders over Saudi air space. But this was later watered down to read that they would simply defend themselves if attacked. The evidence from Saudi sources is that Mr Bunker stuck to the original formula and did not tell Prince Faisal of the change.'
[3] Weintal and Bartlett, pp. 50–1; *Documents, 1963*, pp. 325–7. In his report, U Thant generously recognized that Mr Bunker's talks 'in the end proved fruitful and from them emerged the agreed terms of disengagement'. See also the speech by Crown Prince Faysal at Ta'if, 5 Sept. 1963, *Arab political documents, 1963*, pp. 372–5.
[4] 'Report of the Secretary-General', 29 Apr. 1963.
[5] He had also had experience in the Congo.

to the nature and functioning of United Nations observers in implementation of the terms of disengagement and to report to me with his recommendations as to the size of the set-up that might be required to discharge this responsibility'.[1]

When he arrived in the Yemen and saw the area which the observers were supposed to observe, General von Horn soon realized that U Thant's original estimate of the size of the proposed mission was hopelessly inadequate.[2] 'There were 6,500 square miles of barren waste and mountains', he wrote later, 'through which thousands of trails, tracks, defiles, passes, river beds and canyons known to the mountain people, would have to be observed to seal the routes along which men and arms could make their way (mainly in darkness) from Saudi Arabia into the Yemen. It was an impossible task . . .'[3] Equally alarming was the attitude of the Egyptian authorities to the implementation of the disengagement agreement. Field-Marshal Amer told von Horn on 1 May that 'he wanted to make it clear that the Egyptians had no intention of withdrawing *all* their troops from the Yemen. Whatever international agreements might be reached, a security force would always have to be left to ensure the continuation of the Sallal regime.'[4] When apprised of this information on the following day, the Saudi Arabian foreign minister told von Horn that 'his country was simply not prepared to accept any attempt by the Egyptians to leave security forces in the [Yemen] when, eventually, their army withdrew. Saudi Arabia was going to insist on complete withdrawal; she would take the same attitude towards any Egyptian military personnel left behind in "mufti".'[5]

In spite of this somewhat discouraging picture, the secretary-general decided to press on and, in a second report to the Security Council on 27 May, proposed the establishment of an enlarged mission under General von Horn's command.[6] The problem of its finance was settled when, on 7 June, U Thant was able to announce that Saudi Arabia and the UAR had agreed to defray the costs of the mission.[7] Even so, the Soviet Union insisted that the whole question be put to a meeting of the Security Council on the grounds that it was the latter's function under the Charter to take decisions on 'measures by the United Nations to maintain international peace and security'.[8] At the conclusion of the debate on 11 June the

[1] 'Report of the Secretary-General', para. 5.

[2] In his report, U Thant wrote, 'I have been thinking in terms of not more than fifty observers, a few helicopters, possibly three or four, and a similar number of small aircraft . . . together with the required jeeps and lorries, should suffice.'

[3] General Carl von Horn, *Soldiering for peace* (London, 1966), pp. 310–11.

[4] Ibid., p. 297 (emphasis in original).   [5] Ibid., p. 300.

[6] U Thant report, 27 May 1963 (*Documents, 1963*, pp. 327–8).

[7] U Thant report, 7 June 1963 (ibid., p. 329).

[8] See the letter of the Russian representative to the president of the Security Council on 8 June, *SCOR*, 18th Year, Supplement, document S/5326.

Soviet representative, while expressing his general agreement with the idea of sending a United Nations mission to the Yemen, abstained in the vote on the joint Ghanaian–Moroccan resolution[1] which established the United Nations Yemen Observation Mission (UNYOM), as it became known, on the grounds that no time limit had been placed on the mission's task and that, as Saudi Arabia and the UAR had only agreed to finance it for two months, this might eventually give rise to some difficulties.[2] There seems to have been no sinister political motive behind the Russian action, which was most probably the result of the long-standing Soviet mistrust of independent initiatives by the United Nations Secretariat.[3]

Von Horn felt strongly about the urgency of the mission. As he later noted,

Long before we started I was aware that were we to make any real impression on the Egyptians and the Saudi Arabians, the mission would have to be capable of carrying out its role *efficiently and with the minimum of delay*. Strength—or a show of strength—is the one factor which invariably produces results in the Middle East; and hesitation, any delay in coming into action, would inevitably lead to scepticism and fast degenerate into contempt. Neither side would believe that we were capable of fulfilling our promises.[4]

Unfortunately, there had already been a fairly lengthy delay between the acceptance of the disengagement agreement on 29 April and the passing of the Security Council resolution establishing UNYOM on 11 June. The Saudi Arabian foreign minister had assured von Horn on 2 May that all supplies to the royalists had ceased on 29 April promptly,[5] and while it is hard to ascertain the truth of this statement there is no doubt that the Egyptians were in no great hurry to fulfil their part of the bargain. Thus, although they did begin to withdraw troops in May, they replaced them with fresh units, keeping the total constant at around 28,000 men.[6] By the end of the month, Prince Faysal was warning American diplomats that he would resume arms shipments to the royalists unless the Egyptians carried out their side of the disengagement agreement,[7] and his warning was underlined when, early in June, Egyptian aircraft carried out more raids on Saudi territory.[8]

---

[1] For the text of the resolution, see *Documents, 1963*, pp. 329–30. It was carried by ten votes to nil, with the U.S.S.R. abstaining.

[2] For the Russian delegate's speech of 11 June see *SCOR*, 18th Year, 1038th meeting, *passim*.

[3] The whole question of the constitutional basis of UNYOM is covered in Rosalyn Higgins, *United Nations peacekeeping: documents and commentary, 1946–67*, vol. i, *The Middle East* (London, 1969), Part 4, Sections 2, 4, and 11. In fact, Dr Higgins's chapter is the best single account of UNYOM in existence.

[4] Von Horn, p. 317 (emphasis in original).

[5] Ibid., p. 300.   [6] *NY Times*, 15 May 1963.   [7] Ibid., 1 June 1963.

[8] See the Saudi Arabian complaint to the Security Council in *Documents, 1963*, p. 330. The Egyptian reply (ibid., pp. 331–2) did not deny the attacks.

Von Horn arrived in the Yemen on 13 June with the advance party of UNYOM. The mission was supposed to become fully operational on 4 July, but on the previous day he was forced to report to his superiors in New York that it was still 77 per cent below strength in terms of military personnel, 51 per cent in terms of civilian personnel, and 89 per cent in terms of aircraft.[1] Such shortages, of course, completely hamstrung the mission, and von Horn later admitted that in the early stages, 'apart from Egyptian intelligence, we had no true picture of the bitter fighting raging in the Yemen', a state of affairs that was reinforced by a strict injunction that he was on no account to contact the royalists, in spite of the fact that they controlled large sections of the buffer zone in which his mission was supposed to be operating.[2]

When von Horn returned to the Yemen at the end of July after three weeks' leave, he thought it 'obvious that certain elements in Saudi Arabia had lost patience with our inability to make the Egyptians observe the disengagement terms. Supply convoys across the mountains had been restarted, with or without official blessing, and the Imam's forces had become increasingly active . . .' He did not believe that there was much hope of securing Saudi co-operation. He noted:

At the beginning they had complied with the disengagement terms, but before long they had been driven to the conclusion that this was a very one-sided agreement, because the Egyptians had little or no intention of keeping their side of the bargain. And the complete lack of interest by the United Nations towards any royalist complaints about the bombing and massacres in royalist-held territory by the Egyptians had obviously convinced the Saudis that the high-minded conception of human rights and justice which prevailed on the East River had nothing in common with the basic truths in the Yemen.[3]

It was during July, in fact, that a London newspaper carried the first report by a Western correspondent that the Egyptians were using poison gas in the Yemen.[4]

On 20 August General von Horn resigned as a head of UNYOM. The occasion—an angry exchange of cables with the secretariat over the continuing supply problems, which threatened to jeopardize the mission's entire purpose—was real enough, but it is clear from his memoirs that von Horn was in any case completely out of sympathy with what he saw as a policy of excessive tenderness towards the Egyptians.[5] Although UNYOM continued for another year, until the Saudi Arabian government finally refused to go on paying its share of the costs,[6] his departure marked the real end of any hope that the UN might succeed in mediating

[1] Von Horn, p. 343.   [2] Ibid., pp. 331, 339.   [3] Ibid., pp. 344-5.
[4] *Daily Telegraph*, 8 July 1963. The royalists had already claimed that the Egyptians were using gas. See ibid., 14 June 1963.
[5] Von Horn, esp. Chapter 28.
[6] The Saudi Arabian government almost stopped paying in Oct. 1963.

a settlement of the civil war. U Thant's reports to the Security Council for the remainder of the year provide eloquent testimony to UNYOM's failure either to end the fighting or external aid to both parties.[1] Even his contention, at the beginning of 1964, that the scale of the fighting had been reduced is disputed by at least one highly qualified observer.[2]

In retrospect, it is clear that UNYOM was doomed from the start. In the first place, it was hopelessly small. Von Horn had persuaded U Thant to increase its strength from a planned 50 to 200, but experts reckoned that 2,000 was more like the number really required.[3] Secondly, the disengagement agreement did not cover all parties and all areas of tension. In particular, the border between the YAR and the South Arabian Federation was not included, and the summer of 1963 witnessed a whole series of incidents between Egyptians and republican forces on the one hand and British and Federal troops on the other.[4] Field-Marshal Amer had told von Horn on 1 May that the Egyptians wanted the Yemen–Federation border included in UNYOM's zone of operations,[5] but for reasons which have never been explained, nothing was done about this until the following November, when a British proposal for mutual disengagement was rejected by the republican authorities on the grounds that it would signify acceptance of the existing frontier.[6] By then, of course, it was too late anyway.

Most important of all, however, was undoubtedly the fact that the US government, which was mainly responsible for the disengagement agreement in the first place, was simply not prepared to apply pressure to the UAR in an attempt to make the latter comply with it. This emerges very clearly from the letter of the assistant secretary of state for Near Eastern affairs, Phillips Talbot, to Senator Hickenlooper of Iowa on 26 July 1963, and to which reference has already been made.[7] In his original letter to the secretary of state, Senator Hickenlooper had argued that, not only had Egypt 'neither withdrawn nor diminished its military and other activities' in the Yemen, but there was 'strong evidence that the Egyptians have enlarged the area of attack . . .' In these circumstances, Hickenlooper suggested that the US government 'should give immediate consideration to the question of withdrawal of recognition of the present government of the Yemen' unless the Egyptians withdrew. He added that, if the present situation continued, he would consider tabling a

[1] For U Thant's report of 28 Oct. 1963, see *Documents, 1963*, pp. 334–41.
[2] Dana Adams Schmidt, pp. 171–2. [3] *NY Times*, 3 June 1963.
[4] For the Yemeni complaints see the letters of the Yemeni representative at the UN to the secretary-general on 22 June and 28 Aug. 1963 (*SCOR*, 18th Year, Supplements, S5338 and S5408). For the British rebuttals and counter-complaints of 1 Aug. and 10 Sept. see ibid., S5343 and S5424.
[5] Von Horn, p. 298.
[6] *Times*, 29 Nov. 1963; *Chronology of Arab politics* (Beirut, 1964), vol. i, No. 4, pp. 421–2.
[7] See above, p. 230.

resolution in the Senate to that effect, which might also propose 'such other matters affecting cooperation with Egypt as might be considered proper'—a clear allusion to US economic aid to the UAR.

Talbot's reply provided a revealing picture of the administration's attitude. 'In the first place', he argued, 'the original basis for our recognition of the Yemeni regime still applies. Whether or not the regime enjoys the same degree of popular support is a controversial question . . . [but] this does not mean that those disaffected with the leadership of the new republican regime favour the restoration of the wholly discredited Imamate.' One might have wondered then exactly what it was the royalists were fighting for, had Mr Talbot not already dismissed their opposition as traditional tribal resistance to central authority. 'Second,' he continued, 'we do not believe that withdrawing our recognition would advance US interests.' He went on to explain this largely in terms of the fear that a weak and friendless republican regime would be wide open to Communist penetration. As for the UAR, it 'wants to withdraw its troops from Yemen' and was only prevented from doing so by 'the continuance of tribal guerrilla warfare in the Yemen highlands and perhaps also from the multiplicity of problems facing the new government'. The stronger the YAR became, the sooner the Egyptians would leave. Economic pressure upon Egypt would certainly not be of any help, for 'our experience shows that this type of action does not advance the objectives it is designed to promote, but instead has exactly the opposite result'.[1]

One of the few statements in Talbot's letter with which a more or less dispassionate outsider would probably have agreed was to the effect that 'some observers believe that a broadening of the base of the Yemen Arab Republic leadership might strengthen the hand of the government, reduce tribal disaffection and facilitate a more rapid U.A.R. withdrawal'. Indeed, there was some evidence in the summer and autumn of 1963 that Yemenis of various persuasions were in fact exploring such a possibility, perhaps with the backing of the USA, Britain, and Saudi Arabia.[2] In the absence of any stronger action on the part of the powers involved, this was about the only ray of hope on the Yemeni horizon as 1963 drew to a close.

[1] *Documents, 1963*, pp. 332–4.
[2] *Observer*, 14 July 1963; *Daily Telegraph*, 15 Aug. 1963; *Times*, 18 Oct. 1963; *Economist*, 11 Jan. 1964; Schmidt, p. 200.

PART IV
AFRICA

CHAPTER IX

THE UNITED NATIONS AND THE CONGO
SETTLEMENT, 1962–1963

(a) *Introduction*

AT the beginning of 1962 the Republic of the Congo seemed to be over-
coming the crisis which had afflicted it since it achieved independence
from Belgium in July 1960. The two major threats to its central government in Leopoldville appeared to have been subdued, both with the support of the United Nations force (ONUC) sent in to help resolve the
Congo's problems. In the first place, the challenge from the rival centre
of power set up under Antoine Gizenga in Stanleyville had finally collapsed when Gizenga was brought back to the capital and placed under
arrest. More importantly—since Gizenga had represented a fading risk—
the province of Katanga appeared to have abandoned the secession which
it had maintained since shortly after independence. After nearly two
weeks of fighting with UN troops, its president, Moise Tshombe, had
signed the Kitona Declaration of 21 December 1961, whereby he fully
acknowledged central government authority. Katanga's secession had been
critically damaging to the Congo, since it denied the country revenue from
the province's enormous mineral resources. This was therefore a step
forward of the very first importance.[1]

The achievement of Kitona was much more apparent than real, however. In the first place, ONUC had succeeded in establishing itself in
strength only in Elisabethville, the provincial capital, and not throughout
Katanga, although the acting secretary-general, U Thant, had stated
that this was one of his objectives. ONUC's military position in Katanga
was still far from commanding, and the secretary-general's political
leverage was reduced accordingly. In the second place, the Kitona
Declaration was not as unconditional as it seemed. Although it could be
interpreted as an act of surrender, it soon became clear that it was really
designed as a public affirmation of Tshombe's willingness to negotiate
with the Congolese prime minister, Cyrille Adoula. Moreover, even this
willingness had its limitations, as Tshombe on his return to Elisabethville
announced that he could not speak for the Katangese Assembly which
alone had the right to pronounce on the Declaration. So what had

[1] For Gizenga, see J. Gérard-Libois and B. Verhaegen, eds., *Congo 1962* (Brussels, 1963),
pp. 5–26. The text of the Kitona Declaration is in *Documents, 1961*, pp. 770–1. See also *Survey,
1961*, pp. 513–18.

looked like a hard-and-fast ʳcommitment was in fact nothing of the kind.[1]

In short, the UN action in December had produced not a solution but a compromise. The basic reason for this was that the secretary-general had not been authorized to use force to end Katangan secession. The Security Council Resolutions of 21 February and 24 November 1961 had empowered ONUC to use force only to prevent civil war between Congolese troops or to expel white mercenaries serving in the Katangan gendarmerie. This, in turn, reflected the weight of international opposition to a United Nations equipped to take serious political initiatives. Katanga could count on powerful support from conservative circles in Belgium, even though the Belgian government had recently resumed diplomatic relations with Leopoldville, and indeed it was revenue from the Belgian firm, Union Minière du Haut-Katanga, which financed secession. The policy of the British government in the December crisis had been strongly influenced by extreme right-wing opinion, and on 28 December the British foreign secretary, Lord Home, made a severe attack on the Afro-Asian majority in the General Assembly which undermined the Congo operation. Even the United States administration of President Kennedy, the mainstay of the UN force, felt bound to take into account the formidable Congressional hostility. All these restraining factors had already made themselves felt and were to continue to limit the role of ONUC throughout 1962.[2]

While not universally accepted, this moderation was very widespread, as was proved by the reaction to a Soviet request on 25 January for an urgent Security Council meeting. As the Soviet delegate rightly pointed out, no real progress had been made on the expulsion of mercenaries from Katanga, and, as the head of ONUC, Dr Linner, remarked, the hard core still remained at large. In other words, one of the basic objectives of the Force was unfulfilled. Adoula, however, responded by denying the need for a meeting 'at a time when the situation in the Congo is showing marked improvement', and he was given full backing by the Lagos conference of African states, representing the moderate and conservative sectors of African opinion. In the event, the Security Council met on 30 January, but decided to adjourn without taking any action, by a vote of seven to two.[3]

Linner, none the less, pressed on and tried to extract concessions from Tshombe on this issue and on others, hoping, no doubt, to achieve something before his imminent replacement. He had, on 25 January, asked

[1] For the U Thant statement of 10 Dec. 1961, see *Documents, 1961*, pp. 767–9.

[2] For the texts of the Security Council resolutions and the Home speech, see ibid., pp. 736–7, 763–5, 514–19.

[3] See *SCOR,* 18th Year, Supplement for Jan., Feb., and Mar. 1962, pp. 4–5, 11–12, 52–3, 57, 61–2.

that mercenaries be removed from such towns as Kolwezi, Kipushi, Jadotville, and Kaminaville, and on 7 February he secured Tshombe's agreement to setting up joint commissions to expedite this as well as to a UN military presence in the towns. In return, ONUC would allow the Lubumbashi mining installation to start operations again. On 15 February, however, Tshombe withdrew his consent for UN troops to be stationed throughout Katanga. The joint commissions were established, but came to nothing. Even so, Lubumbashi went into production once more. Katanga had recovered its balance, and the UN had been unable to improve its position one iota.[1]

Katanga's rapid recovery was further stressed by the Assembly's highly qualified acceptance of the Kitona Declaration on 15 February. Tshombe's commitment was described as 'a basis of discussion', and it was emphasized that Leopoldville 'must in future show understanding and take into account the particular characteristics of Katanga'. Among other things, the central government was not to oppose the restoration of Elisabethville's authority over the whole of the province, nor to take any measures 'liable to prejudice the economic and financial situation of Katanga'. Finally, the Assembly reserved the right to ratify whatever agreements might be reached between Tshombe and Adoula.[2]

This resolution plainly served notice on Leopoldville that Katanga was anything but submissive. Moreover, in the debate on 15 January Tshombe even went so far as to denounce 'the Americans who have financed and continue to finance the war and disorders in Katanga' (and, he might have added, who were the principal sponsors of the Kitona Declaration). Nevertheless, the resolution was accepted by Adoula as an approval of the Declaration, and he invited Tshombe to meet him in the capital on 21 February to discuss how it should be implemented. In this he was supported by the United States, who had embarked at Kitona on a policy of bringing the two sides together to produce a Congolese solution to Congolese problems and who chose to ignore Tshombe's provocation in the hope that he would come to terms of his own free will. Few cared to recall that he had attended similar negotiations the previous summer at Coquilhatville, and that the Katanga Assembly had repudiated the agreement he had made there only ten days after its signature. This time, the backers of Leopoldville seemed to believe things would be different.[3]

---

[1] *SCOR*, Jan.–Mar. 1962, 18–20, 28–30. Tshombe's reply is in *Congo 1962*, pp. 343–4. It may be significant that it is not printed in the Security Council records; nor was the statement by U Thant of 9 Jan., which indicates a distinct conflict with Linner's approach. In it U Thant said that the need to consolidate in Elisabethville precluded a hunt for mercenaries elsewhere in Katanga. Text in A. L. Burns and N. Heathcote, *Peace-keeping by U.N. forces* (London, 1963), p. 149.

[2] Text of the Katanga Assembly Resolution in *Documents, 1962*, pp. 857–9.

[3] J. Gérard-Libois, *Katanga secession* (Madison, 1966), p. 234; *SCOR*, Jan.–Mar. 1962, p. 38; *Survey, 1961*, p. 496.

(b) *Breakdown of the Leopoldville talks and the formulation of the U Thant Plan*

The gulf between Adoula and Tshombe was too wide to be bridged, even after nearly ten weeks of negotiation. Adoula remained committed to a Congo in which the centre retained all important governmental functions, while Tshombe continued to press for a solution giving the provinces a far-reaching degree of autonomy. This was the situation during the first round of talks between 18 March and 16 April, when the two delegations were left to face each other alone, and it was no different in the second round between 18 May and 26 June, when Robert K. Gardiner, Linner's successor as head of ONUC, took an active part. Although it was decided to set up four commissions—on military affairs, monetary problems, economic and fiscal matters, and transport and communications—there was complete disagreement on the basic constitutional issue and the conference broke up without even producing a joint communique.[1]

For Adoula, the collapse of the talks was a heavy blow. He had staked his political future on bringing Katanga back into the fold by peaceful means, and now this had manifestly failed, he was wide open to attack from the parliamentary opposition to his left. What was more, he was now governing a country which was rapidly going bankrupt. In the first quarter of 1962, governmental expenditure had soared as high as 4,807 million Congolese francs; receipts had totalled only 1,611 million. The gap could not be closed by a share of Katanga's revenues alone. A drastic austerity programme was also badly needed, but it was still true that the Katangan secession was helping to bleed the Congo to death financially and it was extremely doubtful whether Adoula's regime would survive the crash when it came.

The UN was also in serious financial trouble. Its expenditure on the Congo operation was running at about $120 million a year, over and above a regular annual expenditure of some $86 million. Several member-states, notably France and the Soviet Union, had refused to pay for ONUC or for the UN Emergency Force in the Middle East (UNEF), and the Organization was running deep into deficit. In December 1961 the General Assembly authorized the secretary-general to issue bonds up to a total of $200 million, but as of 30 June 1962 only some $26 million-worth had actually been purchased. In London for talks with Lord Home on 8 July, U Thant was reported as saying that, because of the lack of available funds, the Congo mission would soon have to be wound up.[2] The USA, as the principal backer of both the UN and the Congo, was doing what she could to remedy the situation. In January Kennedy had

[1] For an account of the talks from the UN point of view, see *SCOR*, Apr.–June 1962, pp. 1–93.

[2] *Yearbook of the United Nations, 1962* (New York, 1964), pp. 473–7, 551, 535, 528–9. R. Welensky, *Welensky's 4,000 days* (London, 1964), pp. 259–60.

pledged that his government would buy up to $100 million of UN bonds, but the proposal met with stiff opposition in Congress. Leopoldville was better placed. On 28 June the state department announced the offer of a $10 million grant to subsidize the Congolese import programme, bringing the total aid for the year July 1961 to June 1962 to $51 million. In addition, an international aid consortium was being considered in Washington. Yet valuable as all these initiatives were, they did nothing to resolve the problem of Katanga's secession, and this was still the crucial stumbling-block to progress.[1]

That Katanga was determined to maintain the secession could not be doubted. It is true that on 27 June Tshombe told the secretary-general that his government had decided to make 100 million Congolese francs available to Leopoldville as a token of their good faith, and on 1 July he stated that Katangan delegates to the four commissions which the recent talks at Leopoldville had agreed to set up, would be appointed within the next two days. The offer of the 100 million francs, however, was almost certainly made to embarrass the central government, and, as the *Essor du Katanga* pointed out, it was to be channelled through the UN so that the 'corrupt politicians of Leopoldville' could not get their hands on it. As for the commissions, Tshombe had agreed at Leopoldville that they could not begin work until a joint communique was issued. Since no communique followed the talks, as Gardiner pointed out, there was little point in Tshombe nominating commission members.[2]

The reality of Katangese intentions was disclosed on 11 July, when the second anniversary of 'independence' was celebrated with a large military parade through the centre of Elisabethville. This was followed on 17 July by what had all the appearance of a carefully staged demonstration by Katangese women against an ONUC checkpost, during which a woman and a boy were alleged to have been shot by Indian troops. After two years of UN intervention, Katanga was still as strong and as defiant as ever.[3]

Faced with this defiance, Adoula did as best he could. On 11 July, to coincide with the anniversary of the secession, a law was promulgated creating a new province of North Katanga, thus dividing the existing province into two. On the same day, Adoula once more reshuffled his administration and pointedly refrained from offering any ministerial posts to Katanga. But these were only gestures. The writ of the central government did not yet run throughout North Katanga, which was still largely in the hands of Tshombe's gendarmerie, and Adoula's political weakness was exposed on 16 July when his new ministry fell three votes

---

[1] *Congo 1962*, pp. 365–6.
[2] SCOR, July–Aug. 1962, pp. 21–2, 23–4. *Congo 1962*, p. 400.
[3] SCOR, July–Aug. 1962, pp. 3–7, 26–36.

short of the absolute majority required for recognition by the Chamber of Deputies. The government did not resign, but he was in no position to move against Tshombe.[1]

In these circumstances, the deadlock could only be broken by renewed international action, but the question remained: what form should it take? While in London, U Thant had gone out of his way to stress that as far as he was concerned, military force was ruled out. This still left open the option of pressure by means of economic sanctions, and this was in fact the direction in which both Washington and the UN were tending. The first public indication of what was in the wind came from a statement put out by the state department on the Elisabethville demonstrations of 17 July. In it, the secession was described as 'dangerous to Katanga, dangerous to peace, and dangerous to the development of political stability in one of the largest countries of Africa', and it was disclosed that discussions had been going on for some time on the possibility of a sanctions programme directed against the Tshombe regime.[2] The sanctions were to have one overriding purpose, that is, to undermine Tshombe by depriving him of the revenue obtained from the great European mineral corporations operating in the province, especially the Union Minière du Haut-Katanga. As U Thant was later to put it:

> The core of the Congo problem is that of the secession of Katanga; the problem of the Katangan secession is primarily a problem of finance; the problem of finance, in turn, is the problem of the major mining companies.

This, in his view, was not an over-simplification. It was true that the end of secession would not automatically solve all the Congo's problems, but unless it were brought to an end, the Congo would not be able to become a fully independent and sovereign state.[3]

Three countries were involved in the discussions over sanctions— the USA, Britain, and Belgium—and the first press reports made it clear that it was the Americans who were taking the strongest line. The Belgians, for their part, were reluctant to embark on sanctions for fear of reprisals against the Union Minière by Katangan extremists, and the British were equally hesitant on this score, and on the grounds that the scheme was impractical. The British approach was made clear in a speech to the House of Lords by Lord Home on 25 July, in which he advocated a three-point proposal. Adoula was to draw up a 'genuinely federal' constitution; Tshombe was to share Katanga's revenues fairly with Leopoldville; and the UN must sponsor a programme of financial

---

[1] *Congo 1962*, pp. 53–63, 214–17. Adoula had offered up to three posts to Tshombe in the Leopoldville talks, but then suspended the offer; ibid., pp. 55, 58.

[2] *Times*, 9 July 1962. *Documents, 1962*, pp. 862–3.

[3] *Times*, 4 Sept. 1962. The extract is from the introduction to the secretary-general's annual report, published on 3 Sept.

and technical aid to help the country back to its feet. All these measures should come into effect simultaneously and should be agreed rather than compelled. If pressures had to be applied, then they must be applied equally to both sides.[1]

Home's statement showed a marked British disinclination to distinguish between a legal government and its illegal opponents and for this reason it drew some adverse comment in Washington, where it was said that British policy was influenced by economic interests. The British attitude, moreover, was contrasted with that of the Belgian foreign minister, Spaak, who was reported to be willing at least to try and persuade the Union Minière to hand over its revenues to Leopoldville. Indeed, London appeared to have emerged almost as a spokesman for Tshombe and its partisanship was evident in the lukewarm reception given to Adoula's request on 28 July for UN assistance in drawing up a new federal constitution. This had been criticized partly because the constitutional draft adumbrated in the request was too centralized, and partly because there was no provision for consultation with Katanga in framing the new statute.[2]

The initiative on the constitution, it soon turned out, was only the first in a series of moves made by the UN and Congolese government. On 30 July, U Thant endorsed a request from Leopoldville to the Universal Postal Union to treat Katanga's postage stamps as invalid. This first small step in the direction of sanctions was followed on 31 July by an appeal from the secretary-general to all member states of the UN to 'use their influence to persuade the principal parties concerned in the Congo that a peaceful solution is in their own long-term interest'. If this did not work, he would have to consider 'economic pressure upon the Katangese authorities of a kind that will bring home to them the realities of their situation and the fact that Katanga is not a sovereign state and is not recognized by any government in the world as such'. In the last resort, this might well go to the lengths of an embargo on all commercial and financial relations. Finally, in a letter to Spaak on 2 August, he appealed to the Belgian foreign minister to persuade the Union Minière to turn over to the Belgian government all the revenues currently being paid to Katanga. If Belgium froze these assets pending a settlement, in return the UN would give a pledge to protect the corporation's property against possible Katangan reprisals. This would bring to an end a situation in which the Union Minière had become involved 'whether intentionally or unintentionally, in disruptive political activities which can only be carried on because of the very large sums of money available'.[3]

[1] *Times*, 26 July 1962. *Documents, 1962*, pp. 863–4.
[2] *Times*, 27, 31 July 1962. *SCOR*, July–Sept. 1962, pp. 24–5.
[3] *SCOR*, July–Sept. 1962, pp. 37–40.

These measures were in turn supplemented by concrete actions taken against Katanga at the instance of Leopoldville. On 5 August ONUC announced a ban on all flights into and out of Katanga following a request from the central government. On 7 August the government itself declared that henceforth telecommunications with Katanga were suspended; that all air travellers heading for or coming from Katanga must stop in Leopoldville for visa and immigration checks; and that action was being planned against firms operating both in Katanga and the rest of the Congo. Simultaneously, the Congolese National Army moved into an offensive against the Tshombe gendarmerie aimed at the liberation of the newly proclaimed province of North Katanga.[1]

There is little doubt that these last measures were the sole responsibility of Leopoldville. This was made plain by ONUC on 5 August and what followed was almost certainly an embarrassment to the UN. Adoula, under pressures of his own and doubtless anxious to show that he could do something regardless of his foreign advisers, seized the initiative. The actions taken, however, could be no more than irritants to Katanga, and for decisive measures against the secessionists, the UN still had to wait until the United States, Belgium, and Britain could agree on a programme. This was presented to the UN Secretariat on 9 August by officials of the state department. It was reported to fall into two parts, the first outlining proposals for constitutional reform and revenue-sharing, the second setting out a scheme for the progressive coercion of Katanga. There was said to be full agreement on part one, but still a divergence of view on the sanctions envisaged in part two. Both the Belgians and the British were understood to want to give Tshombe every chance to fulfil his commitments under the programme; the Americans, on the other hand, were convinced that Tshombe would simply bide his time in that case, and time, it was clear, was very much on his side.[2]

Further details of the proposals were revealed by U Thant on 20 August, by which point they had taken on the popular title of 'the U Thant Plan'. The time had come, the secretary-general claimed, to take action under Articles 25 and 49 of the Charter, and the plan offered perhaps the last possibility of avoiding the alternatives of either a UN military withdrawal from the Congo or securing a new mandate to end the secession by all necessary means. If national reconciliation were to be achieved in the Congo, eight major steps had to be taken. They were as follows:

(1) the drafting of a federal constitution within thirty days;
(2) the drafting of laws governing the division of revenues and the use of foreign exchange, and, in the interim, an equal division of revenue between Leopoldville and Katanga together with the allocation to Katanga of at least 50 per cent of the foreign exchange originating there;

[1] *Times*, 6, 8 Aug. 1962.   [2] Ibid., 10, 11 Aug. 1962.

(3) the drawing-up of a plan for currency unification by the International Monetary Fund;

(4) the framing of a plan for the integration of the Katangan gendarmerie into the Congolese National Army, to be worked out within thirty days and implemented within the next sixty days;

(5) the closing of all non-governmental diplomatic and consular missions abroad;

(6) a government reshuffle giving representation to all political and provincial groups;

(7) a general amnesty for political prisoners;

(8) full co-operation by all Congolese authorities with ONUC in the implementation of United Nations resolutions.

This programme was to be presented first to Adoula, and then, with his agreement, to Tshombe. Meanwhile, member-states were to urge both sides to accept it, and at the same time to ensure that no mercenaries or military equipment reached the Congo. If Katanga did not agree, a further appeal would go out to UN members 'to take immediate measures to ensure that their relations with the Congo will be in conformity with laws and regulations of the Government of the Congo'. In addition, U Thant stated that he would make 'a firm request' for the embargo on trade and financial relations mentioned in his appeal of 31 July, and most particularly a ban on Katangan copper and cobalt.[1]

This sounded drastic enough, but there was a great deal more to the U Thant Plan which was not revealed on 20 August. The secretary-general had in fact disclosed in detail only the first half of the plan, that is, the positive proposals for Congolese integration. The second half—the section listing sanctions—was only hinted at and was not made public until 29 November. Under the heading 'course of action', four phases of coercion were envisaged. The first phase covered the period between the secretary-general's adoption of the plan and its presentation to Adoula and Tshombe. During this period, the ONUC military command was to tell Katanga that it intended to have full freedom of movement throughout the province if need be, but that for the time being it was not going to set up new garrisons. At the same time, Adoula was to introduce legislation prohibiting the import or export of unauthorized goods—a clear prelude to the ban on copper and cobalt. Meanwhile, a whole series of measures would be carried out by the UN and by individual member-states. These were:

(1) governmental statements supporting Adoula's constitutional proposals and denouncing Katangan secession;

(2) negotiations between Leopoldville and Brussels for the collection in Belgium of duties on all goods exported to the Congo, including Katanga;

[1] SCOR, July–Sept. 1962, pp. 12–18. Text also in Documents, 1962, pp. 866–71.

(3) the avoidance by ONUC of very low-level flights over Katanga;
(4) immediate consideration by the United States of a small shipment of military equipment for the Congo;
(5) United Nations assistance for the urgent modernization of the Congolese National Army;
(6) additional American aid for Leopoldville once controls were established on the use of foreign exchange, and possibly aid from Belgium and other states as well;
(7) a request from Leopoldville to neighbouring countries for help in preventing the smuggling of arms and other goods;
(8) a further UN appeal for action to stop mercenaries or military equipment from entering the Congo;
(9) an invitation from Leopoldville to the Union Minière to discussions on their future relationship;
(10) an invitation from the United Nations to Belgium and the Union Minière to discussions on the protection of Belgian nationals and Union Minière property in Katanga;
(11) the acceptance by all travellers into and out of Katanga of central government travel regulations.

The second phase covered the ten days which Katanga had been granted to make up its mind on the plan, during which time both foreign governments and the Union Minière were to urge Katanga to accept. If the Katangans seemed likely to reject the plan or play for time, the governments were to warn them that after the ten-day period of grace, they would boycott Katangan copper and cobalt. If, in spite of that, the secession went on, then the screw would be tightened still further. Sanctions might include the withdrawal of Belgian technicians, the suspension of posts and telecommunications, the stoppage of all air traffic in and out of Elisabethville, and a blockade of Katanga's exports and imports by setting up road blocks on the railways leading into the province.

The third phase was scheduled to come into effect if Katanga rejected the plan after the ten-day period had elapsed. Here, the action envisaged was short and sharp. Leopoldville would ask interested governments to refuse to import Katangan copper and cobalt, and they would comply with the request. A fourth phase provided for consultations in the event that Katanga was still defiant when further measures were to be considered.[1]

The non-publication of this sanctions programme, it is reasonable to infer, was decided on in deference to Britain and Belgium, who still emphasized their desire to arrange an agreement by means other than coercion. It is interesting to note, however, that Adoula was supposed to be given only a broad verbal outline of the 'course of action', and that Tshombe was given no indication of it at all. So sanctions were still being

[1] *SCOR*, Oct.–Dec. 1962, pp. 37–42. Text in *Documents, 1962*, pp. 866–71.

played down, although U Thant's statements of 31 July and 20 August had left no one in doubt that they would be brought into play if the occasion demanded it.

The plan was presented to Adoula on 20 August, and in doing so Gardiner made it clear that it was a package to be accepted or rejected as a whole, and that it was not negotiable. On 23 August, Adoula accepted, with the proviso that 'we reserve in advance our freedom of action in case, though its substance may be acceptable, its execution raises difficulties'. He also agreed that it be put before Tshombe and the following day Gardiner flew to Elisabethville to do this. Faced with the combined pressure of Washington, London, and Brussels, and privately urged to accept by his long-time counsellor Sir Roy Welensky, Tshombe gave way. On 2 September he stated that his government wholeheartedly supported the plan, although it only elaborated 'the general principles governing the solutions which will have to be formulated'. This was not an acceptance of the several concrete actions which had been listed in the plan, but U Thant was not disposed to argue and on 5 September he announced that both parties had given their assent. Once again the Congo seemed to be close to a solution of its problems.[1]

(c) *Failure to implement the U Thant Plan*

The process of putting the U Thant Plan into effect began on 10 September with the dispatch of identical letters from Gardiner to Adoula and Tshombe in which he reiterated the programme outlined by the secretary-general on 20 August. The draft constitution was to be completed by the end of September and the Katangans were to be invited to submit their views meanwhile. Three commissions were to be established —on revenue-sharing, foreign exchange, and military affairs—and at the same time the Katangan gendarmerie was to swear an immediate oath of allegiance to the president of the Republic. Both sides were urged to stop all troop movements in Katanga, and Adoula was to bring in amnesty legislation at once and to renew his offer of ministries to Tshombe's party as soon as possible.[2]

All this still had to be implemented, however, and from the very start the task was made doubly difficult by a sharp increase in tension between ONUC and Katanga. On 12 September there was a clash in Elisabethville between ONUC troops and gendarmerie and on 24 September, two Indians were killed by a mine placed on their patrol route. Gardiner had, by this time, amassed evidence that the European mercenaries were once again operating in strength, and that the Katangan air force was being built up to formidable proportions. When taxed with allegations about

[1] *SCOR*, Oct.–Dec. 1962, pp. 30–1, 42–7; *Times*, 27, 31 Aug. 1962; Welensky, p. 263.
[2] *SCOR*, Oct.–Dec. 1962, pp. 48–50.

mercenaries, Tshombe's reply was that 'the affair of the mercenaries is like the tales about sea-serpents or the Abominable Snowman', and he countered with accusations that the UN was interested only in enslaving Katanga or destroying it.[1]

It was against this unpromising background that the American under-secretary of state for political affairs, Mr McGhee, left Washington for the Congo. During the first week of October he was closeted with Tshombe for four days in an attempt to persuade him to come to terms. We are told by one subsequent account that McGhee found the Katangan leader 'contemptuous of the Americans and confident of his own strength', and he was unprepared to make more than a few gestures in Leopoldville's direction. These were the transfer to Leopoldville of the equivalent of $2 million in foreign exchange; the transfer of an equal sum in Congolese francs as the first instalment of its payment of revenues to the centre; the reopening of the Lubilash bridge for railway traffic as a step towards restoring the old route for conveying Katanga's minerals out of the Congo; and the reopening of telecommunications with Leopoldville. All this fell well short of full acceptance of the U Thant Plan.[2]

Even so, Washington seemed disinclined to draw the conclusion that the moment for sanctions had arrived. McGhee had emerged as a spokesman for the moderates within the Kennedy administration, and, as *The Times* saw it, had been sent out 'to apply at least a temporary dampener' to an inflammable situation, even though it placed the plan in jeopardy. We are told that two of Kennedy's White House staff, Dungan and Kaysen, were reluctant to see deeper American involvement, especially since the Soviet threat appeared to have receded. On 14 October the ambassador to the United Nations, Adlai Stevenson, was reported to have given Kennedy an optimistic account of developments.[3]

Others were much less hopeful. Gardiner's report on the growing crisis between ONUC and Katanga was issued on 8 October and was thus available when U Thant met the Congo Advisory Committee on 12 October. The secretary-general seems to have been ready to apply sanctions and the most radical members of the committee apparently wished to go still further and have force used to end the secession. For this purpose they were reported to have called for a meeting of the Security Council. U Thant was opposed to seeking a new mandate from the Council authorizing force, but was apparently sympathetic to the idea of a Council resolution making sanctions mandatory. This he had avoided so far, no doubt partly from fear of provoking a veto.

---

[1] *SCOR*, Oct.–Dec. 1962, pp. 10–13, 1–10, 19, 27.
[2] Schlesinger, p. 504. *Congo 1962*, pp. 391–2. *SCOR*, Oct.–Dec. 1962, p. 134.
[3] *Times*, 22 Oct. 1962; Schlesinger, p. 503; *Times*, 15 Oct. 1962; Burns and Heathcote, pp. 194–5.

Tshombe's refusal to accept the plan was underlined in the days immediately following. The new draft constitution was presented on 16 October to a conference of provincial presidents from which Tshombe was a conspicuous absentee. The revenue-sharing and foreign exchange commissions could not agree on the apportionment specified in the plan, and Tshombe's assent to have his gendarmerie swear the oath of allegiance was made conditional on the prior passage of the amnesty act. It is true that the Katangese initialled a cease-fire agreement for North Katanga on 16 October, and Adoula must bear the blame for repudiating it as well as for not introducing amnesty legislation and offering ministerial posts to Tshombe's party. Yet Adoula's failure to meet the obligations imposed by the plan was far less than Tshombe's and the primary responsibility for its slow progress undoubtedly lay with Katanga.[1]

In Adoula's view, no further delay was now acceptable, particularly as his political position was still precarious. On 8 October Katanga was accused of fomenting secession in the provinces of Kivu and Orientale, and a state of emergency declared in South Kasai, where the separatist leader Albert Kalonji had returned after his recent escape from gaol. Kalonji was recaptured on 2 October but his brief bid for freedom had been an unpleasant reminder of the fragile state of central government authority. So too was the fact that on 10 October it was felt necessary to arrest Christophe Gbenye, one of the principal leaders of the left-wing opposition.[2]

Still the UN did not act, although within the Secretariat pressure for action was rising. On 22 October, Ralph Bunche, the UN under-secretary for special political affairs, arrived in Leopoldville to review the situation, and in particular to devise a contingency plan for the military occupation of Katanga in the event of a further outbreak of hostilities between ONUC and the gendarmerie. But the use of force was still ruled out by Washington. The American ambassador to Leopoldville, Mr Gullion—widely credited with the concept of the U Thant Plan—was later said to have felt at this point 'that the solution was to unleash the UN troops and let them destroy Tshombe's army', but his view was not shared. President Kennedy was convinced that a 'third round' was out of the question in the light of the furore which had followed the two large-scale ONUC military clashes with Katanga in September and December 1961. Nor was the USA prepared to contemplate sanctions at this stage. McGhee on his return from the Congo on 10 October was expected to report that they would be premature, and on 22 October it was indicated that the USA no longer required Tshombe to meet his commitments.[3]

---

[1] *SCOR*, Oct.–Dec. 1962, pp. 31–5, 119–22.   [2] *Congo 1962*, pp. 70–5.
[3] *SCOR*, Jan.–Mar. 1963, p. 54; *Times*, 22 Oct. 1962; Schlesinger, p. 503; Burns and Heathcote, pp. 196–7.

Thus within three weeks the plan had suffered an abrupt decline. It must not be forgotten that Kennedy had other preoccupations. It may well be that his *volte-face* was not altogether unconnected with imminent Congressional elections in which he could expect to face strong opposition from Katanga's supporters, and from 16 October onwards, he had been deep in the Cuban missile crisis. Yet whatever the reasons for the change in US policy, the UN was hamstrung until Washington once again threw its weight behind the Congo operation.

The paralysis of ONUC was amply demonstrated by the exchange of correspondence between Gardiner and Tshombe in the first half of November. On 2 November, Gardiner wrote to Tshombe pointing out that no real advance towards the end of secession had yet been made. On 8 November he visited him in Elisabethville and urged him to accept the plan within a week. Tshombe's reply of 12 November not only gave no ground but embarked on a lengthy and elaborate justification of Katangan policy. Moreover, the very same day Tshombe publicly accused ONUC of looking for a pretext to use force in Katanga. It was clear from the tone of his statement that he was confident of the outcome if fighting broke out, and Welensky gained the same impression when Tshombe came to visit him on 13 November.[1]

In the opinion of Spaak, Tshombe's rejection of Gardiner's personal appeal marked the 'moment of enervation' at which it could be considered that the U Thant Plan had failed. This was not, however, the line taken by McGhee during visits to Brussels and London at this time. He was still, apparently, not thinking in terms of sanctions, and his hand was no doubt strengthened by the well-known reluctance of the Belgians and even more the British to embark on the sanctions programme. So Gardiner's deadline of 15 November came and went with no change in the situation. On 16 November Gardiner again wrote to Tshombe asking him to carry out the plan, and, for the first time since the previous February, demanding both full freedom of movement throughout Katanga and the expulsion of the mercenaries. This indicated a perceptible hardening of the UN attitude, but the most telling feature of the letter was the absence of a threat in the event of Tshombe's refusal to respond.[2]

Needless to say, Tshombe did not respond. All he had to do, it seemed, was to sit back and let the forces of opposition disintegrate. Adoula, for instance, was still in a critical position. The Congolese budget deficit for 1962 was forecast as $160 million and the trade deficit at least $78 million. On 12 November Leopoldville had been placed under martial law after a wave of banditry following the escape of 200 convicts from the Makala prison, and on 28 November a motion of censure on the govern-

[1] *SCOR*, Oct.–Dec. 1962, pp. 35–6, 122–5, 131–7; Welensky, p. 264.
[2] *Congo 1962*, p. 391; *Times*, 15 Nov. 1962; *SCOR*, Oct.–Dec. 1962, pp. 137–40.

ment was passed in the Chamber. ONUC, too, was facing a crisis with the announcement that the Indian contingent would be withdrawn in February. The Indians provided the biggest single element in ONUC and they had so far been the mainstay of the UN presence in Katanga. In their absence the force would be gravely weakened.[1]

In these demoralizing circumstances the USA and Belgium felt it necessary to make some sort of a stand; they were not, it should be noticed, joined by Britain. On 25 November Spaak left for Washington accompanied by Robillart, the managing director of the Union Minière, and on 27 November Spaak and Kennedy issued a joint statement. If there was no substantial progress towards implementing the U Thant Plan by voluntary means 'within a very short period of time', then the programme of economic sanctions would have to begin. To make it clear what this entailed, the plan was published in full on 29 November. The British government, although not having taken part in the warning to Tshombe, was none the less reported to have told him that, if sanctions were applied, it would not oppose them.[2]

Even at this late stage, however, efforts at conciliation persisted. On 28 November McGhee is said to have proposed to U Thant that the plan be modified and an American mission be sent to the Congo under UN auspices. These suggestions were rejected, but a further attempt at an accommodation went on which stemmed from the Kennedy–Spaak statement itself. Indeed, the statement had been intended more as a last appeal to reason than as the prelude to sanctions. Underlying the reference to the accomplishment of the plan by voluntary methods was an attempt to bring Adoula and Tshombe together at the UN headquarters in New York. This was put to Adoula on 4 December, but he would not agree; nor, it seems, would Tshombe either. On 11 December, Spaak, the promoter of this last-minute initiative, declared that Tshombe could 'no longer be considered to be a statesman, but a very powerful rebel'. There now seemed to be no alternative to sanctions.[3]

The reinforcement of ONUC had already begun in preparation for this contingency. Early in November U Thant had asked Greece, Italy, Pakistan, the Philippines, and Sweden for jet fighters, and Indonesia had agreed to send a large contingent of ground troops. On 30 November Brigadier Rikhye, the secretary-general's chief military adviser, left New York for Leopoldville to supervise the build-up, and the same day U Thant's personal position as director of the operation was immensely strengthened when he was unanimously elected as secretary-general in his own right. Most importantly, on 3 December the USA

---

[1] *Times*, 22 Nov. 1962; *Congo 1962*, pp. 94–102.
[2] *Times*, 26, 29, 30 Nov. 1962; *Documents, 1962*, p. 876.
[3] Burns and Heathcote, pp. 197, 203, 198; *Congo 1962*, p. 390; *Times*, 12 Dec. 1962.

threw its weight behind the mobilization by resuming its airlift of UN forces.[1]

The decision for sanctions had in fact been taken. The first indication of this came in a letter from Gardiner to Tshombe of 10 December. At the same time, Gardiner once again demanded complete freedom of movement for ONUC throughout Katanga and warned Tshombe that a drive against his mercenaries could be expected. For this latter purpose the use of force had been authorized by the Security Council and, although Gardiner declared that UN troops would not be the first to fire, he made it clear that, if attacked, they would do much more than simply defend themselves. Henceforth they would 'take the protective measures deemed necessary to avoid a recurrence of the attack', in other words, eliminate the gendarmerie as a military threat. Taken in conjunction with the demand for freedom of movement, this pointed to an ONUC occupation of Katanga if the gendarmerie moved against them.[2]

Gardiner's warning was followed by several other UN and Congolese initiatives designed to set the wheels of sanctions turning. On 11 and 12 December U Thant issued an appeal to Belgium to persuade the Union Minière to cease paying its revenues to the Katangan regime, and urged Portugal, South Africa, and the Central African Federation (through Britain) to prohibit the shipment of Katangan copper through their territories pending a settlement of the revenue question. On 11 December a circular letter from Adoula to seventeen governments called on them to refuse to import Katangan copper and cobalt until the secession was ended.[3]

Faced with all these developments, Tshombe made an extremely important concession, after talks with the Rector of the University of Liège, an emissary sent out by Spaak. On 12 December he told U Thant that Katanga was prepared to transfer all the foreign exchange derived from its exports to the Congolese Monetary Council. The Council should return to Katanga 50 per cent of the residue left after the needs of the Union Minière had been met, but not less than 250 million Belgian francs a month. Apart from the stipulation about the minimum due to Katanga, this met the requirements of the plan in full on this point, and marked a distinct step forward from the position adopted by the Katangans in the commission on foreign exchange two months previously.[4]

Everything, however, depended on the way in which Katanga followed up this move, and the events of the next ten days seemed to show that it was no more than another delaying tactic designed to take the heat out of the situation. On 15 December Spaak asked the Union Minière to send representatives to Leopoldville at once to begin negotia-

---

[1] Burns and Heathcote, pp. 198–9. So far U Thant had been serving the unexpired part of his predecessor's term of office.

[2] *SCOR*, Jan.–Mar. 1963, pp. 30–2.   [3] Ibid., pp. 32–40.   [4] Ibid., pp. 41–2.

tions on foreign exchange, but the Union Minière's reply was that it could not do so unless authorized by Tshombe. This was in line with Tshombe's statement on 18 December that the negotiations would be conducted by an official appointed by himself. This was Van Roey, director of the so-called Bank of Katanga, but on 23 December Van Roey told ONUC that he could not go to the capital because Tshombe had not given him permission. So collapsed the last possibility of averting sanctions, much to the regret of Brussels and of London, which had also been urging Tshombe to reach a financial settlement.[1]

Washington was less dejected. By this time Kennedy's patience with Tshombe had run out and he was ready to give the UN full American backing against Katanga. Early in December, U Thant had asked the USA for more military equipment as part of the general reinforcement of ONUC then taking place. The state department, according to one subsequent account, had proposed that the secretary-general be persuaded to accept in addition 'a squadron of U.S. fighter aircraft, to be flown by our Air Force, thus ending Katanga's resistance in a hurry'. Kennedy, however, was sceptical: the proposal would not be approved by Congress unless the administration could prove there was a Communist threat to the Congo, and manifestly there was not. On 14 December he was prepared to authorize the squadron provided it was not used in combat, that it did not come under UN Command and that both Adoula and U Thant agreed. Both were hesitant and so on 18 December he announced instead the imminent dispatch of an American military mission to the Congo, headed by Lieutenant-General Louis W. Truman.[2]

The decision to send the Truman mission was highly controversial. It smacked of unilateral American intervention in the Congo, and it was criticized on these grounds by both France and the Soviet Union. To the Soviet representative at the UN, Mr Zorin, it was a sign that the United States was 'entering on a role of direct subversion', and it was vociferously attacked by the left-wing opposition in Leopoldville as a major threat to Congolese sovereignty. It could also be seen as a usurpation of the functions of ONUC itself, and there was some truth in this in so far as the mission also marked a significant stage in the development of a purely American military aid programme to the Congo. But its immediate impact was to give a strong boost to the UN at a particularly critical moment, and it was an unmistakable warning to Tshombe that the USA would not brook any further intransigence. Moreover, it came at precisely the time when the General Assembly had authorized funds for ONUC to take it through until 30 June 1963, and when it had accepted the advisory opinion of the International Court of Justice that the expenses

[1] Ibid., pp. 42, 48; *Times*, 17, 20, 24 Dec. 1962.
[2] Sorensen, p. 638; *Times*, 19 Dec. 1962.

of ONUC and UNEF were legitimate expenses of the UN. In all these ways the morale of the Congo operation had been raised high and it was well placed to meet whatever challenge came its way.[1]

(d) *Denouement of the crisis, December 1962–January 1963*

The secession of Katanga came to an end in the middle of January 1963, but it was not brought about by the economic sanctions embodied in the U Thant Plan and set in motion on the previous 10 December. Instead, and quite unexpectedly, the UN was presented with the opportunity of establishing its authority by military means, and it was able to do so in exactly four weeks.

Developments first began to take a new turn on 24 December, when ONUC positions in the centre of Elisabethville came under sustained fire from the Katangan gendarmerie. It is not clear under whose authority the gendarmerie was acting. The order may have come from Tshombe or from one of the extremists in his cabinet such as Munongo; alternatively, the military may have taken matters into their own hands. At all events, after four days of shooting, Tshombe refused to put his signature to a ceasefire order, and in mid-afternoon of 28 December ONUC was instructed to retaliate.[2]

By the evening of 30 December, that is, in little more than 48 hours, ONUC was in control of Elisabethville. This in itself was extraordinary in the light of the fact that in December 1961, the same operation had taken almost two weeks. The speed of the ONUC achievement in 1962 can partly be attributed to the much greater numbers of its forces at the outset of the battle as compared with 1961, but it also showed an ineffectual resistance on the part of the gendarmerie. This is curious when one considers that the gendarmerie had taken the initiative and were functioning at high strength, yet compared with December 1961 their performance was singularly unimpressive and they left the way open for ONUC to make unprecedented gains, around Elisabethville as well as within it. When firing was ordered to cease on 30 December, UN forces had seized Elisabethville, Kaminaville, and Kipushi, and the Katangan air force had been destroyed on the ground.

While all this was happening the UN command was completely out of touch with Tshombe, who had left Elisabethville, probably on 28 December. The following day a statement was issued in his name, threatening resistance 'until . . . our whole economic potential has been destroyed'. On 30 December he appeared in Salisbury, where he was given facilities for a press conference in which he once again called on Katangans to

---

[1] *Times*, 21, 22 Dec. 1962; Burns and Heathcote, pp. 202–5; *Yearbook of the United Nations, 1962*, pp. 541–54.
[2] *SCOR*, Jan.–Mar. 1963, pp. 9–13, 42–5.

fight to the death. From there he proceeded to Kolwezi, one of the last two important mining centres still in Katangan hands.[1]

This was the situation when U Thant gave out a long statement on 31 December in which he said that 'all fighting and firing' had ceased the previous day. This meant that everyone concerned could turn once more to the implementation of the U Thant Plan, but its provisions must be executed quickly, that is, 'in a short period of perhaps a fortnight'. Otherwise, 'other measures might have to be weighed'. The UN was prepared to deal with Tshombe in his capacity as provincial president, and if he returned to Elisabethville he would not be 'interfered with' unless he incited the populace to violence against ONUC.[2]

This declaration of UN policy was greeted with relief by Britain and Belgium, who had been urging Tshombe to go back to Elisabethville and accept the plan. The USA made it clear that she would support further ONUC action if that should be necessary. To underline this support it was announced that the first instalment of a massive airlift of military equipment would arrive during the second week in January, when U Thant's new deadline to Katanga expired. By then ONUC would be in a position of overwhelming military strength.[3]

As it happened, however, by that time Tshombe and his ministers had abandoned the secession and the operation was almost over. Instead of pausing, as U Thant had announced, ONUC had gone on to finish the job. By 3 January UN troops had fought their way through to Jadotville, the major mining centre some 100 kilometres north-west of Elisabethville, and the same day it was admitted that there had been 'a serious breakdown in effective communication and co-ordination between United Nations Headquarters and the Leopoldville office'. At once, Bunche was sent out to make an on-the-spot investigation and report back to the secretary-general.[4]

The explanation later given by Bunche was as follows. The contingency plan he had helped devise in October was in three phases. The first of these envisaged the capture of Elisabethville, the second the seizure of Jadotville and other towns, with the final phase the occupation of Kolwezi. U Thant had called a halt at the end of Phase I and was waiting for the reinforcements promised by Washington before embarking on Phase II—the 'other measures' foreshadowed in his statement of 31 December. But several things had combined to throw the plan out of order. The first was a telegram of encouragement sent after the ceasefire of 30 December, which advised the ONUC command 'to extend their Elisabethville perimeter and to keep the gendarmerie and the mercenaries off balance and on the run'. Following this directive, UN troops

[1] Ibid., pp. 13, 49–50, 60–1.   [2] Ibid., pp. 47–51.
[3] *Times*, 2, 3 Jan. 1963.   [4] Ibid., 4 Jan. 1963; *SCOR*, Jan.–Mar. 1963, pp. 52–3.

moved into Kipushi and Kaminaville and out along the road to Jadotville. As regards Jadotville, it had been expected that they would not be
able to cross the Lufira river close to the town because the road and rail
bridges had been destroyed. The bridges were down, but troops were able
to cross and secure a foothold on the far bank by the evening of 1 January.
It was not until then that U Thant's statement of 31 December was received in Elisabethville and an order sent out that the advance on Jadotville be halted. The commanding officer at the Lufira, however, chose to
go on and by noon on 3 January, Jadotville had fallen.[1]

Much of the confusion surrounding the episode was attributed to difficulties of communication between UN headquarters and the men in the
field. There was a seven-hour time differential between New York and
Elisabethville, messages from the Secretariat had first to pass through
Leopoldville, and the need to encode and decode them meant that there
was often an additional time-lag of at least six hours, even for messages of
the highest priority. This, presumably, accounted for the delay of at least
18 hours in the transmission of U Thant's long statement of 31 December,
but other things were either not satisfactorily explained or were ignored.
Into the first category fell the advance on Jadotville on 2 and 3 January,
and into the second, such questions as why a brief order to halt operations
could not have been sent on 31 December before the secretary-general's
statement was issued. It is also noticeable that Bunche did not deal with
the statement which Gardiner was reported to have made on 30 December,
namely that ONUC was 'not going to make the mistake of stopping short
this time'. This operation, unlike the actions of September and December
1961, was going to be 'as decisive as we can make it'. This may simply
have referred to the intention to move into Phase II after two weeks'
breathing-space, but it could equally have meant that Gardiner intended
to go straight on without a pause until Katanga had surrendered. If so,
then ONUC was pursuing its own policy independent of UN headquarters.
It may, of course, be that headquarters was aware of this but chose to turn
a blind eye to it, but whatever the true explanation of the Jadotville
affair it was damaging to the secretary-general's credibility even though
it showed that the UN was after all composed of human beings.[2]

The capture of Jadotville placed all but one of the Union Minière's
most important installations in UN control. This was Kolwezi, where
Tshombe and his ministers had assembled by 1 January. The question
now facing ONUC was whether Tshombe could be persuaded to return
to Elisabethville and acknowledge that the secession was over or whether
he would put a scorched-earth policy into practice and order the destruction of the Kolwezi complex. Tshombe had put out contradictory statements indicating that he was prepared to do both, but it was felt that he

[1] *SCOR*, Jan.–Mar. 1963, pp. 53–9.   [2] *Ibid.*, pp. 55–6. *Times*, 31 Dec. 1962.

was not a nihilist like some of his entourage and that now his military position was so hopeless, he would submit. This was the course urged on him by the British and Belgian governments and—more peremptorily— by the USA in a statement put out on 4 January. To add to the pressure for a settlement, a representative of the Union Minière arrived in Leopold-ville to open negotiations with the central government on foreign exchange. This was a body blow to the secessionists and it was clear that their threats of sabotage had compelled their chief ally to come to terms out of sheer fright.[1]

It was still not so clear whether the Tshombe regime would follow suit. Tshombe himself came back to Elisabethville on 8 January but the next day once again announced that a scorched-earth policy was still being prepared. He continued to vacillate as, on 10 January, he personally paved the way for ONUC to reopen the railway line between Elisabeth-ville and Sakania on the Rhodesian border and then, on 12 January, suddenly returned to Kolwezi.[2]

On 14 January, however, the announcement came out of Kolwezi that the secession was over, that the UN would be allowed full freedom of movement throughout Katanga and that Tshombe was ready to go to Elisabethville to accept all the provisions of the U Thant Plan. This, at last, was the declaration for which both the Congo and the UN had been striving for two and a half years. It was definitive and there was to be no going back on it. Katanga had been reincorporated into the Republic.[3]

The detailed winding-up of the secession followed quickly. On 15 January Adoula assured U Thant that there would be no recriminations and that Tshombe and the members of his regime would be covered by the amnesty proclaimed on 26 November. With this assurance guaranteed, Tshombe proceeded to work out an agreement for ONUC's entry into Kolwezi, which took place on 21 January. As soon as this had safely happened it was disclosed that on 15 January the Union Minière had assented to hand over all the proceeds from its exports to the Congolese Monetary Council which would remit all the foreign exchange necessary to meet the company's expenses. On 23 January the seal was set on the process of reabsorption when the former Congolese prime minister, Joseph Ileo, arrived in Elisabethville as minister-resident of the central government.[4]

Early in February, U Thant issued his report on the reduction of Katanga

---

[1] *SCOR*, Jan.–Mar. 1963, pp. 61–2, 74; Burns and Heathcote, pp. 217–18; *Documents, 1962*, pp. 877–8.

[2] *SCOR*, Jan.–Mar. 1963, pp. 62–3, 65–6.   [3] Text in *Documents, 1962*, pp. 878–9.

[4] *SCOR*, Jan.–Mar. 1963, pp. 64–5, 74–5, 83–5. The promise of an amnesty for Tshombe drew a bitter protest from President Nkrumah of Ghana, who considered that he should be brought to trial for his part in the assassination of the former Congolese prime minister, Patrice Lumumba, in February 1961 (*Times*, 18 Jan. 1963).

and on the Congo operation in general. Now that the secession was over, a gradual UN military disengagement could begin and increased emphasis placed on technical assistance. The UN could not claim to have solved all the Congo's problems but it had largely fulfilled the various mandates entrusted to it: the maintenance of Congolese territorial integrity and political independence; the restoration and maintenance of law and order; the prevention of civil war; and the expulsion of all unwanted foreign auxiliaries.[1]

U Thant was justified in his assessment. ONUC had held the Congo together, it had minimized the neo-colonial influences operating within its boundaries, it had served to insulate the area from the cold war, and it had been a striking affirmation of the strength of the coalition between the United States and the neutralists of Europe, Africa, and Asia which now dominated the UN. Seen in retrospect the accomplishment is less impressive. The stability given to the Congo did not outlast the withdrawal of the force in June 1964 and it was the United States and Belgium, not a revived ONUC, which were brought in to restore the situation. Moreover, the prime minister who summoned them then was none other than the former secessionist, Tshombe.

[1] *SCOR*, Jan.–Mar. 1963, pp. 92–104.

CHAPTER X

THE PURSUIT OF AFRICAN UNITY

(a) *Introduction*

FOR African states 1963 was the year of reconciliation. The sudden withdrawal of European power from the African continent, leading, in 1960, to the admission of seventeen new states to the UN, had been followed by two years of internecine rivalry both between neighbouring states and between three 'blocs', the Casablanca, Monrovia, and Brazzaville organizations.[1] While the causes of friction had not been removed by 1963, the summit of African leaders at Addis Ababa in May at least succeeded in healing the breach between the rival blocs. In the Organization of African Unity, which was established at the conference, it created an institutional basis for future political and economic co-operation amongst African states.

The ideology of Pan-Africanism arose in response to the prevailing disunity of the African continent which, in the minds of African nationalists, in its turn had been created by the arbitrary partition of Africa by the European powers in the 1880s.[2] It followed—and this was the one point on which there was agreement in principle between Africans—that their independence would only be secure when the last traces of that partition had been removed, and the whole continent had been liberated from 'white minority' rule. Agreement in principle, however, had not led to agreement on the means to be employed to achieve this end and the Pan-African movement had split, first, over the kind of unity to be pursued and, second, over what policies to pursue in relation to the major powers. The so-called African radicals of the Casablanca group, with President Nkrumah of Ghana as their most consistent spokesman, urged, at least in theory, political unification of the continent, and a policy of 'positive neutralism' in foreign affairs. This led them to oppose as neo-colonialist the conservative Brazzaville states, all of which remained closely allied, both militarily and economically, to France. The Casablanca policies were also opposed by a group of moderate states, such as Nigeria, Liberia, and Ethiopia, which, while pursuing policies of non-alignment, were not prepared to accept the radical 'maximalist' approach to African unity. These states had joined with the Brazzaville bloc in

[1] For a more detailed discussion of the emergence of African 'blocs' see *Survey, 1961*, pp. 400–10.

[2] For a useful account of the historical development of Pan-Africanism, see Colin Legum, *Pan-Africanism: a short political guide*, revised edition (London, 1965).

May 1961 to form the loose Monrovia coalition within which members agreed to concert their diplomatic policies and promote interstate co-operation in economic, defence, and social affairs, without making any concessions to supra-nationalism.

At the beginning of 1963 the debate between the supporters of the 'maximalist' and 'minimalist' conceptions of African unity had still not been resolved, as the fierce feud between Ghana and Nigeria, the self-appointed leaders of the two opposing schools, bore witness. But several developments, in both the international and African contexts, had already pointed the way to reconciliation, and indeed, by the end of 1962, agreement had been secured for the holding of an all-African summit conference in Addis Ababa the following May.[1]

Originally it had been in reaction to the Congo crisis and the Algerian war, with their wide-ranging international ramifications, that differences had been revealed among African leaders. In 1962, events in both Algeria and the Congo had, from the point of view of African unity, taken a turn for the better. The announcement of a ceasefire in Algeria in March 1962 had led, almost overnight, to a reduction of tension between the blocs and, in due course, to the successful initiative for an African summit conference.[2] The situation in the Congo had also, to some extent, been stabilized. No doubt, in the eyes of African radicals, continued Western, particularly American, influence with President Adoula's government was far from ideal. But while they could do little themselves to influence the course of events, the occupation of Katanga by UN forces at the end of December 1962, the ending of Katanga's secession in January 1963, and the temporary exile of Tshombe, the secessionist leader, removed the main issues on which they had been agitating for stronger international action. Had the UN force been withdrawn completely by the end of the year, as was originally proposed, and the Congolese government then forced to its own arrangements with the USA and other Western powers for military support to maintain public order, there is little doubt that this would again have provoked bitter controversy. Largely as a result of African protests at the UN, however, the danger of an immediate UN withdrawal was averted, and for the time being the Congo ceased to be a major foreign policy preoccupation of African states.[3]

Furthermore, the cold war struggle for influence in Africa was being conducted in a perceptibly lower key than previously, as demonstrated

---

[1] *Survey, 1962*, pp. 517–18.   [2] Ibid., p. 515.

[3] The proposal to complete UN withdrawal from the Congo by the end of 1963 was a con-sequence of the UN financial crisis following the refusal of several states, principally the USSR and France, to pay their share of the costs of the Congo operation. In the event, although the force was reduced by half, to around 8,000, by mid-1963, the final withdrawal was postponed until mid-1964 (the UN and the Congolese Government sharing the cost) to allow time for alternative arrangements to be made.

by the fact that both the USA and the Soviet Union strenuously avoided taking sides in the border war which broke out between Algeria and Morocco in October.[1] This development, although scarcely recognized at the time, was to provide an indirect stimulus to the movement for African unity. Since neither the USA nor the Soviet Union showed much interest in acquiring new allies, non-alignment inevitably became a less divisive issue in African politics. Their interests in the area were limited, and a body claiming authority over intra-African disputes would, in their view, reduce the likelihood of a direct confrontation between them or with other outside powers in Africa. Thus, despite differences of rhetoric, both super powers were able to welcome the emergence of an African sub-system of international politics.[2]

The Sino-Soviet rift, and the new struggle for influence to which it gave rise, by altering the external environment appears also to have had an indirect effect on the movement towards African unity. By 1963 the Afro-Asian movement, within whose fold most African states had made their international début, was already a spent force.[3] But the prospect of Chinese and Russian delegations endlessly trying to win converts at Afro-Asian conferences, and engaging in fairly unscrupulous practices to achieve their ends, discredited the movement still further, and strengthened the resolve of most African leaders to stay out of the quarrel. 'Imperialism is a by-product of wealth and power', President Nyerere of Tanganyika told an Afro-Asian meeting in February,

> We have to be on our guard against incursions from anyone. Indeed I wish I could honestly say I believe the second scramble for Africa and Asia is going to be a scramble only between capitalist powers. Much too often, the weaker amongst us are regarded as no more than pawns in the cold war conflict.[4]

But if, at the turn of the year, the major international obstacles to unity, or at least to an African summit meeting, had been overcome, the positive pressures in favour of reconciliation had mostly developed within the African context itself. The efforts of most African leaders, in the months before the summit, to patch up old quarrels with their neighbours reflected not so much evidence of a new harmony in African political life as a growing realization of the violence and insecurity which threatened them all. By 1963, the fear of imperialist incursions, a vague but none the less real element of post-colonial psychology, concealed a more acute fear of internal subversion, aided and abetted by neighbouring states. This

[1] Below, pp. 307–17.
[2] Both Kennedy and Khrushchev sent personal messages to the Addis Ababa Conference expressing support for African unity.
[3] For a useful account of the disintegration of the Afro-Asian movement, see G. H. Jansen, *Afro-Asia and non-alignment* (London, 1966).
[4] *Times*, 5 Feb. 1963.

fear lay at the centre of the ideological controversy amongst Africans about the kind of 'unity' towards which they should be working. To the states of the Monrovia group, it was an article of faith that all future African organizations should rest, and be seen to rest, on the principles of 'state sovereignty' and 'non-interference in the domestic affairs of member states', the acceptance of which would effectively bind them to the frontiers inherited from the colonial powers. While in practice the Casablanca states were equally determined to protect specific national interests, in their public utterances the 'radical' leaders had emphasized the revolutionary nature of the Pan-African movement. From the Monrovia view it was precisely because they had sometimes urged the revision of colonial frontiers, as with Morocco's claims to Mauritania or Ghana's to parts of Togo, and had lent their active support to opposition groups in rival states, which professed to agree with their views, that they were suspected of encouraging subversion to accomplish ideological aims.

Yet, by the beginning of 1963, while most states had a record of internal disturbance which their leaders generally blamed on outside interference, the pressure for African reconciliation reflected a common awareness that the real problem was not about frontiers, let alone about ideology, but about the inherent instability of virtually all the new states. Thus, whereas in 1960 African states had split on issues of broad international policy, by 1963 a growing sense of political weakness, and the fear of the sudden *coup d'état* organized from across the border, was a powerful influence in the opposite direction.

(b) *Disintegration of the 'blocs'*

(i) *The Monrovia group: the Togo affair*

President Olympio of Togo was gunned to death in the early hours of 13 January as he was apparently attempting to seek refuge in the American Embassy. At the same time all his ministers, except two who escaped to Dahomey, were arrested after being summoned by telephone in the middle of the night to attend an urgent cabinet meeting. This was the first successful *coup d'état* amongst the independent states south of the Sahara. The issues that it raised, the entry of the army into politics, and internal subversion, posed a threat to all African states whatever their previous political and ideological affiliations, and its repercussions cast a baleful shadow over the preparations for an African summit.

Whatever the underlying reasons for the coup, its immediate cause was never in doubt.[1] The assassination was carried out by a small group of

[1] For a contemporary account of the coup and of the internal political situation in Togo, see Dennis Austin, 'Coup d'etat in the Republic of Togo', *World Today*, Feb. 1963, pp. 56–60.

army officers and NCOs following the government's alleged refusal to enter an open-ended commitment to provide employment and to pay military gratuities to about eight hundred recently demobilized French colonial troops.[1] If, as was claimed later, Togolese exiles in Accra and elsewhere were planning to overthrow the government, it seems unlikely that they had been in contact with the insurgents immediately before the coup, which gave every sign of being a spontaneous and local affair. 'It is because Sylvanus Olympio was anti-militarist that we revolted', one of the military junta said at the time. 'It was our 13 May.'[2] At all events, having acquired power, the junta appeared at first to be unsure about what to do with it. On 14 January, after constituting themselves into an Insurrectionary Committee, they issued a communique denying that the revolt had been motivated by any 'religious or philosophic ideology', or that it had been organized by anyone other than themselves, in or out of Togo. They also pledged themselves to surrender political power at the first available opportunity.[3]

Their task was complicated by the personal nature of Olympio's government. The ex-president's approach to politics had been authoritarian (he had been a successful businessman before he was a politician), and since Togo's independence in April 1960 he had steered a lone course in both domestic and foreign policy. He was one of the few African leaders to insist on a rigidly balanced budget, a policy which affected his attitude towards the army which he regarded as an expensive luxury for a country of the size and resources of Togo. In foreign policy, he had refused to join the Brazzaville group, which he considered too subservient to Paris, but he had also refused to adopt the aggressive attitude of the African 'radicals' towards the great powers. While his political isolation, particularly from the other Francophone states, was no doubt one of the underlying causes of the rebellion, another was the detention in Togo of a large number of political opponents. Olympio's policies had effectively prevented the emergence of any coalition of opposition interests to which the Insurrectionary Committee could hand over.

Faced with this dilemma, the Committee shifted ground, insisting that, despite the weakness of their own political base—the regular Togolese army consisted of about two hundred men—they had led a popular revolt against corruption and injustice and that their immediate aim was 'national reconciliation'.[4] To this end they requested the return from exile of Olympio's two leading rivals, his brother-in-law, the conservative Nicholas Grunitsky, who had been prime minister at the end of the colonial

[1] Daily Telegraph, 18 Jan.; NY Times, 17 Jan. 1963.

[2] Africa Digest, Apr. 1963, p. 173. 13 May was the day of the French generals' revolt in Algiers against President de Gaulle's policy of liberating Algeria.

[3] SWB, ME/1145, 14 Jan. 1963.

[4] Interview with Jean Byer of Abidjan-Matin, quoted in Le Monde, 16 Jan. 1963.

period but who now lived in Dahomey, and the radical Antoine Meatchi, leader of the Northern Union of Chiefs and People, who had lived in Accra and the Ivory Coast since his escape from prison in 1961.[1] At the same time, other radical opponents of the Olympio regime, including Firmin Abaloo and Anani Santos, leaders of the Mouvement de la Jeunesse Togolaise (JUVENTO), a radical breakaway from Olympio's own party, the Comité de l'Unité Togolaise, were released from detention. After a period of uncertainty, while the rival parties jockeyed for position, the task of forming a provisional government was finally entrusted to Grunitsky. He arrived in the capital, Lomé, on 15 January, and after negotiations, in which he obtained the support of all the Togolese political parties, formally dissolved the National Assembly on 17 January, suspended the country's electoral laws, and announced his intention of governing by decree pending the establishment of a new constitution.[2] The role of the Insurrectionary Committee in the new arrangements remained obscure. But there could be no doubt that, in the last resort, Grunitsky would continue to derive his authority from the army and that his position very largely depended on his ability to create jobs of an appropriate status for the unemployed soldiery.

If the army's entry into politics was one aspect which alarmed other African governments, another was the possibility that the coup had been engineered from abroad. The revolt had occurred at a time of acute tension in relations between Ghana and Togo, and the reappearance of Meatchi and his radical supporters, who were believed to have the financial backing of Accra, aroused fears throughout West Africa that the assassination, whatever the formal pretext, might be the prelude to a full-scale Ghanaian intervention.

The dispute between Ghana and Togo dated from 1956, when the former Trust Territory of British Togoland had voted in a UN plebiscite for assimilation with the Gold Coast. The vote had resulted in the permanent separation of the Ewe tribe, whose peoples had previously been divided, since the end of the First World War, between the Trust Territories of British and French Togoland, and who now straddled Ghana's eastern border with Togo. After the plebiscite, Olympio had continued to press for the unification of the two Togolands, and had not concealed his disappointment when, after Ghana's independence, Nkrumah not only ruled out the possibility but, on several occasions, urged Togo to integrate with Ghana as the nucleus of the Pan-African political union to which he was committed.

[1] Meatchi, whose radicalism also reflected traditional northern resentment against political control from the coast, had been imprisoned for two years for incitement to riot during the 1961 elections.

[2] *Times*, 18 Jan.; *NY Times*, 17 Jan. 1963.

The dispute had continued with each side periodically accusing the other of subversive activities.[1] Then, after a brief respite, the result of a mediation attempt by the government of Dahomey,[2] relations between the two countries deteriorated sharply following the attempt on Nkrumah's life in August 1962, which the government of Ghana alleged had been organized from Lomé by exiled members of the United Party. In a note, delivered in Accra on 19 December 1962, the Togolese government denied charges of complicity in the assassination plot and invited Ghana to substantiate them.[3] Ghana replied on 6 January with a warning to Togo of the dangerous international consequences of sheltering and encouraging persons 'conspiring against Ghana while in the pay of foreign agents', and requesting the immediate extradition of three of Nkrumah's principal political opponents resident in Togo, amongst others.[4] To make matters worse, on 8 January bombs were thrown at a mass rally in Ghana, killing four and injuring eighty-four people. The next day the government announced that an examination of fragments of one of the grenades recovered after the incident suggested it to be 'in all probability one of a batch of these grenades manufactured in France and supplied officially to the forces of a neighbouring territory'.[5]

It was against this background that the rest of Africa learned, on the morning after the Togolese coup, that Dahomean and Ghanaian troops were moving towards their respective borders with Togo. Reactions to the crisis were swift. The assassination was condemned by each West African government in turn; indeed, with the exception of Senegal,[6] none showed any sign of recognizing the new regime. At this point, however, only the government of Dahomey, Togo's western neighbour, was in any position to act. Although it was suggested that Ghana was prevented from intervening only by President Maga's warning to Nkrumah that any intervention would precipitate similar action by Dahomey,[7] there is no evidence that Ghana ever contemplated military action. In fact, after ordering troops to the frontier, President Maga had immediately dispatched his foreign minister, Zinsou, to Accra to obtain an official Ghanaian reaction to the crisis. Zinsou saw Nkrumah on the morning of 13 January

[1] See *Survey, 1961*, pp. 414–15.

[2] For details of the various African attempts to resolve the dispute see the interesting account by the first secretary-general of the UAM, Albert Tevoedjre, *Pan-Africanism in action* (Cambridge, Mass., 1965), Chapter V. [3] *Times*, 7 Jan. 1963.

[4] Ibid. The three referred to were K. A. Gbedemah, former Ghana finance minister; Dr K. A. Busia, former leader of the parliamentary opposition, and K. Richardson, general secretary of the United Party. [5] *Times*, 10 Jan. 1963.

[6] The motives for President Senghor's lone stand in recognizing the Provisional Government are unclear. At the time he justified his decision on the grounds that to have done otherwise would have compromised Senegal's position on non-interference in the internal affairs of other states (*SWB*, ME/1149, 19 Jan. 1963). The other states, starting from the same point, withheld recognition partly because they believed such interference to have taken place.

[7] *Daily Telegraph*, 16 Jan. 1963.

and told him that Dahomean movements were merely intended to guard the frontier, a statement which was confirmed the next day in a government communique stating that Dahomey's attitude was dictated 'solely by our anxiety to protect human lives and property. Our country has no intention either to interfere in the internal affairs of Togo or to support any of the factions.'[1] In reply Nkrumah assured Zinsou that, despite his quarrel with Olympio, he could not accept assassination as a political weapon, and that he had no intention of intervening militarily. The next day he sent a deputation to Cotonou to reassure President Maga and to register his support for Maga's efforts towards a peaceful settlement.[2]

Meanwhile, the Nigerian government had taken the initiative in attempting to concert a common African position on the crisis. Nigeria's main fear was not a Ghanaian military takeover, but the widening of the net for Ghana's subversive activities which might result from the establishment in Lomé of a regime closely linked with Accra. After a week of consultations with other West African governments, the Nigerian foreign minister, Jaja Wachuku, announced to the press on 21 January that he had evidence of external intervention in the Togo coup, and that the Nigerian government had decided to convene an emergency meeting of the foreign ministers of the Inter-African and Malagasy Organization— the Monrovia group—'to decide whether African states accept assassination and subversion as a means of getting to power'.[3]

It was at the Lagos Conference (24–26 January 1963), the last meeting of the Monrovia group before the African summit in May, that the problem of subversion emerged as one of the major preoccupations of this bloc, strongly influencing their attitude to all proposals for unity. The outcome, however, demonstrated both the weakness of Monrovia and some of the difficulties that any larger organization, based on the same principles, would inevitably face in attempting to align African policies. On two points the foreign ministers were in unanimous agreement. First, it was agreed to discuss the crisis within the framework of the Lagos Charter, Article III of which, affirming the principles of sovereign equality, non-interference in the internal affairs of member states, and respect for their territorial integrity, formed the basis of the Monrovia approach to African Unity.[4] Second, the foreign ministers gave unreserved support to a resolution deploring the murder of Olympio and condemning 'political assassination as a means of overthrowing the government and rising to power, or as a means of settling political conflicts'.[5]

[1] *SWB*, ME/1145, 14 Jan. 1963.
[2] Ibid. A reference to the ministerial delegation which Maga had sent to Lomé on 13 Jan. to ascertain the facts behind the assassination and to offer help in reconciling the various factions.
[3] *SWB*, ME/1151, 21 Jan. 1963.
[4] Text in *Documents, 1962*, pp. 896–906.
[5] For the text of this, and the other resolutions, see *Documents, 1963*, pp. 434–6.

There agreement ended. The main division to emerge was between those states, led by Nigeria and the Ivory Coast, who favoured a full-scale diplomatic boycott of the Grunitsky regime, and a group of smaller states, including Dahomey, Niger, and the Cameroon Republic, who argued in favour of conciliation. These felt that there was little a diplomatic boycott could achieve and danger that it might make Grunitsky's position untenable and force the provisional government into an extreme position. As the foreign minister of Niger expressed it, 'one does not oppose force with texts nor with a law; another force must impose itself; we have not got those means'.[1]

Despite Nigerian allegations of Ghana's involvement in the coup, which were supported and denied by the rival Togolese delegations which addressed the conference, no firm evidence was produced to support them.[2] The Nigerian foreign minister continued to press for action against both the provisional government and Ghana. It was the Nigerian view that there should be no softening on the position of non-recognition, unless the provisional government took steps to restore the constitution and electoral laws and to organize free elections. In the meantime, it was suggested that to encourage the provisional government to adopt this course as well as to deter Ghana from more active intervention, Nigerian troops should reinforce those of Dahomey on the Togo–Dahomey border. But while the majority of states were prepared, in principle, to study the possibility of joint action against subversion,[3] they refused to support the Nigerian proposal, on the grounds that it would be regarded in Accra as deliberate provocation and would make Ghanaian intervention more, rather than less, likely.

Once it became clear that the Monrovia powers were not prepared to use military pressure, the subsequent debate on recognition became academic. In its resolutions, the Lagos Conference addressed several

[1] *Conference of foreign ministers of the Inter-African and Malagasy Organization*, summary report (*Lagos, 1963*).

[2] The two representatives were Dr Vovor for the Togolese provisional government, and Mally, former minister of the interior in Olympio's government, one of the two ministers to have escaped capture during the coup. Although the foreign ministers finally refused to recognize the Grunitsky regime, Mally was not successful in picking up support. Not only was the evidence he produced in support of Ghanaian complicity—the release of certain political prisoners who had been detained in a previous abortive coup in May 1961—purely circumstantial, but he made a tactical mistake in attempting to implicate the French government. This drew a sharp denial from Paris, and may well have lost him the sympathy of those Francophone states whose relations with the Olympio regime had never been close. In any case, as *Le Monde* pointed out, the charge was inherently unlikely, since the French had recently confirmed, in the context of the Ghana–Togo dispute, that they would stand by their defence agreement with Togo in case of need (*Le Monde*, 26 Jan. 1963).

[3] The governments of Nigeria, Liberia, and Upper Volta were invited to prepare a draft treaty of defence and security, in accordance with Article II (f) of the Lagos Charter for submission to the Council of Ministers at its meeting in Addis Ababa in May. This treaty, however, never saw the light of day, being overtaken by the establishment of the OAU.

recommendations to the Grunitsky regime, which implied *de facto* recognition, but made Togolese participation in the Addis Ababa summit conditional on the prior organization of 'free and democratic general elections', the implication being that failure to uphold the rule of law would bar the Togolese regime from inter-African councils and incur the collective disapproval of thirty-one independent African states. Yet if the Monrovia group could not enforce its will on Togo, it was difficult to see why a larger council would be more effective.

Subsequent events confirmed both the conference's failure to influence the internal political situation in Togo, and the Monrovia group's disintegration. Before the conference adjourned, the foreign ministers set up a mission consisting of representatives from the five states neighbouring on Togo—Dahomey, Ivory Coast, Upper Volta, Niger, and Nigeria—with a mandate 'to clarify the circumstances which surrounded the murder of President Olympio or any external influence which might have incited such a crime and to assist them [the provisional government] as necessary in re-establishing democratic institutions'. Grunitsky informed the conference on 26 January that he was willing to co-operate with the proposed mission, but since his co-operation would depend on the prior agreement of the Togolese army, it was clear that the mission would have very little room for manœuvre. Meanwhile the publication of the Lagos Resolutions, including a recommendation that those responsible for Olympio's assassination should be prosecuted, can hardly have convinced the Insurrectionary Committee of the advantages of co-operation. The mission was due in Lomé on 1 February. At the last moment, however, the governments of the Ivory Coast and Upper Volta decided against participation, presumably because they felt that the only outcome would be to confirm the provisional government in office, a step, which for its own reasons, neither government was prepared to take. Without their support, the Lagos mission collapsed. The remaining three members were received by Grunitsky on 2 February, in what was officially described as a 'frank and cordial atmosphere'; immediately afterwards, however, they withdrew to Cotonou ostensibly to allow Grunitsky 'to inform his countrymen more fully as to the genuine intentions of the mission and thereby allay their anxieties'.[1] The truth was there was nothing for them to do and the mission was never reconvened.

The Togo affair continued to dominate preparations for the Addis Ababa summit within the Brazzaville group. Although their organization, the Union Africaine et Malgache (UAM), was more advanced than either the Casablanca group or the looser Monrovia coalition, to which the 'Brazzaville' states also belonged,[2] it had remained outside the mainstream

[1] *Conference of foreign ministers of the Inter-African and Malagasy Organization.*
[2] *Survey, 1961,* pp. 401–9.

of Pan-African politics. The continuing influence of France in its former West African empire, which had affected the Brazzaville stand against the recognition of the GPRA during the Algerian war, and which found a wider expression through the association of these states with the EEC, under Part IV of the Rome Treaty, separated the Francophone states, at least psychologically, from several of their Commonwealth allies in the Monrovia group, as well as from their Casablanca opponents. However, the refusal of Italy and the Netherlands at the beginning of 1963 to ratify the new convention of association which had been agreed the previous December[1] brought home to the UAM the disadvantage of excessive dependence on Europe, just as the wave of political unrest in West Africa provided an incentive towards greater co-operation with other African states. As the summit approached, the secretary-general of the UAM, Albert Tevoedjre, made strenuous efforts to improve the organization's image in Pan-African affairs, both by widening its membership beyond the former French empire and by persuading the heads of state to adopt a more militant line than hitherto in support of liberation movements in southern Africa.[2] Nevertheless, their main preoccupation continued to be with the problem of subversion, and despite the Secretariat's preparations for a conference devoted to the wider problems of African unity, when the UAM heads of state met between 10 and 14 March at Ougadougou, capital of Upper Volta, the Togo affair, and the question of recognition to which it gave rise, dominated the proceedings.

The inner core of the UAM, the four states of the Conseil de l'Entente, Ivory Coast, Upper Volta, Dahomey, and Niger, had held a preliminary meeting in Abidjan in mid-February following the discovery the previous month of a plot to overthrow Houphouet-Boigny's government in the Ivory Coast. The uncovering of the plot was followed by allegations of subversion. Three ministers were arrested and a special security court was established to try the suspects in secret.[3] Although no firm evidence was produced, the Ivory Coast government appeared to be convinced that the *coup d'état* in Togo was linked with the Abidjan plot[4] and this clearly

[1] For a discussion of the negotiation of this convention, see *Survey, 1962*, pp. 485–7. Although the official explanation for the Dutch and Italian refusal to ratify was that they had to await the results of forthcoming elections, it was generally assumed that resentment over the French veto on British membership of the Community had influenced their decision. The convention was eventually signed at Yaoundé on 20 July 1963, but it was not until 1 June 1964 that it came into force.

[2] His efforts were partially successful. At their Ougadougou meeting, the UAM heads of state admitted the former Belgian Trust territory of Rwanda as the thirteenth member state. They also adopted a strong, if vaguely worded, resolution in respect of their policy towards the African liberation movements: 'The UAM heads of state hereby decide to take concrete measures to liquidate the remaining colonial forts in Africa' (Tevoedjre, p. 19).

[3] *Times*, 16 Jan.; *Le Monde*, 21 Jan. 1963.

[4] At the Lagos Conference the foreign minister of the Ivory Coast, Auguste Debise, had alleged that his government's attitude was dictated, above all, by this link. Much was made of

influenced Houphouet-Boigny's attitude towards the Grunitsky regime. At all events, under the combined pressure of the Ivory Coast and Upper Volta, the Entente states confirmed the Lagos decision to withhold recognition of the Togolese government until the Addis Ababa summit. They were not, however, prepared to wait for the summit to deal with the problem of subversion. The four heads of state agreed to submit detailed proposals concerning this to the UAM conference in March and, in the meantime, to establish a mutual intervention pact amongst themselves. 'It will be sufficient for us', President Yameogo of Upper Volta announced after the meeting, 'to learn that something alarming has happened and we shall be ready to step in.'[1]

The Entente was thus proposing to take action of the kind that Nigeria had proposed at the Lagos Conference, which would inevitably be interpreted by Casablanca as a pre-emptive bid to dictate the terms of inter-African reconciliation. Fortunately, wiser counsels prevailed at Ougadougou, and under pressure from other heads of state, most notably President Senghor of Senegal, the Entente was persuaded to drop its proposal for a joint strike force against aggression and subversion.[2] Paradoxically the argument against regional defence pacts, namely that they would heighten interstate tensions prior to the Addis Ababa summit, also worked against the recognition of the Grunitsky regime, which the majority of Francophone states favoured, but which President Sékou Touré of Guinea still violently opposed.[3]

Although the Togo affair did not have the disruptive effect on the movement towards African unity that had been feared, in a deeper sense the outcome of both the Lagos and Ougadougou Conferences did not augur well for the future. The Monrovia powers, because they formed the majority, as well as being formally responsible for convening the Addis Ababa meeting, would inevitably be in a strong position to insist that membership of any enlarged organization should be made conditional on acceptance of the territorial *status quo*. Yet their control over political events in Africa remained tenuous. It was not that the anxiety, to which the Togo affair gave rise, was unjustified; it was, as the uncovering of plots against the governments of the Ivory Coast and Liberia at the beginning of the year, and the overthrow of President Maga's government in Dahomey and President Youlou's in the Congo (Brazzaville) in August,

the friendship of Amadou Kone, the former Ivory Coast minister of health, who was condemned to death for his part in the Abidjan conspiracy, and Antoine Meatchi, who, during his exile, had often lived at Dr. Kone's house in the Ivory Coast (Tevoedjre, p. 48).

[1] *SWB*, ME/1182, 22 Feb. 1963.

[2] President Senghor arrived in Ougadougou direct from a state visit to Guinea where he had apparently been left in no doubt by Sékou Touré of Casablanca opposition to new regional arrangements. The Entente proposals were also denounced by Accra. *SWB*, ME/1194, 14 Mar. 1963.   [3] Tevoedjre, p. 50.

were to show. But if the forces of unrest within African society, of which these crises were symptomatic, could not be held in check by the adoption of resolutions or even by collective diplomatic pressure, stronger action would have required not only means, but also a political will, which none of the independent African states possessed in 1963.

At the time the main efforts towards African reconciliation were centred on the diplomatic plane. That these efforts continued unabated, despite the upheaval caused by Olympio's death, reflected on the one hand, the disintegration of the Casablanca group, and the consequent isolation of the principal suspect, Ghana, and on the other, the fact that the Pan-African movement was no longer, as it had been a few years previously, solely a West African preserve, which could be held up or carried forward in response to West African pressures alone.

(ii) *The Casablanca group*

By the beginning of 1963, the Casablanca group had already ceased to function as an effective body in African politics.[1] Several causes contributed to its demise. Although its member states had the reputation of forming a radical, ideologically orientated group, the organization had, from the start, attempted to reconcile an oddly disparate set of interests. Morocco was primarily concerned to secure diplomatic support for its claim to Mauritania; while association with the radical Ghana–Guinea–Mali Union was no doubt useful in dealing with the radical wing of its opposition, neither the late King Mohammed's government nor its successor could be described as radical. Similarly, both the UAR and the GPRA had their own reasons for joining the group which had little to do with radical Pan-Africanism. Nasser was able to obtain African support, although it was never more than nominal, for his Israeli policy, while the Algerians valued the association because it afforded their government-in-exile diplomatic recognition. But less than two years after the original conference,[2] the Ghana–Guinea–Mali Union collapsed in all but name, thus removing the dynamic element from the coalition, and, with the exception of Morocco, the group had also ceased to fulfil any useful function for its members.

For both Guinea and Mali the Casablanca affiliation was a barrier to the *rapprochement* which they sought with their French-speaking neighbours. Apart from Sékou Touré's initiative in calling for a summit,[3] itself an indication that he had moved away from the radical wing of the Pan-African movement, his siding with Monrovia over the Togo affair led to a cooling in his relationship with Accra. Although Guinea was not represented at the Lagos Conference, Sékou Touré had been one of the most forthright African leaders in his condemnation of the assassins, calling on

[1] *Survey, 1962*, p. 517.   [2] *Survey, 1961*, p. 403.   [3] *Survey, 1962*, p. 516.

all states to give a 'categorical refusal' to the request of Togo's provisional
government for recognition, an attitude he maintained up to the Addis
Ababa conference.[1] When Nkrumah recognized the Grunitsky regime,
Sékou Touré sent him a telegram expressing surprise at Ghana's decision in terms which made it clear that he shared Monrovia's views on the
dangers of subversion.[2]

Meanwhile, Mali had embarked on a process of reconciliation with her
two Monrovia neighbours—Senegal and Mauritania—that inevitably
undermined her commitment to Casablanca. At the beginning of February it was announced in Dakar that all technical and financial differences
between the two countries resulting from the break-up of the original
Mali Federation had been settled by a joint liquidation committee, an
event which provided the necessary prelude for political reconciliation.[3]
On 16 February Presidents Keita of Mali and Ould Daddah of Mauritania
concluded a treaty at Kayes, just inside the Mali border, in which they
delineated the boundary between the two states. 'The meeting at Kayes
is a symbol', Keita commented, 'future generations must understand that
Africa can only be built by reciprocal concessions.'[4] For Mali, the
Casablanca group was now dead: by recognizing Mauritania, Keita
implicitly endorsed Ould Daddah's refusal to deal with the Moroccan
government so long as Morocco continued to deny Mauritania's existence
as an independent state.

President Nkrumah of Ghana, the remaining member of the West
African radical triumvirate, was thus isolated in his allegiance to the
revolutionary ideals of the Pan-African movement, including the demand
for immediate political unification. Yet Ghana, too, seemed resigned to
the eclipse of Casablanca. African reactions to the Togo affair had demonstrated both Ghana's diplomatic isolation, and, by the same token, the
wide support that existed for a Pan-African organization based on the
Monrovia gradualist formula to which Nkrumah remained deeply opposed. On the other hand, it was clear that the Casablanca group no
longer provided a viable alternative. Despite speculation after the Lagos
Conference that Nkrumah would boycott the Addis Ababa summit, he
evidently realized that in the competition for personal prestige, so
important in African politics, he could only lose by staying away.

In any event, Nkrumah responded with a characteristic mixture of
conciliation in handling his neighbours and ideological assertiveness in
the wider context of Pan-African affairs. Although his government roundly

[1] *Africa Digest*, June 1963, p. 203.

[2] Viz. 'La reconnaissance par le Ghana du nouveau gouvernement togolais, avant l'ouverture
de l'enquête sur les événements du 13 Janvier et avant l'assurance que les coupables seront
punis, risque de servir de nouveau de tremplin aux menées subversives en Afrique' (cited in
Le Monde, 25 Jan. 1963).

[3] *West Africa*, 9 Feb. 1963.   [4] Ibid., 23 Feb. 1963.

denounced the Lagos Conference, Nkrumah was careful to publicize his agreement with President Maga of Dahomey on his handling of the Togo affair.[1] And when, at the beginning of February, a plot was uncovered against President Tubman of Liberia, Nkrumah immediately sent him a personal message of congratulation on his escape.[2] When the acting Ghanaian foreign minister, Puplampu, visited Lagos at the end of February, a visit indicating reduced tension, he announced that the Osagyefo would, despite his differences with Monrovia, attend the African summit in May.[3] At the same time, Nkrumah clearly did not intend to go to Addis as a penitent. In his message to Tubman he had already stated his conviction that 'only the earliest establishment of a union of all African states would save heads of state from constant onslaughts by the enemies of the African liberation movement'. Subsequently, his emissaries visited every major African capital with detailed proposals for political unification.[4] A fuller version of his argument, in which he proposed a bicameral legislature to which the states would surrender sovereignty over economic development planning, as well as monetary, defence, and foreign policy, was contained in his book, *Africa must unite*, the publication of which was timed to coincide with the opening of the Addis Ababa conference.[5] In the political climate of 1963 there was no chance of Nkrumah's proposals being accepted, yet in putting them forward his aim was probably to keep his own dream of a politically unified continent at the forefront of Pan-African debate, and in this he undoubtedly succeeded.[6] Moreover, in the prevailing conditions of political uncertainty, it was not wholly unreasonable to assume that the supporters of revolutionary Pan-Africanism might eventually regain the ascendancy. Already, in several states, those out of power had shown that they were prepared to endorse Nkrumah's programme, against the threat, as one of them put it, that African unity might become 'a sort of trade union of men in power who will seek to support one another to resist popular currents'.[7]

South of the Sahara, it was primarily the pressures on Guinea and Mali towards accommodation with their more conservative neighbours which weakened their coalition with Ghana and undermined the Casablanca group. In the north, it was the incompatibility of Morocco's conservatism with the assertive radicalism of Algeria and the UAR that led to the final collapse of Casablanca. For his part, King Hassan of Morocco had good reason to preserve the Casablanca group so long as possible; increasingly isolated in the Arab world and Africa, he now faced the country's first parliamentary elections in which both opposition parties—the

[1] See above, p. 272. [2] *SWB*, ME/1168, 8 Feb. 1963.
[3] *West Africa*, 2 Mar. 1963. [4] Legum, p. 134.
[5] *Africa must unite* (London, 1963). [6] Cf. Legum, p. 135.
[7] Djibo Bakary, leader of the Sawaba party of Niger, in *Révolution Africaine*, quoted in Wallerstein, *Africa politics of unity* (London, 1968), p. 63.

right-wing nationalist Istiqlal and the left-wing Union National des
Forces Populaires (UNFP)—would undoubtedly exploit any sign of
weakening in the government's position on Mauritania. With no support
from his former sub-Saharan allies, the King depended heavily on relations with Morocco's neighbours in the Maghreb.

Although the constitutions of all three Maghreb countries made some
reference to the idea of a Greater Maghreb, their mutual relations at the
beginning of 1963 could scarcely have been worse. While Hassan was
reported to be anxious to offset Algerian influence by improving his
relations with Tunisia, any move in this direction was blocked by the
Mauritania issue, which had led to a rupture of diplomatic relations when
Tunisia recognized Mauritania in 1960 and sponsored Mauritanian
membership of the UN.[1] Algerian-Tunisian relations had deteriorated
rapidly when, on 18 January, President Bourguiba recalled his ambassador
from Algiers following the Algerian government's refusal to extradite a
Tunisian refugee, condemned *in absentia* for his part in an attempt on
Bourguiba's life the previous month.[2] The resulting situation presented
Hassan with a chance to play honest broker. It was a tribute to his diplomacy, and perhaps also to the residual appeal of Maghreb unity, that
Tunisia and Algeria agreed to discuss their quarrel at a three-cornered
foreign ministers conference in Rabat between 11 and 14 February.

Ostensibly the conference achieved a considerable success. In the
official communique, the foreign ministers agreed to hold regular meetings to realize 'the deep harmony between the foreign policies of the
three countries' and to co-ordinate their cultural, judicial, and economic
policies.[3] While the Algerians still insisted on their right to harbour political exiles, the ministers agreed to allow no activity within their frontiers
that might jeopardize the solidarity of the Maghreb.[4] In an interview on
18 February, Tuhami-al-Wazani, secretary-general of Casablanca,
claimed that the Rabat conference had been 'a victory achieved by the
Casablanca Charter on the road to African Unity'.[5] In reality, the Rabat
meeting had helped to reconcile Algeria and Tunisia, which was not a
member of the group, but had done nothing to improve Morocco–
Algeria relations on which its future hinged. This was not, it is true,
immediately apparent. In March Hassan scored a second diplomatic
success when he visited Algiers, the first head of state to do so since Algerian
independence, and all seemed set for an Algerian–Moroccan *entente*.

[1] *Survey, 1961*, pp. 411–12.

[2] *Economist*, 26 Jan. 1963, suggested that Algerian hostility towards President Bourguiba
(the Algerian consul in Tunis had been instrumental in organizing the escape of the condemned
man) was influenced by Bourguiba's support for Ben Khedda, the former GPRA prime minister,
in his struggle for leadership with Ben Bella.

[3] For the text of the communique see *SWB*, ME/1176, 16 Feb. 1963.

[4] *Economist*, 23 Feb. 1963.   [5] *SWB*, ME/1180, 20 Feb. 1963.

Instead, the two states embarked on a collision course which finally sealed the fate of Casablanca, and led to open war before the end of the year.

Two issues separated the Moroccan and Algerian governments— Morocco's claim, advanced on historical grounds, to parts of the Western Sahara in Algeria and a fundamental incompatibility between Hassan and Ben Bella, which found expression in Ben Bella's repeated refusal to consider the unity of the Maghreb in isolation from the wider movements for Arab and African unity.[1] On neither issue did continued support for Casablanca offer Algeria any significant advantage: on the one hand, active support for Moroccan claims to Mauritania, now a dead issue, might encourage Morocco to press her claims to the Western Sahara, and on the other, it would isolate Algeria at a time when Ben Bella's immense prestige as a revolutionary leader had placed him in a position of influence throughout the continent.

It was against this background that the final eclipse of the Casablanca pact occurred. A meeting of the Joint Supreme Command, originally scheduled for 14 January, was postponed at Algeria's request.[2] It appeared to be only the secretary-general's efforts—he visited all the Casablanca capitals—that finally secured agreement for a heads of state meeting to be held at Marrakesh on 8 May as part of the preparations for Addis Ababa.[3] Meanwhile, the assassination of the Algerian foreign minister, Khemisti,[4] on 11 April, led to the cancellation of the second Maghreb foreign ministers' meeting, thus putting paid, for the time being, to any hope of a formal Moroccan–Algerian *rapprochement*.

As the date of the Marrakesh summit approached, it became apparent that Ben Bella was reluctant to allow Rabat to make propaganda out of a meeting which would take place only ten days before the Moroccan elections. He was also anxious lest, by attending a Casablanca meeting, he would prejudice his influence at Addis where he planned to take a strong line on the need for concerted African support for the Angolan and Mozambique rebels.[5] On 3 May, after Ben Bella had conferred with Nasser during the latter's visit to Algeria, the Algerian government formally requested Rabat to postpone the Marrakesh conference. Since it was already known that neither Sékou Touré nor Keita planned to attend, Hassan had no choice but to accept the Algerian request. Morocco's isolation was complete, and Hassan joined President Grunitsky of Togo as the only two African heads of state not to attend the Addis Ababa summit.

[1] Ibid., also *Survey, 1961*, pp. 411–12.
[2] *SWB*, ME/1180, 20 Feb. 1963.
[3] *La Bourse Égyptienne*, 23, 24 Jan. 1963; *SWB*, ME/1195, 11 Mar. 1963.
[4] The Algerian foreign minister was attacked, apparently by a lunatic, as he was leaving the National Assembly. He died on 6 May without regaining consciousness (*Le Monde*, 13 Apr. 1963).
[5] Ibid., 2 May 1963; *NY Times*, 4, 12 May 1963.

(iii) *East, central, and southern Africa*

In contrast with the complicated pattern in West Africa, interstate disputes, with one important exception, did not create a major problem *vis-à-vis* the Addis Ababa summit within east, central, and southern Africa, the area covered by PAFMESCA.[1] With the summit in view, an original plan to hold a regional conference at Easter was dropped; unlike Monrovia and Casablanca, PAFMESCA had never advanced a specific formula for African unity and did not feel, therefore, a need to co-ordinate policy beforehand. Moreover, the major political preoccupations with which PAFMESCA states were concerned at the beginning of 1963—the dissolution of the Central African Federation, preparations for Kenya's independence, and, in the Congo, the consolidation of central authority after the ending of Katangan secession—neither left those involved with much time to devote to other issues nor were directly concerned with the major themes of Pan-African debate.

Nevertheless, the impact of PAFMESCA on the Addis Ababa conference was probably as great as that of the other groups. In the first place, PAFMESCA had provided the institutional framework within which ideas for an East African federation could be discussed. Secondly, and of more immediate importance, since 1961 PAFMESCA had, from its headquarters in Dar-es-Salaam, provided co-ordinating machinery, and latterly financial assistance, for the nationalist liberation movements in the dependent territories to the south and west. Both of these circumstances directly affected the outcome of the Addis Ababa conference. The fact that the African liberation movements now looked for support to Dar-es-Salaam instead of, or as well as, the older political capitals, was a decisive factor in the siting there of the African Liberation Committee, which was set up by the OAU.[2] Moreover, the fact that federation had been adopted, at least in principle, as one of the long-run objectives of PAFMESCA meant that, in framing an all-African organization, a tacit distinction had to be drawn between 'blocs', which were inadmissible, and regional federations, which might legitimately contribute to a wider Pan-African Union.

The assumption that regionalism was consistent with unity had been strongly denounced by President Nkrumah, and the failure of the Addis

---

[1] PAFMECA, the Pan-African Freedom Movement of East and Central Africa, became in 1962, when its membership was enlarged, PAFMESCA, the Pan-African Freedom Movement of Eastern, Central, and Southern Africa. By 1963 its membership covered the governments of Ethiopia, Somalia, Tanganyika, Uganda, Congo (Leopoldville), Rwanda, Burundi, and Zanzibar, together with nationalist parties, in some instances including rival organizations, from Northern Rhodesia, Southern Rhodesia, Nyasaland, Mozambique, Angola, South Africa, South West Africa, Basutoland, and Bechuanaland. For a detailed discussion of PAFMESCA see Richard Cox, *Pan-Africanism in practice: PAFMESCA 1958–1964* (London, 1964).

[2] Below, pp. 291–5.

Ababa summit to produce a ruling on this issue, represented, in effect, another defeat for his ideas. It was ironical that of all the African leaders, President Julius Nyerere of Tanganyika was perhaps closest to Nkrumah in arguing for full-scale integration as the only means whereby African states might stand a chance of off-setting economic dependence on the outside world and resist the relentless pressure, as they both saw it, of imperialist forces. But whereas Nkrumah had been committed from the early days of Ghana's independence to immediate creation of a continental federation on the lines of the USA, Nyerere prescribed progress towards the same end by whatever means lay at hand, 'either by all-African decisions or by steps towards unity in different areas of Africa'.[1] In June 1960 he had made his celebrated offer to delay his country's independence so that the three territories of British East Africa—Kenya, Tanganyika, and Uganda—could achieve independence together as a single federal unit.[2] Although nothing came of this initiative, the possibility had been kept alive by discussion within PAFMECA, and it was the expansion of PAFMECA into PAFMESCA in February 1962 to include Ethiopia and Somalia, that produced Nkrumah's first public condemnation of the East African movement.[3]

There was, in fact, no discussion of federalism at the African summit, but a week after the conference the three East African leaders, President Nyerere of Tanganyika, Prime Minister Obote of Uganda, and the future president of Kenya, Jomo Kenyatta, announced their intention to federate before the end of the year. The negotiations for an East African federation, in turn, proved abortive,[4] but the possibility of a less comprehensive form of integration remained one of the chief preoccupations of all three states.

In 1963 any discussion of a greater East African federation was held up by the feud between Ethiopia and Somalia, the other two prospective

[1] Julius Nyerere, 'A United States of Africa', *Journal of Modern African Studies*, No. 1, pp. 1–7.

[2] Nyerere's offer was made at the second conference of independent African states, which he attended as an observer.

[3] *Survey, 1962*, p. 515.

[4] It is interesting to note that Ghana's opposition to East African federation appeared to play at least a minor part in the failure of the negotiations. Nkrumah campaigned vigorously against the federation, both before and after the Addis Ababa conference. In *Africa must unite* he argued that 'regional federations are a form of balkanization on a grand scale', adding by way of explanation that 'whereas it may be inexpedient geographically and otherwise for Ghana to join an East African federation, there would be no difficulty for Tanganyika, let us say, joining a political union of Africa'. Although he put his name to the tripartite declaration of intent at the Addis Ababa conference, the only leader openly to associate himself with Nkrumah's ideas was Milton Obote of Uganda, who, from the start, had been least enthusiastic about the federal idea. When later, during the negotiations, Uganda found it impossible to reconcile her national interests with the proposed federation, the government fell back on the Ghanaian view that federations were inconsistent with African unity. See Joseph S. Nye, *Pan-Africanism and East African integration* (London, 1966), pp. 195–203. Nye's book contains a full analysis of the East African negotiations.

members.[1] When both states joined PAFMESCA, membership, in theory, held out the prospect of an East African solution to their differences, although it was clear that they looked to the organization primarily as a forum in which each could lobby support against the other. For Hailé Selassie, the Ethiopian Emperor, PAFMESCA had also provided a platform from which he could press his idea of a wider organization of African states. As the process of decolonization quickened after 1960, it had become clear that, for both internal and external reasons, Ethiopia could no longer maintain her traditional isolation from the rest of the continent; yet just because of this isolation, the basis of an Ethiopian role in post-colonial Africa was not easily found. In a sense, the task of re-conciling the factions provided the Emperor with a role and it is a tribute to his political acumen that he withheld his bid for Pan-African leadership until he was in a strong position to influence the terms under which the reconciliation would be effected. In this bid, PAFMESCA served a double purpose. First, it had allowed the Emperor to identify his govern-ment with the anti-colonial drive to liberate southern Africa, the one issue on which there was no difference in principle between the rival groups. Second, by joining PAFMESCA, Hailé Selassie was able to head off Somali attempts to win support for their claim to the territories of Ogaden in Ethiopia and the northern frontier district of Kenya, both of which had largely Somali populations. With the approach of Kenya's independence, the Somalis had intensified their campaign for a greater Somalia, both within Africa and in direct negotiations with Great Britain. Had they been successful in winning allies for their cause within PAFMESCA, this would have undermined at one stroke the basis—the acceptance of the territorial *status quo*—on which the reconciliation between Monrovia and Casablanca had been contrived.

In the frequent and often bitter exchanges between Mogadishu and Addis Ababa in the early part of 1963, this double interest, to protect Ethiopian territory and Ethiopian leadership in the Pan-African debate, was plainly discernible. At the beginning of March, after a particularly virulent Somali attack, the Ethiopian minister of information defended his government's policy on both grounds:

Ethiopia opposes any Somali demand for land from Kenya or any other country. In so doing it is not Ethiopia's aim only to defend her own rights and interests but also to save African unity and co-operation. . . . The long history of the world fully teaches us that any policy based on tribalism or clan lines is dangerous to peace and co-operation.[2]

Not surprisingly, such arguments made no impression on the Somali government which continued to press its claims at every opportunity.

[1] For the background to the Somali–Ethiopian dispute, see *Survey, 1961*, pp. 412–14.
[2] *SWB*, ME/1192, 7 Mar. 1963.

Nevertheless, as in West Africa, the approach of the summit did act as a restraining influence on both sides. At the beginning of the year the Somalis had attempted to make their attendance at Addis Ababa conditional on a satisfactory settlement of the unfortunate affair of Abdirahaman Husayn, a secretary in the Somali embassy in Addis Ababa whom the Ethiopian government had struck off the diplomatic list on the grounds that he was an Ethiopian national in the pay of a hostile power. Although at first Hailé Selassie refused to make any concession he ultimately relented and at the end of April Husayn was allowed safe passage to Somalia, after seven months' confinement in the Somali embassy in Addis Ababa.[1] On the other side, the Somali government had also recognized the need for conciliation. 'We are always campaigning and fighting for the missing lands to be returned to the motherland', the minister of the interior told an Africa Day rally in Mogadishu on 16 April, 'but in our minds we have never forgotten the cherished desire for African unity.' The decision against attending the African summit had been reversed, he added, as proof that the Somali Republic put the interests of Africa above everything else.[2] As subsequent events were to show, however, the Somalis had merely decided to plead their cause before the higher court of the Pan-African assembly.

(c) *The African summit and its aftermath*

None of the several disputes between individual states proved strong enough to resist the pressures for Pan-African reconciliation. By the time the foreign ministers of thirty-one independent African states assembled in Addis Ababa on 15 May a consensus had emerged on two of the principal issues with which the heads of state would have to deal: it was accepted first that the main purpose of the conference was to replace the existing African groups with a single continental organization based broadly on the Monrovia gradualist formula for African unity, and second, that the conference would adopt, in return for Casablanca concessions on the organizational issue, a common strategy of support for the liberation movements in the remaining areas of colonial rule. The foreign ministers failed, however, in the face of resolute opposition from the Ghanaian delegation, to make any progress with an Ethiopian draft charter providing for interstate co-operation in economic, social, educational, cultural, and defence policy.[3] Kojo Botsio, Ghana's foreign minister, announced that only a continental government would allow the total liberation of the

[1] Ibid., ME/1240, 29 Apr. 1963.
[2] Ibid., ME/1228, 17 Apr. 1963.
[3] The Ethiopian draft was prepared with the assistance of Manuel Trucco, the Chilean ambassador to the Organization of American States. See Boutros Boutros-Ghali, 'The Addis Ababa Summit', *International conciliation*, No. 546, Jan. 1964, p. 9. This article is a useful first attempt at a legal interpretation of the Charter.

continent.[1] This was, of course, the essence of Nkrumah's thesis and throughout the preparatory conference his spokesmen fought a rearguard action to keep the debate open for the summit itself. At the end of the week the foreign ministers had reached deadlock, although they agreed to recommend postponing the drafting of the African Charter to a second conference later in the year.[2]

But if the foreign ministers had failed to subordinate their differences to the wider goal of African unity, it was apparent that the heads of state were determined to succeed. From Emperor Hailé Selassie's opening speech on 23 May to the final ceremony at which the OAU Charter was signed in the early hours of 26 May, the emotional intensity was seldom relaxed. Whatever future historians may conclude, it is clear from the Addis Ababa speeches that the African leaders themselves were convinced that their deliberations represented a turning-point in African history.

The two major decisions—to establish an all-African organization and, contrary to the foreign ministers' advice, to proceed immediately with the drafting of an African Charter—were both effectively settled by Hailé Selassie at the outset. Having first identified the need for a continental organization with responsibilities for interstate co-operation in economic and defence matters, the Emperor concluded:

Let us not put off, to later consideration and study, the single act, the one decision, which must emerge from this gathering if it is to have real meaning. This conference cannot close without adopting a single African Charter. We cannot leave here without having created a single African organization possessed of the attributes which we have described. If we fail in this we will have shirked our responsibility to Africa and to the peoples we lead. If we succeed, then, and only then, will we have justified our presence here.[3]

With the Ethiopian Emperor firmly committed to immediate action, and with the eyes of the world fixed on Addis Ababa, it would have been difficult for later speakers to oppose him. In fact, none tried, and the conference settled down to working out a compromise charter to which all could subscribe.

In his speech, Hailé Selassie had conceded that the ultimate aim lay in full political union, but he argued that, so long as obstacles to political union remained, there was no practical alternative to the establishment of a more limited organization of the kind proposed in the Ethiopian draft charter. In the speeches that followed, this Ethiopian position was substantially endorsed by the majority of those present. Apart from President Nkrumah, only Milton Obote of Uganda spoke in favour of early political unification.[4] For his part, Nkrumah was still unprepared

[1] *Le Monde*, 16 May 1963.   [2] *Times*, 21 May 1963.
[3] 'The Addis Ababa Summit Conference: full text of speeches', p. 5, *Ethiopia Observer*, vol. vii,
No. 1.   [4] Ibid., p. 37.

to make any concessions. It is true that in proposing a Union government, he suggested that this need not involve the sacrifice of sovereignties 'big or small', but since what he proposed was a 'political union based on Defence, Foreign Affairs and Diplomacy, and a Common Citizenship, an African Currency, an African Monetary Zone and an African Central Bank',[1] it was clear that the sacrifices envisaged went far beyond what any independent African state was likely to accept. For the most part the Monrovia powers supported the gradualist approach of the Ethiopian draft, although both Prime Minister Balewa of Nigeria and President Houphouet-Boigny of the Ivory Coast also insisted that, to lay a firm basis for future co-operation and mutual confidence, the Charter would have to contain an unqualified condemnation of political assassination and subversion.[2]

In keeping with the new consensus, the moderate victory in resisting supranationalism was compensated for in the adoption, by virtually all those present, of an uncompromising militancy towards the remaining areas of 'white rule'. The theme that henceforth resolutions condemning colonialism and racial discrimination must be matched by direct action within Africa was developed by leaders from the Monrovia and Casablanca groups alike. President Senghor proposed the application of an economic and diplomatic boycott against South Africa.[3] Prime Minister Obote offered Uganda as a training-ground for freedom fighters from the south,[4] and Sékou Touré demanded, albeit unsuccessfully, that the conference lay down 'a deadline for the end of foreign domination in Africa, after which our armed forces should intervene directly in the legitimate defence of the African continent against aggressors'. He also made the proposal that was subsequently acted upon to combine increased pressure on the major powers at the UN with more positive action, including the establishment of a liberation fund, within Africa.[5] Above all, however, it was Mohammed Ben Bella who caught the imagination of the conference, and of the outside world, with his dramatic plea for immediate and unconditional support for the peoples of Angola, Mozambique, and South Africa in their struggle against colonialism. Without such support, he concluded, the Charter would remain a dead letter. 'So let us all agree to die a little or even completely so that the peoples still under colonial domination may be freed and African unity may not be a vain word.'[6]

The drafting of the Charter was the work of a committee of foreign ministers from Ethiopia, Nigeria, Cameroons, Senegal, Ghana, and the UAR. The final document,[7] reflecting the bargaining between

[1] Ibid., p. 68.
[2] Ibid., pp. 58, 73. In both cases they based their arguments on the circumstances surrounding the assassination of President Olympio of Togo the previous January. Above, pp. 268–70.
[3] Ibid.   [4] Ibid., p. 37.   [5] Ibid., p. 30.   [6] Ibid., p. 53.
[7] For text of the OAU Charter, see *Documents, 1963*, pp. 436–43.

Casablanca and Monrovia, was, it has been noted, 'a curious hotch-potch of principles and purposes, which combined very conservative statements designed to protect the *status quo* in intra-African relations with radical commitments to the outside world'.[1] The Casablanca powers pledged themselves to the principles of sovereign equality (Article III. 1), non-interference in the internal affairs of other states (Article III. 2), and the condemnation of political assassination and subversion (Article III. 5), in return for a commitment from the Monrovia states of 'absolute dedication to the total emancipation of the African territories which are still dependent' (Article III. 6) and an affirmation of non-alignment with regard to all blocs (Article III. 7).

The institutional arrangements were more straightforward. Although Article II states as a purpose the promotion of 'the unity and solidarity of the African and Malagasy states' and calls on members to co-ordinate their general policies in various fields,[2] the institutional framework established under Article VII made no concessions to supranationalism. Final authority was vested in the Assembly of heads of state, to which both the Council of Ministers and the General Secretariat were made responsible. In the case of the other political institution which was to play an important part in the OAU's work—the Commission of Mediation, Conciliation, and Arbitration—the Charter pledged member states to settle disputes peacefully amongst themselves and made provision for the drafting of a separate treaty to establish the Commission itself (Article XIX). The administrative work of the OAU was entrusted at first to a provisional secretariat to be provided by the Ethiopian government assisted by a special committee drawn from six other states.[3]

The OAU's strategy was spelled out in two resolutions, the one on decolonization, the other on apartheid and racial discrimination.[4] Although primarily aimed at the colonial powers, the resolution on decolonization also included a warning to other nations 'that they must choose between their friendship for African peoples and their support of powers that oppress African peoples', an indirect reference to Portuguese membership of NATO which was a long-standing source of contention at the UN between African states and the Western powers. Strongly worded resolutions on colonialism were a standard feature of most African conferences. What appeared to add substance to this one were the specific decisions that accompanied it. Not only was there to be a committee of

---

[1] Catherine Hoskyns, 'Pan-Africanism and Integration', in Arthur Hazlewood, ed., *African integration and disintegration: case studies in economic and political union* (London, 1967), p. 367.

[2] Five specialized commissions were established for this purpose—Economic and Social; Educational and Cultural; Health, Sanitation, and Nutrition; Defence; and Scientific, Technical, and Research.

[3] Niger. Nigeria, Ghana, Congo (Brazzaville), and the UAR (*Times*, 22 July 1963).

[4] *Documents, 1963*, pp. 444–7.

foreign ministers to speak for the OAU at two special Security Council meetings to consider South African and Portuguese policies respectively, which it was decided to request, but the conference also established a nine-member committee, with permanent headquarters in Dar-es-Salaam, to co-ordinate African assistance to the liberation movements and to manage a liberation fund to which all members were required to contribute. Finally, the resolution demanded the breaking off of diplomatic and consular relations with Portugal and South Africa and called for an effective trade boycott of both countries, including a ban on overflying of African territories by Portuguese and South African aircraft.

The resolution on apartheid and racial discrimination likewise served notice on the Western powers that the African states intended to pursue their cold war with South Africa with renewed vigour. Moreover, although both Kennedy and Khrushchev had sent personal messages welcoming the movement towards African unity,[1] the outbreak of the Alabama race riots on the eve of the conference led to bitter criticism of American racial practices and the demand by several radical leaders that some reference to the American situation should be included in the resolution. The final wording was comparatively restrained, including an 'expression of gratitude for the efforts of the Federal Government of the United States of America to put an end to these intolerable malpractices'. But it was clear that the Africans would be looking for more than verbal support in their campaign against South Africa at the UN and would, if necessary, apply pressure on an issue over which the Kennedy administration was particularly sensitive and on which, it went without saying, the Soviet Union would certainly be prepared to capitalize at America's expense.

The remaining resolutions[2] which dealt with African representation at the UN, General Disarmament, and proposals for economic, cultural, and social co-operation, were less noteworthy. However, it was symptomatic of the 'minimalist' approach adopted that the resolution on economic co-operation, which appointed an expert committee to study, in collaboration with the ECA, prospects for an African Free Trade Area or Common Market and an African Clearing and Payments Union, made no mention of the continued association of the UAM states with the EEC. This was a subject on which there were still differences of principle between English and French-speaking states, and it was, therefore, tacitly ignored in the interests of unity.

The successful outcome of the conference created a strong, if temporary, sense of euphoria. The signing of the Charter was the signal for 'a grand reconciliation rite, where all factions solemnly swore that the divisions

---

[1] For the text of the Kennedy and Khrushchev messages, see *USIS* Press Release, 21 May, and *Soviet News*, 24 May 1963.   [2] *Documents, 1963*, pp. 447–52.

of yesterday must come to an end'.[1] Amongst the Arabs, the ceremony
was the scene of a triangular reconciliation between Nasser, Ben Bella,
and Bourguiba.[2] Amongst the sub-Saharan Africans there were similar
declarations of solidarity between those leaders who had failed to patch
up their quarrels before the conference. Sékou Touré vigorously denied
the reports of a rift with Nkrumah, to which their different stands over the
Togo affair had given rise.[3] For his part, Nkrumah heroically refused to
acknowledge defeat and announced:

> The decisions we have taken here have made African unity a reality and we
> can clearly see a Union Government of Africa on the horizon. This is the goal
> which we set ourselves when we struggled in our separate states for independence.
> It is also the compelling force which brought us together in Addis Ababa.[4]

Although the issue of regionalism was not discussed at the summit, immediately afterwards the Monrovia and Casablanca groups were dissolved
and on 4 June, Sékou Touré announced the formal dissolution of the
Ghana–Guinea–Mali Union. Later, on 25 September, PAFMESCA was
similarly disbanded by President Nyerere and its chairman, Kenneth
Kaunda.[5] Only the Brazzaville group refused to disband. On 27 July
the UAM heads of state met at Cotonou to consider the relationship
between their existing organization and the OAU. While the group was
split between abolitionists and conservationists[6] the immediate outcome
at Cotonou was to strengthen the organization by the admission of Togo
as the fourteenth member state. The inclusion in the OAU Charter of a
specific condemnation of political assassination and subversion, the issues
to which the Togo affair had given rise, meant that it was no longer so
important to remain aloof from the Grunitsky regime in order to discourage these activities, and Togo's admission to the UAM, in fact,
prepared the way for admission to the OAU itself when the Council of
Ministers met a week later in Dakar.

At Cotonou, the Brazzaville powers had agreed to work towards
'harmonization and eventually even fusion' with the OAU,[7] and they
maintained this stand at Dakar, resisting successfully a draft resolution
put forward by Guinea which called on all states 'to abrogate, effectively
and immediately, all charters governing previous Groupings and Sub-
Groupings, and to integrate or reorganize their technical bodies within
the specialized institutions of the OAU'.[8] The pressure for dissolution,

---

[1] Tevoedjre, p. 51.

[2] *La Bourse Égyptienne*, 26 May 1963. Nasser also used the occasion to have two meetings with
President Ould Daddah of Mauritania at which he was reported to have assured the Mauritanian
leader of the UAR's *de facto* recognition and invited two members of his government to visit
Cairo for talks on future co-operation.   [3] *Le Monde*, 28 May 1963.

[4] 'Addis Ababa Summit Conference', p. 76.   [5] Legum, p. 138.

[6] Tevoedjre, p. 51.   [7] *NY Times*, 6 Aug. 1963.

[8] For the text of this and the much milder final resolution, see *Documents, 1963*, pp. 453–5.

however, continued after the conference, and at their next meeting in March 1964, also held in Dakar, the UAM heads of state unanimously agreed that the UAM should cease to exist as a political body, although they simultaneously decided to continue its economic, technical, cultural, and social activities within the Afro-Malagasy Organization of Economic Co-operation (OAMCE).[1]

(d) *The OAU and the 'liberation struggle'*

Throughout the period of African rivalries, most African leaders had remained united, in word if not in action, in their opposition to European minority rule in southern Africa.[2] At the Addis Ababa conference they made their first concerted attempt to evolve a common strategy in their campaign against Portugal and South Africa. From then on, the struggle was to be carried forward simultaneously on three fronts. First, those states which still had formal diplomatic or trade relations with either country were committed to severing them,[3] a gesture which by itself was unlikely to make much impression but which was of symbolic importance in the effort to have both Portugal and South Africa ostracized within the international community. Secondly, the Africans proposed to intensify their pressure at the UN, and within the UN specialized agencies, for the expulsion of Portugal and South Africa and the immediate application of diplomatic and economic sanctions.[4] Finally, under the auspices of the newly formed African Liberation Committee (ALC) there was to be an increased emphasis on direct action within Africa, in the first instance against the Portuguese territories of Angola, Mozambique, and Portuguese Guinea, but in principle against the remaining British, French, and Spanish colonies, and South Africa.

In the weeks immediately following the summit, interest centred on the nine-member ALC as the major new element in the confrontation between black and white Africa. The Committee's membership, which included a cross-section of all the pre-OAU groups,[5] suggested that the Africans were in earnest in their determination to provide material backing for the rhetorical anti-colonialism which had long been an established

---

[1] Tevoedjre, pp. 53–4.

[2] See *Survey, 1961*, pp. 415–27; *Survey, 1962*, pp. 490–509.

[3] In Aug. 1963, at the first OAU Council of Ministers meeting in Dakar, the acting secretary-general reported that 'Algeria, Cameroun, Dahomey, Ethiopia, Ivory Coast, Guinea, Liberia, Madagascar, the Sudan, Tunisia, Somalia, Senegal, UAR, Upper Volta have either broken off diplomatic or consular relations as the case may be, or have impounded passports of the nationals, or have prohibited the use of their airfields or ports by the airlines of the two states.' *OAU Council of Ministers, Dakar Conference, 2–11 August 1963. Report of Plenary Sessions* (Lagos, 1963. Restricted).

[4] For the evolution of Afro-Asian pressure at the UN against Portugal and South Africa, see *Survey, 1962*, pp. 490–2.

[5] Tanganyika, Uganda, Ethiopia, Algeria, Guinea, UAR, Senegal, Congo (Leopoldville), Nigeria.

part of UN proceedings. It was clear that the Committee's task would not be easy. Quite apart from a major uncertainty about finance, unanimity amongst the various African factions on the principle of liberation had not previously been accompanied by agreement on the means to be employed to bring this about. In the past, rival nationalist parties of the dependent territories had been able to pursue separate policies-in-exile by putting themselves under the patronage of rival African states. The ideological conflict between Casablanca and Monrovia had, to some extent, been carried over into the liberation movement. While the Addis Ababa resolution on decolonization had appealed 'to all national liberation movements to co-ordinate their efforts by establishing common action fronts, so as to strengthen the effectiveness of their struggle and the rational use of the concerted assistance given them',[1] in practice this was bound to prove difficult. This was partly because divisions within the various nationalist movements often ran deep, and partly because the nationalists were naturally suspicious of outside interference, however benevolent, from a body on which they were not represented.[2]

One consequence of the establishment of the ALC was to raise expectations of support amongst African freedom fighters everywhere. When the committee held its first meeting in Dar-es-Salaam between 25 June and 4 July, it was besieged with petitions from nationalists in virtually every dependent territory.[3] From the outset the committee drew an operational distinction between disputes with Britain and France, which were essentially over the timing of decolonization, and the deeper conflict of principle with Portugal and South Africa. In dealing with Britain, particularly over Southern Rhodesia, the Committee's chairman, Oscar Kambona, announced that the committee would use its good offices to hasten the constitutional process towards self-government, to which the British government was already committed; elsewhere, they would employ 'all means at their disposal' including force.[4] But despite the accent on militancy, Kambona emphasized that neither military nor financial assistance were to be had for the asking. Decisions on the granting of assistance were deferred to the OAU Council of Ministers, while three sub-committees were set up to study the financial, military, and political aspects, respectively, of support for the liberation movements.[5]

[1] For full text see *Documents, 1963*, pp. 444–6.

[2] In this respect the liberation movements probably preferred the more informal arrangements which had operated within PAFMESCA prior to the creation of the African Liberation Committee. Cf. Richard Cox, p. 71.

[3] *Observer*, 30 June 1963. The only exceptions were the three British High Commission territories, Bechuanaland, Basutoland, and Swaziland.

[4] *Times*, 6 July 1963.

[5] *La Bourse Égyptienne*, 9 July 1963. The sub-committees were as follows: financial affairs—UAR, Uganda, Tanganyika; military affairs—Algeria, Guinea, Ethiopia; political affairs—Nigeria, Senegal, Congo (L).

The main outcome of the Dar-es-Salaam meeting was to confirm the policy already laid down at Addis Ababa, under which both military and financial assistance would only be provided where rival nationalist groups had agreed to co-operate. It was with this end in view that the committee established goodwill missions to mediate between the rival nationalists in Angola, Portuguese Guinea, and the Cape Verde Islands.[1]

Angola was to provide the test case for the new policy. Although the Portuguese authorities had succeeded in containing, at great cost to themselves, the African revolt which had spread through northern Angola in April 1961,[2] there remained a 'subverted area' of about 35,000 square miles of thick forest along the northern border with the Congo (Leopoldville), across which guerrillas, some trained in Algeria and others in the Congo, continued to infiltrate. But while Angola was regarded by the ALC as the front line in the liberation struggle, and the most deserving candidate for assistance, all previous efforts to reconcile the União das Populações de Angola (UPA) and the Movimento Popular de Libertação de Angola (MPLA), the two principal nationalist parties, had failed.[3]

The task of the Committee's goodwill mission was further complicated by the fact that both Angolan parties had strong supporters amongst the independent African states. In April 1962 Roberto Holden, leader of the UPA, had proclaimed his Governo Revolucionário de Angola em Exilo (GRAE),[4] whereupon rivals in the MPLA had successfully persuaded Ben Bella, who had previously helped to train guerrillas for both parties, to break off his relationship with the UPA. On the other hand President Adoula of the Congo, while allowing both parties to operate from Congolese territory, had consistently favoured the UPA. When, on the eve of the ALC meeting, Adoula announced Congolese recognition of the GRAE, the immediate effect was to reopen the ideological dispute between those states that had previously belonged to the Casablanca group and the rest. Adoula's announcement was regarded as an attempt to pressure the committee into backing Holden's movement, whose political affiliations were thought to lie with the African moderates, and to forestall a possible Algerian attempt to force the UPA into an association with the 'radical nationalist' MPLA.[5]

[1] Times, 6 July 1963.   [2] Survey, 1961, pp. 419–27.
[3] Survey, 1962, pp. 492–3. There was also a further abortive attempt at conciliation by President Youlou of the Congo (Brazzaville) shortly before the African Liberation Committee meeting in Dar-es-Salaam.
[4] For a discussion of the radical–moderate rivalries in the African liberation movement see Wallerstein, p. 71.
[5] An article by Basil Davidson in West Africa, 26 Jan. 1963, argued that, while the leaders of both parties blamed each other for their failure to co-operate, primary responsibility rested with Holden who had consistently refused all working co-operation with the MPLA, demanding instead that the movement should disband to allow its members to join the UPA as individuals. For a discussion of the political composition of the two parties see Survey, 1961, pp. 417–18.

But although Ghana and Algeria denounced the recognition of the GRAE,[1] it was the Congolese view that prevailed. In part this was due to the collapse of effective opposition from the MPLA at a time when the UPA was unquestionably better organized, both militarily and politically. The MPLA had at first reacted strongly to Adoula's recognition of the GRAE and announced the establishment of a new bureau in Cairo, whose function, apart from fostering closer relations with the UAR, would be to combat Holden's growing influence.[2] However, on 10 July, Agostinho Neto, the MPLA leader, announced that in the interests of African unity he would co-operate with the government-in-exile, although it later emerged that he did not speak for the movement as a whole.[3] The announcement from Dar-es-Salaam that the ALC would make its assistance conditional on the achievement of a common front and that it proposed to assign special responsibilities for the handling of this assistance to states neighbouring on the dependent territories appears to have precipitated an internal crisis within the MPLA.[4] At all events, the ALC mission,[5] which included representatives from Algeria and Guinea, two states that had previously backed the MPLA, was unanimous in recommending to the August meeting of the OAU Council of Ministers both the formal recognition of the GRAE and the channeling of all external support to it. This recommendation was adopted by the OAU and subsequently acted upon by all the African states with the exception of Ghana, whose government became progressively disenchanted with the ALC as time went on, and the Congo (Brazzaville) where President Youlou's government had been replaced in August by a radical regime, which defied the OAU recommendation and welcomed the MPLA after its expulsion from the Congo (Leopoldville).[6]

The failure of the ALC's attempt to mediate between the rival Angolan parties, and the decision to confer legitimacy on the GRAE alone contained obvious dangers for the future. In the short run, however, the agreement reached within the ALC, even if it did not extend to the Angolan nationalists, provided Africans with a reassuring demonstration of the 'spirit of Addis' at work.[7] Unfortunately, there was no sign from

[1] *SWB*, ME/1296, 10 July 1963. It was suggested in Ghana (Radio Accra) that US pressure (the assistant secretary of state for Africa having recently visited Leopoldville) was responsible for Adoula's stand.

[2] Ibid. 　　[3] Ibid., ME/1299, 13 July 1963. 　　　　[4] Ibid., ME/1294, 8 July 1963.

[5] The mission, comprising the foreign ministers of Nigeria, Congo (L), Algeria, Guinea, and Senegal, visited Leopoldville immediately after the ALC meeting in Dar-es-Salaam. *Africa Digest*, Aug. 1963, p. 26. 　　　　　　　　　　　　　　　[6] Wallerstein, p. 163.

[7] At a press conference in Leopoldville on 4 Sept., Holden had claimed that following the OAU's formal recognition of the GRAE, Portugal could no longer use divisions amongst African nationalists 'as an excuse for ignoring the real aspirations of our own people'. Quoted in *Africa Digest*, Dec. 1963, p. 84. However, the Angolan movement continued to be plagued by internal disputes, both within the GRAE and between the UPA and MPLA. Cf. Wallerstein, pp. 164–5.

Lisbon of any weakening in Portugal's determination to retain control of her African empire.

In Portuguese Guinea, as well, the Portuguese authorities remained utterly intransigent. In most respects the two situations were similar. In recent months there had been an increase of rebel activity by the two nationalist parties, the Frente de Libertação de la Independencia Nacional da Guine (FLING) and the Partido Africano de Guine e Cabo Verde (PAIGC), operating respectively from Dakar in Senegal and Conakry in Guinea. On 10 April, after clashes between rebel and government forces, Senegal had requested a meeting of the Security Council to consider alleged Portuguese violation of Senegalese airspace and the bombing of the border village of Bouniak.[1] The Council's debate, which began on 17 April, shed no light on the incident, and it seemed likely, as the Portuguese representative, Vasco Garin, insisted, that Senegal's motives in summoning the Council were political.[2] In any event, when the African states, strongly supported by the USSR, attempted to widen the discussion to a general indictment of Portuguese policies in Africa, the Western powers, whose representatives none the less accepted Portuguese responsibility for the tension in the area, were adamant that the Council should confine itself to the specific incident for which it had been summoned. As Portugal denied the Senegalese charges in their entirety, and as there appeared to be a genuine confusion as to what exactly had happened, this effectively ended the matter. The final resolution, unanimously adopted on 24 April, merely deplored the incident and requested the secretary-general to keep the situation under review.[3] Although, from the African point of view, nothing concrete was achieved, the debate served notice on Portugal, as also on the Western powers, of mounting African pressure in both Africa and at the UN.

As in Angola, the Portuguese authorities reacted by strengthening their defences. At the end of July, the defence minister, General Manuel Gomes de Araújo, described rebel incursions from Senegal as 'inconvenient and disagreeable' but of no other significance.[4] But the arrival of another 2,000 troops to reinforce the 8,000 already in Guinea suggested that the government was playing it safe.[5] Much of the disputed territory favoured

---

[1] SCOR, 18th Year, Doc. S/5279, Supplement for Apr. May, June 1963, pp. 16–17.

[2] In the Portuguese view, the main ground for this claim was Senegal's failure to take any action under Article 33 of the Charter (bilateral action) before having recourse to the Council. Since Senegal still maintained consular relations with Portugal, the arrangement of direct contact need not have raised any great difficulty. For Senegal, as a member of the UAM, however, the advantages of a full hearing before the Security Council were clear: the debate, in which three UAM states (Senegal, Gabon, and Congo (B)) and two Casablanca states (Ghana and Morocco) took part demonstrated their solidarity over the issue of African liberation, thus contributing to the process of African reconciliation.

[3] SCOR, 18th Year, Doc. S/5293, Supplement for Apr., May, June 1963, pp. 30–1.

[4] Africa Digest, Aug. 1963, p. 28.   [5] Times, 18 July 1963.

the rebels, and General Araújo himself admitted that they had already penetrated 15 per cent of the southern province bounded by the Republic of Guinea.[1] Meanwhile, the ALC's attempt to mediate between the rival nationalist parties again ended in failure. The majority of the committee had been in favour of recognizing the PAIGC, as being militarily better placed than FLING to take advantage of outside support. Whether for ideological reasons (PAIGC was an affiliate of the radical MPLA) or simply because the Senegalese government was unwilling to see Portuguese Guinea dominated from Conakry, Senegal vetoed this proposal in the OAU Council of Ministers. The result was a stalemate in which both parties continued to pursue separate policies under the rival patronage of Senegal and Guinea.

Despite these setbacks, the African states remained very much on the offensive throughout the summer. In the diplomatic field, they obtained a number of quick successes. After a ten-day debate, following a walkout by African delegates, the governing body of the ILO decided on 28 June to exclude South Africa.[2] Early in July, another African walkout caused the withdrawal of Portugal from a UNESCO conference, while at the end of July the Economic and Social Council confirmed an earlier decision of the Economic Commission for Africa (ECA) to expel both Portugal and South Africa.[3] But it was on the Security Council, which alone could authorize effective international action, that the Africans pinned their greatest hopes. In line with the Addis Ababa strategy on 11 July the African group at the UN requested two special meetings of the Security Council, the first to consider the situation in the territories under Portuguese domination, the second, South Africa's apartheid policies. In both cases the grounds given were that failure to comply with the long list of General Assembly and Security Council Resolutions addressed to both countries in the past represented 'a breach of peace and security in the African continent as well as a threat to international peace and security'.[4]

The Security Council devoted ten meetings between 22 and 31 July to a debate on Portuguese colonial policy. In addition to Ghana and Morocco, the African representatives on the Council, the OAU was represented by a

[1] *Times*, 18 July 1963.

[2] *United Nations Yearbook, 1963*, p. 598. For details of the debate leading up to the ILO decision see *Africa Digest*, Aug. 1963, p. 24.

[3] *United Nations Yearbook, 1963*, p. 273. African pressure within the specialized agencies continued throughout the year achieving a further success in December when South Africa was expelled from the FAO.

[4] *SCOR*, 18th Year, Doc. S/5347, S/5348, Supplement for July, Aug., Sept. 1963. Para. 7 of the Addis Ababa resolution on decolonization recorded the decision to send 'a delegation of Ministers of Foreign Affairs to speak on behalf of all African states at the meeting of the Security Council which will be called to examine the report of the United Nations Committee of 24 on the situation in African territories under Portuguese domination'. Para. 3 of the resolution on Apartheid and Racial Discrimination recorded a similar decision to 'inform the Security Council of the explosive situation existing in South Africa'.

delegation consisting of the foreign ministers of Tunisia, Liberia, and Sierra Leone and the finance minister of Madagascar, although as non-members, neither they nor the Portuguese foreign minister, Franco Nogueira, who also took part, enjoyed voting rights. The Africans rested their case on a Resolution of 4 April, passed against the objections of the Western powers, by the so-called 'Committee of Twenty four', which the General Assembly had set up in 1961 to maintain the pressure for 'independence for all colonial countries and peoples'.[1] Portugal's continued refusal to co-operate had resolved the Committee to bring the situation to the attention of the Security Council 'with a view to its taking appropriate measures, including sanctions, to secure the compliance of Portugal with the relevant General Assembly and Security Council resolution'.[2]

The debate was along predictable lines. Moreover, since it took place as a result of political pressure at the UN rather than in the wake of a specific military and political crisis there was little chance that it would have any direct impact. Opening the case for the African group, Mr Grimes, the Liberian foreign minister, did his best to anticipate Western objections to the application of sanctions by asserting the Council's responsibility to discern and prevent breaches of the peace. Portugal's continued refusal to recognize the legitimate aspirations of the peoples in her African colonies, the wars of national liberation to which this had given rise, and the flagrant contempt with which the Salazar government had treated UN resolutions, provided, in the African view, sufficient evidence that such a threat existed. 'You should not', Mr Grimes pleaded, 'await an explosion with all its consequences, before you act.'[3] In a letter addressed to the secretary-general on 22 July Nkrumah had stated that 'nothing short of the immediate independence of African territories under Portuguese domination will satisfy us'.[4] Failing such a dramatic reversal in Portuguese colonial policy, the African delegates concentrated, at the beginning of the debate, on lobbying support for the suspension of Portugal's UN membership and the immediate imposition of economic sanctions.

As on past occasions the Africans had the unequivocal backing of Federenko, the Russian delegate. He agreed with the African argument, first advanced in the debate by Quaison-Sackey of Ghana, implicating the Western powers in responsibility for Portuguese policies, through their alliance with Portugal in NATO. 'Such highly provocative behaviour towards the United Nations on the part of the Salazar regime', he said, 'is to be explained first and foremost by the fact that it is acting under cover of the punitive shield of NATO.'[5] Pledging Soviet support for a full

[1] *Survey, 1961*, p. 425; *Survey, 1962*, pp. 330–2.
[2] For text see *GAOR*, 18th Session, Report of the Special Committee, Doc. A/5446/Rev. 1.
[3] *SCOR*, 18th Year, 1040th meeting, 22 July 1963.
[4] Ibid., Supplement for July, Aug., Sept. 1963, S/5366, p. 18.
[5] Ibid., 1047th meeting, 29 July 1963.

programme of diplomatic and economic sanctions, Federenko also demanded of the Western powers a direct and unambiguous answer to the African insistence that they should choose between the friendship of Salazar and themselves.[1]

In reply to African and Soviet accusations, Nogueira reiterated the familiar argument that the overseas territories were an integral part of metropolitan Portugal, and that her policies were in the best interests of the people and in harmony with the UN Charter. If there was violence in her African territories, he suggested, this was the responsibility of outside powers, a charge which Quaison-Sackey freely admitted with the proviso that African support for the liberation movements was fully justified, as proof that a threat to international peace already existed. But Nogueira drew a different conclusion, arguing that the Addis Ababa resolutions contravened the UN Charter and that the onus of responsibility should be shifted from Portugal to the African states:

> During the past few years a new legality has been created, a new conception of law has been brought to international affairs, a new legal structure has been ruling the life, or at least some aspects of the life, of the international community. The interesting point is that such a new notion of international lawfulness works in one direction only, for one purpose only, and for the benefit of some only. . . . When the Republic of the Congo (L) officially establishes military training camps against Angola, it is a lawful act, but if we did the same in some Portuguese territories, it would be an unlawful action. When some people say that they are going to send volunteers against Angola, it is a lawful intention, and they are called volunteers; if we did the same, that would be unlawful, and the volunteers would be called mercenaries.[2]

Nogueira concluded with an invitation to the OAU representatives to visit Angola and Mozambique to study, at first hand, the conditions of the people and their government. For their part, the Portuguese authorities would attach no conditions other than that the visitors should act in good faith and with the impartiality which was to be expected as a matter of course.

If, as Nogueira had suggested, some of the Western representatives agreed with him, none was prepared to say so openly. Nor was there any prospect that the original draft resolution, put forward on 26 July by Ghana, Morocco, and the Philippines, would command the minimum seven votes to pass in the Council.[3] The draft, which described the existing situation as a threat to international peace and security, called on member states *inter alia* to withhold assistance from the Portuguese govern-

[1] *SCOR*, 18th year, 1047th meeting, 29 July 1963. A reference to the Addis Ababa resolution on decolonization. Para. 6 '. . . informs the allies of colonial powers that they must choose between their friendship for the African peoples and their support of powers that oppress African peoples' (full text in *Documents, 1963*, pp. 444–6).

[2] Ibid.   [3] Ibid., 1044th meeting, 26 July 1963, Doc. S/5372.

ment and, in particular, to ban the sale of all arms and military equipment to Portugal. It was not the substance of the draft to which the Western powers objected—they all claimed to be broadly in sympathy with its aims—but its language. Adlai Stevenson explained the US position, which was supported by Britain and France, in a statement on July 26:

Though we agree that the situation in the Portuguese territories gives rise to very serious international friction and might, if continued, endanger the maintenance of international peace and security, we do not agree that a threat to peace already exists. We do not agree, therefore, that the situation falls within the scope of Chapter VII of the Charter, or that the language of any resolution we adopt should so suggest.[1]

In the semantic battle that ensued the Africans eventually settled for a compromise wording, which, while placing the Resolution[2] unequivocally under Chapter VI of the Charter (The Pacific Settlement of Disputes), described the situation as 'seriously disturbing international peace and security in Africa'. Prior to the vote on 31 July, in which they abstained, the British, French, and US delegates explained their positions. All three reaffirmed their sympathy with African aims, itself a testimony to the impact of the African group, and their belief in the principle of self-determination, although the British and French delegates restated their well-known conviction that the administering power, not the Security Council, should decide on the measures appropriate for the implementation of this principle. Adlai Stevenson and Sir Patrick Dean, the British delegate, also confirmed their countries' existing policies under which they did not allow the sale of arms for use in Portuguese overseas territories, and welcomed a provision in the Resolution requesting the secretary-general to ensure its implementation (thus, by implication, authorizing him to initiate negotiations) and to report back to the Council by 31 October.

If the Western position was unsatisfactory to the Africans, it was no less so to the Portuguese. Nogueira left the Council in no doubt as to his government's position on this 'revolting resolution' which he described as morally, and therefore politically, wrong. Throughout the debate, the Portuguese delegation had rejected African charges of repression by reference to the constitutional and other reforms introduced since 1961, and particularly to the 1963 Organic Law for the overseas territories. Although this was couched in general terms, leaving details to be settled individually for each territory, in principle it provided overseas territories

---

[1] Chapter VII, Article 39, provides the authority for enforcement measures undertaken by the Council: 'The Security Council shall determine the existence of any threat to the peace, breach of the peace, or act of aggression, and shall make recommendations, or decide what measures shall be taken in accordance with Articles 41 and 42 to maintain or restore international peace and security.'

[2] For text see *Documents, 1963*, pp. 455–6.

with a greater measure of autonomy and with increased representation in the Corporative Chamber and the Overseas Council.[1] However, any hope that Portugal might be preparing a major change in colonial policy in response to international pressure was dashed by Salazar on 12 August in his first radio and television speech since 1961. In a sustained attack on his critics, in which Russian and American policy in Africa was described as being essentially the same, Salazar took measure of the new militancy among African states, and offered

the closest and most friendly co-operation to those African peoples who would find it useful; and a defence of the territories that constitute Portugal to the limit of our human elements and of our resources, if the African states think fit to turn their threats into acts of war and bring it into our territories.[2]

If there had been any prospect, as the British and American delegates argued, of a useful dialogue between the independent African states and the Portuguese government, it was abundantly clear that there was none now.[3]

The Security Council meeting on Portuguese policy was followed immediately by the second meeting on South Africa. In a letter of 31 July, the South African minister for foreign affairs, Mr Louw, declined to take part on the ground that the matter for discussion, apartheid, fell solely within South Africa's domestic jurisdiction.[4] Far from South Africa posing a threat to international peace and security, Mr Louw accused

[1] The Portuguese government tabled the law in February, following a plenary meeting of the Overseas Council called by the previous minister for overseas territories, Adriano Moreira, in Oct. 1962 (*Survey, 1962*, p. 494). The Council had advised decentralization of matters of primarily overseas interest and recommended administrative changes, including increased representation of the overseas provinces in Parliament. Meanwhile, Moreira, who was generally regarded as a liberal, had left the government in a cabinet reshuffle of Dec. 1962. The delay in passing the law was reputedly the result of opposition from 'integrationists' who aimed at removing all distinctions between the overseas territories and metropolitan Portugal, in order to create one close-knit Lusitanian community.

[2] *Times*, 13 Aug. 1963.

[3] Salazar made a further public speech in defence of his African policy on 27 Aug., when he called a crowd of 70,000 people to 'unite around one word, one reality—Portugal' (*Times*, 28 Aug. 1963). Although later, in response to the secretary-general's request to all member states for information regarding the implementation of the 31 July Resolution, the Portuguese government invited the secretary-general to Lisbon, it was clear that the die had already been cast. U Thant sent his under-secretary for trusteeship and information for non-selfgoverning territories. But neither his discussions, which took place in Lisbon between 9 and 11 Sept., nor the subsequent direct talks at the UN between Portuguese and African representatives, revealed any common ground. For details of these discussions see secretary-general's report of 31 Oct. 1963 (*SCOR*, 18th Year, Supplement for Oct., Nov., Dec. 1963, pp. 55–86).

[4] *SCOR*, 18th Year, Supplement for July, Aug., Sept. 1963, Doc. S/5381. The South African government maintained that consideration of apartheid by the UN contravened Article 2 (7) of the Charter, which states that 'nothing contained in the present Charter shall authorize the United Nations to intervene in matters which are essentially within the domestic jurisdiction of any state or shall require the members to submit such matters to settlement under the present Charter; but this principle shall not prejudice the application of enforcement measures under Chapter VII'.

the African states, quoting Addis Ababa resolutions and speeches as evidence, of subsidizing dissident Bantu, thus obliging the government of the Republic to take increased legislative powers for the maintenance of order and stability.

The debate took place against a background of rising violence in South Africa, which was met by the Verwoerd government with the customary severity. The notorious Sabotage Act of 1962[1] was followed on 1 May 1963 by the passage, against the courageous and lone opposition of Helen Suzman,[2] of the General Law Amendment Act under which the minister of justice, Vorster, was provided with sweeping new powers with which to crush opposition. Under the new Act, the minister was able to detain people for questioning for ninety-day periods without recourse to the courts, and to keep political prisoners in gaol after the completion of their sentences (a provision which he immediately made use of to detain Robert Sobukwe, the Pan-African Congress leader due to be released from prison on 5 May).[3] Moreover, the Act was retroactive. In presenting the Bill to Parliament Vorster said that he intended to impose penalties, ranging from five years' imprisonment to death, on anyone who had pleaded overseas at any time since 1960 that South Africa should be invaded, or who returned to South Africa having been trained abroad in sabotage. Similarly those who had asked for armed intervention before the UN would be held guilty of treason.[4] The International Commission of Jurists promptly called for a strong condemnation of the new Act, stating that

South Africa is now more than ever a police state. In its laws and procedures it is copying many of the worst features of the Communist Stalinist regime. Liberty has gone. Justice is blinded and maimed in spite of the efforts of the Bench and Bar to save such remnants as still remain in that unfortunate country.[5]

But if the civilized world reacted with alarm, there were few signs that the Western powers were ready to accept the Afro-Asian case that the situation had deteriorated to a point where it would justify international action, specifically sanctions.[6] Since it was this that was demanded by the African group in the Security Council, the debate, in its essentials, covered much the same ground as the earlier meeting on Portugal, ending

[1] *Survey, 1962*, p. 498.

[2] Although the opposition United Party supported the Bill as a whole, according to the Party leader, Sir De Villiers Graaf, because it was necessary to put down the 'rising tide of lawlessness', the UP attempted to disassociate itself from the two severest provisions under which ex-prisoners could continue to be detained at leisure and anybody could be detained for ninety days for interrogation. *Africa Digest*, Aug. 1963, p. 20.

[3] *Guardian*, 2 May 1963.

[4] *South Africa Star*, 27 Apr. 1963 (quoted in *Africa Digest*, June 1963, p. 195).

[5] *Guardian*, 15 May 1963.

[6] For a balanced discussion of negotiations over the sanctions issue at the UN, see Dennis Austin, *Britain and South Africa* (Oxford, 1966), Chapter IV.

with the adoption of a Resolution on 7 August which used the same compromise wording, describing the situation as 'seriously disturbing international peace and security' but falling short of an admission that it constituted an actual threat to the peace. The Africans had rested their case for sanctions on South Africa's non-compliance with what was described as the long flow of Resolutions, 'denouncing and condemning the odious system of apartheid'.[1] In addition they drew on two reports from the eleven-member committee which had been established by the General Assembly the previous November to keep South Africa's racial policies under review.[2] The first of these, published in May, had concluded that the new round of repressive and discriminatory measures undertaken in the Republic, together with a continued expansion of the military and police forces,[3] was seriously aggravating the inherent threat to international peace and security, while the second and even stronger report in July recommended the immediate imposition of an embargo on the shipment of arms, ammunition, and petroleum.[4]

There was, however, one major difference between the two debates. Whereas over Portugal, the Western powers, with the exception of Norway, opposed the African demand for a total arms embargo, the US delegate announced that as from the end of 1963, and subject to the honouring of existing contracts, the USA would no longer sell military equipment to South Africa. This, he explained, was a unilateral decision which did not affect the US view that the application of sanctions under Chapter VII 'would be both bad law and bad politics'.[5] Limited as this was when measured against African demands, the American decision[6] nevertheless represented a breakthrough for the Africans in their long struggle to extract something more than verbal support from the West. The draft

[1] *SCOR*, 18th Year, 1051st meeting, 1 Aug. 1963.

[2] The committee was established by the same resolution that had called on member states, for the first time, to impose diplomatic and economic sanctions against South Africa, see *Survey*, *1962*, p. 502. For the text see *Documents*, *1962*, pp. 889–90.

[3] The minister of defence, Fouche, had announced on 11 Feb. that South Africa's permanent defence force, estimated at 23,000, was to be increased by 50 per cent, and that the number of part-time servicemen would also be increased (*Daily Telegraph*, 12 Feb. 1963). Vorster was also reported to have announced a reorganization and strengthening of the police force to make the best use of those civilians who 'had offered to assist the police in combating serious crime and acts of atrocity' (*South Africa Star*, 9 Feb. 1963).

[4] *UN Review*, May 1963, pp. 33–7; ibid., July–Aug., pp. 24–6.

[5] For extracts of Stevenson's statement see *Documents*, *1963*, pp. 456–61.

[6] In his account of the Kennedy Administration, Schlesinger records that the decision was taken on the eve of the Security Council debate on the personal authority of President Kennedy. He ruled in favour of dealing separately with the South African and Portuguese questions, where the US was still inhibited from action by her wish to retain her base in the Azores. The decision appears to have been motivated by the growing conviction, shared in particular by the assistant secretary of state for African affairs, Mennan Williams, and Adlai Stevenson, that following the Addis Ababa meeting, it was necessary for the Administration to back its verbal support of African states with positive action (Schlesinger, pp. 505–9).

resolution tabled by Ghana, Morocco, and the Philippines on 6 August failed to carry in its entirety, the US delegation requesting a separate vote on a clause calling for a trade boycott and export embargo on strategic materials. Even so the Africans could be satisfied when the Resolution, which, apart from reiterating the Council's condemnation of apartheid and calling on South Africa to release all political prisoners, also called for a total arms ban, was passed with only Britain and France abstaining. The secretary-general was asked to report on its implementation by 30 October.[1]

For Britain, traditionally South Africa's principal arms supplier, the US decision, which had evidently not been discussed beforehand, marked an embarrassing departure from the close co-operation that had governed the two countries' stand at the UN over the South Africa question. In Britain, the sale of arms to South Africa was repeatedly challenged by the opposition but the government remained committed to the policy of co-operation in the external defence of South Africa, under the Simonstown Agreement of 1955, the underlying assumption of which, hitherto shared by the USA, had been that the security of the South Atlantic area represented a vital Western interest.[2] Sir Patrick Dean reiterated the British policy of banning the sale of arms which could be used within South Africa to uphold apartheid. But apart from the questionable validity of the implied distinction between weapons suitable for internal and external defence, in African eyes the apparent inconsistency in the British position, in which British spokesmen declared their conviction that South Africa's domestic policies were leading the Republic irrevocably along the road to disaster, while at the same time the government maintained, in the defence field, a relationship based on close co-operation, was now revealed.

As the two powers with the largest trading and investment interest in South Africa, Britain and the USA maintained their common position on the question of sanctions. Both countries remained opposed—and there was no reason to suppose they would lightly revise their position in this respect—to mandatory action under Chapter VII of the Charter. Sir Patrick Dean summarized the Western view with his conclusion that 'the offence of South Africa is not aggression, nor of endangering international peace and security. It is, as I say, a grave offence against human dignity.'[3]

The immediate result of the Security Council Resolution in South Africa was to strengthen both the government's domestic position and its resolve to stand by existing policies. Nevertheless feeling against the

[1] Text in *Documents, 1963*, pp. 461–2.
[2] For a discussion of British policy under the Simonstown Agreement see Dennis Austin, Chapter V.
[3] *SCOR*, 18th Year, 1056th meeting, Aug. 1963. For extracts, see *Documents, 1963*, pp. 462–3.

United States and Britain, who got little credit for her abstention in the
vote, ran high. In September, the foreign minister, Mr Louw, even
suggested that South Africa might unilaterally dissolve the Simonstown
Agreement and discontinue its policy of selling gold on the London market,
although he subsequently admitted that such action would only be taken
in the event of British support for a policy of international sanctions.[1]
In the meantime, as Prime Minister Verwoerd informed a political rally
in Durban on 27 August, the prospect of an arms embargo, while no
doubt inconvenient, created no insuperable problems. South Africa
could, if necessary, produce the ammunition required for internal defence
and South African industry was equipped to meet a larger proportion of
the country's defence production needs than hitherto.[2]

In the months that followed it became clear that the Resolutions of
31 July and 7 August represented not the start of a new and more in-
tensive UN involvement in southern Africa but the limit of what could be
achieved with the co-operation of the Western powers who were safeguarding their existing relationships with Portugal and South Africa.
Although both of these states reacted bitterly against the stand adopted
by Britain and the United States, in practice, as Verwoerd and Salazar
must have recognized, there were no effective counter-measures they
could take.[3] The initiative, as always, rested with the West, and particularly with the United States, even when appearances suggested otherwise.
Had the United States been prepared to allow Afro-Asian opinion to
dictate policy towards Portugal and South Africa, she would have imposed an embargo on both countries in response to pressure in the Security
Council. Instead, the Kennedy regime decided to make no change in its
policy towards Portugal, while on South Africa the decision was taken
prior to, and deliberately independently of, the Security Council debate.

At the time the African states put a more optimistic interpretation on
the turn of events. When on 10 August Mongi Slim, the Tunisian
foreign minister, reported on the outcome of the debates to the OAU
Council of Ministers in Dakar, he concluded that if, as he expected, the
secretary-general reported in October that neither Portugal nor South
Africa had responded positively to the latest Resolutions, the Security
Council would be bound to adopt stronger measures.[4] In the event,

---

[1] *The Star*, Johannesburg, 11, 12 Sept. 1963.   [2] Ibid., 28 Aug. 1963.

[3] Verwoerd's remarks in his speech of 27 Aug. revealed both the inadequacy of South Africa's
retaliatory power and the psychological gulf separating the South African government from the
governments of the Western powers. 'We have pledged our support to the Western nations
who are of our own kind. We are a small nation, it is true, but should they be threatened by
great dangers we would be of value to them. . . . But there is a danger that by adopting their
present attitude towards us, they might push us into the non-committal position taken up by
the African nations of this continent.'

[4] Despite the Western refusal to employ the language of Chapter VII, Slim concluded that
with regard to Portugal 'the Security Council decided to take preventive measures which in-

however, while both the General Assembly and Security Council went on to discuss the situation in southern Africa exhaustively, their debates did little to advance the African cause beyond the point reached by the Security Council in mid-1963.

If, in the Portuguese case, there were at least some signs of movement, they were largely illusory. As we have noted[1] the secretary-general's attempt to make progress through bilateral discussions between African and Portuguese delegations got bogged down over the definition of 'self-determination', the African states maintaining that the rights of the Portuguese colonies had already been settled by the 1960 General Assembly Resolution on decolonization,[2] with the Portuguese insisting that 'self-determination could legitimately take place within a pre-existing national framework'.[3] On 3 December the General Assembly passed by a large majority an Afro-Asian Resolution calling on the Security Council to implement its own Resolution, and decided to keep the question of the Portuguese colonies on the agenda.[4] Three days later, the Security Council met to consider the secretary-general's report, the African group having first issued a statement that, although they were prepared to continue the dialogue with Portugal in principle, the necessary conditions did not exist and they had decided to refer the question to the OAU.[5] The Portuguese continued to insist that their policy was both consistent with the Charter and in the best interests of a multi-racial society in Africa, and the independent African states dismissed both claims out of hand.[6] The final Resolution, introduced on 10 December by Ghana,

contestably fall under Article 40, which in turn comes within the scope of Chapter VII. In taking these preventive measures it will be compelled to take even stronger measures against both Portugal and those States which have not implemented the decision taken concerning the embargo on arms.' On South Africa, Slim was even more emphatic. 'Every member of the Council admitted and declared that this resolution constituted for the Council the last warning that South Africa will receive to adopt a policy which conforms with the principles of Human Rights, with the Charter, and also with human dignity. Consequently if South Africa does not change its policies, the Council will be compelled to take with regard to South Africa.' *OAU Council of Ministers, Dakar Conference*, pp. 83–5.

[1] See above, p. 300.

[2] Resolution 1542 (XV) of 15 Dec. 1960. Text in *Documents, 1960*, pp. 404–6.

[3] The secretary-general's report of 31 Oct. 1963 (Doc. S/5448) contains an account of these discussions. In a submission, the Portuguese foreign minister defended his country's concept of self-determination: 'Portugal did not believe that self-determination could be pre-determined. Portugal believed that there was more than one modality of self-determination just as there was more than one modality with regard to the form of administration of a state. Self-determination to Portugal meant the agreement and consent of the people to a certain political structure, type of state and administrative organization' (*SCOR*, 18th Year, Supplement for Oct., Nov., Dec. 1963, p. 58).

[4] See *GAOR*, 18th Session, Supplement 15, 1963–4, p. 48, A/5515.

[5] *United Nations Yearbook, 1963*, p. 484.

[6] The distance between Portugal and the African states was well described by Alex Quaison-Sackey, the Ghanaian delegate. 'But I might say that when we talk about a multi-racial society we do not mean that any part of Africa should be part of Portugal. Continental pride alone

Morocco, and the Philippines, recorded the Council's agreement that the concept of 'self-determination' was to be understood in terms of the General Assembly's Resolutions on decolonization, and was passed the next day with only France abstaining from the vote.[1] However, the Western powers had first forced a separate vote on the paragraph deprecating Portugal's non-compliance with the 31 July Resolution from which the United States, Britain, France, and Brazil all abstained. Thus while the Resolution obtained the necessary seven votes to carry in the Council, and African honour was thereby vindicated, international action against Portugal was not brought appreciably closer.

The outcome of the debates over South Africa was similarly negative. Although South Africa was more isolated than ever, the Verwoerd regime seemed more impregnable. The fact that the government decided, after initial hesitation, to send a delegation to the General Assembly suggested that it had no wish to court further isolation unnecessarily.[2] On the other hand, as the continued arms build-up, and the succession of political trials plainly showed, they were in no mood for conciliation either. Even the United Party's criticism of the government for running the risk of economic sanctions increasingly lacked conviction. In 1963 the risk was, in any case, never very great: the economic recovery of 1962 was sustained throughout the year, bringing an increase in South African trade with Britain and the United States, her main trading partners, without whose co-operation no policy of international sanctions could work, and whose opposition to such a policy was already on record.

Nevertheless the Afro-Asian group at the UN maintained relentless pressure for sanctions throughout the General Assembly session. The third report of the special committee on apartheid, which appeared on 16 September, contained a fierce indictment of the South African government and concluded with a recommendation to the General Assembly and Security Council, urging both bodies to undertake immediately a programme of diplomatic and economic sanctions including South Africa's expulsion from the UN and its specialized agencies.[3] The report was considered by the Special Political Committee between 8 and 30 October. In addition, the Security Council considered the secretary-general's report on the implementation of its earlier resolution of 7 August. Although South Africa still denied the right of the UN to concern itself with her domestic affairs, the secretary-general was able to draw extensively in his report on a letter of 11 October in which the South African foreign

would never allow us to accept this Portuguese concept of a multi-racial society.' *SCOR*, 18th Year, 1081st meeting, 9 Dec. 1963.

[1] Text in *Documents, 1963*, pp. 465–6.
[2] *The Star*, Johannesburg, 19 Sept. 1963.
[3] *GAOR*, 18th Session, Annexes, Doc. A/5497.

minister had vigorously defended South African foreign policy and accused the African states of threatening the peace:

The steps that South Africa is taking in strengthening its defences should be seen not only in the context of the threats to South Africa by certain African states and in the Addis Ababa resolutions, which are a direct incitement to aggression, but also in the perspective of comparable expenditure on armed forces in other countries of a similar degree of economic and industrial development. South Africa's 1962 defence costs represented 3·77 per cent of the total national output and that represents less than the expenditure of several West European countries of similar economic and industrial development. Moreover those countries, unlike South Africa, enjoy the advantages of membership of a major military alliance.[1]

The African states and their supporters pleaded for a strengthening of the Council's earlier Resolution to include an embargo on strategic materials and the imposition of economic sanctions. The Western powers, however, showed no inclination to accept this demand and the debate was only saved from deadlock by a Norwegian initiative which at least had the merit of keeping the issue open. The Resolution which stemmed from this initiative was adopted unanimously on 4 December.[2] Apart from calling on all states to comply with the Council's Resolution of 7 August, its major new provision was to recommend that a group of experts should be created under the secretary-general

to examine methods of resolving the present situation by the full, peaceful and orderly application of human rights and fundamental freedoms of all inhabitants, regardless of race, colour or creed, and to consider what part the United Nations might play to the achievement of that end.[3]

Thus, at the end of the year, while the odds against any early acceptance of sanctions by the Western powers might seem to have lengthened, the possibility that the group of experts might recommend their application, a recommendation which it would be difficult for the Council to ignore, could not be altogether excluded.

(e) *The OAU and the Algerian–Moroccan war, October–November 1963*

It was ironical that the year which saw African leaders agree to bury their differences and adopt a common position towards the outside world

[1] Secretary-general's report of 11 Oct. in *SCOR*, 18th Year, Supplement for Oct., Nov., Dec. 1963, Doc. S/5438, p. 7.

[2] For text see *Documents, 1963*, pp. 464–5. Although they voted for the resolution, both France and the UK made it clear that they would maintain their policy of supplying arms for external defence, while the US representative explained that, in the US view, the ban on the sale of armament materials, recommended in the resolution, should not include multipurpose items such as petroleum.

[3] At the end of the debate the Special Committee of Experts was set up with Mrs Alva Myrdal (Sweden), Sir Edward Asafu-Adjaye (Ghana), Josip Djerdja (Niger), Sir Hugh Foot (UK), and Dey Ould Sidi Baba (Mauritania) as members.

also witnessed the first armed conflict between two independent African states. The concept of a *pax Africana* lay at the centre of the OAU Charter. Thus, like the Togo affair at the beginning of the year, the fighting that broke out at the beginning of October between Algeria and Morocco in the western Sahara, had serious implications for the continent as a whole, and for the future of the OAU. The containment of the conflict at the beginning of November through a ceasefire, organized under the auspices of the OAU, testified at once to the value of the new organization. And while it is difficult to be certain that, even without OAU arbitration, the war would have taken a different course, there is little doubt that the proscription of war in the Charter, to which they had so recently subscribed, acted as a restraining influence on the disputants, while the existence of an organization representing all Africa was of practical value when both sides wanted a ceasefire but distrusted each other's choice of mediators.[1]

The origins of the Algerian-Moroccan conflict were complex, deriving partly from failures, during the period of French colonial rule, to delineate the boundary, and partly from the sharply contrasting political dynamics operating in each country.[2] We have noted how, earlier in the year, Moroccan fears of Algeria's revolutionary policy and Algerian determination to resist what they regarded as reactionary Moroccan irredentism contributed to the collapse of the Casablanca group and, indirectly, to King Hassan's absence from the Addis Ababa summit.[3] Although at the Dakar meeting of the OAU Council of Ministers, Morocco had been formally admitted to the OAU, Moroccan isolation remained marked, and, as the year progressed, the ideological incompatibility between the Algerian and Moroccan regimes became steadily more pronounced.

Underpinning this general hostility between Rabat and Algiers were several specific differences. As elsewhere in Africa, the boundary problem was essentially a legacy of colonial rule. At the time of the French occupation of Algeria in 1830 there were no fixed boundaries in North Africa, and those that were subsequently negotiated between the French and the then independent Moroccan government were more in the nature of frontier zones, defined according to the occupying tribes, than territorial boundaries in the Western sense.[4] After the declaration of a French

[1] For a useful account of the OAU's role in the Algerian-Moroccan war, on which this section draws heavily, see Patricia Berko Wild, 'The Organization of African Unity and the Algerian-Moroccan border conflict: a study of New Machinery, for Peacekeeping and for the Peaceful Settlement of Disputes Among African States', *International organization*, vol. xx, No. 1, Winter 1966, pp. 18–36.

[2] A summary of the boundary question itself can be found in Anthony S. Reynor, 'Morocco's International Boundaries: A Factual Background', *Journal of Modern African Studies*, No. 3, Sept. 1963, and of the wider political conflict in Édouard Meric, 'Le Conflit Algéro-Marocain', *Revue Française de Science Politique*, No. 4, Aug. 1965.

[3] Above, pp. 279–81.   [4] Wild, p. 19.

protectorate over Morocco in 1912, the colonial authorities established an administrative frontier in the north, known as the Varnier line, but between Teniet-el-Sassi in the Atlas mountains and the Moroccan town of Figuig in the desert area of the south-west, the position remained ill-defined; the French considered this area uninhabitable. It was here, an area occupied mostly by desert tribesmen who knew no frontiers, but claimed by the Moroccan government on historical grounds, that the dispute came to a head in October 1963.

Apart from Morocco's policy of pressing her irredentist claims, Rabat had an economic motive for opposing Algerian occupation of the disputed territory. The discovery of large quantities of iron ore in and around the oasis of Tindouf, and of manganese ore at Jebel Gettara in the Béchar area south-east of Figuig, had given the whole region a new importance. While the Varnier line had placed the Béchar region, and hence the manganese deposits within Algeria, Tindouf had been under Franco-Moroccan military administration until 1952 when it was transferred by the French to Algeria. Algerian control of both areas appeared confirmed when, under the Evian agreements of March 1962 granting independence to Algeria, the French established a joint Franco-Algerian organization to exploit the oil and mineral resources of the Sahara. Morocco accepted this at the time, but soon tried to cut into the Franco-Algerian arrangements by persuading Algeria to accept a joint economic directorate over the western Sahara, in return for which it would presumably be easier for Rabat to surrender territorial claims. But although after Hassan's visit to Algiers in March[1] several conventions were signed providing for economic and industrial co-operation between the two countries, the Algerians were still reluctant to enter firm commitments for joint mineral and industrial projects in the Sahara.[2]

The dispute, already complicated by the introduction of these economic considerations, was further inflamed by Algeria's refusal to honour a commitment, entered into by the GPRA in 1961, to negotiate outstanding frontier problems after Algerian independence. After gaining independence in 1956, Morocco had refused to deal with France over this issue as a demonstration of solidarity with the FLN. In July 1962, however, a secret convention was negotiated in Rabat by King Hassan and Ferhat Abbas, president of the GPRA, in which, in return for unconditional Moroccan support in the independence negotiations, it was stated:

... Le gouvernement provisoire de la République algérienne reconnait pour sa part le problème territorial posé par la délimitation imposée arbitrairement par la France entre les deux pays, qui trouvera sa solution dans des négociations

---

[1] According to the communique issued after the visit 'all the questions in suspense since Algerian independence have been solved in principle'. *Le Monde*, 13 Mar. 1963.

[2] Ibid., 3 May 1963.

entre le gouvernement du Royaume du Maroc et le gouvernement de l'Algérie indépendante . . .

The convention also stipulated that the negotiation was to be carried out by a joint Algerian-Moroccan commission 'dans un esprit de fraternité et d'unité maghrébiennes'.[1]

The text of this convention was not released by Rabat until the end of October 1963, at the height of the conflict, but its existence (its authenticity was never denied by Algeria) no doubt explains the curiously volatile course of Algerian-Moroccan relations between July 1962 and the outbreak of hostilities on 8 October 1963. Shortly after the Algerian referendum the previous year, Moroccan troops had attempted to occupy Tindouf but had withdrawn when they discovered that Algerian forces were already in control.[2] There followed a year of relative calm along the frontier while the Moroccans evidently attempted to persuade the Algerians to honour the Rabat convention. By August 1963 it was clear that Algiers was in no mood for concessions, and several incidents were reported along the five hundred miles of disputed frontier stretching from Colomb-Béchar in the north to Tindouf in the south. The culmination of this critical phase came at the beginning of September with the expulsion of twenty Algerian 'irregulars' from Oujda in Morocco, and by way of reprisal, of twenty-three Moroccans from an Algerian frontier post in the same region.[3] While both sides still seemed anxious to play down these incidents, the Algerians intensified their radio and propaganda campaign with a violent attack, published in the FLN party paper *Al Moujahid*, in which King Hassan was described as a 'marionette' and his closest political adviser, Rida Guedira, as 'the Moroccan Rasputin'.[4]

The crisis was transformed, however, on 29 September when eight thousand Berber veterans of the Algerian Army of National Liberation led by Colonel Mohand ou el-Hadj, joined with the illegal Front of Socialist Forces under Hocine Ait Ahmed in open revolt against the Ben Bella regime. The next day Ben Bella accused the Moroccans of acting in support of the Berber dissidents by massing their troops along the Algerian frontier.[5] At a public rally in Algiers on 1 October he repeated the charges of collusion between the rebels and Moroccan forces and announced the nationalization of all land still in the hands of foreigners.[6]

Faced simultaneously with an internal and external threat, at this stage Ben Bella clearly wished to avoid a showdown. On 4 October, when the Algerian government agreed to a foreign ministers' meeting to

---

[1] *Le Monde* 23 Oct. 1963. The text was released by the Permanent Mission of Morocco to the UN on 20 Oct. 1963.

[2] Wild, p. 23.   [3] *Le Monde*, 6, 12 Sept. 1963.

[4] Quoted in *OFNS*, 16 Sept. 1963.   [5] *NY Times*, 2 Oct. 1963.

[6] Algerian Ministry of National Orientation, *Les Discours du Président Ben Bella* (Annaba, 1964), cited in Wild, p. 24.

discuss the crisis, it seemed that the Moroccans might, after all, obtain their main objective, the implementation of the Rabat convention. On 5 October the Algerian foreign minister, Bouteflika, met with Rida Guedira at Oujda in Morocco. They agreed that relations between the two countries should be normalized by the implementation of the economic conventions signed in May, that Hassan and Ben Bella should meet in Algiers in the near future, that Moroccan troops would be immediately withdrawn from the frontier, and that a mixed commission would meet in Tlemcen in Algeria to examine the border problem.[1] On 7 October the Moroccan defence minister announced the withdrawal of Moroccan troops, in accordance with this agreement, thus allowing Ben Bella to concentrate his military force against the Berber dissidents in the Kabylie mountains.[2] Before the withdrawal could be completed, however, fighting broke out on 8 October. According to Algiers, the first clash occurred when 'uncontrolled elements' attached to the Moroccan forces attacked an Algerian position forty miles south-east of the Algerian administrative centre of Colomb-Béchar, while in the Rabat version, the Algerians had launched an unprovoked attack overrunning the border posts of Hassi Beida and Tinjouf, which, in the Moroccan view, lay one hundred kilometres inside Moroccan territory.[3]

The conflict quickly developed a momentum of its own which obscured the issue of responsibility. King Hassan's first reaction to the Algerian attack on Hassi Beida had been to dispatch his information minister, Boutaleb, to Algiers to seek an assurance from Ben Bella that the incident had been the work of uncontrolled elements in the army and did not represent an official Algerian decision to ignore the Oujda agreement.[4] The outcome of this mission was an Algerian agreement to hold an immediate meeting at Tlemcen to discuss border problems generally, although Ben Bella apparently remained adamant against any discussion of border revision.[5] Meanwhile Hassan was under heavy pressure to resist 'Algerian aggression', and two hours after the Algerian delegation had left for Tlemcen, the Moroccan government announced that it would not attend the meeting.[6] At the same time it was reported that Hassan had informed the cabinet of his determination to defend Morocco's territorial integrity, a decision which served as a signal for a Moroccan counter-attack on Hassi Beida and Tinjouf.[7]

The Moroccan action was well organized and by 14 October the Moroccan army was firmly in control of both the disputed posts. It was at this point that the question of outside mediation first arose. In Algiers, the defence minister, making no reference to Algerian reverses in the field,

[1] *NY Times*, 5, 7 Oct. 1963; *Observer*, 6 Oct. 1963.   [2] *NY Times*, 8 Oct. 1963.
[3] *Le Monde, Guardian*, 10 Oct. 1963.   [4] *NY Times*, 10 Oct. 1963.
[5] Ibid.   [6] Ibid., 11 Oct. 1963.   [7] *Le Monde*, 12 Oct. 1963; *Observer*, 13 Oct. 1963.

announced that Moroccan forces, supported by tanks and aircraft, had invaded the western Sahara to a depth of about fifty miles, and that the Algerian government had invoked the OAU Charter, but would not have recourse to the UN.[1] In the meantime, Ben Bella sent a personal envoy to Marrakesh to attempt a final bilateral settlement of the crisis. Despite his difficulties, he refused to make any concessions on the frontier issue, and after three days the negotiations broke down when Boutaleb announced Morocco's minimum ceasefire terms to be:

(i) an immediate ceasefire with both sides occupying their current positions;
(ii) the immediate appointment of the border commission; and
(iii) preparation for a bilateral summit at which all outstanding issues could be directly discussed.

Boutaleb rejected the Algerian demand for a withdrawal to the positions held before the Moroccan attacks of 14 October on the grounds that the disputed frontier posts were 'purely and simply Moroccan'.[2]

Ben Bella's motives in trying to negotiate a bilateral settlement from a position of weakness remain unclear. Most probably his main concern was to buy time. And in fact even while the negotiations were proceeding, the attitudes of both sides were almost visibly hardening. Replying to Algerian propaganda in kind, Radio Maroc accused Ben Bella of having initiated hostilities in an effort to secure his 'dictatorship' and of spreading fascism throughout Africa, while Hassan toured the southern provinces of Morocco in an effort to build up anti-Algerian feeling.[3] Algerian reactions were even more dramatic. On 15 October Ben Bella announced general mobilization against 'the reactionary coalition' threatening Algeria, and the next day he suspended the National Assembly to allow the deputies to rejoin their units.[4] At the same time Radio Algiers revived an old FLN grievance against Morocco, supposedly buried with the signing of the Rabat convention, by accusing the late King Mohammed V of complicity in Ben Bella's arrest by the French in 1956.[5] Meanwhile, both sides were reported to be bringing up reinforcements and, although the Moroccans were in far better logistic position, the capture on 20 October of an Algerian army helicopter with five Egyptian officers aboard suggested that the Algerians might be preparing to widen the conflict.[6]

Faced with both military reverses and the failure of direct negotiations, Ben Bella's immediate tactic, however, was to shift the attack to the diplomatic level, where Algeria enjoyed the advantage. That the Moroccans were fully aware of their weak diplomatic position was shown on 19 October when they failed to respond forcefully to an Algerian attempt to

[1] *Times*, 15 Oct. 1963; *Le Monde*, 16 Oct. 1963.   [2] *Le Monde*, 18 Oct. 1963.
[3] Ibid., 19 Oct. 1963.   [4] *Times*, 16 Oct. 1963; *NY Times*, 17 Oct. 1963.
[5] *Le Monde*, 18 Oct. 1963.   [6] Wild, p. 25.

open a second front by an attack on the Moroccan village of Ich in un-
disputed territory in the north-east. Although he charged Ben Bella
with trying to escalate frontier incidents into a generalized conflict,
Hassan held his hand, presumably calculating that any stronger reprisal
would gain international support for Algerian charges of Moroccan
aggression.[1]

The full weakness of Morocco's position was revealed once the failure
of direct negotiations opened the way for outside mediation. During the
Marrakesh talks President Bourguiba of Tunisia had addressed telegrams
to both sides urging a ceasefire, an appeal he repeated on 21 October.[2]
But although Morocco agreed to take part in a North African foreign
ministers' conference at Tunis, Algeria refused to negotiate before the
withdrawal of Moroccan troops. Since the Algerians had clearly indicated
their reluctance to implement the Rabat convention over the previous
twelve months, it is hardly surprising that the Moroccans refused to
accept this condition.[3] But if President Bourguiba's mediation attempt
failed, there was no obvious reason why anybody else should be more
successful. Morocco's isolation within the Arab League was shown when
a hastily summoned meeting of the League on 20 October endorsed the
Algerian position by calling for an immediate ceasefire and a withdrawal
of troops to the positions occupied before the fighting.[4] Two days later,
Nasser made a speech at Suez in which he offered to mediate but since he
also deplored the 'aggression committed against Algeria', his offer similarly
stood no chance of being accepted.[5]

It was in this unpromising situation that the OAU faced its first test in
the peaceful settlement of disputes. The outbreak of hostilities had been
viewed with alarm throughout Africa, and Ghana, Mali, and Ethiopia
had all made offers of mediation. The Moroccans were at first as reluctant
to accept OAU mediation as that of any other party and appeared anxious
to take the matter direct to the UN.[6] Their reluctance was, of course,
understandable. On 19 October the Algerian foreign minister repeated his
earlier request for an extraordinary meeting of the OAU Council of
Ministers under Article 12 of the Charter. In declaring Algeria's willingness to abide by the spirit and the letter of the Charter he was, of course,
expressing support for the prevailing African sentiment against the revision of colonial frontiers.[7]

Rabat's eventual conversion to the idea of African mediation was
probably influenced by several considerations, of which discreet US

---

[1] NY Times, 19 Oct. 1963; NYHT, 20 Oct. 1963. [2] Le Monde, 19, 23 Oct. 1963.
[3] Ibid., 23 Oct. 1963. [4] NYHT, 21 Oct. 1963. [5] Le Monde, 24 Oct. 1963.
[6] The Moroccans were reported to have accepted an offer of mediation by U Thant, but
the Algerians maintained their original stand against UN intervention in the dispute (NYHT,
21 Oct. 1963).
[7] Le Monde, 24 Oct. 1963.

pressure in support of Hailé Selassie's efforts,[1] and mounting evidence of Egyptian intervention on the Algerian side, were perhaps the most compelling. In any event, it was finally the combined efforts of Hailé Selassie and President Modibo Keita of Mali that obtained the agreement of both governments to a four-power meeting to be held in Bamako, Mali, without prior conditions.[2]

The outcome of the Bamako meeting, which was held on 29–30 October, fairly accurately reflected the balance between Morocco's military and Algeria's diplomatic strength. The predictable impasse arising from Hassan's refusal to withdraw his troops was overcome by a proposal put forward by President Keita for a demilitarized zone which would be defined by a committee of officers from all four states and supervised by Ethiopian and Malian observers.[3] The final communique endorsed the Algerian request for OAU arbitration but also specifically charged the OAU foreign ministers to study the frontier problem in depth and to make concrete proposals for its settlement.[4] Both Hassan and Ben Bella were thus able to present the agreement as a triumph for their own and for African diplomacy generally. Yet no sooner had they done so, than a fundamental difference of interpretation arose. On his return to Algiers, Ben Bella announced that he had obtained agreement to Morocco's withdrawal from Hassi Beida and Tinjouf, while in Rabat, the Moroccan foreign minister said that Morocco would not evacuate its positions along the frontier.[5]

As with the previous Oujda agreement, the Bamako agreement was overtaken by events before it could be implemented. While the meeting was still in progress there had been reports that Cuban volunteers had arrived in Algiers and were already on their way to the front, while the Cairo daily, Al Ahram, publicly admitted the intervention of UAR naval and military units on the Algerian side.[6] Before the ceasefire could come into effect on 2 November, fierce fighting had again flared up, with both sides accusing the other of breaking the spirit, if not the letter, of the agreement. On 1 November Hassan announced over Radio Maroc an

---

[1] Hailé Selassie arrived in Morocco on a prearranged state visit on 18 Oct. His first attempt at personal mediation seems to have foundered in the face of Algerian and Moroccan intransigence about the conditions under which they would negotiate. The Emperor was opposed, however, to bringing the UN into the conflict, and a joint Algerian–Ethiopian communique stated that before leaving Algiers for Addis Ababa on 23 Oct., he had 'made known his approval' of the Algerian request for an OAU Council of Ministers meeting (NY Times, 24 Oct. 1963).

[2] Le Monde, 25 Oct. 1963.   [3] La Bourse Égyptienne, 30 Oct. 1963.

[4] For full text of the Bamako communique see Documents, 1963, pp. 466–7.

[5] Times and NYHT, 1 Nov. 1963.

[6] The well-informed editor of Al Ahram, Haikal, wrote, 'some UAR navy units headed by the destroyer Suez now share responsibility for protection of Algerian shores while an Egyptian armoured force is now side by side with the Algerian army'. According to Haikal, the UAR forces had been ordered to fight in Algerian land alone and only in defence against aggression from outside (NYHT, 2 Nov. 1963).

Algerian attack on the Moroccan town of Figuig and the withdrawal of
Moroccan troops in the face of heavy Algerian bombardment.[1] The next
day the Algerian foreign minister declared that Algerian troops had only
approached Figuig in reaction to Moroccan incursions around Tindouf
and a Moroccan attack on the Algerian town of Beni-Ounif.[2] Whatever
the truth, militarily the Algerian attack on Figuig made sense since the
town lay within a few miles of the road and narrow gauge railway linking
Colomb-Béchar with central Algeria. Moreover, Colonel Boumedienne,
the Algerian defence minister who was personally in charge of the Algerian
forces at Colomb-Béchar, was reported to be strongly against any softening
in the Algerian position and may well have acted on his own initiative in
an attempt to strengthen Algeria's military position before the ceasefire.[3]

The fighting continued for two days after the official ceasefire and was
finally brought to a halt with the arrival of Ethiopian and Malian observers.[4] The Algerian attack on Figuig created in the Moroccan view an
entirely new situation, and revived Rabat's original desire for a meeting of
the Security Council. At this point it appears that pressure from the
major powers rather than from the African states persuaded the Moroccans
against submitting a formal request for a meeting. Both the US and
French governments were reported to have expressed the hope that the
dispute could be resolved within an African context, a view which was
apparently also shared by Moscow.[5] In any event, on 4 November Rabat
dropped its efforts to obtain a Security Council hearing, reverted to the
Bamako agreement, and requested an early meeting of OAU foreign
ministers.[6]

Opening the foreign ministers' conference in Addis Ababa on 15
November, Haile Selassie said that a failure to settle the Algerian-
Moroccan dispute would deal a crippling blow to the OAU's aims.[7]
While African fears that the Maghreb might become a new theatre in the
cold war were almost certainly exaggerated, an outright failure so soon
after its inauguration would have certainly damaged the organization's
credibility in the eyes of the outside world. Yet it remains uncertain

[1] *Le Monde, Guardian*, 2 Nov. 1963.   [2] *NY Times*, 2 Nov. 1963.
[3] *Observer*, 3 Nov. 1963, reported Boumedienne's view that the conflict 'is not a battle of
frontiers, but a battle between republic and monarchy, a battle between progress and reaction,
a battle between revolution and imperialism'. See also *OFNS*, 8 Nov. 1963.
[4] *Le Monde*, 5 Nov. 1963.
[5] *NY Times*, 4 Nov. 1963. The State Department was also said to have brought pressure to
bear on both the UAR and Spain against any widening of the conflict. Soviet reactions to the
crisis were given in an article in *Pravda* on 17 Oct. in which Victor Hakevski, while accusing the
colonialists of creating a situation which would provide them with an opportunity for intervention, expressed the hope that Algerian–Moroccan relations could be normalized by direct
negotiations between the two countries (*Le Monde*, 18 Oct. 1963).
[6] Ibid., 5 Nov. 1963.
[7] *Daily Telegraph*, 18 Nov. 1963.

whether it was intervention by the OAU, or merely the fact that neither side was properly equipped to fight a full-scale desert war that caused the crisis to ebb away at the end of the year. On one level the OAU conference was highly successful, for while neither side conceded any ground, the spirit of compromise that had marked the May summit reasserted itself, and the foreign ministers were able to contrive a formula which, while admitting the need for a definitive solution in the future, gave neither side immediate cause for complaint, and hence a justifiable reason for breaking the ceasefire. The Commission of Mediation, Conciliation, and Arbitration, provided for under Article XIX of the OAU Charter had not yet been established, and the conference, therefore, appointed a special committee to arbitrate on all aspects of the dispute.[1] By this device, the OAU avoided any general statement on the need for frontier revisions, the Pandora's box of which most African leaders were rightly afraid, but also implicitly endorsed the Moroccan case that, in the absence of any fixed boundary, a problem did exist and could not simply be ignored on the principle of *uti possidetis* as the Algerians proposed.[2]

Since it was the Moroccans who had been reluctant to submit to OAU arbitration, perhaps the major contribution of the conference to the final settlement, therefore, was to reassure Rabat of the possibility of Morocco receiving equitable treatment within an African framework.

But if the OAU arbitration in North Africa provided a reasonably optimistic note on which to end the year, at the same time a reassertion of the principles of African unity was not in itself a substitute for interstate politics of a more traditional kind as African leaders were to discover as they struggled to operate the new OAU machinery. Despite the considerable diplomatic success of the OAU conference the military stalemate between Algeria and Morocco along the disputed frontier persisted. The Bamako ceasefire committee had succeeded in obtaining a ceasefire, but had not been able to create a demilitarized zone which would have involved taking a stand on the substance of the dispute. The end of the year, therefore, saw the Moroccans still firmly entrenched in Hassi Beida and Tinjouf and the Algerians refusing to evacuate the positions they had taken up in the vicinity of Figuig. When the dispute was formally ended in February 1964, it was not as a result of proposals put forward by the special arbitration committee, whose findings were never published, but through an agreement reached in direct negotiations between the two sides.[3] Nevertheless, by creating an atmosphere of *détente* at the critical

[1] Membership of this Committee, which met once in Dec. 1963 but did not get down to work until 1964, was: Ivory Coast, Ethiopia, Mali, Nigeria, Senegal, Sudan, and Tanganyika. For the text of the final resolution of the OAU Conference of Foreign Ministers, see *Documents, 1963*, pp. 467–9.

[2] Wild, pp. 29–30.

[3] Wild, p. 32. This role of the arbitration committee, in whose presence the Agreement was

time, the OAU had proved its worth, and the attitudes of the major powers as well as of the African states themselves suggested that it might develop as a useful instrument for containing and isolating African conflicts from outside contamination.

signed, remains uncertain. It may be that, since Algeria and Morocco had still not resumed diplomatic relations, it facilitated the negotiations.

INDEX

Abaloo, Firmin, 270.

'Abd ar-Rahman ibn Yahya, 220.

Abdirahaman Husayn, 285.

Abdul Karim Zuhur, 198.

Abdullah al-Salim as-Sallah, Colonel (later, Brigadier), 220; attends Arab summit conference, 215; leads the rebels, 218–19; Egypt and, 221, 236; US and, 226, 227, 229–30, 232; criticizes Britain, 228–9, 232–3.

Abdul Rahman, Tunku: and 'Malaysia', 120–1, 122, 123–5, 126–7; in Sarawak, 124; and negotiations with Britain on Singapore base, 127, 128–30; in London talks on 'Malaysia', 132–3; threatens to close Johore causeway, 133; warns Indonesia, 135–6; and time limit for 'Malaysia', 138, 152, 159; meets Sukarno, 150; asks Britain to mediate on Malaysian finance, 154; tries to win over Philippines and Indonesia, 154–5; at Manila summit conference, 155; makes concessions to Indonesia, 156, 163; and confrontation, 163; refuses further talks with Indonesia and Philippines, 163.

Abdul Razak, Tun, 143, 150–1, 154, 155.

Abidjan, Ivory Coast, 275, 276.

Abrassimov, Pyotr Andreevich, 24.

Accra, Ghana, 269, 270, 271.

Addis Ababa, Ethiopia: (1) African summit conference (May) at, 265–6, 285–90; and nuclear-free zones, 15; Russian request for allegiance rejected at, 42; US and, 267, 289, 302, 307; and Togo, 273–4, 276; Nkrumah and, 278–9; absentees from, 281, 308; and regionalism, 282–3, 290; and 'liberation' movements, 291–3, 294; and UN, 291, 296; and Portuguese colonial policy, 298; and decolonization, 298; and South Africa, 301; (2) foreign ministers' conference (November) on Morocco and Algeria at, 315–16.

Aden, 220, 224–6, 228, 232, 234; Aden Trade Union Congress, 225.

Adenauer, Dr Konrad: and Erhard, 3, 32; resigns, 3, 28–9, 32; his fears and disappointments, 8, 16, 21, 23; Kennedy prefers Erhard to, 17; and Moscow Agreement, 21; Khrushchev suspicious

of, 24; discounts Russo-American talks, 26; criticizes sale of American grain to Russia, 28; character of, 29; and Franco-German treaty, 31; visited by de Gaulle, 32.

Adoula, Cyrille: survives threat from Stanleyville, 243; and ONUC, 244; discusses Kitona Declaration with Tshombe, 245–6; his position weak, 246, 256; creates province of North Katanga, 247–8; asks UN to help frame a constitution for Congo, 249; takes action against Tshombe, 250; and U Thant plan, 251, 252–3, 255; refuses to meet Tshombe, 257; and sanctions, 258; and American aircraft, 259; and end of secession, 259; and Western Powers, 266; and Angola, 293–4.

Aflaq, Michel, 194–6, 197, 198, 201, 204–5.

Africa: communism in, 37, 41, 42; scientists in, 41; African Commonwealth states and EEC, 57; reconciliation in, 265–6, 267–8, 276, 277, 284–5, 289, 290, 295, 307; rivalry of *blocs* in, 265; and unity, 265; Francophone states of, 265, 269, 273, 275, 276, 277, 289; fear of subversion in, 267–8, 271, 273, 276, 278; Ghana feared in, 270; 'liberation' movements in, 275, 282, 287–8, 289, 291–2, 295, 298; Anglophone states of, 289.

Africa, central, 282.

Africa, east, 282, 283–4.

Africa, north, Arabs in, 212.

Africa, southern, 3, 275, 282, 284, 304–5.

Africa, west, 271, 275, 277.

Africa must unite, 279, 283.

African Charter, 285–90 (*see also* s.v. Organization of African Unity).

African Free Trade Area, 289.

African integration and disintegration: case studies in economic and political union, 288.

African Liberation Committee, 291–6.

African states: and Portuguese colonial policy, 295–300, 304–5; and South Africa, 301–3, 304–5, 307; and OAU, 317.

African unity, 265, 267; 'maximalist' approach to, 265–6; 'minimalist'

United States of America—*contd.*

African states and, 266-7; does not intervene in Algeria's war with Morocco, 267, 313-14, 315; and Angola, 294; and Portugal's colonial policy, 300, 304, 306; and South Africa, 302-3, 304, 307.

General: policies of, 16, 68-9; 'new frontiersman' approach, 86, 112; Ghana wants Africa to imitate federation of, 283.

Internal: effect of Kennedy's assassination on, 3-4, 30; Congress sometimes opposed to President, 21, 88-9, 112-16, 247, 256; communists in, 45, 46; racial discrimination in, 289.

Military power: Russia afraid of war with, 35 6, 37.

NATO: MLF offered to, 7-10, 14-16.

Nuclear power: confrontation with Russia, 3; MLF in Europe, 7-10, 14-16; nuclear secrets offered to France, 21; no nuclear secrets for West Germany ；26 (*see also* Disarmament *supra*).

Trade: little with Yemen, 224; with South Africa, 306.

UNO: and UN's deficit, 246-7; collaborates with neutralists at, 264.

United States of America, departments and agencies of:

Arms Control and Disarmament Agency, 11, 13.

Bureau of the Budget, 70.

Central Intelligence Agency, 183.

Congress: Congressional Joint Committee on Atomic Energy, 6, 11; over-rigid in negotiation, 13; sometimes opposes Kennedy, 21, 88-9, 112-16, 247, 256; and balance of payments, 69; and equalization tax, 70, 72; antipathetic to India, 87, 113, 114; Patnaik tries for support for India in, 96; and military aid for India, 98, 102; suspicious of Indonesia, 147; and Congo, 244, 256, 259; opposes buying of UN bonds, 247.

Council of Economic Advisers, 78.

Federal Reserve Board, 74.

House of Representatives Committees: Armed Services Committee, 9; Banking and Currency Committee, 73; Foreign Affairs Committee, 97, 114.

Joint Chiefs of Staff, 178, 179, 181, 182.

National Security Council, 181, 182, 184, 234.

OM, 181.

United States of America, departments and agencies of—*contd.*

Pentagon, 13, 22, 23, 178-9; *The Pentagon Papers: the defense department history of United States—decision making on Vietnam*, 178-9, 180, 181, 182, 183, 184.

Senate, 6, 14, 22; Foreign Relations Committee, 11, 22.

State Department: and MLF, 8-9, 19; over-rigid in negotiation, 13; and Test-Ban Treaty, 22-3; on China's invasion of India, 88; and Indian air defence, 104; and South Vietnam, 178, 179, 181, 184; and the Yemen, 229; offers aid to Congo, 247; presents sanctions programme to UN, 250; offers Congo American fighters, 259; and Algeria's war with Morocco, 315.

United States Seventh Fleet, 106.

United Workers Party, Burma, 43.

Universal Postal Union, 249.

Upper Volta, 273-4, 275-6, 291.

Uri, Pierre (cited), 57.

US Balance of Payments in 1963, The, 64, 68.

Ussuri River, 52.

U Thant: and North Borneo referendum, 156, 158-60; and South Vietnam, 177; and the Yemen, 234-6, 239; and Congo objectives, 243, 244; opposes use of force in Katanga, 245, 248, 254; has talks with Home, 246; and sanctions against Katanga, 249, 254, 258; asks for Katanga's revenue to be paid to Central Government, 249, 258; his plan for Katanga, 250-1, 253-4, 255-6, 257, 260, 261, 263; asks for reinforcements for ONUC, 257, 259; confirmed as Secretary-General, 257-8; asks for American military aid, 259; announces cease-fire in Katanga, 261, 262; reports end of secession in Katanga, 263-4; and Portugal's colonial policy, 300; and war between Algeria and Morocco, 313 (*see also* s.v. United Nations Organization—Secretary-General).

Van der Kroef, Justus M. (cited), 125, 137.

Van Roey, 259.

Varnier Line between Morocco and Algeria, 309.

Verwoerd, Dr Hendrik, 301, 304, 306.

Viennot, Jean-Pierre (cited), 193.

Viet Cong, the organisation and techniques of the National Front of South Vietnam, 170, 171, 187, 188.